Collecting Garden Plants

Collecting
Garden
Plants

Jane Taylor

Published in association with the
National Council for the Conservation of
Plants & Gardens

J. M. Dent & Sons Ltd
LONDON

First published 1988
© Jane Taylor 1988

This book is set in 11 on 12 pt Bembo

Printed in Great Britain by Butler & Tanner Ltd,
Frome and London for
J. M. Dent & Sons Ltd
91 Clapham High, London SW4 7TA

Contents

Colour photographs

Foreword by
Dr Max Walters

POPULAR interest in the conservation of nature, as part of a general concern for the impact of man on the environment, grew rapidly in Britain during the 1970's. In 1975 the first international conference on botanical conservation was held at Kew, and the I.U.C.N. threatened plants monitoring centre was established there. These urgent activities stimulated the R.H.S. to hold a Conference in 1978 to consider a range of problems concerning the conservation of garden plants and the gardens in which they grow, and from these deliberations was born the NCCPG.

Foremost among the aims of the new organisation was the promotion of National Collections, in which a range of plants representative of a particular group (usually a genus) of horticultural interest could be grown together as a conservation stock providing a permanent exhibit for education, research and conservation. The National Collections Scheme has now been running for five years, and Jane Taylor's book presents for the first time an account of the Collections and their significance for horticultural botany as a whole.

It has been my pleasure to chair the National Collection Committee during these first five formative years, and to see developing an idea which, though not entirely novel – an earlier, limited scheme of National Species Collections had briefly existed in the early 1950's – has caught 'the spirit of the times' so successfully that we now have a network of over 400 designated Collections throughout Britain. We can, I feel sure, confidently expect that the National Collections Scheme will continue to expand as more individuals and institutions realise the significance of turning their expert knowledge to such good effect. This excellent book will undoubtedly play a part in stimulating the growth and use of National Collections.

Introduction by
Graham Stuart Thomas OBE, VMH, DHM, VMM

WE HAVE long been accustomed to visiting botanic gardens to gain experience in distinguishing between species of plants – that is, the wild plants that are natives of other regions than our own. The same facilities have not been available to those of us who wish to compare the respective values of what we call garden cultivars or 'varieties' of trees, shrubs and plants. The raising and selecting of these for the decoration of our gardens has been going on for hundreds of years through the efforts of nurserymen and indeed gardeners themselves. The result is a bewildering assembly. A recent survey has revealed that over 25.000 species and cuiltivars of herbaceous and rock plants and bulbs are listed by European nurserymen. In the past I have often wondered how order and uniformity could be brought to what is chaos in many genera and at last we can begin to see how this may be achieved.

Dr Max Walters mentions in his Foreword the earlier conferences that led to the formation of the NCCPG by the RHS – the Society which does so much for us gardeners that we are apt to take it all for granted. The scheme and all its ramifications could never have been started had it not been for the RHS and the drive of the Society's treasurer, Lawrence Banks, who has acted as chairman of the NCCPG for ten years, since its beginning. Not only does the RHS house the slender Secretariat at Wisley but this great benefit includes the use of its library and other advantages.

The launching of this very great national scheme has resulted in inevitable and ever growing paper-work connected with the inauguration and servicing of the many Regional Groups and attending meetings throughout the country. The Secretariat has always been run at an absolute minimum owing to financial stricture, despite great generosity from individuals and groups, special trusts and organisations. The dedication of committee members and the Groups is wholly assured but is only part of the effort. The vital life-blood is obviously the cash to finance the scheme.

To this end a new venture has been inaugurated whereby certain rare and new plants may be propagated and sold through normal channels with a percentage of profits going to help swell the funds. This is yet in its infancy. We live from year to year. Links are being formed with the International Union for the Conservation of Nature and Natural Resources (IUCN) and this can only strengthen the work of the NCCPG.

Only by united effort in every way will this great endeavour survive. Having been a Council member at the beginning, and later a Committee member, I have watched it grow and have nothing but admiration for all that has been done. How far we have gone can be gauged by Jane Taylor's book, and I think it excellent that she has set forth these many chapters for us, bringing us right into the picture.

I first met Jane when she and her late husband were looking after the National Trust garden at Coleton Fishacre in Devon. Apart from restoring the garden they were starting a collection of kniphofias. It was at once obvious to me that Jane was a dedicated plantswoman and a skilled horticulturist in general. From this, and no doubt earlier beginnings, has germinated this book, which not only brings to our notice how and why the NCCPG collections started and gathered way, but that they are of great importance.

In reading Jane's pages it is difficult not to become enthused. Enthused about the numerous lovely and rare plants and their relationship to the more common members of their genera. Enthused, too, by Jane's suggestions about how to use plants to their best advantage and with best cultivation. And how can we not enthuse about the keen spirit of the collection holders to whom we owe so much? I believe that the mere establishing of the collections will not be the end-product, but that having so many representatives of a genus in one place, the result will be a great sorting-out of name-confusions and new evalution of cultivars to our lasting benefit. There is a daunting task awaiting everyone but my experiences with the older roses proves that, with patience and perseverance, much can be done.

Whatever may be the outcome of the national collections we could not want a better advocate for them than the author of this book. Throughout the pages she gives us much from her observations and experiences connected with botany, history, and the art and craft of gardening so that all our gardens will benefit. I feel sure the book will gain the success which the time and effort spent on it so richly deserves.

General Introduction

THIS BOOK is about plants for your garden; about collecting them, about the people who collect them, and about the National Council for the Conservation of Plants and Gardens. This is an organisation dedicated to saving garden plants and responsible for coordinating, as we shall see, a national, country-wide scheme of garden plant collections. The book is also about selecting the best plants for a particular purpose or position in your garden, and how the National Collections scheme can help. It is not, except incidentally, about garden design, which is quite another subject. There are excellent books on garden design from which one can learn about keeping the centre of a composition open and uncluttered, or about creating a central axis; about balance and perspective and the use and abuse of curves. Then, too, many people have a good eye for line and, without necessarily knowing why, can lay out a pleasing design on the ground, playing with pegs and string and lengths of hosepipe until it looks right to them. Others may be content with an inherited garden style, changing only the planting detail rather than the basic design.

I think that this stage in the creation of a garden, vitally important though it is, is often a good deal easier to negotiate than the next: establishing a style of planting – planting as furnishing, that is – that will enhance and complement the basic layout of structural or foundation planting, hedges and screens, grass, stone, water perhaps. This means selecting plants with care, but if we are to select, we need to know what the choices are. Between the somewhat limited selection of plants available from garden centres, and the vast range listed in works of reference, there is a great gap, not easily filled by the gardener who wants just the right plant for a particular spot and prefers not to end up with what his neighbours have chosen.

Many garden owners, baffled by the possibilities, play safe and buy plants that they have seen in a garden centre, illustrated in a book, or on television, and then place them in their gardens by segregating them into categories: the rose garden, the herbaceous borders, the spring or summer bedding, the shrubbery. This kind of planting, derived from fashions prevailing in Victorian times, is still fostered to some extent by the popular gardening press, but it scarcely satisfies the keen gardener for long.

Several of the most enthusiastic gardeners I know are primarily collectors eager to grow and know as many plants as can be persuaded to fit into their gardens, or perhaps specialising in certain groups of plants; maybe even progressing from enthusiasm to enthusiasm as one genus or group of plants is mastered and another demands attention. Though they would mostly modestly deny it, they are plantsmen; and the more acquisitive they are the greater the risk that their gardens will lack coherence, consisting at the extreme of a collection of plants assembled without regard for their overall effect in the garden. At the same time most plantsmen, even if they do not consciously consider grouping their plants for effect, grow them as nearly as possible in the conditions that suit them, and thus a kind of unity develops based on common cultural needs.

At the other extreme from the plantsman is the designer, who selects his plants purely as elements in the picture he seeks to create. He may aim to blend colours and textures, with flowers or foliage or both, or he may think in landscape terms, where the interrelation of shapes and spaces is all-important. In either event the tendency is to a very disciplined style of planting at best, and in less competent hands the result can be a dull and unimaginative composition. This will be especially likely if the designer (be he a professional landscape architect, or merely the chap planting up his own garden) adopts a safety-first attitude; for if the effect that is sought is to be achieved at the minimum of risk of failure, only well-tested, familiar ingredients will be used.

Somewhere between the plantsman who is above all an avid collector and the disciplined designer is the kind of gardener who has been described as artist-plantsman. There is in Britain a long tradition of good garden design and planting by such well-known and influential writers and garden-makers as William Robinson, Gertrude Jekyll, A. T. Johnson and Lawrence Johnstone, and in our own time Graham Stuart Thomas and Christopher Lloyd among others. It is my belief that in their work, and that of their disciples, are the most satisfying gardens to be found, those where a blending of the two extremes is achieved. Successfully to combine the two is a most difficult thing. In all of us, probably, the collector and the artist are at war, though one side may have the other pretty thoroughly suppressed, and the conflict is exacerbated by our timid self bleating to the bold experimenter in us 'But what will the neighbours say?' or 'think of the expense'. How much more rewarding to persuade all these different selves to live in harmony, so that the collector may yield to an impulse buy without feelings of guilt, while back in the garden the artist, instead of thinking 'What *am* I to do with this now I've got it?' in a helpless manner, goes constructively to work to fit it into the garden picture he has created thus far. Bearing in mind that in any group there will be several possibilities, this should not be too difficult, given that he has a reasonably open mind. And how thrilling when the newcomer is found the very place that most enhances its own particular appeal and that of its new neighbours.

It is the special quality of British gardening at its best to achieve this balance between picture gardening and plantsmanship, helped by a generally benign climate and the *tournure d'esprit* which sees a garden as an entity in a continuous process of evolution rather than a static artefact in the French style.

Professional garden designers may lament the absence of a genuine modern style of gardening in Britain, but they are unlikely to be able to impose one that makes no allowance for this attitude of mind and for the collector's instinct that welcomes plants as individuals, not as items of décor.

Among the great garden-makers who have helped to form our present-day taste in planting our gardens, Gertrude Jekyll's constant preoccupation in the design of gardens was, in her own words, 'to form beautiful pictures'. Her books are packed with stimulating ideas and, though few of her actual planting schemes remain, some have been restored, and through her writings her influence has been immeasurable. Some of her suggestions, it is true, are apt to give rise to a sense of frustration; their pre-war largeness of ideas is rather at variance with our present-day lack of both acreage (in many private gardens at least) and labour. Yet time and again there crops up an association of plants, a point about cultivation, or one of her contrivances which is eminently usable today. In *Colour Schemes for the Flower Garden*, perhaps her best-known book, it is the hardy flower border that chiefly claims her attention – though it is more truly what we should now call a mixed border, with shrubs, bulbs and annuals as well as hardy perennials and tender bedding plants. In this book, as in her others, there is, too, a good deal about the rather more relaxed style of planting which is surely her lasting memorial, making use of a wide range of plants to create a picture that will be pleasing to the eye at all times while foregoing the concentrated impact of the June border, the main flower border that needed unremitting attention to provide a mass of colour from July to September, or the individual gardens devoted to one or two genera or colours.

Not that, in her skilled hands or those of the other gardeners of the late nineteenth and twentieth centuries to whom we owe so much, the more informal style of planting was dull in the very least. Now this is not the place to give a history of the last hundred years or so of gardening, even if I were qualified to do so, but since I believe that the type of planting I am about to describe is the one with which many gardeners feel most at ease, I think the debt should be at least acknowledged. This natural style, though not actually evolved by William Robinson, was much advocated by him in his writing, and his books are still read, still relevant. Both Robinson and another influential gardening journalist, A. T. Johnson, a generation younger, wrote about the natural style in general terms, comparatively seldom giving specific plant groups as examples. In this they differed not only from Miss Jekyll, whose books contain many plans and descriptions of actual borders and gardens within gardens, with full details of their components, but also from later writers such as Vita Sackville-West. Now that we are so much more mobile than a generation or two ago, innumerable people visit Miss Sackville-West's garden at Sissinghurst (too many, it seems, for the well-being of the garden itself) to see at first hand the plant groups she wrote about. Probably at least as influential is the garden at Hidcote, created by Lawrence Johnstone before the Hitler war. Though the planting in both these gardens is informal, the profusion of flower and foliage is set firmly in a largely formal design. This takes them a step or two away from the Robinsonian naturalism of rock garden and woodland garden (though Hidcote has its own miniature 'Westonbirt' of informally arranged trees and shrubs) but many of the ingredients are the same; the principle of combining trees, shrubs, perennials, bulbs is one of wide application. This is, in fact, gardening in four layers, as described by Graham Thomas in several of his books. The upper layer, of course, is formed by trees. Beneath their shade, and beyond it, in the sun, are shrubs of varying heights forming a permanent framework, inter- and perhaps under-planted with perennials and bulbs, while here and there climbers use the shrubs and trees as support, as they would in nature. This is a style of gardening which can greatly reduce maintenance by providing efficient ground-cover; but even where the ground is not permanently covered by growing plants, or by a mulch of dead leaves or compost – perhaps because of the addition of annuals and tender bedding plants to the mixture – gardening in layers has much to offer. It is, after all, nature's way. Provided due regard is paid to the preferences of each plant in terms of soil, situation and climate, the mutual protecton offered by the plants to each other is far more likely to be beneficial than otherwise, and indeed will probably increase their tolerance of conditions that are less than ideal in other ways. Plants that are doing well, obviously, make for a more satisfying garden picture than miserable invalids or struggling runts. Just as important is the fact that this sort of gardening gives much wider scope for devising plant associations than if the plants are segregated into categories.

The plantsman-collector will hardly miss the evident fact that here is a style of gardening which will enable him to wring the maximum return from every scrap of his probably far too small garden. Here, let us say, is a stalwart shrub, superb perhaps in its season but unexciting at other times;

why not drape a clematis over it, or *Aconitum volubile*? Among this group of ferns could be planted some spring bulbs, their dying foliage concealed by the ferns' new fronds in late spring. That idea, as any Jekyll reader will recognise, is taken straight from a chapter in the Colour Schemes book, and a glance at the plan that goes with it reveals that many other spring flowers are included in a border which would be a plantsman's and an artist's delight equally. There is, I believe, no reason for a plantsman's garden to be a mere higgledy-piggledy collection of unrelated individuals. Read E. A. Bowles's entrancing *My Garden* trilogy if you doubt this. You can hardly fail to be captivated; he writes far better than Miss Jekyll and he proves that the plantsman can create many satisfying garden pictures. Is it heresy to suggest that because he put the needs of his plants before their value as so much decoration, the results may have looked better to the sensitive gardener than the 'colour patch' style of planting?

Then there are these words, written by Christopher Lloyd: 'I invariably buy on impulse. Not for me the cool and rational approach. You'll never catch me saying "Charming, but I haven't a place for it". If I like the plant and think I can succeed with it, then I buy and deliberate afterwards.' That from one who, on the evidence of his writing about plants and of his garden, is probably as aware as anyone today of (his own words again) 'this business of juxtaposition and setting, which makes all the difference between a jumble and a picture'.

There are, of course, fashions in gardening as in anything else, and gardening in layers – referred to by a friend as 'tenement gardening' because it fits so many plants into a given area by using garden space vertically as well as horizontally – associating plants by common ecological needs, is widely practised today. (It also comprises some minor fashions that have been adopted, not always successfully, through lack of under-standing or practical experience perhaps, by the popular gardening press and the trade. There is most notably a ground-cover lobby recommending a range of plants, not always the most suitable for the purpose, as the answer to almost any weed problem.) A special kind of difficulty is encountered by those who must garden in keeping with the period of a house or a surviving garden design. There are many gardens open to the public, owned by The National Trust or other institutions or by private individuals, where currently fashionable styles of gardening can have no place. Such gardens are often labour-intensive; and purists may wish to grow only those plants which were extant in the era of the particular garden, as well as adhering to the appropriate style. It is not always easy to obtain the exact variety of plant that is needed for such schemes. So we find not only the gulf between the commonly available plants and those that the plantsman-collector or the designer may be seeking for their different reasons, but also the need for specific varieties that may have been dropped, long since perhaps, by the trade.

Britain's National Collections of garden plants exist, in part, to help fill this gap. Until the National Council for the Conservation of Plants and Gardens was formed, and the National Collections scheme established, the collecting instinct of Britain's gardeners was in the main uncoordinated, and sometimes undirected. Now, as we shall see, a national scheme is coordinating, formalising and initiating collections of garden plants. The Collections are in a sense living museums, aiming to gather and hold, against swings in taste and fashion, a representative range of garden plants past and present, all the plants of a kind together – all the hollies, say, or every sort of Korean chrysanthemum. The more complete a Collection becomes, the more it can fulfil another important function, that of evaluation; thanks to the magpie instinct of the owners of National Collections we, the gardening public, may have guidance in selecting from the best plants available. This in turn implies yet another function of the National Collections: to act as reserves of living material of as wide a range of plants as possible, which can be made available for propagation and distribution as a commercial demand makes itself felt. I stress 'commercial demand' as, however desirable it might be to make all the plants in a National Collection available to anyone who wants them, there are just not the resources for this, and so the Collections must act, on the whole, as reserves of stocks rather than as general suppliers.

Though I have touched on several of the functions of the National Collections I have not yet said exactly what they are or how they originated. To do this I must go back a little, to 1978 when the Royal Horticultural Society called a conference on the conservation of rare and threatened garden plants. Though many gardeners, both amateur and professional, had been doing their best to save endangered plants that particularly interested them – as it might be double primroses, or more widely the plants imprecisely known as 'cottage garden plants' – this haphazard approach to conservation had two major drawbacks. It was comparatively undirected, without any real coordination of effort, and it left many categories of plants as vulnerable as ever because they were unfashionable. The RHS conference culminated in the formation of the National Council for the Conservation of Plants and Gardens, an organisation whose aims are expressed in its somewhat cumbersome title (usually shortened to the initials NCCPG). The NCCPG now consists of a small central coordinating staff based at the RHS garden at Wisley, and a nation-wide membership of keen volunteers whose activities range from visiting gardens and raising money by local events, to recording plants and gardens locally, propagating and distributing uncommon plants, and forming group National Collections or helping the owners of privately or publicly owned National Collections.

The National Collections are seen by many people as one of the most important aspects of the work of the NCCPG. The ultimate aim is that every genus or group of garden plants should be represented by at least one designated National Collection, and better still by two in different parts of the country, with different climatic conditions. Already, though many groups of plants are not yet adopted, there are over 400 National Collections in existence. Some of them are mature and fairly complete collections that were already well-established when the NCCPG was formed; others are very new, and owe their existence at least in part to the enthusiasm which the NCCPG has engendered in the gardening world.

The National Collections are not the only work of the NCCPG, though they are closely associated with many other facets of the NCCPG's conservation efforts and in some cases have been its chief inspiration. For example, the success of the National Collections scheme has aroused great interest internationally, and led to discussions with international botanic gardens on the principles of National Collections and how similar schemes could be set up in other countries. The NCCPG is now cooperating with the International Union for the Conservation of Nature, though the IUCN, as its name implies, is concerned only with wild species, not with garden varieties. However, very many of the plants grown and cherished in British gardens are species, and some of them have become uncommon, or even threatened, in their native habitats. Take, for example, *Acer griseum*, the paperbark maple, described later in the chapter on the *Acer* National Collections. Despite obduracy in the matter of ripening good seed in this country, it is now commonplace in British gardens and fairly widely available commercially. In its native China it has been reduced to populations of saplings only, as mature trees are felled by the local inhabitants for firewood. Thus, though a protected tree, it is under threat and conceivably could be saved thanks to the plant collectors who first introduced it. A more exotic plant to our eyes, now that the paperbark maple has become widely grown in Britain, is the so-called Chihuahua plant, *Tacitus bellus*, a small succulent almost extinct in its native Mexico but offered by a conservation-conscious seed house in Britain, Thompson & Morgan (who carry their interest in the work of the NCCPG to the lengths of accepting responsibility for their own National Collection, of annual poppies).

Because, even within the fairly circumscribed framework of the National Collections scheme, collaboration with the IUCN is an immense task taxing resources to the limit and beyond, it has been approached systematically. It was decided to tackle a global problem country by country, starting with New Zealand, partly because the NCCPG has formed valuable contacts in that country and partly because there exists, in Britain, keen interest in plants from New Zealand. *Olearia* and *Senecio* are just two genera with many New Zealand representatives that feature in these pages. Taking the wider view of every New Zealand plant listed in the IUCN Red Data Book of endangered plants, the NCCPG determined so far as possible which of them are growing in British gardens. Knowledgeable growers of New Zealand plants were then consulted for an assessment of their garden-worthiness; for the NCCPG must not lose sight of its brief, which is to conserve *garden* plants. The result of the New Zealand study was the discovery that 12% of threatened New Zealand plants are growing commonly in British gardens. It must be stressed that the NCCPG is in no way involved with the reintroduction of endangered plant species to their native habitats; that is the responsibility of the IUCN and of botanic gardens.

Now that the National Collections scheme is well established, and constantly expanding, it is becoming increasingly important for scientific research; for scientists can now research all, or most, of the plants of a particular genus at one location. A valuable example is the *Linum* Collection, on which work related to cancer research is being conducted.

The Royal Horticultural Society not only provided the initial impetus that led to the formation of the NCCPG; it remains one of its major supporters, providing office facilities and services at Wisley. As well as financial assistance, the RHS gives practical support by holding a number of National Collections and by assisting National Collection holders with the preparation of herbarium specimens. Traditionally, herbarium specimens have been prepared of wild-collected plants almost exclusively, but for about twenty years the Wisley herbarium has also become the repository for specimens of cultivated plants, drawing especially on the plants grown in trials at Wisley itself and on plants which receive awards at the flower shows at Vincent Square. To these have now been added an increasing number of plants from the National Collections. As the National Collections herbarium specimens come to represent a wider and wider range of garden plants, so they will be of increasing use to those wishing to study a particular genus or group of plants. The specimens will also help to combat one of the most acute difficulties facing most National Collection holders: the lack of good descriptions of cultivated plants. Until the introduction of specimens of cultivated plants to the Wisley herbarium, there was for garden varieties no equivalent of the 'type specimen' of wild species; and few garden plants are described with any completeness, making identification extremely hazardous. Now, reference points can be established for more and more garden varieties, so that future generations will need less and less to rely on vague descriptions of the 'pink, 2 ft, June' type backed up by perhaps fallible human memory. Diana Miller, in charge of the herbarium at Wisley, writes that 'as the collections build up, apparently new plants will be able to be checked with named existing cultivars and a decision made as to the validity of a new name. Plants thought to be lost might be retraced by comparison with older herbarium material and problems with awards recommended to plants at the flower shows may be resolved more easily and with a greater degree of certainty.' To make identification still more certain, detailed descriptions, colour references and where possible photographic records are also included. The National Collection herbarium specimens are distinguished by easily recognisable labels.

Another large project, though not open-ended in the same way as the herbarium scheme, is the project funded by the Leverhulme Trust for a specific period, during which one hundred genera are being researched to establish, first, which garden varieties have been raised, introduced or grown in British gardens during the past one hundred years or so, and second which of these are still extant. From the data their rarity status can, tentatively at least, be established, though it must necessarily be a somewhat subjective assessment.

Other financial support has come from the government: the Department of the Environment has recognised the importance of the NCCPG's work by making a generous contribution to administrative costs.

It is not, of course, purely financial support that is needed, essential though it be. Tangible support is increasingly being offered by the nursery trade, in a variety of ways. Several nurseries hold their own National Collections; a great many more assist with plant propagation and distribution, a vital part of the NCCPG's endeavours. The NCCPG plant sales, organised by the groups, are increasingly perceived, by the gardening public and the nursery trade alike, as wonderful hunting grounds for the unusual, uncommon or rare, and the trade contribution has been immense. Nor is collaboration with the trade limited to rediscovered or rare plants. The first plant to be introduced by the NCCPG to raise funds to promote conservation work is a new variety, a double yellow *Gazania* named 'Yellow Buttons', introduced from South Africa and given to the NCCPG. In collaboration with the trade it has been increased from the first singleton plant to commercial quantities and offered to the general public; from each plant sold the NCCPG benefits.

Other collaborative endeavours are being pursued, such as the propagation and distribution of many old dianthus held in a National Collection, but until now commercially unavailable; they are propagated by Birmingham University staff and sold through the NCCPG. The National Trust is also a source for collaboration in distributing rare plants, and many National Collections are held in National Trust gardens; though, despite the similarity of name which sometimes confuses, the National Collections scheme is not 'part of the National Trust'.

The Consumer Association and the NCCPG work closely together on many projects, with the NCCPG advising on many horticultural matters for the Association's magazine 'Gardening from Which?' and the Consumer Association reciprocating with financial support, duplicates of photographs taken of National Collection plants, and joint displays at flower shows throughout the country, to promote both organisations. At the Bristol Flower Show in 1988 a three-cornered stand was the joint effort of the NCCPG, 'Gardening from Which?' and Cannington College, displaying their National Collection of abutilons. The Consumer Association is also responsible for its own National Collection, *Achillea*, grown at Capel Manor in Hertfordshire.

As well as the direct financial support of the Department of the Environment, government assistance has come to the NCCPG in other ways. Manpower Services Commission subsidised employees have carried out specific tasks to assist the secretariat, most notably with research on behalf of National Collection holders in the early days of the scheme. More recently in a joint venture at the Ayr and Arran show the NCCPG stand organised by the Ayr and Arran Group of the NCCPG and the central secretariat, was sponsored by the Consumer Association; the plants needed to form the display were raised by trainees from the Youth Training Scheme at Moorpark under Mr Bill Ivey. With plant material donated by NCCPG members, National Collections and the National Trust for Scotland's School of Gardening at Threave, these inexperienced trainees propagated enthusiastically and were rewarded with a Gold Medal.

Specialist horticultural societies are increasingly joining hands with the NCCPG in a variety of ways: there are several National Collections held collectively by, for example, the Hardy Plant Society or the Cyclamen Society, and the British Pteridological Society is closely involved in several of the National Collections of fern genera. There is a wealth of expertise, professional and amateur, in the specialist societies and this is increasingly made available to the NCCPG as the societies advise on the finer points of cultivation or identification of their chosen plants.

As well as specialist societies, many different kinds of institutions and individuals hold National Collections. There are botanic gardens and horticultural colleges with Collections, local authority parks departments, arboreta both private and public, the National Trusts, and nurseries large and small; and as well as these there are many Collections in the hands of private individuals both amateur and professional. Some are cared for in private gardens by owner-gardeners, some are the result of collective efforts by members of NCCPG local groups, and there is even, as we shall see, a Collection looked after by a class of Surrey schoolchildren.

As a result of this diversity of endeavours, and especially perhaps because of the success of the National Collections scheme, the NCCPG is widely perceived as the only credible organisation in the world involved in garden plant conservation.

Trees

Introduction

IN THE days of the great landscape gardens of the eighteenth century, trees were planted in abundance: our native trees, most of them destined to reach great size. In the nineteenth century exotic trees, especially conifers, began to reach our gardens; many were the monkey puzzles, cedars and wellingtonias planted as lawn specimens in Victorian gardens, or in parks. It was not until well on into the nineteenth century, and during this century, that most of the smaller trees we now take for granted were first introduced: the crabs, rowans and whitebeams, magnolias, and later the Japanese cherries and maples. There is still, surprisingly perhaps, no National Collection of Japanese cherries, but the other trees just mentioned are all represented in two or more National Collections; with birches, *Betula*, they comprise the five genera – *Malus*, the crabs; *Sorbus*, the rowans and whitebeams; *Magnolia*, and *Acer*, the maples – included in this section on trees for your garden.

They have much to offer, these trees, apart from their generally convenient size for today's smaller gardens. Like the bigger trees which preceded them in more spacious days, they may have considerable beauty of form; they are frequently very decorative in foliage, and many offer fine autumn colour; in flower, fruit, or both in due season, they may make a spectacular display; and some have fine bark as yet another attraction.

Form

Trees vary greatly in form, from the narrow columnar or conical outline that is chiefly, but not solely, seen in conifers, through domed or rounded crowns, to the broad fan of branches of many magnolias and cherries, and the widespreading canopy or weeping branches of certain varieties. Whether you are choosing a specimen tree or planting part of a group,

3

the form of your tree, the outline and density of its branches, its winter tracery, are all at least as important as the colour and abundance of its flowers or fruit, or the brilliance of its autumn colour. These are all fleeting effects, while the shape and poise of your tree will be with you all year. Do you want the firm solidity of a magnolia, with its large leaves and weighty, spreading branches, or will the delicate outline of a birch be more appropriate? Will the charm of their blossom or the brightness of their fruits compensate for the comparatively dull shape of many crabs? How will that domed, almost mushroom-like Japanese maple seem in winter without its elegant foliage? These are all points which deserve ample consideration before you choose your trees; and the fewer trees you have space for, the more essential it is to make the right choice, for in a surprisingly short time even a small tree will grow large enough to dominate your plantings.

Foliage

Most of the trees discussed in this book are deciduous (a few magnolias are not), so their leaves are with us for half the year at least; far longer than any season of flower or fruit. Some trees have exceptionally elegant or attractive foliage – the Japanese maples of course are grown for almost nothing else – while in others the leaves contribute very little to the beauty of the tree. On the whole, no-one could claim fine foliage for the crabs, unless you like the purple tones of some varieties. Personally I find these extremely hard to fit into any planting scheme, but many people would not agree. The ferny leaves of the rowans, on the other hand, or the broad, restful grey foliage of whitebeams, have great allure even without their autumn colouring attributes. Most birches have fairly small leaves which bring a gentle old-gold or lemon yellow tone to the autumn landscape, softening the brilliant reds, oranges and purples of the maples and rowans. Many magnolias have noble foliage, both the deciduous kinds and the evergreen; few trees are finer than a great specimen of *M. delavayi* with its huge, sea-green bloom-backed leaves, but this is a tree for favoured climates only, elsewhere a wall shrub and very worthy of such a position.

An added value to be gained from the trees which put on fine autumn colour is to be found in the carpet of fallen leaves beneath the canopy branches. It pays, in autumn, not to be tidy-minded. Indeed, just the same is true of fallen petals in spring.

Bark and beauty of stems

Of the trees included in this book, only the birches and some of the maples are generally grown for their attractive bark. Birches offer not just the white or silvery-grey bark of our native, and many other, birches, but also yellow, russet, apricot, tan and shaggy black trunks. The snake-bark maples are a group with usually green bark, striped and streaked with white, while there are also maples with red or coral stems rivalling the Westonbirt dogwood for winter brilliance; and the lovely peeling, tan or rich brown-barked *Acer griseum*, the paperbark maple.

As well as the colour and texture of bark, there is pleasure to be gained from the shape of tree trunks. The classic standard tree on its perfectly straight stem may not always be the best choice; a leaning or picturesquely bent or gnarled trunk may have its own charm and informal appropriateness. Then too we may wish for a multi-stemmed tree, or for a small closely-planted grove – birches lend themselves particularly well to either treatment. A large magnolia, too, springing multi-stemmed from ground level, can be very fine. Obtaining such a tree may be difficult; the nursery trade is organised to produce standards rather than many-stemmed trees, and you may need to acquire a young sapling and rear your own.

Flower and Fruit

Flowering trees are understandably popular, and of the five genera considered here two are grown above all for their flower: the magnolias and the crabs. The effect they make is quite different one from the other. Magnolias bear large flowers, often in great profusion it is true, but each flower appears as an individual with its own characteristic form, as of a chalice or goblet, a bowl, or the multi-petalled starry flowers of *Magnolia stellata*. The individual flowers of crabs are much smaller and relatively formless, making their impact by their sheer quantity. They bring white or pink or purplish tones; and magnolias especially, flowering in the main earlier than the crabs, relieve the masses of yellow of spring; but as a result, their placing needs to be considered very carefully. Few things are more painful to the eye than an indigestible lump of bright yellow forsythia (and perhaps even some orange berberis) with purplish-pink magnolias.

As with fallen autumn leaves, so with spring blossom; the carpet of waxy petals beneath a magnolia, or of the tiny petals of the crabs, mirroring the flower still held on the branches above, greatly enhances the picture they make in the garden scene.

For autumn fruit the rowans are supreme, with the whitebeams and some crabs also making a contribution. Our native rowan or mountain ash fruits too early, bringing an uncomfortable feeling that autumn is upon us a full month or so before its time. By the time the Chinese rowans display their fruit it is truly autumn and their great bunches of yellow, orange or scarlet, or of crimson, pink or white fruits, are a welcome feature of the misty autumn landscape with its crisp mornings and occasional brilliantly clear days.

Siting

When choosing a tree for a particular position – or a position for a particular tree, for it often happens that way round especially in the gardens of keen plantsmen – there is more to be considered than simply the outline and size of the tree, its soil preference, its colour of flower, fruit or autumn foliage. It is worth considering the relation of the sun, in its passage across the sky, to the chosen tree. Where will its shadow fall at various times of the day? The long shadows of a tree across a lawn, moving with the hours, are a very important part of the picture it makes in the garden. Then, too, it is worth remembering that foliage, especially in its autumn colours, is enhanced by the sun shining through it, while the colour of bark and berry needs, to attain its full value, to have the sun falling upon it; backlit, the trunk and the fruits will appear merely dark shapes on a light background. Suitable backgrounds may need contriving to set off the flowering display of your chosen tree, or it may be best to arrange for the blossom to be seen against the sky. The fine *Magnolia campbellii* at Sharpitor near Salcombe on the south Devon coast owes much of its impact to its position on a terrace at a lower level than much of the garden, so you can not only look into, rather than up at, its flowers, but also see them against a backdrop of sea and sky. It is worth a special journey in March to see this lovely tree in flower. The brilliant colours of maples and rowans in autumn gain greatly if set among quiet-toned evergreens, as with the Japanese maples at Westonbirt growing with dark green spires of *Calocedrus*, or seen against groups of conifers, as also at Sheffield Park, where reflections in the lakes give yet another dimension.

Acer

MAPLES have been cultivated for many hundreds of years for their beauty of foliage, form or bark. Some are large, robust and handsome trees; of these, the Norway maple and sycamore, at least, are familiar to us all. At the other extreme are the fine-leaved forms of Japanese maple which in youth often form little mushroom-shaped shrubs, and in old age may make graceful and delicate small trees. Between are a host of species. Maples can furnish our gardens with autumn colour or brilliant spring foliage; or with beauty of bark or vivid winter stem colour. Some display a delicacy, or a boldness, of leaf form; a few are handsome in flower, and several are admired when carrying their striking winged seeds. Many of the finest maples, none the less, are scarcely known to gardeners, outside a handful of enthusiasts.

The handsome, hardy and vigorous Norway maple, *Acer platanoides*, a large-growing tree, is suitable for almost any soil and is decorative when bearing its yellow-green flowers before the leaves appear, as well as in foliage. There are variegated forms, such as 'Drummondii', purple-leaved kinds like 'Goldsworth Purple' or 'Crimson King', a seedling of 'Schwed-leri' which itself has bright red young foliage ageing to green in summer. 'Lorbergii' has deeply cut leaves and the unusual, white-speckled leaves of 'Walderseeii' dry when pressed to a translucent creamy-yellow with the veins picked out in deep green.

The best known garden form of sycamore, *Acer pseudoplatanus*, is 'Brilliantissimum', with bright shrimp-pink spring foliage. Sadly, it then fades to a sickly, chlorotic yellow. 'Prinz Handjery', with similar bright pink young growths, is a better plant; the summer foliage, a healthy green, is backed with dove-purple, and the tree grows with more enthusiasm than the painfully slow 'Brilliantissimum'. Hedgerow sycamores often display quite brightly coloured spring growths, but all too often, in my experience, this is inconstant; the sapling marked last spring may well,

7

this year, be a plain green like all its fellows. Returning to the cultivated forms, there is a variegated sycamore, and two golden-leaved kinds, 'Corstorphinense' and 'Worleei'. The purple-leaved sycamore has crossed with *Acer heldreichii* (from the Balkan States and Greece) to produce, at Blagdon in Northumberland where one of the National Collections of maples is grown, an interesting seedling with purple-backed foliage.

The Caucasian *Acer cappadocicum* also has its gold and purple-red forms, and 'Tricolor' with young foliage variegated red, pink and cream. Its Chinese form var. *sinicum* is striking in autumn when decked with its bright red fruits. At Hergest Croft in Herefordshire, where the other National Collection of maples is grown, is a seedling from *A. cappadocicum* 'Aureum' planted in 1978; it is both red and gold and could be worth a clonal name. Other maples that, like *A. cappadocicum* var. *sinicum*, are worth growing for their winged seeds are *A. tataricum*, pinkish in fruit, and the red-seeded *A. trautvetteri* from the Caucasus, a tree with bold foliage emerging from brilliant crimson buds.

Some of the snake-bark maples have bright autumn fruits, but their chief attraction lies in their striped and marbled bark. A rare snake-bark is *Acer morrisonense* from Taiwan, a fairly hardy tree despite its origins, with red bark, striped with white, bright red twigs, and long racemes of showy fruits. At Hergest this tree varies greatly in its resistance to the climate; two out of three die, but it is so decorative that it is worth persevering with. Also rare in cultivation is *Acer laxiflorum* from China, with green snake-bark. *Acer forrestii*, slightly less uncommon perhaps, is closely related; its beautifully shaped leaves are held on red petioles. It is remarkable for the way in which it sends out long, arching, and relatively unbranched stems from the trunk in all directions to form a three-dimensional fan. More familiar in our gardens is *Acer capillipes*, a beautiful and hardy tree with coral-red young branchlets; the older bark is brownish-green with the characteristic white snake-bark stripes. Bold three-lobed leaves turn to bright shades of orange and red in autumn: though on the heavy soil at Blagdon (glacial boulder clay over carboniferous limestone) autumn colour is less reliable than at Hergest Croft.

Acer davidii is a fine, and variable, snake-bark maple represented in cultivation by several different forms. The Ernest Wilson form is compact in growth, with green bark, striped in white, and dark green foliage. George Forrest's form is looser in growth, with red, white-striped bark and bright purplish-red young shoots. *A. davidii* 'Serpentine' has much smaller leaves as seen at Blagdon, where also is a seedling grown from a seed collected by Lord Ridley on Mt Omei in 1981.

Another well-known snake-bark maple is *Acer grosseri*, green-barked, and its form *hersii* with more distinctly lobed leaves. *A. tegmentosum*, and the better-known *A. rufinerve*, are Asiatic snake-barks (the first from Korea

and eastern Siberia, the second from Japan) with green, white-striped bark
and a white bloom on the young shoots. *A. rufinerve* takes on bright
crimson and yellow autumn colour, in contrast to the more restrained
yellow of *A. tegmentosum*. There is a curious form of *A. rufinerve* with
white-marbled foliage, *f. albolimbatum*; unusually for a variegated form it
comes true from seed, varying in the extent of the white spotting and
flecks, and is somewhat apt to revert. Closely related to these is *A.
pensylvanicum*, from, as its name implies, eastern North America; exem-
plifying, with *A. rufinerve*, the parallelism of Appalachian and Far Eastern
floras. *Acer pensylvanicum* is handsome in autumn when its large, three-
lobed leaves take on yellow autumn colour. Desirable as it is, it is surpassed
by its exquisite but temperamental form 'Erythrocladum', in which the
young stems are bright coral pink. In winter it rivals the coral-bark maple,
'Senkaki', but has not its constitution; most of us who have planted
'Erythrocladum' have lost it at least once before persuading it to grow.
By contrast the snake-bark maple called 'Silver Vein' is a good doer.
Lord Ridley considers this to be a hybrid between *A. pensylvanicum*
'Erythrocladum' and *A. davidii*, Ernest Wilson form; but other authorities
give it as a form of *A. rufinerve* and state that it originated at Hillier's
Nurseries. Whatever its origin it is a fine thing with beautifully marbled
bark.

One of the best loved maples is *Acer griseum*, grown chiefly for its
shaggy bark, peeling and flaking in orange and tan layers. It makes at best
a shapely tree, with trifoliate leaves, silvery glaucous beneath, that turn to
bright crimson and scarlet in autumn. At the same time it is often hung
with abundant, though scarcely showy, fruits, but very few of these are
viable; so that it remains, if not rare, still fairly expensive and generally
planted as a single specimen, a treatment it well deserves. *Acer griseum* has
some near allies with similar foliage composed of three leaflets, which are
beautiful trees deserving to be planted far more frequently. *A. nikoense*
from Japan has hairy foliage which turns to vivid shades of scarlet, crimson
and orange in autumn. It grows slowly to form a tree of up to 50 ft. At
Hergest are two forms: the type collected by Henry in China has larger
leaves with brighter glaucous backs, and rich claret autumn colour with
no hint of yellow; the type introduced by Maries has grown much more
slowly and its leaves are paler and somewhat smaller. It is a large bush
rather than a tree and turns yellowish-red in autumn. *Acer triflorum* is rare
and slow-growing, needing perhaps hotter summers than it experiences
here. It usually colours to brilliant scarlet in autumn, and has ashy-brown
peeling bark. *Acer henryi*, rarest of the cultivated trifoliate maples, grows
at both Blagdon and at Hergest, and survives at Westonbirt Arboretum
(about which more later) lying on its side. Another rare trifoliate maple
of which there are good specimens at Hergest is *Acer mandschuricum* which

produces quantities of seeds, none viable. Yet another maple which remains very rare in cultivation, partly because it is difficult to propagate, is *Acer giraldii*, which grew for many years unrecognised at Hergest – it looks somewhat like a sycamore but has a white plummy bloom on the young shoots.

Several maples mimic, more or less convincingly, other trees. *Acer catalpifolium* is a tender Chinese species that has leaves somewhat like the Indian bean tree; *A. carpinifolium*, least maple-like of all the acers, has foliage like a hornbeam and *A. crataegifolium* resembles a hawthorn in leaf. This last has a pretty variegated form, 'Veitchii', with pink, green and white foliage. *A. distylum* is sometimes called the lime-leaf maple. The vine-leaf maple, *A. circinatum*, is a shrubby species from North America which colours brilliantly in autumn and is attractive in spring flower, the wine-purple sepals and whitish petals contrasting with crimson bud-scales. *Acer negundo* is the box elder, though evidently neither a box nor an elder; the foliage is compound and coarsely toothed, with perhaps a remote resemblance to that of elder. It is a species which has given rise to several garden cultivars, including the much-planted 'Variegatum' which is so frequently ruined by reverting green-leaved branches overpowering, with their greater vigour, the parts with cream-edged foliage for which the tree is chosen. Yellow-leaved and yellow-variegated forms are known; a strange kind with much reduced, linear leaflets is known as 'Heterophyllum'; and 'Violaceum' has the young, purplish branches covered with a glaucous bloom. It has the further merit of attractive coral flowers. Even better in flower than this is *A. diabolicum purpurascens*, a Japanese species with the most striking flowers of any maple, bright coral clusters.

Most maples, though they dislike very dry soils, are equally intolerant of boggy conditions. A few are found, in nature, growing in quite wet soils; such as *A. rubrum*, the red maple, national emblem of Canada. Several garden forms of the red maple have been selected, of which a new and exceptionally fine one is 'October Glory', outstanding in its rich crimson colouring.

Acer saccharinum, the silver maple, is closely related to the red maple. The silver maple is a large tree of great beauty, with long pendulous branches that stir in the slightest breeze, revealing the silvery underside of the leaves. Confusingly, the sugar maple, from which maple syrup is chiefly obtained, is botanically *A. saccharum*. Its close ally *A. nigrum*, the black maple, is sometimes considered as a subspecies of the sugar maple, but Lord Ridley points out that it is unique among maples in having stipules.

Many of the maples I have so far mentioned are of Eastern or American origin. Apart from the sycamore and Norway maple, other European species include *A. campestre*, the field maple (the only maple native to

Britain), with pinkish young foliage. Like so many maples, this too has produced different garden forms, with yellow, red or variegated foliage. The wild species, however, is a very pretty tree that scarcely needs such artifices. *Acer opalus* is a handsome European species which is particularly striking in bright yellow flower produced even before those of *A. platanoides*. So too is the Caucasian *A. velutinum* with vivid candle-like spikes of yellow flowers. Quite distinct from most maples are the Mediterranean species, *A. sempervirens* and its near allies *A. syriacum* and the Cretan *A. obtusifolium*. All are shrubby rather than tree-like, and nearly evergreen with leathery, small leaves. At Hergest are two *A. sempervirens* grown from seed from a tree in the Jardin des Plantes, Paris, itself raised from Tournefort's original tree. In deference to their origins these shrubby maples are given sheltered positions in the lee of a wall at Blagdon.

Some of the most beautiful maples are distinctly tender but are suitable for gardens in mild areas, and several are grown at Blagdon in cold glasshouses, where they are threatening to push off the roof. Perhaps the least tender and the most beautiful is *A. pentaphyllum*, from China, with long, slender five-fingered leaves, glaucous beneath, on scarlet petioles. It is rare in the wild and far from common in cultivation, though fairly easy to raise from cuttings. The Himalayan *A. campbellii* has elegant palmate foliage. Close to it is *A. flabellatum*, with seven to nine leaflets, and its variety *yunnanense*, both rather hardier. *A. kawakamii* will also grow outside in sheltered sites, though native of Taiwan; an attractive maple with triangular leaves drawn out to a long slender point. *Acer serrulatum* is another Taiwanese species still under glass at Blagdon, awaiting trial outside for hardiness.

Several of the tender evergreen maples have foliage of very different character, leathery and unlobed. The mature leaves of *A. oblongum* can be as much as a foot long; bright green above, they are glaucous-white beneath. Its close ally *A. lanceolatum* is from Hong Kong. The related *A. paxii* has three-lobed leaves, also glaucous beneath. *A. hookeri* and the similar *A. sikkimense* have red branchlets and dark glossy green foliage. Another Himalayan species is *A. laevigatum* with sword-shaped, bright green leaves. *A. craibianum* is a tender species with three blunt, forward-pointing lobes to each leaf, almost like *Sassafras*; the young growths are crimson, making this a most desirable little tree for the mildest gardens.

It must be evident from the maples I have so far mentioned that the genus *Acer* is much given to producing aberrant forms, some of which are very beautiful; others should undoubtedly have been strangled at birth. Of all the species of maple, none is more diverse in its manifestations than *A. palmatum*, the Japanese maple. Minute variations in foliage form and colour have been selected and named, especially in Japan, so that there are several hundred named kinds now in cultivation. They – or a selection of them, at least – are kept as a separate National Collection at Westonbirt Arboretum in Gloucestershire. With them are grown their near ally *A. japonicum*, the full moon maple, and its far fewer variants.

With so many hundreds to choose from, I can do no more than mention a few of the Japanese maples that are now available to British gardeners. An old and still popular kind is *Acer palmatum* 'Osakasuki', with bright green foliage turning reliably to brilliant scarlet, crimson and flame in autumn. Many Japanese maples have purple foliage, and 'Bloodgood' is outstanding with deep red foliage, turning bright crimson in autumn when it is hung with vivid red seeds. In common with other named clones this must be propagated vegetatively, by cuttings or grafting; but 'Atropurpureum' of commerce is often seed raised, so the seedlings have no right to a cultivar name.

The Dissectum group of Japanese maples form dome-shaped shrubs with pendulous branches, often growing wider than high, and finely cut foliage, feathery or fern-like in appearance. The green-leaved forms are collectively known as *A. palmatum dissectum viridis* and the purple as *A. palmatum dissectum atropurpureum*. 'Crimson Queen' is an outstanding selection with deep red foliage turning scarlet in autumn. 'Burgundy Lace' is another good plant with finely-cut leaves, and 'Chitoseyama' is enchanting in spring when the young, much-divided leaves are vivid pink, later turning to deep claret and then, in autumn, to bright crimson. A group with the leaflets reduced to slim blades, classed as the Linearilobum group, includes the lovely 'Villa Taranto', with green, white and pink foliage. Several other Japanese maples, with leaf shapes varying from the basic palmate outline to the finely-cut dissection, have unusual colouration, with variegations of pink, cream, yellow, red or white. 'Butterfly' is recommended for its upright habit and pretty foliage, green flecked with cream. Less unnatural in aspect are the forms with bright spring foliage that later turns to green: 'Corallinum' in shrimp-pink spring garb, and 'Shishio Improved' with small crimson leaves maturing to green, are just two of these. Another, which never makes a big plant, is 'Katsura', with orange, yellow and pink spring foliage, green in summer, flame and yellow in autumn.

Not all the Japanese maples are grown for their foliage alone. One of the most admired is 'Senkaki' ('Sangokaku') which is a plant for winter effect above all. Known as the coral bark maple, it rivals *A. pensylvanicum* 'Erythrocladum' with its vivid coral-red winter twigs. In leaf it is neat and delicate, palest green in spring and brilliant yellow flushed with apricot and pink in autumn. At Blagdon a big plant of this is set against the blackish-green foliage of a large Irish yew; 'Senkaki' well deserves a contrivance such as this to reveal its full beauty. Less brilliant than 'Senkaki' but a fine thing none the less is 'Aoyagi' with vivid green-barked branches.

Acer palmatum 'Ribesifolium' is a very variable cultivar. At Hergest is a narrow upright form some 40 ft tall, highly rated there when it turns a rich russet brown very late in autumn. Elsewhere it often makes a rather shapeless bush with distorted leaves and little virtue.

The full moon maple, *Acer japonicum*, has been more restrained in its variants; there are a mere dozen or so. 'Aconitifolium' is a beautiful tree with deeply divided, feather-edged leaves turning scarlet, claret and carmine in autumn in harmony with its wine-purple fruits. 'Aureum' is desperately slow growing, but worth your patience, forming a small rounded tree densely packed with butter yellow foliage, turning orange-red in autumn. At Hergest a much-admired combination of colour and form is *Acer japonicum* 'Aureum' with *Taxus baccata* 'Aurea' and behind them a good, not too garishly blue form of *Cedrus atlantica glauca*.

At Westonbirt it is the vine-leaved form of *Acer japonicum*, 'Vitifolium', that is more frequently seen than the parent species. The vine-leaved maple is more vigorous than *A. palmatum*; as its soft green leaves unfold some specimens produce a conspicuous crop of small red flowers in drooping clusters. But it is primarily planted for its autumn colour, which begins to show in September with shades of yellow, followed by scarlet, deep pink, gold, crimson and ruby red, set off by some remaining green leaves, which finally in late October turn to claret red.

At Westonbirt, as at Hergest and Blagdon, the maples grow in informal settings, in grassy glades and with other shrubs and trees. The Japanese maples fit well into more gardened settings equally, perhaps with hostas, evergreen azaleas, slow-growing (rather than dwarf) conifers, forms of *Pieris* with their bright spring foliage and sprays of white lily of the valley flowers, and the like; with underplantings of some of the many small things that enjoy light shade and the moist, leafy soil that best suits the maples: wood anemones, trilliums, ferns, and so much else.

The National Collections

The National Collections of maples are held at Hergest Croft Gardens, Kington, Hereford (Mr R. A. and Mr W. L. Banks); at Blagdon, Seaton Burn, Newcastle upon Tyne (Viscount Ridley); and at Westonbirt Arboretum, Tetbury, Gloucestershire (The Forestry Commission).

The first maples were planted at Hergest by Dick Banks's grandfather in the second half of the last century. His son, Dick Banks's father, was however the great planter of this genus and many others, including birches (see Chapter 000), planting all he could get hold of, scouring the nurseries of England, Scotland and Ireland as well as France, Belgium and Holland. He was also in touch with several other owners of gardens such as Balfour of Dawyck, E. A. Bowles, and Coltman Rogers of Stanage nearby. When the Hergest plants were catalogued by Bruce Jackson about 1930 there were eighty-six entries covering thirty-six species of Acer. Bruce Jackson also introduced a number of new plants from Woburn, Aldenham (The Hon. Vicary Gibbs) and Colesbourne (H. J. Elwes). The Hergest maples were designated as a National Collection in April 1981.

By contrast the collection of maples at Blagdon is in the main much younger, though already around 200 different maples are represented there. Most of the plantings date from the early 1970s or later. The Blagdon maples were designated as a National Collection in September 1983.

The Japanese maples at Westonbirt Arboretum were designated as a National Collection in March 1982. Westonbirt is a Victorian arboretum laid out with a garden designer's eye, and in particular with autumn colour in mind. The planned climax of colour in late October derives chiefly from maples, cercidiphyllums, and deciduous species of Euonymus, set against the varying greens and contrasting form of mature conifers. Texture and translucency, space and density all contribute to a composition which draws the crowds in their thousands. Almost uniquely in this country, many of the Japanese maples at Westonbirt have grown beyond the mere prettiness of youth to their full-grown grace and beauty. John White, Curator of Westonbirt Arboretum, suspects that some of the oldest trees there, although unnamed, may be old surviving cultivars. Before the present revival of interest in maple cultivation on a commercial scale the practice at the Arboretum was to plant rows of seedlings in the nursery and select perhaps two in a hundred for their autumn colour and form. These were planted out in the early sixties to form the now world-famous Acer Glades. There are also many cultivars at Westonbirt, thanks to the collection mania of Sir George Holford, founder of the Arboretum, whose notes Bruce Jackson drew upon when compiling his catalogue of the trees and shrubs at Westonbirt in 1927. Here it is stated that trees of Acer japonicum 'Vitifolium' in the Acer Grove were certainly, then, forty years old.

Betula

BIRCHES are a much less diverse lot than the maples. Their appeal lies in their curious and beautiful bark, and often in their untamed grace. Our native silver birch, *Betula pendula*, is as lovely as any, with its silvery-white, scarcely peeling bark and graceful habit. Like all birches it is variable in habit, and to some extent in bark characteristics – some (such as var. *obscura* from Poland) fail to develop the waxy betulin which gives birches their white bark. The lovely form known as 'Tristis' is the most graceful of all, of narrow outline, decked with curtains of slender hanging branchlets, their purplish-brown colouring contrasting with the tall white trunk. In areas of heavy snowfall all the birches are of the 'Tristis' type, their pendulous branches shedding the snow where the less graceful types might snap beneath its weight. 'Tristis' becomes large in time; for a small garden the determined weeper 'Youngii' might be more suitable, though seldom does one see a plant looking other than slightly grotesque, a kind of graceless vegetable gnome perched on a white stem. Prettier, but also slow-growing, is 'Purpurea', a silver birch of normal habit with coppery-black foliage.

In the wild, forms of silver birch with more or less deeply cut foliage appear from time to time; some have been propagated by grafting and given a distinguishing name. The name most often encountered is 'Dalecarlica', but it appears that most, if not all, cut-leaved birches in commerce and even in cultivation are in fact forma *crispa*, a tree which lacks the elegance of the true 'Dalecarlica' with its deeply-cut, fern-like foliage.

Birches are much given to hybridising, and natural populations show wide variations, with some species apparently grading almost imperceptibly into others. Thus identification is often hazardous, and the hapless gardener's choice beset with difficulties. Take the very white-barked birch we all think of as *Betula jacquemontii*. Tony Schilling, of Wakehurst Place (Kew Gardens' country outpost) and Kenneth Ashburner, a nurseryman

15

specialising in birches, have recently published their findings on the status of B. *jacquemontii* and B. *utilis*, considered by many gardeners and botanists to be two separate species, distinguished by the colour of their bark and the number of veins in the leaf. However, it seems that in the wild the very white-barked B. *jacquemontii* from the western Himalayas merges gradually into the orange-brown or chocolate-barked B. *utilis* from Nepal, Sikkim and Bhutan. Tony Schilling and Ken Ashburner consider that there is a direct correlation between climatic conditions and bark colour: the betulin-saturated, white-barked trees grow at high altitude in dry zones, with high light intensity and low temperatures; the brown-barked birches in areas of very high rainfall. Some very lovely, white-barked birches are offered commercially as B. *jacquemontii*, but names to look out for in future if you want to be sure of obtaining a fine white-stemmed birch are 'Grayswood Ghost' and 'Inverleith', the latter name proposed for the beautiful 'B. *jacquemontii*' which grows at the Royal Botanic Garden in Edinburgh. This is now considered to be a second-generation hybrid, with blood of perhaps B. *pubescens* (the downy birch, our other native birch) or even of B. *papyrifera*, the paper birch from North America. Whatever its parentage, it is a superb tree, and the infusion of European or North American blood may make it more suitable for the British climate than pure B. *utilis* var. *jacquemontii* from Kashmir.

Further east again, in western China, grows *Betula albo-sinensis*, greatly admired for its apricot-orange, peeling bark. One with a fine dark mahogany bark grows vigorously among a group of *Rhododendron fulvum* at Hergest, where one of the National Collections of birches is grown. Also at Hergest are two hybrid birches with similar, tan-coloured bark. These have proved distinct enough to be worth naming and propagating, yet only by chance did they survive long enough to show their characteristic colouring. One of a group of beech trees separating two parts of the azalea garden at Hergest had to be cut down; next year on the bare ground there came up a tremendous crop of tree seedlings. There were conifers, *Sorbus*, *Stranvaesia*, cotoneasters, elms and above all birches. They were all allowed to grow for a few years, when the twenty or thirty which showed most sign of being white- or silver-barked were planted out separately. The rest were left where they were growing, to be disposed of later. A few years later one of these rejects, still unfelled, produced a stem of a colour between cinnamon and honey, which shows up at a distance and is always much admired. It was named 'Hergest'. Another, slightly darker and not quite so striking, has been named 'Haywood' after the common beyond the garden at Hergest. At Blagdon, where the other National Collection of birches is grown, similar colouring appears on a seedling of B. *tianschanica*, coppery-tan in bark, with horizontal creamy-white lenticels.

Betula ermanii, from the Far East, has creamy or apricot-white bark, thinly peeling, with buff-pink lenticels. It is suited to very thin, poor, rocky soils, though like any other birch it will thrive on a good well-drained soil. *B. costata* is similar; but here again the naming of birches is in some confusion. A tree at Hergest Croft, labelled *B. costata*, is in fact the Grayswood form of *B. ermanii*, with very striking creamy bark. At Blagdon a small *B. costata* has warm cinnamon-apricot bark, marked with vertical striping in a deeper, slightly glaucous-bloomed coppery tan.

One of the most un-birch-like birches is related to *B. costata*. This is the Caucasian *B. medwediewii*, which grows into a big, wide-spreading shrub with thick stems, scarcely peeling bark and large alder-like leaves which die off pale yellow in autumn. A resemblance to alder is recognised in the specific name of *B. alnoides*, from the Himalayas; this, like the allied *B. luminifera* (a Chinese species) is reputed to be tender. Lord Ridley and Dick Banks, in China together, collected seed of *B. luminifera* in a car-park outside a restaurant. The seed sown at Blagdon, Lord Ridley's seat, germinated, and saplings of this collection now grow at both Blagdon and Hergest Croft.

None of these three birches has particularly striking bark, and we need to turn to other eastern species to discover more trees worth garden space for their white or coloured stems. Such is *B. platyphylla*, of which two geographical variants are in cultivation. *B. platyphylla szechuanica* from China has dusty white bark that sheds onto the hands like ancient distemper, and is of rather stiff, graceless habit. *B. platyphylla japonica* has larger leaves than our native silver birch. Though it comes into leaf about three weeks earlier than other birches it seems resistant, none the less, to spring frosts, at least at Blagdon. The bark on mature trees of *B. platyphylla japonica* is pure white, but for many years it remains brown on young trees, before beginning to peel to orange and apricot. Another very early-leafing birch is the Far Eastern *B. davurica*, which is normally vulnerable to damage from spring frosts. But as Dick Banks, of Hergest Croft, points out, hardiness is very difficult to determine. Why will one plant die, when another next door survives? The reason may be clonal differences, or different shelter from sun or wind from a particular quarter, or perhaps differences in the state of activity or maturity of growth in similar plants. It is unwise to be didactic about the hardiness of any species, and *B. davurica* is a case in point. At Hergest are trees of great size and beauty with rugged flaky trunks with a hint of pink in them; these trees thrive, unaffected by spring frosts. Are they somewhat hybridised, or do they come from a climate as unreliable in winter as our own? Another three plants of *B. davurica* – now reduced to just one miserable specimen – looking much like others from south Russia, get caught by cold every spring and looked like witches' brooms as a result. Recently Kenneth Ashburner presented Hergest with three plants from Hokkaido, hoping they might be hardier. They were planted in a group. One died, one was untouched, and one badly damaged. Much the same could be recounted about many other plants. In one garden there may be a splendid specimen, in another a wretched one, especially when they have been grown from wild seed rather than vegetatively propagated from selected clones.

Betula davurica has affinities with the North American paper birch, *B. papyrifera*, which varies greatly in bark characteristics, some seedlings maturing to show spectacular peeling white stems while others, even whole populations in the wild, may remain brown. The paper birch is larger in leaf than our native silver birch, and has not its graceful habit. The papery, peeling bark is impervious to water, and has had many uses: as roofing, for canoes, or to make drinking utensils. Another North American birch is *B. caerulea-grandis*; unlike the widespread paper birch this one is restricted, in the wild, to maritime provinces of New England and Nova Scotia. A sapling of this, the blue birch, at Blagdon has rich apricot-tan bark, with a faint white bloom of betulin.

The yellow birch, *B. lutea*, is more widespread in eastern North America. It makes, ultimately, a sizeable tree with yellowish-brown, shiny peeling bark. From similar areas comes the river birch. *B. nigra*, which grows equally well in ordinary or in swampy soil. The river birch has shaggy flaking bark, pinkish buff ageing to near black on mature trees, which usually form two or three trunks forking low down.

Birches and azaleas make good companions at Hergest. Their foliage gives just the right sort of dappled shade and surprisingly their shallow root system does not seem to dry the ground too much for the azaleas. In the two recent hot dry summers the birches suffered more than the azaleas, when the sap failed to reach the tops to keep them in good leaf, though there were no casualties in spite of no watering. The autumn colours and white stems give great charm to the area, though to keep it at its best the stems must be scrubbed periodically to keep green algae and lichens at bay.

Not all birches are tree-like and suitable for such plantings. The dwarf birches, exemplified by the familiar *B. nana*, are alpine and montane shrubs from Eurasia, America and Greenland. *B. nana* forms low thickets of shrublets with tiny, circular leaves. This is the only shrubby birch likely to be found in commerce: others that are in cultivation, but scarcely likely to be offered commercially, are *B. humilis* and *B. glandulosa*, which both grow rather taller than *B. nana*. This smallest of birches is easily raised from cuttings, but is not necessarily easy to establish; several specimens have died at Hergest, perhaps from drought; in the wild it grows in moist places. When it thrives it is a pretty shrub for informal settings, as it might be with dwarf willows, or with heathers such as *Erica ciliaris*, which seems to appreciate damper conditions than most heaths.

From this bewildering confusion of names, which birches can you confidently plant in your garden? The only certain way of getting just what you want, if you are looking for a particular bark colour, say, is to see the tree from which your plant has been vegetatively propagated; young plants do not show the attractive features which develop later. One of the loveliest is the very white form of '*B. jacquemontii*', to be called 'Inverleith'. Good forms of *B. albo sinensis* var. *septentrionalis*, with cinnamon stems covered with a faint plummy bloom, are also much sought after. Then there is the creamy-barked *B. ermanii*, Grayswood form. If you have a really damp corner, do not disdain the river birch, *B. nigra*, for all that it takes a long time to show its characteristic shaggy brown bark. Any of these birches will lend to your garden a distinction that will never be achieved by a plot with Young's weeping birch in one corner.

The National Collections

The National Collections of Betula are held at Hergest Croft Gardens, Kington, Herefordshire (Mr R. A. and Mr W. L. Banks) and at Blagdon, Seaton Burn, Newcastle upon Tyne (Viscount Ridley).

The Hergest birches were designated as a National Collection in April 1981. Many of the trees were already mature specimens, planted by Dick Banks's father, who collected all he could, scouring the nurseries of England, Scotland and Ireland, France, Belgium and Holland. He was also in touch with owners of other gardens, such as Balfour of Dawyck, E. A. Bowles, and Coltman Rogers of Stanage nearby, who wrote the article on birches in the RHS Journal of 1928 where he mentioned a number of the Hergest plants. The plants at Hergest were catalogued by Bruce Jackson in about 1930; Jackson also introduced a number of new plants from Woburn, Aldenham (The Hon. Vicary Gibbs), and Colesbourne (H. J. Elwes). More recently Dick and Lawrence Banks have received plants raised from wild seed from Kenneth Ashburner and the Ness Gardens (Hugh MacAllister). The Banks family have been assisted in identifying their birches by Kenneth Ashburner, Tony Schilling, Roy Lancaster, Lord Ridley and Carl-Axel Janssen of Sweden.

Most of the birches at Blagdon are young plants; the National Collection here was designated in September 1983. Lord Ridley has been planting extensively, both birches and maples and many other genera contributing to a young but already very interesting arboretum. At Blagdon, too, birches of known wild origin are being planted.

Magnolia

MAGNOLIAS present a paradox. Aristocratic in appearance, and just demanding enough in their requirements to add to their reputation as exotic trees, not for the multitudes indeed but only for the few, they are botanically primitive by comparison with the other trees we have considered: the maples, birches, rowans, whitebeams and crabs.

In fact, most magnolias are by no means difficult to grow. Their reputation has perhaps suffered from the one problem that may arise, apart from failure resulting from attempts to grow them in unsuitable soil. Magnolias can be a little tricky to establish if their fleshy roots are damaged during their dormant season; unable to restore their damaged tissues while not in active growth, the roots instead may decay, and the young tree may die. The remedy is simple. If there is any risk of damage to the roots (and how often, even from a container, can one plant a tree without the slightest root injury?) then your magnolia should be planted only in spring – late in April or May, depending on your individual garden climate – when the roots will be actively growing and able quickly to make good any injury. It goes without saying that you will carefully and cleanly cut back any root that you inadvertently wound. Best results come from planting magnolias when still very small: as little as a foot or so.

Magnolias grow best in neutral to acid soil, though most will tolerate slightly alkaline soils and a few will even grow well on chalk. Most need a cool, moist, leafy soil (though some do not seem disturbed by summer drought, always a hazard in the British climate), and thin, poor soils are not the ideal conditions. This means that, at the Savill & Valley Gardens in Windsor Great Park, where there is an astounding collection of magnolias, John Bond, Keeper of the Gardens, has to take special care to improve the soil so the magnolias can give of their best. His technique is to mulch them heavily with well-rotted manure every three years; and, of course, to prepare the soil very thoroughly before planting. One winter I drove around the Valley Gardens with John Bond looking at his collection and at the beds he was preparing for some new plantings. Already in place, and several years old, were some magnolias. They had been planted in a grassy glade, and though looking well enough, were small and stunted. Plants of the same age in Savill Gardens, planted in carefully made beds in enriched soil, were twice, three times the height of these little trees. John Bond was remedying this by carefully lifting the turf and digging beds around the starved magnolias, taking care to injure their roots as little as possible, then enriching the soil with leaf mould and well rotted manure. 'They'll jump away next season with this treatment' John told me; and I've no reason to doubt his judgement, based on years of experience. This is perhaps the place to remind ourselves that, unless in such exceptional circumstances, the soil around magnolias should never be cultivated; a regular top-dressing of leafy compost will feed the roots, keep them cool, protect them from injury by a carelessly handled fork, and suppress weeds.

The collection of magnolias at Windsor Great Park has no particular history; magnolias were extensively planted from the beginning, for both the Savill and Valley Gardens are woodland gardens, and magnolias are ideal woodland trees and shrubs. Thus they are everywhere, associated with other woodland plants: *Pieris*, *Rhododendron* and many others. At Bodnant in north Wales, too, where the other Magnolia National Collection is held, magnolias are dispersed through the garden. Here both soil and climate are very different; in the place of Windsor's thin Bagshot sand and low rainfall (no more than 22 ins a year on average) Bodnant enjoys an acidic boulder clay and shale, and a rainfall of 40 ins a year; perhaps not everyone's ideal, but many growers of rhododendrons, magnolias and the like regard 40 ins as a minimum.

Magnolias fall into various groups, both botanically and horticulturally. Let us begin with everyman's magnolia, the Soulangiana hybrids. Both hardy and free-flowering, their great flowers appearing on the bare branches in spring and consequently liable to frost damage, they are tolerant of a wide range of soil conditions, of atmospheric pollution and even, to a greater extent than any other magnolia, of wind. This range of hybrids was bred in France from a cross between – to use the names more familiar to gardeners, if not those currently regarded by botanists as correct – *M. denudata* and *M. liliiflora*; the original cross took place in the early part of the nineteenth century. Since then many named Soulangiana hybrids have been introduced, and the best – as viewed by the National Collection holders and other magnolia growers – are not necessarily the most commonly grown. The original *M.* × *soulangiana* has upright creamy white tepals flushed pink or purple at the base (tepal is the term used to denote the petals and sepals of magnolia flowers, which are commonly indistinguishable from each other). Name kinds vary from pure white to fuchsia-purple, white within. 'Alba Superba' is a good pure white opening earlier than the type; better, perhaps, is 'Brozzonii', a later-flowering white with, sometimes, lime-green shading on the outside of the tepals and a faint flush of carmine at the base. The best-known dark-flowered cultivar is 'Lennei', very late flowering, with flowers like huge purple tulips, white inside. 'Lennei' has a characteristic floppy habit, making a big sprawling bush rather than a tree. A newer deep purple-flowered kind is 'Burgundy'. Better known than this is 'Picture', which makes a more upright tree than 'Lennei' and has immense red-purple flowers borne even on little plants of well under man height. 'Grace McDade' is a seedling of 'Lennei' that has inherited its flopping habit, but has very large pure pink and cream flowers borne quite late. 'Sundew', which is perhaps a 'Picture' seedling, has very large white fragrant flowers sometimes shaded with almost coral pink tones. 'Sundew' was raised by Amos Pickard of Canterbury in Kent; at Windsor Great Park there is a great range of Mr Pickard's F2 'Picture' seedlings, many with gemstone names: 'Opal' in palest blush white, 'Ruby', reddish pink with a white picotee edge, paeony-red 'Garnet' and several others, being tried and compared by John Bond. These are just a few of the Soulangiana hybrids, and not all are easily to be bought, but you should not find it too hard to obtain 'Lennei' or 'Brozzonii'. One of the beauties of magnolias is the white or purple carpet of thick, waxy petals that spreads beneath them as the flowers fall, echoing, at the best moment, the still numerous blooms on the bare branches. Later the leaves emerge in pale, yellow-green, looking almost chlorotic; but this is a natural phenomenon and they will soon deepen in colour to their normal summer green.

Magnolia denudata (correctly, now, *M. heptapeta*), a parent of the Soulangiana hybrids, was the first to be brought into cultivation, and remains one of the most beautiful, with large pure white fragrant flowers, at first goblet-shaped; later the thick-textured petals spread widely. Sadly this exquisite shrubby tree, the Chinese yulan, is susceptible to spring frosts, especially if stimulated into growth by the treacherously mild spells we often have in February and March. The flowers appear in early spring on the leafless branches, in great numbers; small wonder that the Chinese planted it so freely in their temple grounds. In our gardens it is beautiful when simply set against dark evergreen foliage, as it might be that of phillyreas or hollies.

The other parent of the dependable Soulangiana hybrids is *M. liliiflora* (now correctly *M. quinquepeta*), most often encountered in the form 'Nigra'. A large shrub rather than a tree, this magnolia has narrow buds opening to a long succession of tulip-shaped flowers of deep wine-purple, creamy-white within. They appear much later than those of *M. denudata*, among the emerging leaves. Like so many magnolias, *M. liliiflora* has aromatic young wood and bark; its flowers are also scented.

The exquisite *M. salicifolia*, the willow-leaved magnolia, not only has aromatic bark and wood, but the leaves too are fragrant, usually of aniseed though sometimes of lemon verbena. The small, pure white flowers, which are produced in great abundance on the naked wood in April, are powerfully fragrant with a scent not unlike that of the old mock orange, *Philadelphus coronarius*. *Magnolia salicifolia* forms a slender, twiggy tree with narrow leaves; it is hardy and easy to grow and with its elegant charm makes the larger-flowered, stouter-growing Soulangiana hybrids seem a little obvious. Various hybrids, with broader leaves and less delicate in aspect, are going about as *M. salicifolia*, and some of them can be seen at Windsor Great Park. The closely allied *M. kobus* can hardly compare with the willow-leaved magnolia; it is a vigorous and robust magnolia with white flowers borne in April or earlier. Seedlings of *M. kobus* often take many years to reach flowering size; but good forms may be raised from cuttings and will flower more promptly.

The star magnolia, *M. stellata*, is so closely related to *M. kobus* as to be considered by some botanists to be no more than a multi-tepalled form of that species. However this may be, to the gardener *M. stellata* is quite distinct, the favourite magnolia for small gardens, making a twiggy bush that flowers freely when young. All through the winter it is decorated with its furry-coated, blonde flower buds, that open in early spring to the familiar many-tepalled pure white or pale pink, starry flowers. The variety 'Waterlily' has many extra tepals, opening from pink buds to very fragrant flowers; but it seems that the name 'Waterlily' has been applied to three or even four different plants, so there is some sorting out to do here in the National Collection. Similarly with the pink *M. stellata* 'Rosea', which is applied to two different plants, one American, one Japanese. 'Royal Star' is a distinct form with much larger flowers, borne on a vigorous bush with healthy deep green foliage. *M. stellata* is an adaptable species, tolerating most soils especially if well laced with peat, less sensitive to wind than many, and able to regenerate quite freely if cut back. It lends itself to some very pretty associations, as it might be with the blue of *Omphalodes cappadocica*, or of the common grape hyacinth, at its feet. Because of the hint of blush pink that so often suffuses the flowers the star magnolia is best kept away from the stronger colours of spring, the bright yellows of forsythia or the scarlet and vermilion of flowering quince.

From seed of *M. stellata* 'Rosea' a fine magnolia was raised at Windsor Great Park and named 'Neil McEacharn' after the owner of the garden at Villa Taranto in which the parent plant was growing. This has made a tree, with many-petalled flowers like those of the parent. It is now regarded by many magnolia experts as a form of *M. × loebneri*, the group name given to hybrids between *M. kobus* and *M. stellata*. The Loebner hybrids all make small, slender-branched trees with starry flowers borne on the bare stems; they are tolerant of most soils including chalk, and begin to flower when still small. There are now several named kinds. 'Ballerina' is in effect a tree-like *M. stellata*, with the same starry, fragrant white flowers. Slightly taller, flowering a little earlier, is 'Merrill', with semi-double white flowers. 'Leonard Messel' has received the Royal Horticultural Society's highest award, a First Class Certificate; forming a more open tree than the others, it bears many-petalled flowers, fuchsia-pink in bud and creamy white suffused with soft lilac pink on opening. These have the advantage of being more frost-resistant than the white-flowered kinds. Like *M. salicifolia*, the Loebner hybrids have small leaves, casting a dappled shade rather than the denser gloom of the large-leaved Soulangiana hybrids; they thus make ideal companions for camellias and rhododendrons.

Another group of offspring of various forms of *M. stellata*, crossed with *M. liliiflora* 'Nigra', or *M. l.* 'Reflorescens', are the 'girls' which John Bond showed to a curiously unappreciative committee at the Royal Horticultural Society's show at Vincent Square not long since. Bred in America, these are a race of hybrids intended to flower later than *M. stellata*, so that they would be less liable to frost damage. There are eight of these girl-named magnolias, all grown at Windsor Great Park: 'Randy' and 'Ricki' flower in late April, 'Ann' in mid April; 'Judy' is slow growing and almost fastigiate in habit. 'Betty' has large flowers in mid to late April and 'Susan' has sweetly-scented flowers. 'Jane' flowers late, in early May, but before 'Pinkie', the palest of this range of hybrids, which all have wine-purple flowers, creamy inside. It is hard to choose between them, but perhaps the vote should go to 'Pinkie' for its very late flowering season, or 'Susan' for its sweet perfume and deep claret-red colouring, or to the very free-flowering 'Randy' which makes an almost columnar tree.

Lovely as are the magnolias so far described, they cannot compare with the great Asiatic tree magnolias. Supplementing the National Collections is a project to conserve these large-flowered magnolias, conducted by several of the most successful magnolia growers in the country, who have identified the ten rarest and most important magnolias whose future in cultivation is currently threatened, and have arranged for them to be propagated. The name that first comes to mind is *Magnolia campbellii*, a large, wide-spreading, often multi-stemmed tree that occurs in the wild in the Himalayas, at altitudes where the dominant vegetation, apart from magnolias themselves, is composed of oaks and tree rhododendrons. The tree itself is pretty hardy, certainly in the south of England; but its immense bowl-shaped flowers appear as early as late February in some seasons, and even in bud are apt to be damaged by frost. A mature tree, covered in its great, glowing pink flowers, is an unforgettable sight. But note that word 'mature': *M. campbellii* usually takes twenty-five years or more to reach flowering size. However, there are several forms, and some flower at an earlier age, as will be noted as they are mentioned.

As usually seen in this country, *Magnolia campbellii* has clear pink flowers, but it seems that in the wild the white form, f. *alba*, is the commoner. There are some superb specimens of *M. campbellii alba* at the Valley Gardens, raised from seed from Nepal in 1962, the year in which the pink-flowered form first flowered at Windsor Great Park. A deeper rose pink form has been named 'Darjeeling'; the original tree grows in the Darjeeling Botanic Garden in India. A seedling of this, also with richly toned, almost crimson flowers, has been named 'Betty Jessel'; later flowering than most, it should be a good choice for gardens where spring frosts regularly damage the earlier-flowering kinds.

Other named kinds of *Magnolia campbellii* have in them the blood of *M. mollicomata*, at first regarded as a distinct species but now reduced to a subspecies of *campbellii*. *M. mollicomata* (as I will call it for brevity's sake) occurs further east than *M. campbellii*, in open forests of fir, with a dense undergrowth of cotoneasters, daphnes, dipeltas, viburnums and woodland rhododendrons. From the gardener's point of view, the plants differ in certain quite significant aspects, not least of which is the tendency of *M. mollicomata* to reach flowering size at a much earlier age. The colour of *M. mollicomata* is less pure than that of *M. campbellii*, a chilly mauve-pink in place of *M. campbellii*'s clear, warm tones. The shape of the flowers differs too, that of *M. mollicomata* always nearer to the cup and saucer shape than to the cup without saucer of *M. campbellii*, where the outer tepals often fail to reflex. Further, *M. mollicomata* makes a spreading, bushy tree where *M. campbellii*, though also wide-spreading and often multi-stemmed, tends to grow tall. In the garden *M. campbellii* seems not merely to tolerate, but actually to seek the sun by growing out and away from sheltering walls or surrounding shrubs, whereas *M. mollicomata* appears to prefer cooler, woodland conditions. At Windsor Great Park, *M. mollicomata* cannot stand comparison with *M. campbellii*, which is far finer in colour.

Some forms of *M. mollicomata*, however, have provided very fine trees. One group raised from seed collected by George Forrest, and planted in two Cornish gardens and one in Sussex, proved to have huge flowers of an astonishing violet-red fading to deep lilac-purple, borne on trees of upright, almost fastigiate form. The tree at Lanarth in Cornwall has been propagated and grown under the name 'Lanarth'; seedlings come fairly true to type but must not, of course, be designated as 'Lanarth', a name that should be applied only to the original tree and its vegetatively propagated offspring.

From crosses between *M. campbellii* and its subspecies *mollicomata* other notable trees have been raised. Some of these were bred at Kew by Charles Raffill, whose name is attached to the first of his seedlings to flower – at Windsor Great Park, in 1959, aged thirteen. It has the large, intense pink flowers of *M. campbellii*, with just a hint of the purplish tones of the other parent. Another of Raffill's seedlings was sent to Caerhays, a famous Cornish magnolia garden, where it flowered in 1966 at the age of twenty, causing quite a stir among those who saw its huge, crimson-pink flowers, white on the inner surface, with pink veins. It was named 'Kew's Surprise'.

Magnolia campbellii has been used as one parent in another famous cross, *M.* × *veitchii*: the other parent is the lovely white *M. denudata*. There were six progeny of the cross, and all flowered by the time they were fifteen; only two were kept, one white, named 'Isca', and the other pink. This tree, long known simply as *M.* × *veitchii*, should now bear the distinguishing clonal name 'Peter Veitch'. The trees are tall and vigorous, with handsome foliage and flowers produced in great abundance. Unfortunately they are very prone to wind damage, as the wood is extremely brittle. A third form of the cross, a chance seedling from a nursery in California, has deep wine-red flowers and has been named *M.* 'Veitchii Rubra'. All the *M.* × *veitchii* hybrids have chalice-shaped flowers that are said to have a distinct fragrance of bluebells.

Other magnolias in this Asiatic group are less well known. *M. sargentiana* is a tall, upright tree with slender branches, taking a generation to reach flowering size. A large tree in a good season is a wonderful sight, decorated with large, many-petalled rose pink flowers that open wide, almost like a huge pink *M. stellata*. Its variety *robusta* is more often planted; it comes into flower at an earlier age and forms a big shrubby tree with loose, almost untidy-looking flowers that nod one-sidedly; sometimes as much as 1 ft wide, they are white flushed with mauve pink. They apparently have a strong spicy scent, and I'm told that, in artificial light, the surfaces of the tepals glisten as if dusted with a very fine artificial glitter. Despite its large leaves, *M. sargentiana robusta* is surprisingly wind tolerant, and the flowers are also thick-textured enough to be more than usually weatherproof. A particularly fine specimen of *M. sargentiana robusta* grows at Bodnant; it received the coveted First Class Certificate in 1947.

M. dawsoniana is a twiggy dense tree with flowers very like those of *M. sargentiana*, borne only after twenty years or so and at first only a few at a time at the top of the tree; with maturity they increase in number and are borne nearer eye level. Like those of *M. sargentiana*, the flowers of *M. dawsoniana* are ragged and floppy, and nod on the branches; the outside of the tepals, which is coloured, is half hidden and you look up into the white, faintly lilac-tinted inner surface of the flowers. *M. dawsoniana* 'Chyverton' is a fine form, named for another famous Cornish magnolia garden; it has bright crimson backs to the tepals, and this intense colouring glows through to the white inner surface. The whole thing is enhanced by deep crimson stamens. All the trees of *M. dawsoniana* at Windsor Great Park stand out in summer by virtue of their dark green, leathery leaves and rounded bushy habit, more pronounced where they grow fully in the open.

Last of the pink Asiatic tree magnolias represented in the National Collections is *M. sprengeri* and its forms. As with *M. campbellii*, there are pink and white forms, the white (*M. sprengeri elongata*) rather like *M. denudata* in flower, with a purple stain at the centre. Two forms, one with pure white tepals and the other creamy-white, are known in cultivation, both growing at Bodnant. However, it is *M. sprengeri* 'Diva', the pink-flowered form, and its seedlings which create a sensation in flower. Here we have a smallish tree which bears, in April, fragrant flowers very like a smaller version of those of *M. campbellii*, of a rich carmine which shows to best advantage on the erect flowers. They appear later than those of *M. campbellii* and are thus less likely to be spoiled by frost. Several seedlings have been raised to flowering size; not all of them equal to their parent. One that bears comparison is 'Claret Cup', with rosy purple flowers, paler inside fading to white. Better still is 'Copeland Court', in rich clear pink. Yet this seedling was nearly destroyed before it ever reached flowering size. Though its rescue was performed long before the NCCPG was conceived, the story well illustrates the aims of the organisation. The seedling tree was presented to a former Bishop of Truro and planted in his garden. On his death this property was sold, donated to Truro Cathedral School and renamed Copeland Court. When in 1960 the governors of the school decided to build another residential block, the headmaster realised that the tree would have to be sacrificed and contacted Neil Treseder, a noted magnolia grower, who recounts the story in his book *Magnolias*. Mr Treseder and the head gardener decided to risk transplanting the tree, by then 15 ft high; this they did with the greatest care. Inevitably it suffered a check, but this may have hastened its maturity, for it first flowered not long after the move. Windsor Great Park too, has its own 'Diva' seedling, named 'Eric Savill' for the man who created the gardens.

M. sprengeri 'Diva' and *M. sargentiana robusta* were deliberately crossed in the famous Cornish garden at Caerhays Castle, and the first seedling flowered at age fourteen, amply rewarding the head gardener who performed the cross. 'Caerhays Belle' has enormous thick-textured clear salmon pink flowers freely borne.

A group of hybrid magnolias deriving from the Asiatic species are the Gresham hybrids, bred as a deliberate attempt to combine the beauty of *M. campbellii* and the hardiness of *M. denudata*. The method chosen by

D. Todd Gresham was to cross *M.* × *veitchii*, which is half *M. campbellii*, with *M. denudata* to produce a race of one-quarter *M. campbellii* hybrids. About fifty were raised, described by their raiser as 'svelte brunettes'; several were named, rather repellently, with such epithets as 'Raspberry Ice' and 'Peppermint Stick'. 'Vin Rouge', less off-puttingly named, is a worthwhile foliage plant with bronzy red young leaves and dark wine red flowers. Despite its name 'Raspberry Ice' is in fact a good thing, with luminous pink flowers borne late, with those of 'Lennei'. Other hybrids were raised by Todd Gresham from *M.* × *veitchii* 'Peter Veitch' and *M.* × *soulangiana* 'Lennei Alba', described as 'buxom, full-bodied, nordic blondes' (I'll spare you the rest of the commercial). 'Rouged Alabaster' has bowl-like flowers up to 1 ft across, rose pink in colour. 'Sayonara' is a very large-flowered white and 'Manchu Fan', another white, is in effect a faster-growing, more tree-like version of *M. denudata*. The punningly named 'Heaven Scent' is a good fragrant pink that seems to perform well in English gardens.

Following these Asiatic tree magnolias comes the season of a group of shrubby magnolias with nodding flowers, saucer-shaped and displaying their great boss of crimson or purple stamens. Four species and a hybrid, with another, allied hybrid, comprise this group and one or other of them can be grown in almost any soil conditions from chalk to acid, leafy woodland soil. Though tolerant of some lime, *M. sieboldii* is one to avoid if your soil is chalky. It has not the largest flowers of this group, nor the most fragrant, but their season is very long, from May to August; set horizontally among quite large leaves, glaucous backed, they are followed by striking crimson, fleshy fruits which split to reveal scarlet seeds. *Magnolia globosa* is the least common, and perhaps the least garden-worthy, of the group, forming a huge spreading bush with bold handsome foliage, but rather small flowers that do not open widely, and are easily browned by rain or even dew. *M. sinensis*, on the other hand, bears large, very fragrant white flowers in May and June on a small bushy tree that can be pruned to shapeliness. Compared with the Asiatic tree magnolias, this is worth raising from seed, taking a mere five to seven years to reach flowering maturity. So too does *M. wilsonii*, perhaps the most distinct of this group. It makes a little, somewhat upright, tree with narrow, more pointed leaves of deep sea-green colouring. Though tolerant of some lime in the soil, it prefers a cool root-run in part shade. *M. wilsonii* flowers chiefly in May and June, its nodding flowers white with red to purple stamens, and sweetly scented; another crop of flowers sometimes appears in August. The most vigorous, and the most chalk tolerant, of the set is the assumed hybrid between *M. wilsonii* and *M. sinensis*, given the name *M.* × *highdownensis* from the chalk garden at Highdown in Sussex where it was first recorded. It is like a more vigorous *M. sinensis* in growth, with slightly smaller, nodding, fragrant white flowers. Seedlings of *M. wilsonii* at Windsor Great Park have appeared identical in leaf to *M.* × *high-downensis*, and some botanists assume it to be merely a form of *M. wilsonii*, while others regard it as a natural hybrid; and certainly at Windsor Great Park there are nearby trees of *M. sinensis* whose pollen could have fertilised the seed of *M. wilsonii*.

With *Magnolia hypoleuca* (*obovata*) we come to a noble summer-flowering tree belonging to a group represented in both America and Asia and distinguished by the way in which the leaves are clustered in whorls at the end of the shoots, whence the American name umbrella tree. The Asian *M. hypoleuca* has large leaves, silvery-white beneath (this is the meaning of the name 'hypoleuca') on a rather gaunt tree which bears large, powerfully scented suede-textured flowers of pale creamy buff colouring, with a boss of crimson stamens. The medicinal magnolia, *M. officinalis*, has smaller flowers with less colourful stamens, but is even more fragrant. A pink-flowered form at Windsor Great Park was at first attributed to this species, but is now thought to be a form of *M. hypoleuca*. The third Asian member of this group, *M. rostrata*, unlike the other two, has a thick coating of rusty fur on its buds and young leaves. A tall tree in the wild, it has curious stout shoots, heavily marked with the enduring scars left by the leaf stalks, and noble foliage, coppery fawn when young and glaucous beneath. The whitish, melon-scented flowers are rather like those of *M. campbellii* but are half hidden by the great leaves, and are very frost-tender; while the leaves and branches alike are distressingly apt to be damaged and torn by wind. The tree is just too tender for Windsor, and is very much a plant for Cornish or Irish gardens.

From America comes the related *M. macrophylla*, with even larger foliage, vast papery-textured leaves light green above and glaucous-white beneath, arranged in the typical umbrella fashion. The creamy-white flowers of *M. macrophylla* fade to buff and parchment tones. With these huge leaves it must have a cool, moist, well-nurtured soil and all the shelter possible from wind, which can so easily bruise and tear the foliage. A variety of *M. macrophylla*, var. *ashei*, is both slightly tender and very uncommon in English gardens. At Windsor Great Park, it does well, finding the hotter, drier summers more to its liking than the cool, damp Cornish climate that suits other magnolias so well. Its white flowers are powerfully scented.

Also American is *M. tripetala*, a tree with strong-smelling creamy-white flowers followed by striking rose-red fruits with scarlet seeds, and quite large leaves in parasol-like whorls; a frustrating tree to grow as it is very brittle and frequently suffers wind damage. New shoots regenerate freely from the base, but it is hard to keep it as a well-shaped tree. Not a tree for the average garden, therefore, especially as the flowers are said to smell of goat. The wood, too, is smelly, and with its spongy texture is hard to cut cleanly.

M. × watsonii (now correctly *M. × wieseneri*) unites the two groups of summer-flowering magnolias just considered; its parents are stated to be *M. sieboldii* and *M. hypoleuca*. It forms a small bushy tree with waterlily-like buds, opening to large, nodding or upward-facing globular flowers of creamy-fawn colouring and suede-like texture, with a large central cluster of crimson stamens. The scent of these flowers is far-reaching on the air, a rich warm perfume slightly reminiscent of pineapples. Another magnolia that joins these two sections is 'Charles Coates' (*M. sieboldii* × *M. tripetala*) which is much what one would expect from these two parents: a large-leaved tree with fragrant creamy-white flowers, with a conspicuous red boss of stamens, appearing in May and June.

Every magnolia I have so far considered is deciduous. Of the evergreen magnolias we can grow in this country, by far the best known is *M. grandiflora*, the American southern magnolia or bull bay. Often seen trained as a wall shrub, it can also be grown as a free-standing tree in the south of England, given shelter and full sun, and few evergreen trees that will grow in such a wide range of climatic conditions are more magnificent. As so often, it is worth choosing your variety with care. *Magnolia grandiflora* seedlings are likely to take twenty years or more to reach flowering size, but precocious forms have been selected, named and propagated. Some horticulturists maintain that these kinds flower at a young age because they are raised by vegetative methods from trees of flowering age; however this may be, in practice the expectant gardener is more likely to be rewarded promptly than if he plants a seedling tree. The varieties most likely to be encountered include 'Exmouth', popular for over two centuries. It makes a vigorous, upright-growing tree with long narrow leaves, rusty-felted beneath when young, and flowers freely from July to autumn if given plenty of sun. 'Ferruginea' has shorter leaves, with the typical glossy dark green upper surface and a more lasting, thicker coat of tan fur beneath. 'Goliath' is shorter and broader still in leaf and has large globular flowers. All forms of the bull bay are deliciously fragrant, with a rich warm scent strongly laced with lemon.

The sweet bay, *M. virginiana*, is an American species that is happy in moist soils, though not boggy ones, despite its alternative name of swamp laurel. Some forms are deciduous, others evergreen; all bear creamy-white sweetly-scented flowers from June to September. The leaves, smaller than those of *M. grandiflora*, are glaucous-white on their undersides. Seedlings have been raised from crosses between the sweet bay and the bull bay, and one such, 'Maryland', is commercially available. A spreading, shrubby tree, it was selected for its hardiness and freedom of flower; in leaf it is exactly like *M. grandiflora*. 'Maryland' is recommended by John Bond;

the sandy soil of Windsor Great Park, if heavily laced with good humus according to John's invariable practice, seems to suit it well. It flowers as a very young plant and the flowers are equal to any *M. grandiflora*.

Another hybrid of *M. virginiana*, this time with *M. tripetala* – already described – is *M. × thompsoniana*. Although it predates the first of the familiar *M. × soulangiana* types by several years – it originated in the London nursery of Archibald Thompson in 1808 – it remains undeservedly little-known. Unlike the smelly pollen parent *M. tripetala*, *M. × thompsoniana* bears fragrant flowers, three times the size of those of *M. virginiana* and appearing over a long season. It is virtually evergreen in mild areas, but is capable of surviving quite severe cold. As Neil Treseder observes in his book *Magnolias*, given these 'qualities of hardiness, fragrance and long flowering, it is surprising that propagation of this hybrid seems to have been almost completely neglected by British nurseries'.

If you have the climate for it, in maritime Devon or Cornish gardens with shelter from wind, say, or inland a suitable high, sheltered wall, few trees are more magnificent than the evergreen *Magnolia delavayi*, a Sino-Himalayan species. Its massive leaves, up to 1 ft long and 6 ins wide, are stiff textured, deep sea green with a fine greyish bloom. The flower buds are huge but open only briefly, often at night, so the tree never makes a great floral display. If you should be so lucky as to garden where there is a mature specimen of *M. delavayi*, however, as I have, you will find it worth climbing the tree, working up through its dense canopy beneath which no vegetation survives, merely a jungle-like forest floor of fallen, leathery-textured coffee-brown leaves, to reach the flowers. On close inspection they turn out to have the texture of suede, of a delicate primrose yellow, with an exotic and heady perfume. Despite its huge leaves, *M. delavayi* is surprisingly tolerant of wind, but in a sheltered position the lovely bloom on the leaves is unblemished. It is hardier than my comments might suggest, and can regenerate itself if badly damaged by frost.

Even in a chapter of this length, I cannot do justice to the immense collection of magnolias at Windsor Great Park, or the superb trees at Bodnant, where 'against the house, in the formal garden, and in the wild garden they are equally appropriate'. (RHS Journal, 1940)

The National Collections

The National Collections of magnolias are held at Bodnant Garden, Tal-y-Cafn, Colwyn Bay (The National Trust) and at the Savill and Valley Gardens, The Great Park, Windsor, Berks (Crown Estates Commissioners).

The Bodnant magnolias were designated as a National Collection in April 1981; those at the Savill and Valley Gardens in July 1982. Both collections are mature and well-established, including fine specimens of many different species. The soil and climatic conditions in the two gardens are very different. At Bodnant the magnolias grow in acidic boulder clay and shale and enjoy a rainfall of 40 ins a year on average. At the Savill and Valley Gardens the thin Bagshot sand and low rainfall of around 22 ins a year mean that constant care must be taken to improve the soil, to topdress with leafy compost, and to irrigate thoroughly in dry soils.

Many of the Bodnant magnolias were planted against walls, and given this shelter even the large-leaved Magnolia delavayi proved a success. Several of the great pink-flowered Asiatic magnolias enjoy similar shelter, and even M. nitida, original seedlings from Chinese seed sent from Caerhays, grew successfully on a wall. The Windsor magnolias are treated – as are many at Bodnant – as woodland plants, succeeding best when grown in cultivated beds rather than in grassy glades. They were originally planted in the Savill and Valley Gardens to form second-storey plants as a foil for, and shade canopy over, the many rhododendrons grown there. Most of the original planting of magnolias at Windsor took place just after the Hitler war, so that they are now, forty years on, fine trees. New kinds are being added whenever possible.

Malus

MANY crab apples have sterling qualities that put them in the front rank as flowering or fruiting trees for smaller gardens. It may be a little harsh to say that they lack charisma; that their virtues are to some extent those that make them (like some thoroughly good people one knows) worthy but just a touch dull. I hope in studying the crabs for this chapter, and subsequently in writing it, to convince myself, and thereby you, that there are some good things to be had in the genus *Malus*.

Thus, my first draft for this chapter was sent to Dr & Mrs Robinson, the holders of one of the National Collections of *Malus*. It came back with the comment against 'just a touch dull': 'Surely not!' Justifiable reprimand, I now see; for indeed, though I still cannot say they have my heart as, say, magnolias or rowans, in studying the crabs I have come to see that they have much charm, if not charisma.

The other National Collection of *Malus* is at Granada Arboretum (Manchester University), where also is the National Collection of *Sorbus*, and it is in this latter capacity that we shall visit Granada. Here is what Helen Robinson, of Hyde Hall in Essex, has to say about the crabs' performance on heavy London clay. 'When we started gardening at Hyde Hall, our first plantings were mainly cherries, but having been given a collection of *Malus* in 1968, we soon realised what very good garden trees these were with their prolonged flowering season, with the added bonus of autumn fruit and, in some cases, colour. *Malus* do well on clay soils which tend to be wet in winter and dry out in the summer. In our part of Essex, rainfall seldom exceeds 20 ins and therefore growth in all species is slow for the first years. As soon as root growth penetrates the subsoil, there is sufficient moisture available to maintain good growth.' From this we can deduce that the crabs are not faddy, but are tolerant of soils that would try the temper of many other flowering trees. Virtually any soil, but for a bog, will suit them, including chalk and other alkaline soils; they are less happy on thin sandy soils. However, I have myself grown several different crabs in dry, acid, stony, humus-starved coal-mine waste, where they put up an excellent performance of growth, flowering and fruiting each year on 'soil' that scarcely, until I began to garden it, supported stunted heather and sparse, downland turf.

Most of the crabs I grew were chosen for their fruit before their flowers, and this tendency of the genus to produce highly ornamental, and often edible, fruits, from which an excellent jelly can be made, gives it in some respects an edge over the more glamorous cherries, to which the crabs are closely related and some of which they can rival in flower. Their flowering season, too, is generally late enough to escape damage from spring frosts. Yet another attribute of many varieties of crab is their purple foliage; rated a virtue by some, it is in the eyes of others a positive drawback, a blot on the escutcheon of an otherwise esteemed genus. I will try and remain open-minded, but I do think on the whole that the purple crabs, like the purple plum or sycamore, the copper beech and others, are too solid a mass of indigestibly hard colour to fit happily into most landscapes. As a garden tree, carefully associated with its neighbours, a purple-leaved crab can be more easily assimilated in a small-scale design than as part of a larger scheme where it can throw out the balance by its overweighted intensity of colour. And, of course, as we shall see, the dark pigment extends to the flowers and fruit, so that we find in the crabs richer, deeper colours than in the Japanese cherries, which stop at deep pink. There are no true reds, except 'Almey', among the crabs; all the deeper-coloured kinds lean towards purple, and this too limits their use in the garden to compositions based on this range of colours; they clash horribly with yellow.

The crab that put the purple pigment into the garden forms with dark foliage is *Malus niedzwetskyana*, which has red young growths, and purple-red flowers followed by large plum-red fruits. Even the wood is suffused with pigment; a young branch, cut, is seen to be red all through. This crab is not a good garden tree, however, even if you could pronounce its name with enough confidence to order it; it is subject to one of the ills that sometimes beset crabs, the disease known as scab. Happily many garden varieties, including coloured descendants of this susceptible species, are resistant to scab. Another threat to the well-being of crabs, while we are on the subject of diseases, is fireblight: potentially serious, since this is a notifiable disease for which there is no treatment, and affected trees may have to be destroyed. Helen Robinson told me, however, that Hyde Hall is in the worst area for fireblight; their *Sorbus*, *Pyracantha* and *Cotoneaster* all suffer badly, but 'we have *never* seen it on *Malus*'. The Robinsons are fortunate too in that scab is 'insignificant in our garden'.

Which are the best purple-leaved crabs to choose, if such you desire? The best-known are probably 'Eleyi', which is very susceptible to scab, and 'Lemoinei', very good of its kind. Brighter in foliage than the parents, they are similar to 'Aldenhamensis', differing in the shape of the rich plum-purple fruits. The last, too, though flowering later than 'Eleyi', is especially pretty because the leaves emerge even after the flowers. Both form small trees with spreading rounded heads. 'Profusion' is another, with purple young foliage paling to bronze-green, and deep claret-purple fragrant flowers also paling rapidly, followed by deep red fruits. Sadly, 'Profusion' is subject to canker. It is surpassed by 'Liset', a little tree with deep red flowers that hold their colour better. 'Liset' is said to be very resistant to scab. 'Neville Copeman' is another fine crab; a seedling of 'Eleyi', it is far more striking in fruit, bearing large deep crimson crab apples.

Another set of crabs deriving from *M. niedzwetskyana* is the Rosybloom group, raised in North America but less rebarbatively named than many garden plants from across the Atlantic (we've already met Magnolia 'Peppermint Stick'; and fancy calling an aristocratic paeony 'Cheddar Cheese'!). The Rosyblooms were bred to cope with Canadian winters but, as Bean dryly observes: 'the ability to withstand seventy degrees of frost is not a necessary attribute so far as British gardens are concerned'. However, many of this group are beautiful in flower and have decorative fruits that make good jelly. Among them are 'Almey' and 'Simcoe'. Both have copper or purplish young growths, and the summer foliage of 'Almey' has a bronze cast. The flowers of 'Almey' are bright red, free of muddy purple tones, with a whitish, star-shaped centre, and quite large; the little fruits are bright orange flushed with carmine. 'Simcoe', which has received awards for both flower and fruit, has large rose-pink flowers, not of such a clear tone as 'Almey', and vinous-red fruits. Both are copiously produced on a vigorous crab forming an open, even-shaped round tree.

For sheer mass of bloom you can hardly beat *Malus floribunda*, well named by the botanists. This forms a small tree with arching branches, almost weeping beneath the weight of the massed flowers. In bud they are deep rosy red, opening to pink and paling through blush to white. This Japanese crab is often seen as a rather untidy tangle of branches; it benefits from regular winter pruning, which simply consists of removing entirely crossing branches and those that are spoiling the shape of the tree. A hybrid of *M. floribunda* is the lovely 'Excellenz Thiel', best grafted on a tall stem to display its weeping branches. It is also very beautiful grown as a bush or half-standard, to make a mound of colour. *Malus spectabilis* is another flowering crab that is aptly named; for this is a small tree – taller than *M. floribunda* however – that over a full month in April and May produces quantities of large semi-double, rosy pink flowers, paling to blush. Perhaps a hybrid of this, 'Van Eseltine' is of upright, columnar habit, suited to small spaces, and has similar large, double rosy pink flowers. Neither has much to offer in the way of fruits or of autumn colour. 'Katherine' grows rather weakly and is best as a bush, though at Hyde Hall it has done very well, making a neat small tree which would do credit to any garden. This is another crab with large double flowers, pale pink fading to white, showing up well against dark green foliage; tiny yellow flushed red fruits follow.

Little *Malus sargentii* is another Japanese crab; it forms a low, wide-spreading bush perhaps 6 ft high, with profuse pure white, scented flowers set among dark green leaves, and cherry-like, vivid crimson-red fruits. The foliage colours quite well in autumn, to yellow and orange. With its compact habit and masses of flower it is a valuable shrub for a small garden and one into which I should love to fling a clematis to add yet another season of interest to the crab's spring and autumn show. It would look well on a bank, spreading its skirts over the sloping ground.

Moving west, China offers us several good crabs, including one that looks almost cherry-like. This is *Malus hupehensis*, a rather upright tree of stiffish habit with glossy bright deep green leaves, and fragrant white flowers opening from pink-tinted buds in May; or rosy pink in the form *rosea*. Its currant-like fruits are greenish-yellow flushed with red where the sun strikes them. In China the leaves are apparently used to make 'red tea', but whether the curious red tea one can buy in specialist shops in this country is *Malus hupehensis* I know not. The Hupeh crab can be raised from seed, and will come true; it produces its seeds apomictically, like many of the rowans; that is, viable seed is set without fertilisation. Given this convenient attribute, it should be grown more often; especially as so great a plantsman as E. H. Wilson, whose name is associated with many outstanding plants, considered it the finest deciduous flowering tree he had introduced.

Another group of Chinese crabs are grown more for their fruits than their flowers. *Malus toringoides* is a most graceful little tree with lobed leaves and creamy-white flowers, followed by beautifully coloured fruits, quite small, yellow flushed with scarlet where the sun reaches them. The closely related *M. transitoria* has slightly smaller fruits, and performs very well in difficult conditions at Hyde Hall. Another Wilson introduction, the large-leaved *M. yunnanensis*, adds to its great crops of red, cherry-sized crabs with white dots, flaring autumn colour of scarlet and orange. The somewhat similar Japanese *M. tschnonoskii* flowers with no great freedom, and has dull-coloured fruits – when it condescends to produce them at all; (the tree at Hyde Hall fruits regularly) – but this handsome erect tree redeems itself by producing superb autumn foliage of 'bronze, crimson, orange, purple and yellow' (H. S. J. Crane, writing about crabs in the RHS Journal, 1961).

I have mentioned, in passing, fragrance. A few crabs are outstanding for their scent, none more than *Malus coronaria* 'Charlottae'. This North American crab blooms late, in May, its large semi-double pink flowers scented like violets. More than this, it often colours brilliantly in autumn, making it a valuable addition to the select band of two-season trees for small gardens, though sadly it is very subject to canker. Though it is seldom mentioned, some of the crabs usually chosen for fruit have sweetly, if not strongly, scented flowers. Such, in my experience, is 'Dartmouth', which bears large crops of red and yellow bloomy fruits from which a fine jelly can be made. 'John Downie' is probably the best-known of the fruiting crabs, an erect tree with pink and white flowers appearing in late May and followed by masses of large, conical fruits, scarlet and orange in colour. 'Cheal's Crimson', another reliable performer, has orange and red fruits. A lesser known variety is 'Montreal Beauty', with large orange-scarlet fruits following sweetly-scented, large white flowers just faintly blush-tinted. The rich crimson scarlet fruit of 'Veitch's Scarlet' is said to have a 'brisk, pleasant flavour'. I like 'brisk' for that astringent sourness.

At least two of the Rosyblooms, mentioned earlier for their hardiness and vigour, are outstanding as fruiting trees. 'Chilko' and 'Cowichan' have rosy pink flowers and large glossy crimson fruits. Among the red-fruited kinds, I must mention two that hold their fruits, exceptionally, almost right through the winter. 'Crittenden' has pale flowers and shiny, deep red fruits, slightly smaller than those of 'Red Sentinel', which fruits so freely that the branches are weighed down. In colour the fruits are bright cardinal red with a high gloss, and are held till after Christmas when the redwings and fieldfares arrive. The appealingly named 'Red Jade' is an American-raised crab which bears copious quantities of its small red fruits on drooping branches; a good little tree to associate with the yellow-fruited kinds.

There are several yellow crabs to choose from. Outstanding among them is 'Golden Hornet', an upright medium to large tree with single white flowers massed along the branches, followed by heavy crops of bright yellow fruits, slightly larger than cherries, that hold for many weeks. 'Golden Hornet' is one of those useful crabs with stiff, upward-growing branches, fitting into the smallest space. Another yellow-fruited crab that does well at Hyde Hall on that difficult clay is 'Gibbs' Golden Gage'.

The fragrance of some of these fruiting crabs may derive from *Malus prunifolia*, a wild species of uncertain origin, perhaps Siberian, which in its variety *rinki*, has both yellow and red-fruited forms. The yellow-fruited kind was given an award by the Royal Horticultural Society when shown from Kew Gardens. The yellow is very handsome though perhaps less so than 'Golden Hornet', which has *rinki* in its parentage. Another good yellow of this kind is 'Cheal's Golden Gem', with large pure white flowers and small yellow fruits, ripening in September. Like 'Cheal's Crimson' (which was originally offered as a variety of *M. prunifolia*) this is an old cultivar, dating from around the time of the Great War.

Another good yellow-fruited crab has blood of *Malus sieboldii*, a small tree or large shrub from Japan, allied to *M. floribunda* but with a shorter season of flower: though for all that a very pretty tree with pale to deep pink flowers in April and a graceful, arching habit. The hybrid, 'Wintergold', has very glossy foliage and small yellow fruits on long, slender stalks, holding until Christmas. This is a good, compact tree for a small garden.

Of course, these are just a few of the many crabs, both wild and cultivated, that grow in the National Collections. The lists, from both Hyde Hall and Granada Arboretum, are impressive, and yet Mrs Robinson tells me that 'since being given the opportunity to hold one of the *Malus* Collections for the NCCPG we have collected material of a further seventy species and cultivars, making a total of one hundred and thirty six'. Clearly there is nothing for it but to visit one of the collections and see for yourself the range and variety that crabs can offer.

The National Collections

The National Collections of Malus, *the crab apples, are held at Hyde Hall, Rettendon, Chelmsford, Essex (Hyde Hall Garden Trust – Dr & Mrs Robinson) and at Granada Arboretum, Jodrell Bank, in Cheshire (Manchester University).*

The Granada Arboretum crabs were designated as a National Collection in April 1981. The Arboretum is a comparatively new one, begun in 1972 with the basically educational aim of providing as comprehensive a collection as possible of trees and shrubs of aesthetic, horticultural and scientific interest. Thus its aims coincide closely with those of the NCCPG. The heavy boulder clay and open site, exposed to cold drying winds in spring and winter, imposed certain limitations, but the crabs cope well with these conditions.

The National Collection of crabs at Hyde Hall is also a youngish collection: the garden was begun twenty-five years ago, and the crabs designated as a National Collection in July 1982. Here, too, the soil is heavy, London clay that turns sodden in winter and dries hard in summer; the annual rainfall rarely exceeds 20 ins. Despite this the crabs grow well; growth in the early stages is slow, but as the roots penetrate the lower levels the growth improves.

Sorbus

THE BIG genus *Sorbus* includes the mountain ashes or rowans and the whitebeams, the service trees and a few oddities that do not fall into these groups. In this one genus, therefore, are included some of the finest trees for small gardens. They are hardier and less finicky about soil conditions than many maples, and have less greedy root systems than birches. They are less striking in flower than crabs and magnolias, the other two groups of trees to be considered in this book; but in leaf they are considerably more attractive than the crabs especially. The large-leaved forms of whitebeam can rival the big-leaved rhododendrons or magnolias for foliage effect, and are much easier to grow; the pinnate-leaved rowans, attractive all season with their ferny foliage, are often spectacular in autumn garb, which is less likely to disappoint in 'off' years or less than ideal soils or climates than that of the maples. Added to their autumn colour is the effect of their clusters of vivid fruits: red, orange, vermilion or yellow in one group of rowans; white, pink or crimson in another. Almost their only drawback is the unpleasant, fishy smell of their flowers.

Botanists have separated the genus *Sorbus* into various sections, of which the chief are section Sorbus (Aucuparia), the rowans; section Aria, the whitebeams; and section Micromeles. One of the finest collections of *Sorbus* in the country is at Winkworth Arboretum in Surrey, where many kinds are planted on a steep hillside. Walking along the paths that lead through the trees, you can look down on those below or up into the ones above; as the sun strikes through the autumn-tinted foliage, or lights up the coloured fruits, the play of light and shadow contributes to a memorable visual experience. Here you realise that, to get full value from autumn foliage, you will see it with the sun before you; but against the light the clusters of fruit are mere dark blobs, and you should turn to see them with the sun upon them.

41

There are many rowans at Winkworth, but it is the whitebeams and section Micromeles that are designated as a National Collection, so I will consider these first. *Sorbus aria* is our native whitebeam, found in southern England on chalk hills. In spring the young, unfolding leaves are silvery-white and look like small magnolias, and later in summer, though the upper surface of the leaf turns dark green, the underside remains white, so that the whole tree seems silvery-grey when stirred by the wind. In the wild, whitebeams commonly grow with yew, whose dark, almost black-green foliage makes an ideal contrast and suggests that, in the garden too, whitebeams are best sited against a dark background. The flowers, typical flattish heads, off-white in colour, are of no particular merit, but in fruit the whitebeam is beautiful, its clusters of scarlet berries set among tawny or dull gold autumn leaves. There are several forms of whitebeam; perhaps the finest is 'Majestica', with large leaves up to 6 ins long and larger fruits than the wild species. 'Lutescens' is especially lovely in spring, when its young leaves are densely furred with creamy-white on both surfaces. In habit it is compact and conical. Its name might lead one to suppose that its mature foliage is yellowish; but for this we must turn to 'Chrysophylla', which has rather narrow leaves, lime green in summer and clear yellow in autumn. A form found wild in Bosnia with almost circular leaves, 6 ins or so long, is known as f. *cyclophylla*; a superb foliage tree well worth seeking out.

The common whitebeam is hardy and adaptable, tolerant of severe winds and of atmospheric pollution, and thriving on any soil, including of course chalk; though perhaps less happy on thin, dry, acid soils. The Himalayan whitebeam, *Sorbus cuspidata*, is an even more beautiful tree, but a little more exigent, preferring sheltered woodland conditions and tending to be short-lived. Shelter is necessary in part because its huge leaves are borne on rather fragile petioles that snap easily in the wind. Where it is happily sited few broad-leaved trees are more striking in foliage; the leaves, up to 10 ins × 5 ins, are creamy-white or silver-grey beneath. The tree has an open, even gaunt habit, with few, stout branches, rather like a tree magnolia; the young branches, like the under surface of the leaves, are covered with white cobwebby down. In fruit *S. cuspidata* cannot rival the common whitebeam, but its foliage takes on unusual, if sombre, autumn tints of muted browns and tans.

A better doer than the Himalayan whitebeam is 'Wilfrid Fox', named for the creator of Winkworth Arboretum. Possibly a hybrid between *S. aria* and *S. cuspidata*, this fine tree is happier than its putative Himalayan parent in exposed situations. Another outstanding whitebeam of uncertain origin is commonly known as 'Mitchellii', but should properly be called 'John Mitchell'. It has almost circular leaves, about 5 ins × 4 ins, glossy green above and white beneath; a handsome foliage tree of tougher constitution than *S. cuspidata*. It may be a form of *S. thibetica*, which grows stiffly upright; 'John Mitchell' forms a rounded head in maturity.

Included in section Aria is one of the most interesting and, to my eyes at least, most beautiful of all the entire-leaved sorbus. *S. megalocarpa* is a Chinese species that forms a low, widespreading shrubby tree with stout, rich brown branches, fat, sticky reddish winter buds, and large leaves very like those of the loquat, with deeply impressed veins. Its autumn colour is variable from warm brown to sombre crimson; the large fruits have been likened to partridge eggs, russet-brown and lightly speckled. In flower it is very striking, bearing loose clusters of creamy flowers on the bare branches in late February and March when a mild spell spares them from frost damage. Sadly, this desirable tree is hard to obtain and not easy, at least in my experience, to establish. I can think of few trees of which I would rather inherit a mature specimen.

Two closely related and very ornamental whitebeams, *S. graeca* and *S. umbellata*, are by some authorities considered to be two forms of the one species, *S. umbellata*. Growing at Winkworth, side by side as planted by Dr Wilfrid Fox, they can be seen to be quite distinct in habit. *S. umbellata* is a much-branched shrubby tree, with jagged leaves very silvery-white beneath, and late-ripening fruits of greenish yellow flushed red where the sun strikes them. The Winkworth *S. graeca* is much more upright in habit, with dark red fruits ripening two months earlier, in September, and leaves grey rather than white beneath.

Closely allied to the whitebeams is the delightful and little-known *Sorbus chamaemespilus*, a slow-growing shrub with short, stiff branches, cobwebbed with white wool in youth. The flowers are rosy pink, and the fruits bright red, among orange and gold autumn colour. With two distinct seasons of effect, and its neat dwarf habit, it better deserves a place in a small garden than many more widely-planted shrubs.

With *Sorbus alnifolia*, we come to the first, alphabetically, of the trees in section Micromeles that are grown at Winkworth Arboretum. The section is an interesting and very varied one centred in the rainier parts of the Sino-Himalayan region, and includes at least two – some would say more – trees of great merit and interest. Anyone who saw the magnificent vase of *S. alnifolia* in fruit at one of the Royal Horticultural Society's autumn shows a year or two ago will surely agree that this is a species deserving to be grown much more widely. It forms a sizeable tree of pyramidal outline with beech-like grey bark and slender twigs forming a delicate winter tracery, obscured in summer by dense layers of thin-textured foliage overlapping like that of hornbeam, which it much resembles; though the specific name *alnifolia* asserts a resemblance in leaf to alder. The dense clusters of white flowers appear in May and are followed by widely-spaced fruits, egg-shaped and deep pink or soft orange-scarlet in colour. In autumn the foliage takes on similar tones of apricot pink or orange-scarlet. There is a very fine tree of *S. alnifolia* at Winkworth and here too grows *S. zahlbruckneri*, (*S. alnifolia submollis*), which somewhat resembles *S. folgneri* (next to be described) but represents a botanical conundrum: cultivated plants demonstrate characteristics that place it in section Aria. *S. folgneri* is a most elegant little tree with slender, semi-pendulous branches, white-felted when young. The leaves are slender and pointed, dark green above and silvery-white felted beneath; they droop in loose clusters and 'on windy days a tree of *S. folgneri* can usually be detected by the characteristic shimmering of its half-silvery leaves.' (ms of Dr Wilfrid Fox, creator of Winkworth Arboretum, quoted by Bean). In a good year the foliage turns to (Dr Fox again) 'golden pink on top ... brilliantly incandescent.' Typically, the small oval fruits are red; in the form 'Lemon Drop' they are yellow.

Still in section Micromeles, one of the rarest sorbus growing at Winkworth is *S. japonica* var. *calocarpa*, with somewhat pear-shaped, orange-yellow fruits.

Sorbus meliosmifolia is a small shrubby tree of no great merit except in early spring, when its young foliage unfolds in shades of metallic pink, apricot and bronze. Its scented flowers are borne very early, in April, and the ribbed foliage sometimes takes on sombre crimson autumn tints. Rarer even than this is *Sorbus epidendron*, represented by two specimens at Winkworth and one at Edinburgh Botanic Garden, and perhaps by no others in Britain; though the Edinburgh tree, at least, is I believe being propagated for planting elsewhere. The young foliage is copper or bronze-tinted; in summer the large leaves are dark green above, whitish beneath, and distinguished by their deeply impressed veins. The white flowers may be quite showy, often forming a loose conical spray. The specific name *epidendron* indicates that this sorbus may be found in the wild as a shrubby epiphyte – that is, growing on trees; both the Winkworth specimens are of shrubby habit, but the Edinburgh one is more tree-like.

Intermediate between the whitebeams and the rowans are a group of sorbus that probably originated as hybrids, though some at least behave like species and breed true from seed. *S. hybrida* is one such, demonstrating the character of apomixis, which is fairly frequent, as we shall see, among the rowans. (Apomictic reproduction occurs when viable seed is set without fertilisation, so that the offspring are identical with the parent.) *Sorbus hybrida* is a small, upright tree with partly lobed, partly pinnate leaves – the upper half lobed, the lower half with one or two pairs of free leaflets – dull green above and greyish white beneath. The selected clone 'Gibbsii' has larger fruits, brilliant crimson-scarlet and freely borne, that weigh down the branches. The Swedish whitebeam, *S. intermedia*, is a tough and wind-resistant tree of tidy, symmetrical habit, its green, grey-backed leaves lobed in the lower half and coarsely toothed in the upper. The autumn colour is a warm yellowish brown, to set off orange-red fruits. *S.* × *thuringiaca* is of rather stiff habit, especially in the variety 'Fastigiata'. It has longer leaves than *S. hybrida* and does not breed true from seed. None of these is in the first rank as ornamental trees, but they have their value as shapely, gale-resistant trees for the outer reaches of large gardens where wind is a problem.

Botanically, the service trees fall into different sections, but I shall take them together here. The service tree itself, *Sorbus domestica*, is quite widely grown as a street tree in Europe but seldom planted in this country. It is of European origin and was for some time considered to be a rare native of Britain also, but it now seems that the famous specimen growing in the Wyre Forest was deliberately planted. Affectionately known as the 'old sorb', this tree was first noted in 1678 and was, sadly, burnt by a local vagrant in 1862. Fortunately, even in the nineteenth century there were those who were concerned to save rather than exploit our flora, and a direct descendent of the tree was planted in 1916 on the original site. There is a fine specimen of the service tree, also a descendent of the 'old sorb', at Oxford Botanic Garden, a seedling planted about 1850. Beside it is another, planted around 1790. These two trees represent two forms of the service tree, f. *pomifera* with apple-shaped fruits and f. *pyrifera* with pear-shaped fruits, the seedling from the Wyre Forest tree. With its handsome pinnate foliage and large flowers the service tree is highly ornamental, if not as striking as the best of the rowans.

The wild service tree, *S. torminalis*, is decidedly native to Britain, as well as Europe, north Africa and south-west Asia. It is undeservedly uncommon in cultivation, though at one time its fruits, which can be eaten, like medlars, when bletted, were more appreciated than now. In south-east England they were known as 'chequers' and may have given their name to many of the Chequers Inns. The foliage of the wild service tree is very handsome, large, boldly cut like that of the American red oak, and shining green, turning dusky red and bronze in autumn. *Sorbus latifolia* is the Fontainebleau service tree, another species that is thought to be of hybrid origin, coming true – by apomixis – from seed. One parent was certainly *S. torminalis*, the other some member of the *aria* group. As its name implies, the Fontainebleau service tree grows wild in a small area of France centred on the Forest of Fontainebleau. The foliage is glossy green above like that of the wild service tree, but closer in shape to the *aria* types, roundish in outline, and white felted beneath. It has typical white flowers in May and rounded, brownish red fruits. Other interesting sorbus of this type occur as rare British natives: *S. bristoliensis* is an attractive shrubby tree with brighter, orange-red fruits, known only from the Avon Gorge near Bristol; *S. devoniensis* is nearer in aspect to *S. latifolia* but differs in its longer leaves. As its name implies, it grows wild in Devon; its fruits were once sold in Barnstaple Market. Yet another, *S.* × *vagensis*, is a natural hybrid between *S. aria* and *S. torminalis*, and thus of similar parentage to the Fontainebleau service tree; but this one was named originally from a tree at Symonds Yat in the Wye Valley, the only area where it occurs in the British Isles. An interesting and very rare hybrid of this kind, *S.* × *magnifica*, grows at Winkworth; like *S. torminalis* it colours well in autumn, but the leaves are barely lobed and are woolly beneath. Though not outstanding as ornamental trees, all these different service trees are historically interesting and could perhaps be planted more frequently as commemorative trees.

Many of the sorbus in sections Aria and Micromeles are grown at Granada Arboretum, at Jodrell Bank in Cheshire. Here, however, the whole genus has been designated as a National Collection; thus the rowans are included. In this section are a great many trees of such beauty that it is curious that so few are commonly grown. As already noted, they fall into two groups: those with orange or vermilion fruits, often varying to yellow; and those with white to crimson fruits.

The most familiar of the orange-red fruited kinds is our native rowan or mountain ash, *Sorbus aucuparia*, a variable species, beautiful in the wild but in its typical state hardly worth garden space: its fruits ripen in late August, bringing a hint of autumn unseasonably early in the year when our thoughts are still with summer. Furthermore, they are quickly stripped by birds, and the foliage drops early without colouring. Forms of the common rowan, however, are worth growing for other attributes. 'Asplenifolia' has deeply incised, lacy foliage, and 'Dirkenii' is clear yellow in young leaf. 'Beissneri' is similar in leaf to 'Asplenifolia', but its beauty lies chiefly in its bright bark, coral red or terracotta on young branches and coppery tan on the older wood. The foliage turns in autumn to shades of honey gold in contrast to the coral red petioles. Like the Hergest birches, it will probably need scrubbing in wetter, western gardens to remove obscuring lichens and mosses.

An amber-yellow fruited form of *S. aucuparia* is offered as 'Xanthocarpa', and 'Apricot Lady' is similar, with apricot yellow fruits and bright green foliage, colouring richly in autumn. There is an unappealing fastigiate rowan of besom-like aspect called, predictably, 'Fastigiata' and at Granada grows a tree of narrow outline with yellow fruits dubbed 'Upright Yellow'. 'Sheerwater Seedling' is of upright habit with large clusters of orange-vermilion fruits. Dr Benton, Curator of the Granada Arboretum, tells me that a group of Aucuparia hybrids that he is very impressed with are the North American 'Lombart's Choice Hybrids' obtained from Seafield Nurseries. 'The variety "Kirsten Pink" is a most attractive twiggy, small-leaved form with shell-pink fruits, and this, and the varieties "Scarlet King" and "Vermilion", are all growing well. The latter two are much more Rowan-like in their overall appearance but have spectacular fruits.'

Most of the North American rowans are dull when compared with the Far Eastern species, and I shall dismiss them briefly. A possible exception is *S. americana*, a smaller tree than our native rowan with similar, but later-ripening, scarlet red fruits and, on acid soils, better autumn colour of scarlet and apricot.

Demonstrating the parallelism between North American and Far Eastern species that we have already encountered in *Acer* (with *A. pensylvanicum* and *A. rufinerve*), the nearest ally of *S. americana* is the Japanese and Korean *S. commixta*. In cultivation this is seen as a tree of upright habit with bright red fruits and bright autumn colours of scarlet and flame. The rowan known as 'Embley' is similar, colouring rather later in autumn. It has commonly been called *S. discolor*. With their narrow outline they make fine street trees, or single specimens in limited space; where there is more room they can be grouped to good effect. 'Ethel's Gold' is probably a seedling of *S. commixta*; it has amber-gold fruits that last well into winter.

The most widely planted of the yellow-fruited rowans is 'Joseph Rock', a superb small tree of similar upright habit to *S. commixta*. It has neat, glossy dark green foliage that turns to claret purple, crimson and scarlet in autumn, setting off the creamy-primrose and honey-gold fruits that hang long, in large clusters. The status of this tree is still uncertain; it was raised from seed collected in the wild by the eponymous Dr Rock in 1932 and may be a natural hybrid, or may belong to *S. rehderiana*, an interesting species that seems intermediate between the red- and the white-fruited species of rowan. Whatever its botanical status, as a garden tree 'Joseph Rock' is hard to fault, except that it seems particularly prone to fireblight. Sited against a dark background the pale fruits are given full value once the leaves have fallen; or it may be equally striking silhouetted against a clear blue autumn sky.

The cumbersomely named *S. esserteauiana* makes a small tree resembling in outline an old apple tree. The young leaves are copper-coloured, and in autumn the foliage turns reddish; orange-red fruits are borne in large clusters, ripening late and holding well. The more attractive form is the yellow-fruited 'Flava', but it can scarcely compare with 'Joseph Rock'. Far more striking are two Chinese species that should be much more extensively planted. *Sorbus sargentiana* is easily distinguished by its bold foliage, with large leaflets that unfold in coppery-bronze tufts from fat mahogany-red sticky buds like those of the horse chestnut. In autumn the tree is spectacular, with huge clusters of matt orange-scarlet fruits and bright orange-vermilion foliage colouring in November. *S. scalaris* is even more distinct in leaf, with leathery-textured, narrow, closely set leaflets giving it almost the aspect of a huge fern, enhanced by the copper tones of the unfolding foliage that almost reminds one of one of the big blechnums. In maturity *S. scalaris* forms a spreading tree, weighed down in autumn by its big clusters of glossy vermilion-scarlet fruits that follow wide heads of creamy flowers. On acid, sandy soils especially, the foliage in autumn turns to scarlet and flame.

The red-fruited rowans cannot be relied upon to come wholly true from seed, though many will produce a fair proportion of seedlings that resemble the parent. Sadly this is not true of *S. scalaris*, which almost invariably produces hybrid offspring. By contrast, the white-crimson fruited rowans are almost all apomictic, so that their seedlings resemble the parent. This group contains some very beautiful small trees. One of the loveliest and most distinct is *Sorbus cashmeriana*, easily and quickly raised from seed so that it should be much more often grown. Unusually among rowans it has large, pale pink flowers in May; these are followed in autumn by clusters of marble-sized, soft, pure white fruits on the bare branches, ignored by the birds and hanging until they turn to brown mush. *S. × hostii* is another with pink flowers.

The white-fruited forms of *S. hupehensis* are now considered by Dr McAllister, of Ness Botanic Garden, to be referable to *S. glabrescens*. Whatever their taxonomic status, both the white and the pink-fruited forms are trees of the highest merit, with beautiful glaucous foliage, sometimes coppery-bronze when young, and often dying in autumn in shades of pinkish orange flushed with claret purple. The fruits are small and hard, white or crimson-pink, and last well into winter, after the leaves have fallen. This is another tree that deserves careful siting, where in summer its subtly-coloured foliage can be seen at close quarters and in autumn its fruits set against a dark background. Various pink-fruited selections of this fine rowan have been named; they tend to have even more glaucous foliage, colouring to claret and crimson in autumn.

Sorbus vilmorinii is a small and elegant tree of spreading shrubby habit with an even greater tendency than most sorbus to form several main stems. In leaf it is very pretty, with numerous small leaflets giving a ferny effect; the foliage turns to crimson and claret-purple in autumn. The fruits are enchanting, clusters of small rosy-crimson berries that slowly pale through pink to blush-white, and last long into the winter. 'Pearly King' is similar, though with fewer leaflets its foliage is less attractive. Dr McAllister attributes it to *S. rehderiana*, clearly – since he also considers it to include 'Joseph Rock' – a variable species. *S. vilmorinii* comes true from seed ('Joseph Rock' does not) and can also be grown from cuttings. In some gardens it self-sows freely, and I have found *S. hupehensis* to do so as well. Similar again to *S. vilmorinii*, but with pure white fruits, is *S. prattii*, making a little round-headed tree or many-stemmed shrub. This species, too, can be relied upon to come true from seed. With their neat, compact or tabular habit, delicate foliage and pretty fruits, they are small garden trees of the greatest value, suitable for a variety of settings. I should like to see them, for example, providing height and contrast in some of those overdone planting of heathers, with which in both colour and character they seem to me to assort ideally.

On a much smaller scale the same is true of a most delightful dwarf shrub in this pink-fruited section of rowans. *Sorbus reducta* is a suckering shrub that forms a small thicket of stems between 6 ins and 2 ft in height, set with glossy green leaves that turn to claret-crimson in autumn, among pink or blush-white fruits. It grows best in moist, peaty soil, such as suits dwarf rhododendrons, with which, as well as heathers, it associates very well. Smaller still than *S. reducta* is the uncommon *S. pygmaea*: more properly now to be known as *S. poteriifolia*, but do not on that account confuse it with *S. poteriifolia* of gardens, a small tree rather resembling *S. vilmorinii*. The true *S. poteriifolia* is a minute shrublet barely 6 ins high, semi-herbaceous, with running roots. It has rosy-pink to crimson flowers and white fruits. Its rarity is due no doubt in part at least to its reluctance to accept captivity; its running tendencies make it almost impossible to grow in a pot. In the wild it is said to grow in micaceous schist, and I know of at least one grower who succeeded with it for several years in a gritty, leafy compost in a large trough, which also housed a gentian or two and some tiny rhododendrons. I should add that these little rowans are not grown at Granada Arboretum, where the trees have to make their own way in turf; but no account of the genus *Sorbus* would be complete without a mention of them.

One of the finest rowans is not represented at Granada Arboretum, possibly because it is too tender. *Sorbus insignis* is a striking foliage plant, suggesting, as Bean puts it, 'some evergreen species from a subtropical rainforest.' Each leaflet is up to 5 ins long and 1 in wide, or even more; borne in, usually, two to five pairs per leaf, each of which may be 10 ins or so long. The larger-leaved forms, with fewer leaflets, mostly from collections in Yunnan and Burma, are on the whole the most tender, and have been separated as *S. harrowiana* but are now considered to fall within *S. insignis*. The small white, pink or reddish fruits are insignificant, but as foliage plants these tender rowans are unsurpassed, and are well worth trying in any sheltered woodland garden in the south of Britain.

Happily most sorbus are more tolerant of a wide range of climate and soil conditions than this noble species. Whether you garden on chalk or peat, on clay or sand, there is a sorbus that will grow for you; whatever the size of your garden.

The National Collections

The National Collections of Sorbus are held at Winkworth Arboretum, Nr Hascombe, Godalming, Surrey (The National Trust), and at Granada Arboretum, Jodrell Bank, in Cheshire (Manchester University). Recently a third Collection has been designated at Durham Agricultural College; this will develop into a duplicate Collection paralleling that held at Winkworth Arboretum.

The Winkworth Collection is limited to sections Aria and Micromeles, although many other species also grow there from section Aucuparia. Section Aria represents the whitebeams. The Collection was designated in April 1981 and consists of mainly mature trees, planted by the creator of Winkworth Arboretum, Dr Wilfrid Fox, who bought the land in 1937. He planted many trees of different genera, but Sorbus were a particular interest of his, and his collection quickly won renown. The soil is not ideally suited to whitebeams, being poor, dry and sandy, particularly thin on the steep slopes, but with careful cultivation they can be induced to grow well.

The Granada Arboretum is a comparatively new one, as noted at the end of the chapter on Malus. The Sorbus Collection was designated in March 1982, and comprises all sections of the genus. Like the crabs, the rowans and whitebeams cope well with the soil and climate at Jodrell Bank. The trees all grow in turf, rather than in cultivated beds, but the competition from the grass does not seem to affect them adversely.

Shrubs

Introduction

SHRUBS have long been used, in different ways it is true, to define and shape our gardens. Two or three centuries ago they were considered almost solely as backgrounds, whether clipped into formal shapes that denied them any individuality, or grown free but close-packed in shrubberies. During these centuries, however, and especially during the nineteenth and early twentieth centuries, new and beautiful shrubs were introduced from North America, the Southern Hemisphere, Japan and China. These introductions added a great range of plants to the precious evergreens of Mediterranean origin, laurustinus and bay, Portugal and cherry laurels, and our own few native evergreens – holly, yew and box – that were so appreciated by early gardeners in their efforts to cheat winter. As well as these evergreens, many of the deciduous flowering shrubs we now take so much for granted were introduced during this period. Slowly shrubs began to be appraised as individuals with their own characteristic beauty of form, foliage, fruit and flower; particularly perhaps the last, so that now it is shrubs that are the mainstay of many gardens even where flowers and colour, above all, are sought.

The garden centre movement has reinforced this dependence – it is hardly too strong a word – on shrubs, for few hardy perennials look well growing in containers in the spring season which sees the peak of garden centre sales. At this time, on the other hand, many shrubs are in flower, and the garden centre customers can 'see exactly what they are getting'. Of course this creates another imbalance, and partly accounts for the complaint that shrub gardens are dull and colourless from June onwards. Yet this need not be so. Even among the tiny selection of shrubs included in this book, there are those that will provide summer as well as spring colour. If you accept dwarf conifers and rhododendrons as each, in their own way, special cases, then of the remaining genera two are essentially spring-flowering – forsythia and pieris – and two will provide later colour:

cistus for high summer and ceanothus from spring through until autumn. Two others, the olearias and their close allies the shrubby senecios from New Zealand, have much fine foliage to offer as well as daisy flowers, in some species the chief attraction. And there are many others. This is not to say that, in my view, shrubs should be used to the exclusion of all else to provide year-round colour. As I said in my introductory chapter, many gardeners find the greatest satisfaction in combining shrubs and trees with perennials, bulbs and ephemerals in close association to form changing garden pictures.

The Choice

Thanks to the plant collectors who introduced so many new shrubs to cultivation, from all the continents of the world, we have an enormous range to choose from. With the natural tendency of the human mind to categorise, we may find it helpful to think of these perhaps as evergreen or deciduous; as primarily grown for flower or for foliage; as plants for hot, dry conditions, for exposed seaside places or for cool woodland soils.

Another broad division that I like to consider is the contrast between formal and informal, or put another way between domesticated and untamed shrubs. Of course, depending upon their companions and their settings some may sit equally happily in either category, but broadly speaking the more highly bred plants call for a domesticated or formal setting.

It is, however, the conditions the plants need that have the greatest practical impact upon our garden planning. Even if we think that a cistus and a pieris might look well together, we are unlikely to make them both grow happily in the same position; either the Mediterranean sun-lover or the native of cool, acid soils will suffer where the other succeeds. In exposed seaside gardens, wind-buffeted but relatively frost-free, many Australasian composites will make a first line of defence against the salt gales which would destroy the most frost-resistant shrub lacking their protective coating of wax or felt. Others, given some shelter, are magnificent foliage plants much coveted by gardeners from colder inland areas; planted in frosty pockets, they soon die, or worse still linger on, their stunted growth and desiccated leaves testimony to their misery. But in general, whether inland or by the sea, it is wind that is the worst enemy of British gardens, and plants that thrive in exposed spots are especially precious.

Cistus and ceanothus both need sun and well-drained soil, and to them could be added plants from later sections of this book: some narcissi, tulips, the South African kniphofias or red-hot pokers, sedum, dianthus, penstemons and some asters, bulbous nerines also from South Africa, and the silvery-leaved *Lychnis*. With kniphofias, dianthus, asters and nerines we come to plants that have received the attentions of the hybridisers, and this leads us on from cultural needs to aesthetic considerations. To this group of sun-lovers, then, we could add forsythias, the large-flowered clematis hybrids, and, from the section on trees, the flowering crabs and whitebeams; though these would need an enriched soil and the clematis a cool root-run as well, which could be provided by the shrubs; and both the crabs and the whitebeams would fit equally well in less tamed settings. Needless to say, shrubs and perennials that are not treated in this book would also find their place in this domesticated setting: lilac and mock orange, old shrub roses and paeonies, delphiniums and Korean chrysanthemums among them.

Pieris and rhododendrons, on the other hand, need an acid soil, cool and leafy, and some shelter from scorching sun and drying winds. They would assort with the maples, birches and rowans, with magnolias too; while among them primroses and snowdrops, foxgloves and some thalictrums, arisaemas and some spurges would find suitable growing conditions. At the woodland edge many species of clematis and some narcissi would grow happily and look well, and in moister soils ligularias and lobelias would add vivid colour in high summer.

Dwarf conifers are a mixed lot, varying from prostrate or spreading junipers that assort well with sun-loving Mediterraneans, to exclamation marks much abused as contrast to heathers, or tiny bun-like objects fit only for rock gardens or troughs. I don't feel I can generalise about dwarf conifers, but will consider in the chapter devoted to them different ways of combining them with other plants, leaving you to make up your own mind whether you approve or not.

Shrubs as Individuals

Shrubs have different roles to play in the garden scene by virtue of their form and habit. Just as much as trees, they need careful placing: nothing is to be gained by treating them as the components of a herbaceous border, massed and grouped by size and colour. All too often the outcome of this approach is a Parks Department haircut: 'pruned' to a neat outline, the shrubs lose all their individuality and very likely much of their flower as well, for the annual clip-over is often performed without regard for the flowering season of the shrub.

There are shrubs which are dominant in character, with fine foliage and a noble deportment, demanding that they be treated as individuals. Such, for example, are many rhododendrons. It is sad to be faced, as I was in a garden where once I worked, with large old rhododendrons so crowded in by their neighbours that their characteristic outline was distorted beyond recall. They need not be grown in chilly isolation, but are the better for not being cramped.

Others, such as cistus, are gregarious, ideally suited to growing in close boscage to form dense, ground-covering masses emulating their native *maquis*. Yet others, of which forsythia may be taken as an example, are formless, and whether massed or grown singly need a firm supporting cast and a unifying underplanting of shrubs and perennials. Whether as specimen shrubs, components of a close boscage or part of a mixed planting, however, it is as individuals that I shall consider the shrubs in the next eight chapters, with suggestions for their use in the garden.

Ceanothus

BLUE-FLOWERED *Ceanothus* captivate all who see them. As Arnold-Forster observed in his classic *Shrubs for the Milder Counties*, they are 'some of the most treasured decorations of our gardens'. Few shrubs that we can grow successfully in our gardens offer such a range of blues, from the china-blue of *Ceanothus thyrsiflorus repens* to the deep, almost gentian tones of *C. impressus*; with grey-blue; 'the faint blues of wood-smoke or chalcedony' (Arnold-Forster again); blues both light and dark with a softening hint of purple; clear lavender, mauve-pink and various shades approaching white.

Many have evergreen foliage and most grow rapidly. Added to their colour this makes a list of attributes that might add up to the perfect garden shrub, were it not for that question mark over hardiness, so frequent with desirable plants. For *Ceanothus* are mainly natives of California, forming an important constituent of the vegetation known as chaparral – the brush of the Californian foothills. Here, in poor, stony, fast-draining soil, many species grow with native oaks, *Arctostaphylos*, and *Yucca whipplei*, on exposed banks among rocks and gravel; often they colonise the scars left by the builders of new roads. Others, for example *C. incanus*, *C. leucodermis* and *C. papillosus*, are found in broken woodland, *C. incanus* even where the soil is quite moist. *C. incanus*, in fact, is quite unlike the common image of a ceanothus; it has creamy-white flowers in spikes, greyish leaves and stems covered with a white bloom. It also has formidable 2 ins spines. It is a very beautiful shrub.

It is this usual preference for dry soil that led Roy Cheek, who has been largely responsible for one of the two National Collections of *Ceanothus*, to plant them at Cannington, in Somerset, against a wall raised well above a road, on dry, fast-draining soil where previously there had been a collection of old plums, that no doubt had robbed the soil of most of its nutrients. The ceanothus that replace the plums are planted in natural relationships, in sequence, the hybrids growing – so far as possible – between their parents. For the student of *Ceanothus* this means that Roy Cheek's plantings constitute virtually a living key to the genus.

There is much also to interest the keen gardener to whom botanical relationships are of less importance than garden effect. Both Roy Cheek and Neil Lucas, who has built up the other, much younger National *Ceanothus* Collection at Torquay, in the hospital grounds, stress the value of an experimental approach to the genus. Traditionally, the evergreen species have been grown as wall shrubs in all but the warmest gardens, and their rapid growth has led their owners to trim back the shoots as they encroached on windows and spread over paths. This treatment, or maltreatment, shortens their lives; and this short life expectancy is the other black mark many gardeners place against ceanothus – unfairly perhaps, in the case of a shrub that grows so quickly and of which most kinds are so easy to propagate and hence to replace. At Cannington the ceanothus are allowed to billow out, to flop to the ground if they will, to root down if they can, and to grow without constraints. Many of the ceanothus of the original planting are still thriving, enormous and full of bloom.

At Torbay Hospital Neil Lucas has asked himself whether to give the ceanothus maximum protection against a wall, or try to simulate more natural growing conditions by planting on dry sunny slopes. In mild, but moist, coastal Devon the soils are in the main fairly rich, and it is easy to see why the ceanothus should behave differently from their native counterparts in California.

Especially worthy of wall space are C. 'Burtonensis', a hybrid or perhaps even a form of *C. impressus*, distinguished by its small, almost circular leaves; and *C. × veitchianus*. Some of the more spreading kinds make superb ground cover in exposed places: *C. thyrsiflorus repens*, of course, and 'Yankee Point', with mid-blue flowers. The naming of ceanothus, as available commercially in this country at present, is very muddled, and one of the tasks of a National Collection holder is to sort out such confusions so that an intending purchaser may be sure of getting what he wants and not an imposter. Take *Ceanothus thyrsiflorus repens*. Often recommended as ground cover, this is a plant which I had always known as exceptionally vigorous, quickly making 10 or 12 ft of growth sideways, with a height of 3 ft or so; with shining, thumb-nail sized dark green leaves and powder-blue flowers in spring. Neil Lucas uses plants of this name extensively as ground cover in the hospital grounds, originally obtaining his plants from local nurseries. Three distinct forms can be recognised. The first is a very vigorous, open bush which when established covers 4 ft in a season, and varies in height to about 4 ft. The second is of medium vigour, more dense but still fast-growing, and flowers well. The third is a very compact dense mounded bush covering itself with flower, and only a third the size of the others despite being planted in a similar position. A fourth form, much lower growing and extremely prostrate, could turn out to be *C. thyrsiflorus prostratus*.

C. × veitchianus is another name to look at warily. The original plant was introduced from the wild, a probable natural hybrid rather than a true species, by William Lobb in 1853. A fine tall shrub of 10 ft or so, it has bright cobalt blue flowers and glossy leaves. You will often find it labelled 'C. dentatus' or 'C. dentatus floribundus', and to make matters worse plants labelled 'C. veitchianus' may actually be *C. × lobbianus*. This, as you might well surmise, owes its name to the same William Lobb who introduced it, too, in the 1850s. It has similar bright blue flowers. Yet another in this complex of similar plants is *C. floribundus*, found again by William Lobb, in 1850, and sent to Veitch's nursery in Exeter. Exactly where he collected it is not known, and it has not been found in the wild since. Worse – for from the gardener's point of view it was a superb plant with flowers 'of a particularly vivid shade of mazarine-blue' (Bean) – it may no longer exist at all. In 1936 W. J. Bean stated, in *Trees and Shrubs Hardy in the British Isles*, that descendents of the original had been found in Devon, but by the time that great work was revised (Vol. 1, A–C, came out in 1970) the comment is 'whether any vegetative offspring of the Veitchian plant still exist is not certain'. What *is* certain is that there is confusion between *C. floribundus* Hook (probably the Veitch plant); *C. floribundus* of gardeners; *C. dentatus floribundus* which may or may not be the Veitch plant, *C. dentatus* itself; and *C. × lobbianus* which is sometimes grown as 'C. dentatus'; not to mention *C. × veitchianus*, with which this nomenclatural paper-chase began.

The ordinary gardener might ask 'What has all this to do with me?' Well, quite a lot. Take that example of the ground-covering *Ceanothus thyrsiflorus repens*. It could matter a good deal if you expect something a couple of feet across and high, and get the 12 ft monster that I grew. The big fellow looked superb with *Cytisus × praecox*, a mound-forming broom 4–5 ft high and wide smothered in pungently scented cream flowers in spring, with the palest greeny-primrose flowers of 'Ukon', a Japanese cherry, in the background. The little ceanothus, to emulate this colour grouping, would need to be paired with *Cytisus × kewensis* instead. Set the blue of the ceanothus against an early rose species such as butter-yellow *R. ecae* or paler *R. hugonis*, or my favourite big *R. × headleyensis*, and you'd need, again, to choose one of the bigger *C. thyrsiflorus repens*. Then again, *Ceanothus thyrsiflorus* itself, rather than its procumbent form, is tall, even up to tree size of 20–30 ft: magnificent giving shade to a group of pale deciduous azaleas, as in the wild it grows with the white azalea *Rhododendron occidentale*. Arnold-Forster, who did a great deal to popularise ceanothus in our gardens, found its pure blue 'rather lightless in a mass … helped by a touch of contrasting colour, such as the yellow and red of honeysuckle or the reds of *Vitis henryana*'.

'Cascade' is probably a form of *C. thyrsiflorus*, a tall, fairly tough shrub with arching branches of powder-blue flowers in May and June. At Mount Stewart in Northern Ireland it combines charmingly with a white-flowered daisy bush – here the rare *Olearia erubescens* is used, but *O. × scilloniensis*, with its greyish foliage and massed daisies, would do as well and is easier to get hold of. Another good hybrid that would combine with the olearia, and perhaps too with the deep yellow saucers of *Fremontodendron*, is 'Puget Blue'.

Most evergreen ceanothus flower in spring, beginning with *C. arboreus* in February. Some, however, extend the season well into summer and autumn, among them 'Autumnal Blue' and 'Burkwoodii'. The first is a hybrid of *C. thyrsiflorus*, and flowers from July to October, light blue in colour. 'Burkwoodii' has richer blue flowers and the same valuable season; it is less hardy than 'Autumnal Blue'. They combine well with a rose such as pale yellow, single 'Mermaid', or as part of an all-blue planting to make a soft haze of colour, with *Agapanthus*, *Ceratostigma*, *Perovskia* and *Caryopteris*.

Let's return to *C. arboreus* and its forms, that flower so early but are large and somewhat tender shrubs needing wall protection. Named kinds are 'Ray Hartman' and 'Winter Cloud', this one giving the hint that, in California, they can be expected to flower from January. In this country *C. arboreus* may just flower as early as February. 'Trewithen Blue' is a deeply coloured form that is quite widely available; a pity we cannot yet say the same about 'Treasure Island', which is apparently dark blue in flower and grows to a manageable 8 ft or so.

C. papillosus is more easily obtainable; I've already mentioned its form 'Puget Blue', and 'Concha' is another. Nicest of all, in my view, is *C. papillosus* var. *roweanus*, a low-growing shrub seldom over 3-4 ft, with brilliant blue flowers and long, narrow, sticky leaves, a striking and beautiful plant compact enough for a low wall. Other low-growing, or even prostrate, ceanothus are worth a try. *C. gloriosus*, with lavender-blue fragrant flowers, is a creeper several feet wide with solid-textured dark green toothed leaves. It is a coastal species, ground-hugging near the shore but taller inland. *C. divergens* is semi-scandent, so when you grow it near other shrubs you can expect to see its blue flowers and wavy-edged leaves appearing among its neighbours' branches. Another species which veers away from the purer blues is *C. purpureus*, 2-4 ft high, with long rigid reddish-brown branches and superb holly-like leaves. The red-purple buds are followed by lavender-purple flowers and large red seed pods. *C. prostratus* is rather tricky, growing flat to the ground, hence its Californian name of squaw carpet. It comes from high altitudes, where it spends the winter under snow cover, which prompted Neil Lucas to plant it, not in mild and normally snowless Torquay, but on the edge of Dartmoor, where it promptly succumbed to a snowy winter.

What other ceanothus are scented, apart from *C. gloriosus*? *C. arboreus* is supposed to be fragrant, and so is *C. cuneatus* – but this is of little garden value, with unimpressive dull-white flowers. *C. ramulosus* and its variety *C. r. fascicularis* are said to be honey-scented, and Neil Lucas has grown plants from Californian seed, which have yet to flower: so we don't yet know if they will have this characteristic away from their native country. Conditions are very different here, and a plant such as *C. rigidus* which is scented in California may not be so here. It is a subject requiring more research and a good nose. There is no doubting, however, the cinnamon-scent of the leaves of *C. velutinus*, particularly when crushed. Incidentally, should there ever be a shortage of soap, ceanothus flowers when rubbed in water make a lather which is apparently a good substitute. *C. rigidus* is worth growing anyway, scent or no scent, for its rich royal blue flowers; and it has a charming white form called 'Snowball'. Sadly, both are tender and must have wall protection. A hybrid of *C. rigidus* is the admirable and easy 'Delight' with rich blue flowers in long sprays in spring; perhaps from its other parent, *C. papillosus*, comes its greater hardiness.

Another singularly beautiful but rather demanding ceanothus is *C. cyaneus*. Making a shrub of around 10 ft and flowering, normally, in May and June, it has large long sprays of hazy blue flowers that may continue to appear well into autumn: I photographed it at Cannington, full of flower, in October. In the wild it grows in association with *Romneya californica*, the Californian tree poppy, and the combination of the just off-blue ceanothus with the large, satiny white poppies enhanced by their central golden boss of stamens would be worth trying to emulate here. The snag to *C. cyaneus* is its dislike of root disturbance, which may make it hard to establish. 'La Primavera' is apparently an easier hybrid, but where to obtain it? Neither this, nor many others that were mentioned in Rensselaer & McMinn's book *Ceanothus* – cultivars of European origin such as 'Mme Furtado', 'Rosamund', and 'Sapphire' – have yet been rediscovered. Maybe they survive in old European gardens, but without accurate planting records how should we identify them?

At Cannington the evergreen species and hybrids are grown on south- and west-facing walls. In recognition of their greater hardiness, the decidu-ous kinds are relegated to the east wall of the large enclosed garden where they grow. Instead of a botanical sequence, the deciduous kinds, being in the main a fairly homogeneous group of hybrids, are ranged in a colour progression, from pink at one end through white to blue at the other.

Without doubt the best known ceanothus of this group is 'Gloire de

Versailles', a charming and valuable shrub with smoky blue flowers in 4–6 ins sprays on violet stems in late summer and autumn. Because it, and its kindred hybrids, flower on the shoots of the current season's growth they can be hard-pruned each spring. Thus they fit admirably with the now traditional mixed border, joining, among the flowers of summer, such shrubs as *Caryopteris × clandonensis*, hardy fuchsias, *Hebe speciosa* hybrids, *Tamarix ramosissima* (*T. pentandra*), *Hypericum* 'Hidcote' and many other essentially rather formless, but easy and colourful shrubs. The gentle hazy blue of 'Gloire de Versailles' will cool down hot reds and yellows, of crocosmias or day lilies perhaps, or combine seductively with lavenders, mauves and purples, including large-flowered clematis, nepeta, *Salvia virgata nemorosa*, pale phloxes, and early Michaelmas daisies. Deeper blues include 'Indigo' (the deepest of all, but less hardy than most) and 'Topaze'. 'Henri Desfosse' has red young stems; 'Delilianus' is sky blue and 'Leon Simon' paler still. The deeper blues like 'Indigo' blend well with a deep crimson rose such as 'Fellenberg'.

One parent of this group of deciduous hybrids is *C. americanus*, a white-flowered, hardy, deciduous ceanothus of interest chiefly as being the first to be introduced to this country, in 1713; and for being used, after the Boston Tea Party, as a substitute for tea. Next in the colour-graded plantings at Cannington come the pinks, which can be charming, or washed out and muddy, depending partly on soil and partly, no doubt, on the companions you choose for them. As always, the less-than-clean, mauvy pinks need careful handling. 'Ceres' has large sprays of lilac pink flowers; 'Marie Simon' is rose pink, and 'Perle Rose' is the brightest – at its best – in carmine rose. The name 'Pinquet Guindon' is mentioned by Arnold-Forster, and appears in Hillier's *Manual of Trees and Shrubs*, described as being a peculiar shade of lavender suffused pink; but Hillier's must have ceased to supply it some time ago, for it is still on the search list for the National Collections. These pink ceanothus combine enchantingly, as I once saw in a small Gloucestershire garden, with similarly coloured deutzias, such as June-flowering 'Contraste' in mauve-pink with a deeper, purple stripe down each petal; but if you prune your ceanothus too hard too late they probably wouldn't make it in time to coincide with the deutzia. A better bet might be the lilac-pink *D. longifolia* 'Veitchii', which goes on flowering into July. Whatever the companions you choose for them, the deciduous ceanothus are good tough shrubs, if correspondingly less exciting than the evergreen kinds which must remain too tantalisingly tender for cold northern gardens.

The National Collections

The National Collections of Ceanothus are held at Somerset College of Agriculture and Horticulture, Cannington, Bridgewater, Somerset; and at Torbay Hospital, Lawes Bridge, Torquay (Torbay Health Authority).

The Cannington Collection, one of several National Collections held at the College, was designated in April 1981. Most of the plants forming the core of the Collection were already well-established, part of an earlier planting of Ceanothus and various Leguminosae – the pea family – including species of Indigofera, Caesalpinia japonica and so on. These, like the Ceanothus, were plants that were expected to grow willingly in the poor soil left after some old plums had been grubbed out. In time the leguminous shrubs were removed, leaving the Ceanothus to grow to full size.

The plants at Torbay Hospital are much younger, and are being added to each year as new areas need landscaping. There is a wide variety of sites, from steep banks needing trouble-free cover, to areas in paving or gravel where attractive landscaping is regarded by the hospital authorities as an important element in patient care, with sheltered courtyards and walls for the most tender species and exposed sites at the satellite hospitals where other species can be tested for hardiness.

Cistus

THE CHELSEA Physic Garden, half hidden by tall walls, between Royal Hospital Road and the Embankment, has been a botanic garden for over 300 years. Three centuries of cultivation have left the soil well drained and rather hungry; the sheltering walls and south-facing site give the garden a special climate of its own, trapping every scrap of heat in summer between the walls, which give cosy protection in winter. Thus it is that Mediterranean plants grow especially well in the Chelsea Physic Garden; the big olive tree is famous, and in the summer of 1976 it even managed to ripen a good crop of its fruit. There is a stand of Kermes oak (*Quercus coccifera*), too, at the Chelsea Physic. This little evergreen shrub with neat, holly-like leaves, also a native of the Mediterranean, is the host plant of the Kermes insect, from which scarlet dye was obtained before chemical dyes were invented.

In such company the cistuses find themselves entirely at home. They are all natives of the Mediterranean region, many in Spain and Portugal; all are evergreen, and have quite large, rose-like flowers in white, or shades of pink, mauve or magenta, giving them their common name of sun rose. They are, indeed, larger cousins of the little, brightly-coloured rock roses which are often also called sun roses, *Helianthemum*: but the resemblance is superficial only, for the rock roses and sun roses belong in a family of their own, not the rose family at all.

Cistus are often recommended for dry, poor soils, even for thin soil over chalk, and in such soils, in the hottest and sunniest sites our country can offer, they will thrive. I was surprised, therefore, to find many growing at Chelsea Physic Garden in a bed lightly shaded by trees. Duncan Donald, curator of the garden, told me that many species do in fact grow in light shade at woodland edges in the wild, and in a climate as nearly continental as that of the Physic Garden he felt it was worth trying to grow his cistuses in like conditions. The overhead canopy also gives a little extra winter protection, so what the cistuses lose in summer sun, with its beneficial ripening effect on the wood, they may gain in winter warmth; while the rooty soil provides still better drainage. Most of us would still, I think, plant our cistuses in full sun, perhaps at the foot of a south-facing house wall where their evergreen foliage would make an attractive year-round furnishing, decorated in summer with copious flowers. These each last just one day; by evening the ground beneath the bushes is carpeted with petals, but the next morning more buds open to deck the shrub again.

First choice, perhaps, for an important position – such as the foot of house walls, by a patio, at the corner of a much-used path – would be one of the cistuses with aromatic foliage. As Duncan says, there can be few scents more evocative of Mediterranean holidays than the resinous fragrance of cistus foliage, at its most marked on warm summer evenings. The gum which produces this aroma is used in perfumery, and at one time in medicine; known as ladanum, it is extracted mainly from two species. *C. ladanifer*, the gum cistus, and *C. creticus*, about which we shall hear more later. *C. ladanifer* is rather upright in habit, with narrow leaves, clammy with resin: a propagator's nightmare, as your fingers and knife get stickier and blacker with every cutting you make. Its flowers are exquisite, white with a conspicuous maroon-red blotch at the base of each petal, in the usual thin, almost tissue-paper texture of cistus flowers. They are borne singly, the largest of any cistus, though rivalled by the beautiful *C. palhinhae* which sets its great, pure white flowers against abundant dark green foliage. *C. ladanifer* and *C. palhinhae* are closely allied; the second grows on the limestone promontory of Cape St Vincent in the Algarve, while the gum cistus, with a wider distribution, stops short at the limestone, but seems not to mind lime in our gardens.

Many of the cistuses we grow are natural hybrids; one of the best, inheriting from the Gum Cistus the shiny, fragrant gum and from its other parent a greater resistance to cold, is *C.* × *cyprius*. The tough and hardy *C. laurifolius* has also passed on to this offspring its clustered flowers, borne three to six on a stem, white with the blood-red blotch inherited from the gum cistus. *C.* × *cyprius* is tall and vigorous, spreading with age; in winter its foliage turns to a chilly, leaden grey-green.

Another child of *C. ladanifer* is *C.* × *aguilari*, found wild in the Iberian peninsula and in Morocco and first introduced by Sir Oscar Warburg. To the Warburgs, father and son (Dr Edmund Warburg), we owe much of the present popularity of the genus. In the early 1800s *Cistus* were widely grown, and 112 different kinds are beautifully illustrated in Sweet's *Cistineae*, published in 1825-30. Several of those he described were illustrated from plants growing in the Chelsea Physic Garden, then known as the garden of the Apothecaries' Company, under its curator, Mr William Anderson. Later, however, cistuses lost much of their popularity. In the second half of the nineteenth century a good deal of research on the genus was conducted at Antibes; many hybrids were raised artificially which helped botanists to determine that several cistuses described by Sweet and others as species were in fact hybrids. This work was almost unknown in England, and by 1930, when Sir Oscar Warburg's account of *Cistus* appeared in the RHS Journal, he was evidently writing of a group of plants largely ignored by gardeners. 'There is evidence, from Sweet's book,' he wrote, 'that round about 1840 cistuses enjoyed much popular esteem in England, though principally as plants for the cold greenhouse'.

The Warburgs travelled widely in the Mediterranean and introduced several new *Cistus* species and hybrids, including *C. × aguilari* already mentioned, a tall hybrid with white flowers and vivid green leaves, their edges neatly crimped. Sir Oscar raised a blotched form of *C. × aguilari*, christened 'Maculatus', which has more decidedly resinous leaves than the pure white flowered form. It received an Award of Merit in 1936.

At about the same time as the Warburgs were popularising *Cistus*, Captain Collingwood Ingram (better known for his devotion to Japanese cherries which earned him the nickname Cherry Ingram) introduced *C. palhinhae*, and crossed it with its near relative *C. ladanifer*. The results of the marriage were several fine cistuses, whose worth was recognised by the RHS Award of Merit. 'Paladin' (AM 1946) and 'Pat' (AM 1955) both have large white flowers, maroon-blotched; the later 'Blanche' (AM 1967), as its name implies, has pure white flowers. They are slightly tender, like their parents, but are bushier than the rather thin-habited *C. ladanifer* Another child of *C. palhinhae* is 'Elma' (AM 1949), also raised by Captain Ingram from a cross with the hardy *C. laurifolius*. Indeed, as the laurel-leaved cistus has cropped up before in this text, it is high time I described it. Like most of those I have considered so far, it gives off a resinous or incense-like aroma in hot weather; it is tall, tough and hardy, and bears its creamy-white flowers in clusters up to 9 ins long. *C. laurifolius* is none too easy to raise from cuttings, but grows very easily from seed, and this makes it invaluable as evergreen cover in large masses for soils too hot and dry for most evergreens.

Cistuses are mostly very fast-growing, and this makes the denser-habited kinds valuable as ground cover plants on dry soils, especially as many develop by throwing out new layers of growth over the old. Their rapid growth also makes them suitable as fillers between more permanent shrubs, that grow slowly to a large size.

Too many people, in my view, think of ground cover plants as low-growing only; yet any plant that grows densely enough to exclude weeds can reduce maintenance, which is one aim of ground cover; another, not unnaturally, is to clothe the ground *decoratively*, and this the *Cistus* family is well qualified to do. There are, indeed, low-growing cistuses in plenty.

The flattest of all is *C. salvifolius* 'Prostratus', a honey of a plant with trailing stems that mound up to about 1 ft in height, decked with creamy-white flowers, stained yellow at the base. It is ideally adapted to draping down a rock face or a dry wall, perhaps in company with another trailer or weaver of not too assertive tendencies, as it might be *Borago laxiflora* with nodding, wide-open bells in pure china-blue (cut the borage ruth-lessly back after flowering, lest it choke the cistus), or the satiny, lavender-blue saucers of *Convolvulus mauretanicus*.

Cistus salvifolius itself is equally valuable on a larger scale, to about 2 ft high and several wide. It sows itself freely in many gardens, rapidly carpeting a dry bank if given its head. If you have a large and difficult slope of dry soil to cover, this and some spreading junipers could quickly do the job for you. I would be tempted to add, too, two delightful pink-flowered cistuses. Most 'pink' cistus lean firmly towards mauve or magenta (and none the worse for that) but *C. parviflorus*, and its offspring *C. × skanbergii*, both have flowers of pure and appealing dog-rose pink, set among grey-green foliage. *C. parviflorus* is the showier, with broader foliage and large flowers, but *C. × skanbergii*'s tiny flowers have great charm; both are pretty hardy and form wide, low mounds. They make pretty companions for white and pink Scotch roses, silvery foliage of artemisias, santolinas and the like, lavender, and the soft dusty purple *Salvia officinalis* 'Purpurascens', with *Erysimum* 'Bowles's Mauve', a perennial shrubby wallflower with blue-grey narrow leaves and tall spikes of bright lavender-mauve flowers.

Of similar habit is the admirable *C. × corbariensis*, progeny of *C. sal-vifolius* from which it inherits white flowers, yellow-stained at the base. They open from very pretty rose-pink buds, over a longer season than many cistuses, which mostly tend to produce a concentrated burst of flower for a comparatively short time. In winter, in poor soils, the foliage of *C. × corbariensis* turns to a warm russet-purple. A group of several cistuses, this and the grey-green *C. parviflorus* with bright apple-green *C. × aguilari* and *C. × cyprius* of the lead-grey winter garb, make a charm-ing picture in winter, never mind their summer floraison.

Another hybrid offspring of *C. salvifolius* is *C. × florentinus*, rather larger in size than *C. × corbariensis*, with tan-coloured buds and narrower foliage inherited from its other parent, *C. monspeliensis*. A neat and free-flowering white cistus, *C. monspeliensis* is the only one of the genus known to have sported to a yellow-flowered form, recorded by Sir Oscar Warburg and found again by Mr & Mrs Harold Read in 1984. All other known yellow-flowered cistus are now considered by taxonomists to belong to the related genus *Halimium*. The National Collection does not at present cover *Halimium*, though Duncan Donald thinks it would be appropriate to include not only *Halimium* but also *Helianthemum* (species only); many of the latter were originally described by Philip Miller, the famous curator of Chelsea Physic Garden and author of the famous Dictionary which first appeared in 1731. Here I want to mention only the bigeneric hybrids classed as × *Halimiocistus*. There are four or five, some of which occur in the wild. × *Halimiocistus sahucii*, which is *C. salvifolius* × *Halimium umbellatum*, a white-flowered species, is a first-rate low, spreading, tough little shrub with narrow dark green leaves and square-petalled pure white flowers, less than an inch across, but profusely borne. It was introduced by Sir Oscar Warburg. × *Halimiocistus ingwersenii* is in effect a slightly larger version with hairier leaves, flowering over a longer season. The gem is × *Halimiocistus wintonensis*, and its recent form 'Merrist Wood Cream'. Here we have a shrub which is somewhat tender, and none too easy to grow unless exactly suited, but worth any effort for its large, cupped white flowers with a broad blood-red zone around bright yellow centres.

With the mention of blotches I must lead myself back to the cistuses, and specifically to white-flowered *C.* × *lusitanicus* 'Decumbens' which, like every other blotched true cistus, gets its bold maroon markings from *C. ladanifer*. It is aptly described by Bean as 'one of the elite of cistuses, valuable for its low, spreading habit and for bearing its flowers freely over a long period.' *C.* × *verguinii* is another of this kind, less hardy perhaps but very appealing. Though there is no doubt that this and many other cistuses are distinctly tender, there are plenty that in suitable conditions, with impeccable winter drainage, are perfectly hardy in the south at least. I grew many cistuses, all those indeed, except the Ingram hybrids, that I have mentioned thus far, as well as many of the pink-flowered kinds yet to be described in this chapter, in a garden in Gloucestershire where many survived the great freeze of 1981-2. Several were totally undamaged, including *C.* × *corbariensis*, *C. parviflorus*, *C.* × *skanbergii*, *C. laurifolius*, *C. hirsutus* (a pretty, hairy-leaved species with white flowers) and *C. salvifolius* 'Prostratus'. Most of the others were damaged but not killed, and grew away well in the spring. *C.* × *verguinii* was stone dead by spring and so was *C. palhinhae*. The lowest temperature recorded that winter in my garden was −22°C, which is 40°F of frost, not just once, but night after night. To me, at least, most of the cistuses have proved themselves hardy enough to try almost anywhere if soil conditions are suitable.

Among the pink-flowered cistuses, which I have hardly mentioned as yet, only *C.* × *purpureus* was killed in 1981-2. This is scarcely surprising, as it inherits its tenderness, as well as its bright chocolate-maroon blotch, from *C. ladanifer*. Its other parent is *C. creticus*, from which it has its rosy-purple colouring. It is a good thing, with narrow, greyish leaves and large bold flowers. A hardier form is 'Betty Taudevin', with even brighter flowers.

Only *C.* × *purpureus* and its cultivar, of the pink cistuses, have blotched flowers. *C. creticus* itself, the other species from which ladanum gum is extracted, is a variable species (the names *C. villosus* and *C. incanus*, it seems, both belong here also) which covers a wide geographical range in the Mediterranean. I have frequently raised it from seed; indeed, it self-sows abundantly, even into a lawn, and the resulting plants have varied in foliage, flower and habit. Some have greyer, woollier foliage than others, and the leaf shape varies considerably, while in flower they may range from pale rose pink to quite a strong near-magenta. *C. albidus* is hardier than *C. creticus* and has white woolly foliage setting off quite large flowers of pale lilac-pink, a charming shade that looks well with santolina, rosemary, and sage both purple and green, a blend of Mediterranean shrubs echoing the *maquis* vegetation – the thickets of scrub that grow where maritime pine has been felled.

A charming low-growing magenta-pink cistus is *C. crispus*, not often seen in its true state with wavy-edged, deeply veined leaves. In gardens its hybrid with *C. albidus*, 'Sunset', is more often seen, a little shrub with insistent magenta flowers, superb if you can take the colour: I can, and love 'Sunset'. Another pink-flowered hybrid of *C. crispus*, this time with *C. palhinhae*, is the very fine 'Anne Palmer', raised by Captain Ingram.

Cistus 'Silver Pink' is one of only two cistuses to have received an Award of Garden Merit; the other is tough old *C. laurifolius*, which is thought to have been one of the parents of 'Silver Pink'. The hybrid has grey-green foliage and large, clear pink flowers, with more blue in them than *C. parviflorus* it's true, but no hint of magenta. It is immensely popular – perhaps because it is so regularly offered in garden centres – with the gardening public; not with me. It needs a better soil than most to grow well, so it may be my fault that I never took to it.

Most of the cistuses I have described are readily available in nurseries and garden centres. Duncan Donald considers that the genus has less known 'gems worthy of attention: for example, *C. symphitifolius*, although one of the least hardy species (it is a native of the Canary Islands), makes a stunning large-flowered, upright-growing shrub when given adequate winter protection.' *C. osbeckifolius*, also from the Canary Islands, was killed in 1984-5 in the Chelsea Physic Garden. But as cistuses grow fast, are in the main easy to raise from cuttings, or seed for some of the species, are evergreen and have great beauty of flower, it is surely worth trying any that may come your way.

The National Collection

The National Collection of Cistus *is grown at the Chelsea Physic Garden, 66 Royal Hospital Road, London SW3.*

Tucked away between the Embankment and the Royal Hospital Road, behind high sheltering walls, the Chelsea Physic Garden is among the oldest botanic gardens in England; it was established in 1673 and retains its original epithet, 'physic' at that time meaning 'pertaining to things natural'. The reputation of the garden was greatly enhanced under the care of Philip Miller, appointed Gardener in 1722; he was one of the greatest horticulturists of his day, and author of a famous Dictionary of Gardening.

Mediterranean plants grow well in the sheltered climate of the Chelsea Physic Garden, and except for the most tender, Cistus *are no exception. However, the Collection is a young one, designated in September 1983, and few of the plants are yet of any size. However,* Cistus *of various kinds have long been grown in the Chelsea Physic Garden; some of the specimens so beautifully illustrated in Sweet's* Cistineae *were taken from plants in this garden, and* Cistus *are known to have been popular at this time, the first half of the nineteenth century.*

Dwarf Conifers

TRUE dwarf conifers – those that in a gardener's lifetime will hardly grow beyond a height of 18 ins or so – are few; conifers that grow extremely slowly are more numerous. Both in garden centres, and in the National Collection, there are conifers that will in time become anything but dwarf. The advantage of the National Collection over the plants you see in the garden centre is that at Windsor Great Park you will be able to see clearly the difference in size of plants that, as young container-grown stock ready for sale, were all about the same size in the garden centre. If you garden on the grand scale of the Savill or Valley Gardens in Windsor Great Park, it hardly matters if a so-called dwarf conifer rapidly reaches 6 or 8 ft high, or across; in the small gardens that most of us have, it matters a lot.

Lately the popularity of dwarf conifers has increased tremendously, in tandem with the vogue for heathers, for the two are often planted in combination. This, by now a cliché mixture, is promoted as labour-saving, yet the no-work garden of this kind is something of a myth. The trouble is that heathers are not labour-saving. If they are to look good they need regular propagating and replanting. If not regularly clipped back they get leggy and let the weeds through. At the same time I don't want to decry the combination entirely; merely to sound a note of caution and to suggest alternatives. Perhaps the saddest part of a cult like the heathers plus conifers plantings is that all too often it is misused, plonked down in featureless suburbia, away from the heathlands where it could look entirely appropriate.

The dwarf conifers in the National Collection are grown in a very open situation, in irregularly-shaped cultivated beds. They could not cope with any competition in the impoverished Bagshot sand of Windsor Great Park, but they are seen in their natural setting of rough grass and heather, Scots pine and birch; native vegetation. The grasses are the fine, thin-bladed kinds, not the coarse lush greenery of heavier or damper soils. The beds are given a heavy mulch of bark chippings, pine needles, or leaf mould, kept well topped-up so weeds have little chance to grow, and those that do can be pulled out quickly and cleanly, the mulch falling away from their roots. With the conifers, in the beds, are garden varieties of heaths and heathers, but also many other companions: shrub roses give height and contrasting form, with flower and vivid fruit in their seasons. Berberis and dwarf hollies, *Cistus* (a little tender, but valuable in mild gardens), *Hypericum*, shrubby potentillas, *Pernettya* with big, bright, long-lasting berries in autumn and winter, *Arctostaphylos*, brooms and a delightful golden-leaved gorse. The common theme is informality. All these, you will note, are plants of untamed aspect, with flowers unaltered by the breeders' art. The shrub roses are not the bourbons and damasks, cabbage roses and moss roses that have enjoyed a revival of popularity lately, but wild species, neat of leaf and discreet of flower, making their chief impact in autumn when their hips seem the more brilliant for their sober background of greens, greys and bronze, the colours of the conifers. Evergreen azaleas and daphnes would also make good companions, and over low, spreading conifers such as some of the junipers, small-flowered clematis can be grown, as we shall see in another chapter.

Dwarf conifers have enjoyed earlier surges in popularity, and several famous names are commemorated in the National Collection; most notably, perhaps, that of Murray Hornibrook, who in the 1920s and 30s largely sorted out the confusion then reigning in the nomenclature. Dwarf conifers had first been popular in the mid-nineteenth century as an extension of the many arboreta then planted; their later popularity, revived by Murray Hornibrook and later by others, was chiefly the result of the new interest in rock gardening. In our own time Humphrey Welch has done much to resolve many of the nomenclatural muddles that had once again arisen since Mr Hornibrook's day; while no-one, probably, has done more to popularise dwarf conifers than Adrian Bloom, of Bressingham Gardens.

For ground-cover – another gardening buzz-word of our day – the prostrate or spreading junipers are among the best of all plants, and unlike many other conifers they thrive in all types of soil including chalk. On a fairly large scale the feathery, grey-green *Juniperus sabina* 'Tamariscifolia' makes a dense mat as the branches build up in layer upon layer. 'Blue Danube' is a form of *J. sabina* with more or less prostrate branches that root as they grow, set with light grey foliage. The Japanese shore juniper, *J. conferta*, is especially attractive with apple-green foliage on almost prostrate branches that build up to a pleasingly textured surface. In some gardens this has fallen prey to a disfiguring disease, and the similar *J. taxifolia* var. *lutchuensis* may be a better choice; the more so as its yew-like foliage is softer and less prickly than *J. conferta*. The very flat-growing *Juniperus horizontalis* is a North American species that makes long branches densely set with branchlets bearing blue-grey foliage. Selected forms include 'Bar Harbor', which turns to mauve in winter and, with its upturned side branchlets, has an almost deep-pile effect. 'Douglasii' takes on even deeper tones of plum-purple in winter. Lower in growth and very dense is the intensely blue-grey 'Wiltonii' or 'Blue Rug'. For a similarly dense, but more compact bright green juniper, choose *J. procumbens* 'Nana', which becomes lightly bronzed in winter. This is just about neat enough in growth to be worth planting to trail over a rock face or down a small bank in the larger rock garden.

To grow with heathers, instead of or as well as the upright exclamation marks so often recommended (I'll mention a few later), try the larger junipers that grow at an angle of 45° or so. 'Grey Owl' makes a loose mass of thin branchlets set with tiny grey-blue leaves, and looks well with small-leaved species roses such as *R. farreri persetosa*. This, if grown in full sun and a rather poor soil, takes on purple and bronze tones which set off the tiny bright pink flowers. The big junipers such as the hybrid 'Pfitzeriana', with deep green foliage, and its 'gold' counterpart, 'Pfitzeriana Aurea' with lime-yellow new shoots, make wide-spreading bushes that in time will cover a lot of space, so that they are scarcely dwarf, but more compact forms have been selected, such as 'Old Gold', which holds its colour well all year, becoming bronzed in winter.

There is a fairly new, compact form of *Juniperus squamata* known as 'Blue Star', with silvery-blue foliage, forming a dense spiky mound. This assorts well with pink-flowered cistus, as it might be the low-growing, hardy, grey-leaved *C. parviflorus* with delightful dog rose-like flowers.

The common juniper has many variants, and an especially attractive one is *J. communis* 'Depressa Aurea', low-growing, with arching, bright yellow new shoots in spring ageing to deep gold in autumn and warm bronze in winter. It blends well with some of the coloured foliage heathers, the bright oranges and scarlets, which can be hard to fit into the landscape without some emollient allied colour nearby. The common juniper also offers one of the best upright forms to set among heathers for height, or in matched plantings for more formal settings. The Irish juniper is *J. communis* 'Hibernica', a dense column of deep green foliage; but not suitable for windswept sites. Other good upright junipers derive from the Chinese juniper (*J. chinensis* 'Stricta' with soft, blue-grey foliage) or from *J. scopulorum*, the Rocky Mountain juniper, which has given rise to the ultra-popular 'Skyrocket', a very narrow column of silvery-grey foliage. Perhaps the best loved of all is the Noah's Ark juniper, *J. communis* 'Compressa', a little, dense, green column that grows extremely slowly and is seldom seen much over 2-3 ft in height. Even this, however, can

outgrow a modern, small rock garden in its, or its owner's lifetime. I
know of a specimen in a Welsh garden, sixty or seventy years old and
well over shoulder high, still dense but suffering from slight middle-aged
spread, so that it has no longer a slender flame-like outline. Not many of
us are likely in these restless days to stay in the same house, caring for the
same garden, for sixty years, so the Noah's Ark juniper is still a safe bet
to plant in any rock garden, preferably grouped rather than alone, or
tucked down below the summits of the rock. In nature trees of this outline
would not be seen on the heights, where the wind would distort and stunt
them; here we would do better to choose a small prostrate form to flow
down the rock, or a little tree of naturally irregular outline such as one of
the dwarf pines. If it should be damaged by wind you can prune it to
accentuate the natural distortion. *Pinus mugo* is the mountain pine, a
variable plant which has given rise to such forms as 'Gnom', 'Mops' or
the botanical variant var. *pumilio*. Our native Scots pine, *P. sylvestris*, has
a form known as 'Beuvronensis' which forms a rounded, densely-branched
shrub.

Many of the dwarfest conifers are of the shape usually described as a
bun, little rounded shrublets. Several derive from the Lawson's cypress
that is so familiar as a hedging tree, or from other species of *Chamaecyparis*.
Such is *C. lawsoniana* 'Minima Aurea', a little rounded plant composed of
upright fans of yellow foliage, paler in winter. This interestingly textured
surface gives it more interest, in my eyes, than the dense and mossy buns
of 'Gnome' in bright green or the darker green 'Gimbornii'. *C. l.* 'Pygmaea
Argentea' is another little bun-shaped conifer with silver-tipped, blue-
green foliage, attractive in winter. One of the smallest of all conifers is *C.
pisifera* 'Nana', a minute bun of congested dark green foliage. *C. obtusa*
'Nana' is larger, forming a flat-topped bush; the dark green foliage is
arranged in cup-like sprays. The balsam fir, *Abies balsamea*, has a form
'Hudsonia' which forms a shrublet of similar outline, rounded and flat-
topped, with short dark green needles, whitish beneath. Spruces and firs
are closely related and the black spruce, *Picea mariana*, gives us the form
'Nana' which is of similar aspect. *P. abies* 'Nidiformis' derives its name
from the hollowed top, suggesting the shape of a bird's nest; it has
attractive bright green foliage and drooping branch tips. 'Little Gem' is a
tiny mound with very short bright green foliage; 'Gregoryana' and the
darker-needled 'Echiniformis', the hedgehog spruce, are also very slow-
growing, dense, bun-shaped mounds. Then there are two tiny, ball-
like forms of the Japanese cedar, *Cryptomeria japonica* 'Vilmoriniana' and
'Compressa', both with tiny light green leaves turning fox-brown in
winter.

All these little, slow-growing conifers are best planted with the slowest
and most compact of alpines, such as the Kabschia saxifrages perhaps, and

tiny bulbs – the miniature tulips; *Narcissus asturiensis*, the smallest of all trumpet daffodils at 3 ins or so; scillas perhaps, though these can be invasive by self-sowing; and the tiny, restrained, bright blue *Allium sikkimensis*. Larger and more rumbustious rock plants, aubrietia and arabis and the like, will in no time swamp the baby conifers before they have time to make any significant growth.

Even ultimately slightly larger conifers need to be watched carefully in their early stages. If you plant *Picea glauca albertiana* 'Conica' for its perfect cone-shaped outline, it would be sad to see it damaged by an over-enthusiastic neighbouring plant poulticing it with foliage. This bright green spruce has the neatest and most perfect cone shape of all the slow-growing conifers, and when it has attained some size it looks well with dwarf shrubs of spreading habit such as the smaller-leaved evergreen azaleas, or one of the more compact, mushroom-shaped Japanese maples.

Several slow-growing thuyas make good companions for heathers, azaleas, dwarf berberis and the like. *Thuya occidentalis* 'Rheingold' remains popular for its old-gold foliage, turning to orange and russet in winter. Similar in colour but very much smaller is the little conical *T. plicata* 'Rogersii', tiny enough to join the pygmy buns already described; the yellow foliage is tipped with orange and deepens to bronze in winter. 'Stoneham Gold' is eventually tall, though very slow-growing; it is colourful in winter and suited to the heather garden. These are forms of the western red cedar, a tall timber tree in the wild; the other American *Thuya* is *T. occidentalis*, of which 'Rheingold' is a form. From China comes *T. orientalis*, of which 'Rosedalis' is a pretty form of rounded habit and soft texture, with clear yellow new shoots ageing to pale green and then to grey-purple in winter. The spikier 'Meldensis' is violet and russet-brown in winter, and does not have creamy young shoots. Closely related to the thuyas – formerly included in that genus, indeed – is the Japanese *Thuyopsis dolabrata*, which has a nice low-growing form, 'Nana', that forms a wide, flat-topped bush of rich green turning bronze in winter. It seems much more shade tolerant than many conifers.

Other good, medium-sized slow-growing conifers are to be found in the Sawara cypress, *C. pisifera*, and the Hinoki Cypress, *C. obtusa*. By a long way the best known is *C. pisifera* 'Boulevard', a loose cone of soft, light blue-grey foliage which turns to a sad brown on limy soils. 'Boulevard' also dislikes wind and dry soils, as well as lime, and many of the delightful baby plants purchased in garden centres must disappoint their owners, but at its best it is a pretty thing, and with due attention to soil and wind protection will grow well as a tub specimen for several years. *C. pisifera* 'Plumosa Rogersii' makes a dense cone of soft bright yellow foliage, paler in winter; 'Squarrosa Sulphurea' is larger, bright sulphur-yellow in summer and light blue-green in winter. *C. pisifera* also produces forms with whipcord branchlets, 'Filifera' and its yellow counterpart 'Filifera Aurea', which both make low, widespreading bushes with pendulous branches. In colour the yellow form assorts well with dwarf blue-flowered rhododendrons. The Hinoki cypress has given us some forms with foliage borne in flattened, fan-like sprays, such as 'Kosteri' which is bright green in summer, bronzed in winter. Don't be misled by the name *C. obtusa* 'Nana Gracilis' into thinking that you have something as slow as 'Nana', which reaches barely 18 ins. 'Nana Gracilis' will finally be almost ten times this height, but grows slowly and is very appealing with its larger shell-shaped sprays of dark glossy green foliage. *C. obtusa* 'Tetragona Aurea', though ultimately of similar size, is very different with its congested moss-like foliage, rich golden yellow in sun.

The blue spruces, *Picea pungens* 'Moerheimii', 'Koster', Hoopesii' and the like, are often planted for their vivid silvery-blue foliage, though in time they become quite large. Theirs is not the easiest colour to place and needs a fairly formal setting, well away from plants of untamed appearance. 'Glauca Prostrata' is a nice form with sideways spreading branches. One of the best of the larger scale conifers is *Sequoia sempervirens* 'Adpressa', with grey leaves tipped with cream. This has a tendency to produce upright shoots which must be cut out to keep it low-growing; but fortunately, unlike most conifers, it does not resent hard pruning and can even be cut right back to the main stem to start growing again. Another prostrate spreading conifer which is extremely rare in the wild, though now well secured in cultivation, is *Microbiota decussata*. Green in summer, it turns brown in winter, warm and cosy or dead-looking according to your frame of mind.

The common yew, *Taxus baccata*, has several slow-growing, widespreading forms that make attractive garden plants, but most of them grow quite large fairly rapidly. 'Standishii' is of upright habit, slow-growing to form a dense column of bright yellow foliage. One of the oddest of all conifers is the small, slow-growing yew called 'Amersfoort': with its thick, almost circular leaves set on sparse, stubby branches it looks very like *Olearia nummularifolia*; the sort of plant with which you can puzzle your garden visitors.

The hemlock spruces are evergreen trees with elegant drooping branches, North American natives preferring acid moist soils. *Tsuga canadensis* has several dwarf forms worth including in a collection of conifers; such as 'Jeddeloh', with pale green leaves, a low squatty bushlet of bird's nest form. 'Bennett' is compact and semi-prostrate, with fan-like or drooping branches; but it will in time grow to as much as 6 ft.

In the *Podocarpus* family we find several unusual and attractive conifers. Many *Podocarpus* species form trees or large shrubs, but *P. nivalis*, the alpine totara, is an almost prostrate species from New Zealand with leathery, pale green leaves. From Australia comes *P. alpinus*, a dense low bush thickly set with dark green yew-like foliage. The bold-leaved *P. macrophyllus* has a compact form, var. *maki*, which may reach 6 ft in ten years. Also from the antipodes, *Dacrydium laxifolium* is the pygmy pine from New Zealand, a prostrate species with tiny leaves, olive-green to blue-grey in colour turning purplish in winter. From the mountains of Tasmania comes *Microcachrys tetragona*, a sprawling bushlet that would look well among stones in the rock garden. It has whipcord foliage and tiny egg-shaped, red, translucent fruits. Most *Phyllocladus* species become fairly large in time, but the dwarf *P. alpinus* var. *minor* will reach no more than 3 ft in ten years. It bears the usual foliage of its genus, broad bluish phyllodes quite unlike the usual conifer needles or scales; in spring it is colourful when set with crimson female strobili: the little catkin-like clusters of flowers.

The rate of growth of conifers varies greatly, not only from variety to variety, but also within the same variety in different soils and climates. In a rich soil, with abundant moisture, even a slow-growing conifer may accelerate and embarrass its owner in a few short years by its unwonted size. Also, although slow growing, 'dwarf' conifers go on growing for a long time and ultimately may become quite large, as anyone who has seen the Nisbet collection at Wisley or visited the Botanic Garden at Glasnevin, Dublin, will realise. At Glasnevin is a collection of dwarf conifers donated by Murray Hornibrook in about 1921, and now dominating the rock garden. The choice of a conifer for any site must be a compromise, based not on its ultimate size but on its useful life in that position. If you choose a very dwarf conifer and plant it very small, it will be years before it makes its effect; but if you want a larger specimen for immediate impact you will have to pay a lot for it – even if you can find it. Your alternative is to choose a stronger-growing kind that will make a much quicker effect, and be prepared to replace it after five or ten years. You can slow its growth meanwhile by lifting and replanting it every two or three years – a better method of checking it than pruning – and this will give your little tree a root system ideal for moving later to a new site. Thus you need not regard your conifers as disposable; rather as transportable. From the rock garden you could move your conifers to the heather bed, say, or assort them with species roses or cistus, as John Bond has done at Windsor Great Park, when they are large enough neither to look incongruous nor to get smothered. Remember to water your conifer very thoroughly, both before and after moving, which you will ideally do in early autumn. In dry weather following a move, spray or syringe the foliage as often as possible.

Though lifting is preferable to pruning for growth control, this is not to say that pruning is unnecessary. It is done for two reasons. One is to keep the plant within bounds, but the other and more interesting, even challenging kind of pruning is formative, to ensure that your little plant grows as it should, well balanced, shapely and in character. On the really tiny plants you may need to use nail scissors (especially as the rule for successful formative pruning is 'little and often'); but I very much doubt if John Bond has time for such niceties, and his conifers all look well, shapely and handsome.

The National Collection

The National Collection of dwarf conifers is held at the Savill and Valley Gardens, Windsor Great Park, Berkshire (Crown Estate Commissioners).

Most of the conifers in the Collection are slow-growing rather than truly dwarf. Many are grown in large, cultivated beds with an accompanying cast of suitable companion shrubs. The various beds in the Valley Gardens are named for people who have in some way been associated with dwarf conifers. Thus there is the Hornibrook Bed, after Murray Hornibrook who, in the 1920s and 30s did so much to sort out the confusion then reigning in the nomenclature of dwarf conifers. The Valley Gardens collection started with two lorry-loads of plants from Hillier's Nurseries, a generous gift from the late Sir Harold Hillier, and another from Sue Farquhar and Elizabeth Strangman's father's collection immediately after his death, described as a magnificent collection, the cream of the dwarf conifers. R. S. Corley's fine collection was bought a little later. There are, of course, Strangman and Corley Beds now planted in the Valley Gardens.

Another great name in dwarf conifers is that of Humphrey Welch, who in the 1960s sorted out many of the nomenclatural muddles that had arisen since Murray Hornibrook's day. Sadly, after many vicissitudes, Mr Welch's tremendous collection did not get transferred to the Crown Estate Commissioners after he moved away from Devizes, where his Pygmy Pinetum had become so well known. Mr Welch was able to give some plants to the Savill Gardens, and others were bought for the Collection; while Mr Welch's immense knowledge was freely given.

The dwarf conifers at Windsor Great Park were designated as a National Collection in July 1982.

Forsythia

You might wonder what there is to say about forsythias. Surely there aren't so many different kinds: the bright yellow and the paler one, and 'Beatrix Farrand' perhaps, with its extra large flowers. Certainly all forsythias bear a strong family likeness, but there are thirty-two cultivars and species in the National Collection, with more added as material becomes available.

This is one of the newer Collections, at least so far as the plants themselves are concerned; unlike many of the other fairly complete National Collections, it was not based upon an existing collection but has been entirely assembled in the last few years. Richard Webb, of Webb's Nurseries near Droitwich, where the collection grows, wrote to Chris Brickell (then Director of Wisley Garden) on 11 August 1980 offering to help the NCCPG as a way 'of doing our bit for the plants which provide us with our livelihood'. Thus, though the Collection is young, Mr Webb was among the first to come forward from the nursery trade to offer his help. 'We chose forsythia', he told me, 'as it appeared manageable and flowered at a time when we had most visitors. By June 1982 we had assembled twenty-four cultivars. The Collection was planted in October 1982 and produced a fine show for the first time in spring 1985.'

Generally, when writing about the plants in National Collections, I have considered the wild species first and then the garden hybrids derived from them. With *Forsythia* I propose to begin with a group of hybrids, which includes the most familiar and widely-grown varieties of the genus. These are the hybrids between *F. suspensa* and *F. viridissima*, both of which we shall meet later; collectively they are known as *F. × intermedia*. First noted in the latter part of the nineteenth century, this cross produced at the turn of the century the plant that many gardeners undoubtedly think of as *the* forsythia. 'Spectabilis' is a vigorous, indestructible shrub that in so many gardens every spring smothers itself with bright yellow flowers.

Good as it is of its kind, there are many better forsythias for small gardens, and if a visit to the National Collection persuades a few garden-owners to plant a forsythia other than 'Spectabilis', Richard Webb's work will have been worthwhile. The comparison, for interested visitors, will be the easier because the collection is planted with a view to study not aesthetics: 'I have purposely left the forsythias as individual free-standing shrubs adjacent to each other for purposes of comparison, so they are a "collection" and not a garden design'.

If you find the strong yellow of 'Spectabilis' too harsh for your taste, you could turn to 'Spring Glory', a seedling of the old, pale yellow 'Primulina'. 'Spring Glory' bears sulphur yellow flowers very freely on a shrub of more modest size, perhaps 6 ft, as against the 10 ft or more of 'Spectabilis'. I am not sure if this is the same as 'Spring Beauty'* in the National Collection, which 'appears very floriferous with a good clear yellow colour without the harshness of many of the other varieties.' Much older than 'Spring Glory' is the pale yellow 'Densiflora', a compact variety with pale yellow flowers crowded on to the branches. Of more recent introduction than this, dating from 1935 ('Densiflora' is a late nineteenth century cultivar) is 'Lynwood', a sport of 'Spectabilis' that is finer than its parent, but still seems to take second place to it in gardens. It has large, rich yellow, broad-petalled flowers profusely borne. New varieties of *F. × intermedia* that are still being assessed in the National Collection are 'Goldzauber' with large deep yellow flowers, 'Northern Gold' and 'Minigold' with strong yellow flowers on a compact shrub. I wish the people who introduce plants would think of something other than 'gold' for all these bright yellows! Also newly received at Webb's is a plant listed as *F. × intermedia* 'Spectabilis Variegata', described as having attractive variegated foliage (there is at least one very unattractive variegated forsythia going about, a measled horror that looks merely diseased). Few forsythias have much to boast of in the foliage line, and Richard Webb goes so far as to say that 'few genera are so uninspiring left by themselves from May to February, and so we have underplanted with herbaceous ground-cover and winter flowering ericas to add further season interest. In addition I shall try a variety of summer flowering climbers which can be cut to the ground annually in winter to brighten up the forsythias in summer: *Clematis viticella* varieties, *Tropaeolum speciosum* and *Eccremocarpus*.'

'Tremonia' is a variety with better foliage than the usual forsythia offering. Here we have a shrub which has yet to flower in the National Collection, but which is quietly pleasing all season, thanks to its attractive, finely serrated leaves. Whether you think it worth garden space when

---

* When I queried this with Mr Webb, he told me that 'Spring Beauty' had come to him at one remove from Harlow Car, whose records are apparently mute as to its origins.

there are more striking foliage plants to be had is another question; perhaps if it settled down to flower as freely as its brethren it might be a different matter. Another that does not flower significantly is 'Arnold Giant', which in addition is hard to propagate; not a shrub likely to make much commercial impact. However, it has historical interest as the parent of at least two superb offspring. 'Karl Sax' is a bushy forsythia with rich canary yellow flowers that are held horizontally to display their deeper yellow throats. The other name that is met in this context is 'Beatrix Farrand', which appears to have become attached to a plant that has no right to bear it. The 'Beatrix Farrand' of commerce is a very vigorous, tall plant with extremely large, soft yellow flowers, more nodding than those of 'Karl Sax' but with a similar deeper yellow throat. In the National Collection the flowers are rather sparsely borne, and the plant has unattractive foliage even by forsythia standards. Carefully grouped with other spring-flowering shrubs, however, it can be good. For a group that will emphasise the deeper amber tones in the throat of the pseudo 'Beatrix Farrand's big flowers, try setting it with *Berberis darwinii*, with a ground planting of *Euphorbia griffithii*, in the form 'Fireglow' or 'Dixter', both of which have coppery-red bracts. For a sharper-toned group, the forsythia (whether this imposter or another in the × *intermedia* gaggle) could be combined with lime green and yellow tones of *Milium effusum* 'Aureum', golden feverfew, doronicums, the acid-green *Euphorbia polychroma* and the like. There are two approaches that you can take to these masses of strong colour offered by most of these forsythias: enhance and intensify them, as here; or cool and contrast them with emollient colours. This, I think, works better with the paler, gentler toned forsythias, where white and blue can be used more happily than against the more powerful yellows.

One of the parents of the *F.* × *intermedia* hybrids, *F. viridissima* is not often seen now, as it cannot compare with its progeny nor with the other species with which it was crossed to produce them. It is a stiff, upright-growing shrub flowering in April, rather after the hybrids, the flowers quite large and of the habitual bright yellow. A geographical variant, *koreana*, also grows at the National Collection; it has slightly larger, brighter yellow flowers. *F. viridissima* survives as a name to most of us only in the tiny form 'Bronxensis' which, at 2 ft or so at maturity, is small enough for a rock garden. Give it full sun to see a crop of its pretty primrose-yellow flowers, which at Kew are set against the slate-blue fuzz of *Ceanothus rigidus*. It is quite a pet if you can induce it to flower. Allied to *F. viridissima* is the only European species, *F. europaea*. It is a very rare relict species, confined to a small area in the Balkans, and is frankly not worth garden space though of interest to botanists.

With *Forsythia suspensa* we come to a valuable early-flowering shrub that can be trained on a high wall (even a north-facing one, where it will put out a good crop of flowers) or allowed to grow unsupported, when it tangles itself into a fairly solid mass of branches up to 10 ft or so. Various forms are recognised of this Chinese shrub that has long been cultivated in Japan. *F. s.* var. *fortunei* is of more erect habit than the other forms, with upright or slightly arching branches, less graceful than var. *sieboldii* which has slender shoots, arching right over and rooting down where they touch the ground; a useful quality that makes it a good plant for covering a steep slope. It will even scramble up into a neighbouring tree or large shrub. *F. s.* var. *sieboldii* looks well with other vigorous shrubs of spring, *Berberis darwinii* again perhaps, one of the amelanchiers, maybe even the glossy-leaved *Viburnum* × *burkwoodii*, though the pink of its buds may not please everyone against the yellow forsythia. Nicest of all the *F. suspensa* kinds is *atrocaulis*, with dark purple stems and bronzed young foliage and lemon-yellow flowers; a selection called 'Nymans Variety' is of more upright habit and flowers later, a very beautiful forsythia with wide, soft yellow, nodding flowers. It makes a good companion for *Chaenomeles* 'Simonii', a spreading shrub with deep blood-red flowers and, above, the white flowers of *Amelanchier* or, at its own level, the starker white of *Spiraea arguta* and a solid ground-covering plinth of *Erica mediterranea* 'Alba'. A wild collected form of *F. suspensa* came to the National Collection from Roy Lancaster, who found it near the Ming Tombs in China. It has not yet made its way into commerce, and perhaps never will; Richard Webb says that 'sadly this plant does not appear to match the romantic promise of its source'.

Also soft yellow in colour, but producing its flowers much earlier, in February and March, is *F. giraldiana*. Here we have a large spreading shrub of up to 12 ft high, too large for the average garden and not quite in the first rank but, for its very early flowering, worth planting in larger gardens. Richard Webb considers, indeed, that 'the soft yellow of *F. giraldiana* in February is outstanding'. Flowering not much later than this is *Forsythia ovata* and its variants: small, compact shrubs that have a subdued charm and none of the blatancy of the bigger *F.* × *intermedia* kinds. *F. ovata* reaches not much above 5 ft and has yellow flowers in early March. The Japanese form, f. *japonica* and its variety *saxatilis* are very similar to *F. ovata*, though f. *japonica* flowers about four weeks later. Marchant's, a famous nursery that reached its apogee between the wars, offered two 'forms' of *F. ovata*, Lemon and Gold (as descriptive, not cultivar names) and perhaps the *F. ovata* in the National Collection, described as having amber yellow flowers, is the same as Marchant's 'Gold' form. A new introduction called 'Ottawa' has pale yellow flowers appearing very early, on compact growth. Their colouring is soft enough to assort with the bright mauve-pink flowers of *Rhododendron* Praecox, with a ground-planting of *Erica carnea* 'Springwood White'. With *F. ovata* 'Tetragold', smaller-growing with deep yellow flowers, you could grow a flowering quince of compact habit, the chalk-white double sloe perhaps, and bright blue *Pulmonaria angustifolia* at their feet. *Forsythia 'ovata robusta'* is a mysterious plant not very like *F. ovata* itself, stronger-growing with deep yellow flowers, perhaps a hybrid. The same is probably true of 'Arnold Dwarf', said to make effective ground-cover 2-3 ft high and spreading to 6 ft across; but at Webb's Nurseries it has grown very slowly and flowers sparsely. When they do appear the flowers are quite a pretty shade of soft yellow, but if it will neither flower nor grow with any enthusiasm it looks like an also-ran, especially as there are such pretty forms of *F. ovata* about.

It is good that the National Collection of such a genus is held by a commercial firm. Garden centres have tended to offer only 'Spectabilis', in one of those circular arrangements whereby the only forsythia commonly sold is the one that everybody knows, which they know because it is the only one they ever see offered for sale. Now, perhaps, there is a chance that we may be able to buy some of these more attractive, more compact forsythias that will accommodate themselves so much more suitably and discreetly in a small garden.

The National Collection

The National Collection of Forsythia *is held at Webb's Garden Centres Ltd, Wychbold, Droitwich, Worcs (Mr Richard Webb).*

It was an early Collection to be designated, in April 1981, one of the first in the hands of a commercial nursery. The Collection was actually planted in October 1982, and made a fine show for the first time in spring 1985. Despite being so young, it is already fairly complete, and is planted for study purposes rather than with any aesthetic aim. This will make it easy for visitors to the Garden Centre to compare the different forsythias and choose the one best suited to their gardens.

Olearia

IT MAY seem curious to find the National Collection of a genus of shrubs regarded, in the main, as tender, sited in northern Scotland. But the garden at Inverewe, where both *Olearia* and *Senecio* (which will be discussed in a later chapter) are grown as National Collections, is on the west coast, its climate tempered even so far north by the Gulf Stream. Though west coast gardens even in southerly counties can feel bitterly inhospitable to humans because of their moisture-laden air, they are relatively frost-free and offer congenial homes to plants intolerant of severe frost but well able to withstand Atlantic gales.

Many olearias are extremely wind-resistant, due in large part to their thick, leathery leaves, which may be protected by a waxy or downy coating, adaptations to just such climatic conditions and not uncommonly found in Australasian plants.

In *Trees and Shrubs Hardy in the British Isles* Bean observes that although only one, *O. × haastii*, is generally hardy, over sixty species and hybrids of olearia have been in cultivation outdoors in the British Isles and of these 'about twenty five are hardy enough to survive the average winter in all but the coldest parts'. This is well in excess of the number likely to be grown in the average garden, but it suggests – and this is confirmed by my own experience in growing about forty taxa at one time or another – that many gardeners are missing out on a genus with great appeal. *O. × haastii*, indeed, which is the only olearia known to many gardeners, is also indubitably the most boring, with small crowded leaves dark green above and off-white beneath, and white flowers fast turning grubby, in July and August. As a coastal hedge, it is splendid, taking any amount of salt wind buffeting and seldom needing clipping. Quite as tolerant of seaspray, and far more handsome, is *O. macrodonta*. The foliage mimics holly in form, though not in colour, for it is of silvery-green, white below. Like many olearias it is musk-scented. The floral display is tremendous, the bush disappearing under wide white heads of daisies. Once well-grown to small-tree form, *O. macrodonta* displays attractive peeling buff and fawn bark, and is worth pruning up better to show the stems. Forms 'Major' and 'Minor' live up to their names: 'Minor' is a pet suitable for quite tiny gardens, and 'Major' has been measured at 22 ft high and 48 ft across; in each case everything, leaves and flower-heads, is in scale. 'Rowallane hybrids' are said to be *O. arborescens* (for which read on) × *O. macrodonta*; they have the holly-like leaves of the second, but flower-heads hanging out like the first-named putative parent. Closely allied to *O. macrodonta* is *O. ilicifolia*. Despite its name, the 'holly-leaved' *O. ilicifolia* is less holly-like than *O. macrodonta* with narrower, wavy-edged, sharp-toothed leaves greyish above, white-felted below. Like *O. macrodonta* it is musk-scented; white flowers appear in midsummer. It seems as hardy as *O. macrodonta*, but less accommodating in cultivation.

Others nearly as frost-hardy are the thoroughly confusing bunch found in *O. avicenniifolia* on the one hand, and as *O. cheesemannii*, or *O. cunninghamii*, or *O. rani* on the other. The first is a big shrub with unexciting oval, somewhat pointy leaves, grey-green or olive above and off-white below, flowering in late summer. Earlier to flower is the plant dubbed 'White Confusion', a name expressive of the emotions that assail the novice amateur of olearias when he tries to unravel this group in his mind. Similar again, with blunter leaves and larger flower-heads, is the plant for long known as 'O. albida' (which it is not; we shall meet the true thing later) and now given the name 'Talbot de Malahide' in honour of the man who did so much to bring Australasian plants, and especially olearias, to the notice of the British gardening public.

But that it flowers in late spring, *O. cheesemannii* is to horticultural eyes much like a scaled-down version of *O. avicenniifolia*. This is not to say it lacks charm; indeed, with its abundant white scented daisies in early summer it is a very worthwhile plant. Another nice thing which may be a child of *O. avicenniifolia* is *O.* 'Waikariensis', grown for its grey foliage. It has been known, also, as *O. oleifolia*, the olive-leaved olearia, and indeed the generic name of the genus derives from *Olea*, olive, suggesting the silvery appearance of many members of the genus, reminiscent of olive trees – and not from some Irish O'Leary. Better to pronounce the name Olearia, not O'Leary-a.

Pleasant though *O.* 'Waikariensis' is, it is eclipsed by 'O. mollis', a name of no standing botanically when applied to the shrub known thus to gardeners. Here we have a compact shrub as silvered as *Convolvulus cneorum*, though waxy-leaved whereas the Mediterranean plant is satin-textured. It derives from a cross between *O. ilicifolia* and *O. moschata*, a small shrub whose name admits to the musky odour it shares with others of the genus. This parent has small leathery leaves thickly, stickily felted to give a grey-white effect, hidden at flowering time under masses of white bloom. It must be said that in maritime climates such as that of Inverewe, these 'small shrubs' have made immense domes, 9 ft × 15 ft.

Definitely less hardy than *O. avicenniifolia*, but still able to survive inland, as a shadow of their west-coastal selves, when sheltered from cold frosty winds, are *O. arborescens* and the quite similar *O. furfuracea*. The leaves of *O. arborescens* are thinner-textured than those of *O. furfuracea*, wavy at the margins and glossy green above, 'silvered below with a satin sheen; flowers in loose drooping plumes all over the bush, white with darker centres' (W. Arnold-Forster, *Shrubs for the Milder Counties*.)

O. furfuracea flowers before *O. arborescens*, in early rather than late spring (though I don't think my memory is at fault when I recall flowers in high summer) and has more appealing foliage, thicker-textured, very wavy at the margins, glossy green above and white below.

Most olearias are very easy to root from cuttings: *O. furfuracea* and others grow away happily from slips stuck in the open ground in summer and simply covered with a plastic cloche. The same is not true of one of the most desirable of all in the genus, *Olearia lacunosa*. Forming, in mild areas, a large rounded shrub, it is set with long, slender, dark green leaves, with a geometrically precise impressed, right-angled venation and pale tan underside. Again, W. Arnold-Forster's impressionistic description cannot be bettered: 'extraordinarily strong and hard, with clear-cut design and the firmness of a thing fashioned in metal'. Despite its reputation for obduracy in the matter of growing roots, I succeeded with two of six sent to me in October, only to have them succumb to another hazard of the rare, desirable and portable: theft. Almost as lustworthy, and not so recalcitrant, is *O.* 'Zennorensis', offspring of this and *O. ilicifolia*. Here the narrow olive-green leaves are set with many small sharp teeth along the margins. Despite its exotic appearance it is amazingly tough, well able to cope with the Atlantic battering it receives at Eagles Nest in Cornwall. Its rarer parent is said to prefer moist soil, but another wind-resister with leaves as different as could be grows in the wild on 'clefts and ledges of sunbaked schistose rocks ... with *Veronica hulkeana*' (W. Arnold-Forster). *Olearia insignis*, formerly *Pachystegia insignis*, forms a low spreading bush with almost prostrate stems and oval to near-circular, olive-green leathery leaves, thickly felted in white, tan or buff beneath. The flowers are large for the genus, like 3 ins ox-eye daisies.

Admirable as a tall, front-line filter for salt winds, but very frost tender, is *O. traversii*, with blunt silvery leaves. Of the larger growing, larger-leaved kinds grown for foliage effect, however, few can compare with the true *O. albida* and especially, *O. paniculata*. The first has large, undulate-edged leaves, but is hopelessly frost tender and has probably been killed even on Tresco by the recent hard winter. *O. paniculata* is almost always mistaken for a pittosporum with particularly fine, large, fresh apple-green leaves with wavy edges. A shrub in colder areas, if it survives at all, *O. paniculata* will make a respectable tree with peeling bark where the climate is mild enough – I have climbed into the lower limbs of such a tree in an Irish garden. The flowers are scarcely noticeable, but that they waft a delicious perfume in their late autumn season. Arnold-Forster refers to a purplish-leaved form, but I cannot imagine this to be an improvement on the fresh peridot-green of the type. *O. paniculata* is from New Zealand, like so many of the genus; all these, whether from North or South Island, tend to adapt better to British conditions than the mainland Australians. Of these, *O. argophylla* is an especially handsome foliage plant preferring mild moist shade, where its silvery felted unfolding young shoots gleam like an exotic version of the young flames of whitebeam on our native chalklands. The sticky *O. viscosa* seems to be botanically close, a small, lance-leaved shrub of no great garden merit.

From New Zealand comes *O. colensoi*, of which W. Arnold-Forster's description is so tantalising that one longs for the hardier forms hinted at by Bean to be introduced from high altitudes to replace the tender Stewart Island stock at present in cultivation. The leaves are, it seems, large and leathery, 'like grey green velvet' when unfolding in June; the young shoots in April are brilliantly silvered.

There is not room here to consider all the odd, and often oddly attractive species of *Olearia* that are probably only to be obtained through exchange, so I will move on to consider the remaining groups within the genus, those that mimic other plants and those that, unlike all those we have so far met, have showy coloured flowers. As they are so distinct from others in the genus, let me save these for the last and introduce before them some of the copycat species.

Take, for example, *Olearia solandri*. This looks for all the world like a better quality *Cassinia fulvida*, itself also a New Zealand shrubby composite. It has the same yellow stems set with little needle-leaves, yellow-felted beneath. Where the cassinia wafts a smell of fermenting honey at flowering time, *O. solandri* is redolent of heliotrope. None too frost-hardy, it is quite happy in buffeting salt winds. Also needle-leaved, but greyish rather than yellow of complexion, are *O. odorata* and the longer-needled *O. virgata* var. *lineata*. This latter is especially graceful, with long, whippy stems set with gappy whorls of leaves. *O. virgata* var. *lineata* forma *dartonii* is broader and bolder of foliage, each leaf nearer the size and shape of those of English lavender.

Also quite unlike the usual run of daisy bushes are those which bear, not needle foliage but tiny stubby, almost circular leaves close-set on the branches. *O. nummulariifolia* is the most familiar of this group, with leaves glossy green above, yellowish below. Like *O. solandri*, its flowers are heliotrope-scented. *O. nummulariifolia* var. *cymbifolia* has longer leaves with rolled-back margins, and is of greyer cast; *O. coriacea* is larger in leaf, each up to half an inch wide and very thick-textured.

My experience of the heath-like *O. floribunda* is limited, for I found it extraordinarily difficult to root from cuttings so I never actually grew a plant of it. But if one could persuade it to thrive it would join the other mimics in foxing all but the most experienced gardeners, so like a tree heath, or perhaps a *Fabiana*, is it when not in flower. *O. algida* from Tasmania (not to be confused with *O. albida*) is similar, of greyish cast. Like all Tasmanians it does well at Inverewe. *O. ramulosa*, also Tasmanian, is very tender, but a grand sight when in full, white plume of flower.

These heath-like olearias are scarcely likely to attain the popular appeal of the kinds that, more than most, deserve the epithet daisy bush, flowering like so many white or coloured Michaelmas daisies in late spring or early summer. These derive from the *O. phlogopappa* complex, from the southern Australian mainland and Tasmania. The original introduction was white-flowered; later Harold Comber introduced from Tasmania forms, known collectively as the Splendens group, with pink, mauve, purple or blue flowers. Like the white-flowered kind they have foliage of greyish cast, almost entirely obscured at flowering time by the mass of daisies. 'Master Michael' is a good deep violet-blue; others are apt to be designated as Pink Form, Mauve Form and so on. With their soft leaves they are by no means so wind resistant as others in the genus. A hybrid in the group is the startlingly white *O. × scilloniensis*, which at flowering time in late spring forms a dazzling mound of bloom, and later makes a quiet, grey-leaved background to summer flowers. In suitable climates it is a shrub lending itself well to mixed border culture with other softish shrubs that can be pruned fairly hard after flowering, or in spring, to retain their desired size and neatness of form.

Olearia frostii, from Victoria, Australia, has an undeserved reputation for tenderness that seems to persist despite the efforts of those who, like myself, have brought it through bitter winters unscathed, to promote it as a hardy shrub. Over neat, grey woolly foliage *O. frostii* bears large, solitary flowers of clear pale lilac. Any plant which is this attractive in leaf and flower, and survived −22°C night after night with minimal protection, must be worth considering as a hardy ornamental, yet it remains unaccountably scarce.

The two Chatham Island species with large, beautiful flowers are less accommodating, apparently needing a moist atmosphere, fearing cold drying winds but unperturbed by salt gales. *O. semidentata* has slender, pointed leaves, white woolly beneath, and young shoots shining white. Large solitary daisies open deep lilac in colour, and as they expand they fade, the play of colours enhanced by the violet purple disc of each aster-like flower. *O. chathamica* is broader in leaf, with pale violet ray florets fading to white around the dark purple disc. Closely allied is the rare *O. angustifolia* with narrower leaves and white flowers.

There are plants, these two Chatham Island daisy bushes among them, which are far finer in the wet and windy north-west than in the southerly climates preferred by gardeners for their own if not invariably their plants' comfort. But the genus *Olearia* comprises enough members sufficiently adapted to sheltered inland conditions to merit wider attention.

The National Collection

The National Collection of Olearia *was designated in April 1981. It is held at Inverewe (National Trust for Scotland) in north-west Scotland, and comprises at present fifty-four taxa, so must rank as among the most complete National Collections in existence; for not many more than sixty species and hybrids have been in cultivation outdoors in the British Isles. However, Peter Clough, who has a vast experience of west coast gardening from Tresco in the Isles of Scilly to his present post at Inverewe, writes that 'the total known taxa for a full collection is somewhere in the region of 107, so we have far to go, even though we are to our knowledge the largest collection in Europe. To obtain a full collection we must turn to source material in New Zealand and Australia. We have obviously tried seed from Botanic Gardens in these areas, but generally have had no success with the addition of species in this way, as the seed is more often than not sterile or with no viability. To proceed further we really need vegetative material from New Zealand and Australia and should probably proceed this way.' A propos of* O. avicenniifolia *'White Confusion', Peter Clough writes 'the whole of the genus is to many totally "White Confusion", but it is surprising how one gets used to their variations when a collection is grown in close proximity to one another. We can definitely identify any of our plants from a single leaf.' For example, he refers to 'the characteristic brown stained petiole base on the upper surface of the leaf of* Olearia furfuracea.

Pieris

JOHN BOND, in whose care one of the National Collections of *Pieris* finds itself (in company with rhododendron species, dwarf conifers, magnolias and several others not treated here), has an experimental turn of mind; he likes to acquire and 'trial' all the new cultivars he can of the plants he is interested in. Both the Savill and the much larger Valley Gardens, of which John Bond is the Keeper (for the Crown Estate Commissioners; the gardens are in Windsor Great Park) are largely woodland gardens, and *Pieris* is a genus of evergreen shrubs that thrive in these conditions. Moist, peaty or leafy soil, or the Great Park's light, sandy, lime-free soil, to which are added quantities of good leafy humus, suit these plants and give them the cool root run they need; while the canopy of trees provides light shade and wind shelter. For *Pieris* have two outstanding attractions: their spring foliage, which is often brilliantly coloured, but can be susceptible to frost or wind scorch while unfolding; and their sprays of lily of the valley flowers, produced early in the year.

For many years even the great tree and shrub nurseries listed only a handful of *Pieris*. Most of these had fine spring foliage, scarlet, pink, cream or bronze, and all were white-flowered. Then one or two kinds with pink-flushed flowers were introduced. Lately many different kinds have come to us from Japan, New Zealand and the United States, and John Bond has been assiduously importing them and growing them to see how they compare with each other and how they fare in the English climate.

By contrast, the other National Collection of *Pieris*, at The High Beeches in Sussex – also a woodland garden – is limited to species. Anne Boscawen, who with her husband, and remarkably little other help, maintains this immaculate and beautifully designed, spacious garden, told me why they had chosen to have their *Pieris* designated as a National Collection. 'We have many plants with different foliage – all presumably wild seed as they were here before 1932, and we wanted to learn more about them. We have a few hybrids and clonal varieties but we feel that to collect all the available hybrids and cultivars would not be possible here. Our garden is essentially designed landscape and we do not have facilities for trial grounds. What we can do is to record fully, with all known facts, the plants we do grow, and we have maps available, and lists. We are also starting to collect pressed herbarium specimens of the plants in our collection.'

Thus the two Collections are in many ways complementary. They have in common custodians who are dedicated record keepers; but on the one hand we have the old, possibly in some cases original collections from the wild; on the other the new, compared and contrasted so that the gardener who has room for only one or two can make his choice.

The species that has given rise to most of the cultivars we now have available to us is *Pieris japonica*, an evergreen shrub from, as its name implies, Japan, growing to perhaps 8 or 10 ft in time, with sprays of white flowers appearing very early, in February and March. John Bond finds it needs almost full sun to flower freely but, at the same time, it must have some shelter as very severe frosts will damage the flowers. Recently a large number of new forms have appeared on the market: John lists nearly fifty in his collection, which is not yet quite complete. They include some very lovely pink and red-flowered forms. 'Blush' was the first of the pinks; its fairly deep pink flowers are borne quite freely even in shade and are set among neat, dark green leaves. 'Pink Delight', in John Bond's view, 'looks like a winner', with its deep pink flowers in pendulous racemes. 'Flamingo' is an astonishing colour, a deep dusky red. The pink-flowered *Pieris* can look well in groups with such plants as *Rhododendron* Praecox in bright magenta-purple (avoiding 'Flamingo' which is too near red to blend well with this colour), *Daphne mezereum*, and *Prunus* 'Okame' perhaps, with vivid pink flowers; underplanted, if you want to pursue the pink theme, with bergenias or *Erica* × *darleyensis* 'Cherry Stevens' in thundery purple-pink or the paler 'Arthur Johnson'. The purple tones in the rhododendron, daphne and heaths emphasise the pink of the cherry and pieris, making it seem less blue, nearer to a clean, pure pink. Another pink pieris that is often disappointing is 'Daisen': it is dumpy and lacks grace; and the pretty pink flowers are produced sparingly in stumpy racemes. 'Christmas Cheer' behaves similarly and certainly does not flower at Christmas, so far at least. But in a garden in Maryland, USA, 'Daisen' is outstanding for its luxuriant, bright green foliage and distinctive spreading habit; though in that climate, it needs plenty of shade and a very moist, humus-rich soil. Perhaps 'Daisen' is simply not a plant for the English climate, though it would be interesting to see how it performs in a mild, moist Cornish garden.

There are good selections of white-flowered *Pieris japonica* to be had too; a name one hears more and more often is 'Dorothy Wyckoff'. Here is a tall, slender *Pieris* with good sprays of white flowers opening from warm brown buds that decorate the bush all winter. In Maryland, this shrub also displays deep-plum to garnet-red, glossy winter foliage. Another new cultivar, 'White Cascade', has particularly long flower sprays.

Most *Pieris japonica* forms have bronzed young growths, attractive indeed but lacking the brilliance of the *Pieris formosa* kinds. Exceptionally, 'Scarlet O'Hara' has quite bright young foliage on a tallish, slender shrub. *P. japonica* 'Rosea' is the name borne by a plant which John Bond likens to the squat 'Daisen', but that it has attractive peach-pink young growths. The young foliage of 'Bert Chandler' is often said to be salmon pink at first, paling through cream to white before taking on the usual green coloration by midsummer. The plants that John Bond grows under this name have clear yellow young growths, very pretty but easily damaged by spring frosts.

Entirely un-pieris-like is the odd little shrub named 'Little Heath Green', with tiny narrow leaves arranged in whorls along the slender stems. Other oddities are the dwarf forms 'Bisbee's Dwarf' and 'Pygmaea'. Not unlike these in appearance is the dwarf species *P. nana* from Japan; now placed in a subgenus of its own, *Arcterica*. It grows barely 3-4 ins high. A small form of *P. yakusimensis* also exists; it has quite large flowers and forms a low mound of pale green foliage. Seedlings from this seem not to maintain the dwarf, widespreading habit. All these little plants would make good companions for small rhododendrons and little shade-loving plants in a shaded rock garden with moist acid soil, or in the peat garden.

An exception to the limited season of *Pieris* is the white-edged *P. japonica* 'Variegata'. There are very few plants with variegated foliage that are suited to the woodland garden, other than hollies and hostas. *P. japonica* 'Variegata' is a fine variegated shrub for shade; you may indeed prefer to give it enough shade to inhibit its flowering, as the combination of white flowers and creamy variegations is not a very happy one. The young foliage in spring is touched with pinkish bronze. Even those who, like myself (a bias I will betray throughout this book, no doubt), are wary of variegations, find this acceptable to lighten a dark corner. In time it makes a big shrub. There is also, for smaller spaces, the variegated 'Little Heath' (of which the curious 'Little Heath Green' is the plain-leaved form).

Until the pink and red flowered forms of *Pieris japonica* began to make their impact, it was the forms of *Pieris* with scarlet spring foliage that we all wanted to grow, and some forms of *P. formosa* remain, at their best, unrivalled for brilliance of foliage in the woodland garden. The epithet *formosa* does not indicate that it comes from Taiwan (Formosa); it means 'beautiful, handsome'. The species is widespread in Nepal, the Eastern

Himalayas, Assam, Burma and south-western and central China. Covering such a wide range, it is a variable species and several superb forms have been selected. The best known clone is 'Wakehurst', which has brilliant sealing-wax red foliage in spring, fading through pink and yellow to light green; and sometimes flaring up again in a paler echo of its spring colouring in August. In late spring large sprays of white flowers, of the usual lily of the valley shape, add to the spectacle. 'Wakehurst' is quite widely available and, as testified by its First Class Certificate (1930), is one of the finest woodland shrubs for milder gardens; the Forrestii Group are all nearly as good but other clones are harder to come by. 'Rowallane', for example, has butter-yellow young foliage, remaining yellow until late summer, in contrast to the scarlet of 'Wakehurst'. These forms of *Pieris* combine delightfully with plants that enjoy similar conditions, such as *Enkianthus*, a shrub of layered habit with little orange-pink urn-shaped flowers; with rhododendrons, of course, especially the choicer species: but do avoid hybrids with blue-pink or magenta-purple flowers – whites and pale yellows make a happier blend of colours; and with the white stems of *Betula jacquemontii* or among snake-bark maples, perhaps. For a striking contrast, run *Clematis alpina* through a *Pieris*, to set the nodding, lavender-blue flowers of the clematis among the scarlet young leaves of the shrub. But let your *Pieris* grow to a good size first, and see that the clematis does not overwhelm it.

'Forest Flame' is an apt name given to another *Pieris* which is readily available, and a better choice for the average garden, with its vivid scarlet spring foliage fading through pink and cream before adopting its summer green, and large, drooping sprays of flower. 'Forest Flame' is widely available in commerce; but even better is 'Firecrest', which is fast becoming known for its similar virtues. Both 'Forest Flame' and 'Firecrest' received Awards of Merit at the same RHS Show in 1973 for young growth and, a very rare happening, 'Firecrest' was given a Second Award of Merit in 1981 for flower. Both were undamaged at Windsor Great Park during the severe winter of 1981-2, whereas 'Wakehurst' is rather more susceptible to cold, and the two newer cultivars of *P. formosa*, 'Charles Michael' and 'Jermyns', are both – especially 'Charles Michael' – decidedly unhappy in cold spells. 'Forest Flame' and 'Firecrest' both have blood of *Pieris japonica*, which gives them their extra toughness. So, perhaps, has 'Grayswood', which flowers extremely freely and forms a compact and yet graceful shrub. John Bond has tried it in light shade and in full sun, where it flowers most freely, with warm brown buds an attractive feature in winter. In light shade the flowers are less abundant, but are held in long graceful pendulous sprays. The spring foliage is coppery bronze and not to be disdained.

A plant which came to Windsor Great Park many years ago as *Pieris japonica* 'Grandiflora Purity' was then described as being very dwarf, but has in fact comfortably reached over 3 ft in height, though maintaining a compact habit. It flowers with great freedom, the white flowers borne in upright spikes in March and April. Despite the name it bore on arrival at Windsor, John Bond believes it to have affinities with *P. taiwanensis*★, a very hardy, small-growing species with white flowers in upright spikes. Lacking the bright spring colouring of so many other Pieris, this one is hardly worth space in the garden unless your climate is too harsh for the better kinds.

Not everyone is enthusiastic about *Pieris floribunda*, a tallish (6 ft) species that makes a wide spreading bush in time. The foliage, admittedly, is dull green and never puts on the bright spring livery; but in full flower, covered with its erect white panicles, opening from green buds, it can be a fine sight. The older the plant the shorter and stubbier the flower spikes, until they are no more than an inch or so in length. This North American species has a selected form with much longer panicles, known as 'Elongata'; but the spikes of this, too, may dwindle as the plant ages until barely distinguishable from the normal type. As first shown to the RHS in 1938, 'Elongata' had spikes up to 8 ins long.

★ Anne Boscawen points out that this plant closely resembles some forms of *P. japonica*. Collected in Taiwan in 1918 by E. H. Wilson and often labelled *P. taiwanensis*, a species now merged in *P. japonica*.

The National Collection

The National Collection of Pieris *species is grown at The High Beeches, Handcross, Sussex (The Hon. Edward & Mrs Boscawen). At the Savill and Valley Gardens, Windsor Great Park, is the National Collection of* Pieris *including cultivars.*

The High Beeches Collection was designated in October 1981. It consists mainly of mature plants, many of them possibly raised from wild-collected seed. There are no plans to add cultivars to this Collection.

By contrast the Collection at the Savill and Valley Gardens, designated in November 1985, already at the time of designation included a great many cultivars. John Bond, Keeper of the Gardens, has a policy of importing and growing for trial all the cultivars he can obtain of the plants in which he is interested, provided of course that like Pieris *they are suited to the open woodland conditions of the Savill and Valley Gardens. The Collection is already an almost complete living museum of all known* Pieris *cultivars, and John Bond is actively seeking the last few needed to complete the Collection.*

Rhododendron

THE GENUS *Rhododendron* is a large one, with around 800 species, of which about 500 are grown in this country. Then, of course, there are hundreds of hybrids and cultivars as well. Clearly, taking on the whole genus would be beyond the capacities of any single National Collection holder, so *Rhododendron* is being tackled in more manageable chunks. The major rhododendron National Collection is the species collection at Windsor Great Park, with various tender species being grown at Brodick on the Isle of Arran (subsections Falconera and Grandia) and at Inverewe (subsection Barbata) and the forms and derivatives of *Rhododendron forrestii* at Bodnant. The other National Collections so far designated within the genus *Rhododendron* are of different groups of azalea; these are horticulturally distinct from the mainstream of rhododendrons and will not be considered here.

The basis of the collection at Windsor Great Park (Savill and Valley Gardens) is the Tower Court collection, assembled by the late J. B. Stevenson with help from the old Rhododendron Association, a small and rather exclusive (the modern word would perhaps be élitist) group of great rhododendron growers. On Stevenson's death in 1949, his widow attempted to keep the collection going, but she had not enough help and decided her only course was to sell it. The collection was valued at £11,000 – remember this was in 1951 when £11,000 would buy you a respectably-sized country estate – the buyer to remove the plants. They were bought by the Crown Estate Commissioners, and transferred with great care over three years.

If the only rhododendrons with which you are familiar are the hardy hybrids, shrubs with showy trusses of flower and boring, laurel-like foliage, then the species collection at Windsor Great Park should change your perception of the genus. Here, arranged in a botanical classification in their sections (formerly known as series: the revised classification of

99

Cullen and Chamberlain is followed at Windsor, and all the labels agree
with the new nomenclature), are a great range of rhododendrons of all
sizes from the little 'yaks' to shrubs of tree-like proportions, and big bushes
of the large-leaved species, with their look of having strayed from some
primeval jungle. Because far the greater number of visitors to the Savill
and Valley gardens come in late spring, when the rhododendrons and the
renowned Punch Bowl planted with evergreen azaleas are in flower, they
miss all the wonderful foliage effects of the rhododendrons. If you visit in
July, say, or even in December, you can take in the beauty of the
rhododendron foliage, and the lovely undulating terrain in which the
plants are set, without the distractions of flower colour.

The geographical heartland of the genus *Rhododendron* is the Sino-
Himalayan region, at altitudes above 8,000 ft. In the areas where rhododendrons are abundant, the climate is appalling by our standards: mist
shrouds the slopes and peaks and rain falls frequently in summer, while
snow blankets the land, and protects the rhododendrons, for up to six
months of winter. It is surprising how well even the large-leaved rhododendrons do on the dry, thin Bagshot sand and – by rhododendron
needs – arid climate of Surrey, but then John Bond, who is in charge of
the gardens, believes in irrigation and mulching. However disbelieving
we humans may be, the average British climate is far too dry in summer
for many of the plants we try to grow, and even in the wet western isles,
as it might be at Brodick, or the west coast as at Inverewe, the distribution
of the rainfall, which in total is much higher than at Windsor, is wrong
for the plants: too much falls in winter and too little in summer. For all
that, the climate of the coastal north-west is more suitable for the large-
leaved rhododendrons and both Brodick and Inverewe are known for the
quality of their plants.

The lesson, then, is that if you want to grow good rhododendrons, you
need not only an acid soil with abundant humus, but also a willingness to
irrigate in dry spells, and a determination to keep your soil well covered
with a loose, leafy, moisture-retaining mulch. A blanket of stodgy manure
is not what rhododendrons need: their fibrous roots lie very near the
surface in a close root ball, and need air as well as moisture.

For those who are interested there are many specialist publications on
the genus, giving the familiar classification into series or the revised
grouping into sections. I propose to be very subjective and selective in
discussing the National Collections of rhododendrons and will certainly
not plod through 500 species. What I want to do is pick out some of
the characters that make certain rhododendrons particularly interesting,
exciting, attractive – those qualities that add up to a 'garden worthy'
plant – and select species that best illustrate these attributes. And because
I have stressed that rhododendron species have much to offer beyond their

flowers, I shall begin with those that are worth growing for their foliage alone.

Several rhododendrons have a felt-like covering, known as indumentum, to the underside of the leaf. This indumentum is often of a rich rusty tan, sometimes paler buff or fawn, and sometimes silvery white. *Rhododendron bureavii* has dark green foliage backed with a bright rust-red felt. Perfectly hardy, it is slow-growing and compact; its flowers are unexciting white or pink bells but, with such striking foliage, flowers seem almost redundant to the observer, if not to the plant. *Rhododendron fulvum*, again, has a cinnamon-brown indumentum backing its very dark green leaves; it makes a taller and more open shrub with small pink flower trusses in March. At much the same season appear the luminous deep scarlet flowers of *R. mallotum*, a species which even in gardens where frost destroys the flowers is worth growing for its handsome foliage, dark green and wrinkled above, tawny red beneath. It makes a fairly tall, narrow shrub and, like so many rhododendrons except the very small-leaved ones, needs some shade. Any of the smaller-leaved maples make ideal companions for these tawny-felted rhododendrons, and if you are lucky enough to inherit a fair-sized specimen of *Acer griseum* you will find that its peeling, mahogany and tan bark echoes the rust-red felt. At ground level, lacy ferns and cyclamen can happily inhabit the leafy ground between the roots of the rhododendrons.

A compact shrub with fawn or pale brown indumentum, *Rhododendron lanatum* has pale yellow bells spotted with red in April. Closely related to this is *R. tsariense*, a smaller shrub with small rounded leaves, bright rusty brown beneath, and white or blush flowers. A clone with the name 'Yum Yum' won an Award of Merit when exhibited by Major General and Mrs Harrison; Mrs Harrison was the former Mrs Stevenson, and it has been said of her, in tones of some envy, that she married two great rhododendron collections.

Some of the best rhododendrons for indumentum are found among the large-leaved species and, in ideal conditions such as those of Brodick or Inverewe, the largest of these may produce enormous foliage, each leaf 18 ins or more in length. *Rhododendron fictolacteum* has very dark green, shiny leaves, up to a more modest 12 ins in mild, moist, westerly climates; the undersides are covered in a rich chocolate brown felt. The flowers are white, blush pink or lilac to rose pink, blotched with maroon and frilled at the edges, borne in rounded trusses. It is a hardy species, now regarded as a subspecies of *Rhododendron rex*, which has larger leaves with a paler, fawn or greyish indumentum. Slightly less hardy, *R. arizelum* (*R. rex* subsp. *arizelum*) has fine cinnamon or fox-red indumentum, and is strikingly contrasted, in the Valley Gardens, with the bright lime yellow foliage of *Acer japonicum* 'Aureum'. The flowers of *R. arizelum* are variable in colour from cream to primrose, sometimes flushed with pink, or shades of warm pink from salmon through apricot to deep rose. A larger shrub closely related to *R. arizelum*, *R. falconeri* is a noble plant with leaves up to 12 ins long, densely felted beneath with rust-red indumentum. The flowers of *R. falconeri*, creamy-white to near yellow, last longer than those of any other known rhododendron: up to a month. It, too, is better suited to mild westerly gardens, but if you garden near the coast in the south or east of the country and can contrive plenty of shelter you may well succeed with it. Much the same conditions are needed by *R. eximium* (*R. falconeri* subsp. *eximium*) with deep cinnamon-brown indumentum persisting for at least a season on the upper surface of the leaf, and flowers in shades of pink. All these are members of subsection Falconera, grown as a National Collection at Brodick.

About the best-known big-leaved rhododendron, I would guess, is *R. macabeanum*, a member of subsection Grandia, which is also grown as a National Collection at Brodick. A big shrubby tree, this splendid and remarkably hardy species has big, broad, leathery leaves with whitish or silvery-grey undersides and – in the best forms – dense trusses of yellow bells with a crimson-purple blotch, in March and April. Less excitingly, the flowers may be washed-out creamy-primrose. Another lovely feature of *R. macabeanum* is the bright red bud scales which make the expanding growth buds in spring look like red candles, opening into silvered young leaves. Do beware of inferior seed-raised plants: the best flowers go with the best foliage, and it is worth paying extra (quite a lot extra) for a good form, rather than settle for poorly coloured flowers.

The largest leaves of all belong to another member of subsection Grandia, *Rhododendron sinogrande*: up to 2 ft long, shiny above, buff or grey-felted beneath. Big fat bells of creamy-yellow, crimson-blotched flowers in enormous trusses appear in April and May, after *R. macabeanum*; and unlike 'macabe' good flowers and good foliage tend not to go together. In mild, moist, sheltered gardens a big *sinogrande* is the noblest thing the genus *Rhododendron* has to offer.

The leaves of *Rhododendron hodgsonii* (subsection Falconera) are among the handsomest in the genus, up to 1 ft long, dark green with an almost metallic sheen above, buff or foxy brown beneath. In flower *R. hodgsonii* is variable, from dirty, muddy mauve or rose-purple to a much more pleasing pink; sometimes sweetly scented. It is a hardy species suitable for most sheltered gardens in this country and, as if this catalogue of qualities were not enough, it also has beautiful bark, well described by Peter Cox (*The Larger Rhododendrons*) as 'creamy, mauve shot green, pink to cinnamon, peeling in large sheets'. Several other species also have lovely bark, and should be grown near a path, unobscured by surrounding vegetation, so you can not only feast your eyes but also indulge your sense of touch by stroking the lovely limbs of your rhododendrons. Among such delights is *R. arboreum* (of which the subspecies *cinnamomeum* also has fine woolly cinnamon-coloured indumentum and, usually, white flowers), a tree-like species as its name implies, displaying its rough peeling bark. In flower colour, *R. arboreum* is very variable and, as a general rule, the colours regarded as most desirable, the true deep blood-reds, are more tender than the pink or white-flowered forms. All bear fairly small flowers in tight trusses. This is a smaller-leaved species than those we have so far considered, and in some forms the underside of the leaf is shining silver.

There is no such variation in the colour of *R. barbatum*, a splendid species with dense trusses of rich scarlet flowers, which has given its name to the subsection Barbata which is grown as a National Colection at Inverewe. Despite its exotic appearance this rather gaunt, tree-like rhododendron is hardy in the south, given shelter, but best in the moist north-west; indeed Inverewe is renowned for the quality of its *R. barbatum*. In leaf it is not particularly fine; it rates a mention here, rather than later for its flowers, because of its good bark, maroon and purple peeling to a smooth, blue-grey surface. *R. barbatum* may flower as early as February, or as late as April. The exquisite *R. griffithianum* produces its immense scented, lily-shaped flowers in May. They may be white, sometimes spotted with green, or sometimes veined or flushed with pink, deepening even to deep rose pink. It is beautiful even without its lovely flowers, when the eye, undistracted, is likely to appreciate its peeling bark, ranging from fox-red, tan and cinnamon-brown to fawn and grey-bloomed deep green.

The bark of *Rhododendron thomsonii*, too, gives year-round pleasure. Here we have a species of quite different aspect, with almost round leaves, bright blue-glaucous when young, dark green at maturity but remaining blue-white or glaucous-green beneath. The foliage makes a lovely setting for waxy, blood-red or deep wine-red flowers, appearing in April and May. The smooth, peeling bark is fawn and buff, grey, apricot and creamy-pink in colour. Although birches should be planted with rhododendrons only with caution – they cast a suitable dappled shade but have far-ranging, greedy roots – where there is sufficient moisture to take the risk I like to see *R. thomsonii* among birches that have pinkish bark; warm apricot-white *B.ermanii* or cinnamon-pink *B. albo-sinensis sep-tentrionalis*, say. Add a primrose-yellow, cowslip-scented corylopsis, the April-flowering *C. veitchiana* perhaps, for a charming woodland cameo.

The leaves of *R. wardii* are of similar shape, rounded or fatly oblong, and almost sea-green in colour, to set off very pretty pale cup-shaped flowers, varying from pale creamy-yellow or primrose to lemon and sulphur, often set off by a basal blotch of crimson-maroon. It flowers as late as May, and is hardy in the south, needing only dappled shade.

As its name implies, the leaves of *R. orbiculare* are virtually circular; they have glaucous undersides. It is a shrub which ought never to flower, for the broad, stout-bodied bells are a dismal shade of magenta-pink. I am not one of those who shun magenta: but *R. orbiculare* gets it wrong. Not so *R. williamsianum*, with much smaller leaves, 10p-sized and almost as round but for their heart-shaped bases; bronze when young, they are dark green at maturity with whitish undersides. The little bells, two to four in a cluster, open in April and are of a charming shade of pale pink. When well-grown, in an open sunny position, but with ample moisture at the root and shelter from cold winds, it makes a dense, wide bush about shoulder-high at most.

Rhododendron thomsonii is not the bluest-leaved rhododendron by any means. There is a lovely group of quite small-leaved, aromatic rhododendrons with intensely glaucous-blue young growths maturing to sea-green, and waxy, *Lapageria*-like flowers in shades of mustard or amber yellow, tangerine-orange, dusky vermilion, muted pink or sombre plum-crimson. Many are now grouped in *R. cinnabarinum* that formerly were considered separate species. *R. cinnabarinum* Roylei Group have large plum-coloured flowers with a faint bloom on the surface; from Windsor Great Park came the selection 'Vin Rosé', which won an Award of Merit in 1953. The Concatenans Group (formerly *R. concatenans*) have, in the best forms, vividly glaucous-blue foliage and orange-yellow flowers. Closely related to *R. cinnabarinum* is *R. keysii*, which has narrowly tubular flowers in flame red or scarlet with yellow-green lobes, reminiscent of the similarly coloured flowers of *Fuchsia splendens*.

Also with glaucous-blue foliage, *R. oreotrephes* has quite different flowers, little bells varying from cool lavender to warm rosy mauve. It is quite hardy and flowers in May, after the frosts. The foliage may have a slight aroma, reminiscent of the much smaller-growing *R. glaucophyllum*. Here we have a little shrub with leaves intensely glaucous-white beneath, and with a strong smell of saddle-room, which may repel you or fill you with nostalgia. In flower, *R. glaucophyllum* is delightful, its rosy-pink bells appearing in May. A most desirable form, var. *luteiflorum* (now I think elevated to species rank as *R. luteiflorum*) has lemon-yellow flowers. So too does the entirely lovely *R. lepidostylum*, a low, wide-spreading shrub with bright glaucous-blue, bristly-hairy foliage. On a much smaller scale again is *R. impeditum*, which has tiny steel-blue leaves and deep lavender-blue flowers. There are many of these charming dwarf or compact rhododendrons with 'blue' flowers, some small enough for rock gardens, in peaty soil of course, others excellent medium-sized shrubs for woodland edges, or the simulated garden equivalent. *R. augustinii* is one of the taller blues, up to 6 or even 10 ft. Like so many rhododendron species, it is variable and the deeper, nearer to true-blue forms, which are usually considered the most desirable, are also apt to be the most tender. Many good clones originated in the Tower Court collection in the days of Colonel Stevenson.

Even more variable in flower colour is *R. campanulatum*, which may be white, blush, pink, mauve to purple, or blue-lavender. The leaves, which are fairly large though nowhere near the giant size of the large-leaved species, have a dense sienna-brown felty indumentum and, when young, are often very glaucous-blue; especially in the variety *aeruginosum*. *R. campanulatum* flowers in April, earlier than the mainstream of hardy hybrids but by no means so early as many other species. If you have a suitably mild climate, or are prepared to gamble that, every so often, the weather will be kind at just the right moment, you could grow some of the very early-flowering species. Some of those I have mentioned already flower fairly early: *R. barbatum*, *R. mallotum* among them. One of the most delightful of all rhododendron species, not bold in leaf nor large and vivid in flower, but with that indefinable quality we call charm, is *R. lutescens*. Here we have a rather open-habited medium-sized shrub with coppery-red young foliage, and clear pale yellow flowers, quite small, appearing in February or March. The form 'Bagshot Sands', with primrose-yellow flowers, is a Tower Court plant. There is also a delicious pink form, not a pure or a blued pink but a subtle pale peach or skin pink. By comparison with *R. lutescens*, the tree-like *R. calophytum* is big and butch, with long narrow leaves up to 12 ins long; it can be spectacular in flower, with big trusses of white or pink bells heavily blotched with deep crimson at the centre, borne in March or April. Its close relative *R. sutchuenense* is less tall, with leaves almost as big and larger flowers, not so clean in colour, coming a little earlier than those of *R. calophytum*.

At the other end of the rhododendron season are some fine late-flowering species, *R. discolor* for example. A tall Chinese rhododendron, *R. discolor* has white or faintest blush flowers opening as late as the end of June or early July. Even later is *R. auriculatum*, a big shrub with large leaves characteristically lobed at the base, and fragrant white flowers in July and August. Nor need late-flowering rhododendrons bear only white flowers. Those of *R. griersonianum*, appearing in June, are a beautiful shade of geranium lake, among narrow pointed leaves which are fawn-felted beneath. The quality of red displayed by *R. griersonianum* needs the tender, slightly yellowed green of young fern fronds, the royal fern if you can manage it or the shuttlecock fern, *Matteucia struthiopteris*, to set it off to best advantage, in dappled shade, sparse enough to allow much of the sun to filter through to illumine the flowers.

Another good, June-flowering red is *R. eriogynum*, now in *R. facetum* under the new classification. Sadly, it is not hardy outside mild, moist gardens, but there is well worth growing, not only for its scarlet flowers but also for the silvery-furred young leaves which appear late in the season. Also believed to be tender when first introduced, *R. spinuliferum* has proved pretty hardy in the south. It is quite un-rhododendron-like with its tubular, tight-mouthed brick, tangerine or scarlet flowers and smallish, puckered leaves. April and May is its season, and it grows to 6 ft or more. At much the same season flowers *R. neriiflorum*, its crimson-scarlet bells set among near oblong leaves, bright glaucous-white beneath.

With space fast running out, I must mention a few more smallish species, and most notably of all *R. yakushimanum*, an immensely and justifiably popular species that forms neat rounded bushes, with narrow leaves, seeming narrower still as their margins are turned down and in; the undersides of the leaves are densely felted in grey-white or tan. Most people rave over *R. yakushimanum* in flower, but it looks, to me, merely smug, with tight little trusses, tight as a newly-set overdone perm, in apple-blossom pink fading to white. In the Valley Gardens is a large bank of seed-raised *R. yakushimanum* which makes a fine effect out of flower, and no doubt causes 'ahs' of admiration in May.

By contrast with the wide-ranging Windsor Collection of *Rhododendron* species, which includes just about everything that will grow in the climate, or with the great bushes of large-leaved species at Brodick and Inverewe, the Collection at Bodnant in North Wales is both narrowly defined and limited to little rhododendrons, those of the *forrestii* alliance. This is a small group of species varying from prostrate shrubs to little mound-forming bushes. They like to creep along mossy rocks, cool banks or even half-rotted tree stumps or logs, in settings where they can receive some shelter from spring frosts which easily destroy the first flush of growth and its flower buds. *R. forrestii* itself is best known in its form *repens* (Repens Group in the new classification), with – when it bears them at all – the fleshy narrow bells in scarlet-crimson that characterise this group of species. Similar in flower, but usually more upright or mounded in habit, is *R. chamae-thomsonii*. Many hybrids have been raised using one or other of the members of this alliance (often *R. forrestii* Repens itself) to produce a range of low, red-flowered hybrids. None is better known than 'Elizabeth', raised at Bodnant, and always popular for its quite large, brilliant scarlet bells on a low-growing, mounded shrub. Its prostrate form is known as 'Creeping Jenny' or sometimes just as 'Jenny'; another Bodnant plant, this. From another stable came 'Carmen', a most lovely small shrub with neat, dark green foliage and deep cardinal-red bells of waxy texture. 'Baden Baden' and 'Elisabeth Hobbie' are two good German-raised dwarf red rhododendrons with *forrestii* Repens blood, while one of the best from Germany is 'Scarlet Wonder', less dwarf than some, with bright red flowers and good foliage. Though, on the whole, I try to urge people to experiment with species rhododendrons rather than staying with the more familiar hybrids, in the case of these little red-flowered shrubs I think most would agree that the hybrids are the better garden plants, flowering more reliably and more tolerant of periods of drought. I have seen whole rock faces covered with the creeping stems of *R. forrestii* Repens left exposed and bare, decorated only with dead branchlets, after a droughty summer that killed the rhododendron stone dead.

The National Collection

The National Collection of Rhododendron *species is grown at the Savill and Valley Gardens, Windsor Great Park, Berkshire (Crown Estate Commissioners). The National Collection of* Rhododendron, *subsections Falconera and Grandia, is grown at Brodick, Isle of Arran (National Trust for Scotland) and that of subsection Barbata at Inverewe (National Trust for Scotland). The National Collection of* Rhododendron Forrestii Alliance *is grown at Bodnant, Colwyn Bay (The National Trust).*

Although the climate of Berkshire is too cold for the tender species of Rhododendron, *most hardy or near-hardy species are represented in this immense Collection. Even the large-leaved species grow here, though not seen at the spectacular size of leaf and stature of plant that they achieve in the milder, wetter climate of Brodick or Inverewe. At Windsor, the rhododendrons are arranged in their botanical classification, section by section, in large beds on an undulating site. The nucleus of the Collection was the Tower Court collection, assembled by the late J. B. Stevenson with help from the old Rhododendron Association. On his death his widow was, after a year or two, obliged to sell the collection; it was bought for £11,000 by the Crown Estate Commissioners, and carefully transferred to its new home over the next three years, between 1951 and 1954. There have been many additions to the collection since, in an attempt to make it as complete as possible given the climatic limitations of the site. A canopy of forest trees provides broken shade and wind shelter. The* Rhododendron *species at Windsor Great Park were designated as a National Collection in July 1982. Both the Scottish Collections, at Brodick and Inverewe, were designated in July 1986. Although there are many rhododendrons both large and small at Bodnant Garden, only the small group known as the Forrestii Alliance is designated as a National Collection; the Collection was accepted into the scheme in April 1981.*

Senecio

SENECIO is a huge genus including such undesirables as groundsel, a handful of superior perennials for our borders, succulents, a hardy climber to decorate our autumn gardens, and a fairly clearly defined group of shrubs from New Zealand. It is these last which form the National Collection held at Inverewe, where they grow in company with the olearias they closely resemble both botanically and horticulturally.

Their promiscuity in cultivation as in the wild leads to problems of identification; it has been suggested that most of the plants in cultivation in Britain are hybrids. Certainly the plant known as *Senecio greyi* in many British gardens, and as *S. laxifolius* in some, falls in fact within a group known as the Dunedin hybrids. The very common silver-leaved garden shrub, hardy in many areas, should now be known as *S.* 'Sunshine'. The group as a whole derives from the two species just named, with infusion from a third, *S. compactus*.

With its ovate, grey leaves, white beneath, and heads of cheerful clear yellow daisies in summer, *Senecio* 'Sunshine' scarcely needs description. It is one of the most useful of grey-leaved shrubs, hardly enough for most British gardens, submitting happily to a severe pruning to keep it compact and within bounds. Indeed, it is the better for such treatment, carried out either in spring, if flowers are not wanted, or after the flowers begin to fade if you enjoy its bright floraison and your chosen colour scheme will not be disrupted by yellow in summer.

'Sunshine' is by far the most widespread and well-known of the Dunedin hybrids, as a plant if not by that name. It appears to be *S. compactus* × *S. laxifolius*; others in the group with *S. greyi* blood have not yet been named. It may be that to talk of *S. laxifolius* and *S. greyi* as separate species is a solecism. Though the forms of each species regarded as typical are distinct, they are linked by a range of intermediates in both

109

North and South Islands of New Zealand, and may merely form the extremes of a single widespread and variable species.

Be that as it may, the plant known as *S. greyi* is found in North Island, and is a beautiful shrub with leaves densely white-felted beneath, and with a felted margin above, a feature which does not occur in the Dunedin hybrids. The flowers are the usual clear bright yellow. *S. greyi* is less hardy than the Dunedin hybrids and, indeed, may not exist as such in British gardens. *S. laxifolius* is also very rare in Britain. In the wild it is lower-growing than *S. greyi*, with leaves white-felted beneath and, at first, grey above. Yellow flowers are borne in pyramidal heads in summer.

The third species that contributes to the Dunedin hybrids, *S. compactus* is a small shrub also but more compact in habit, as its name implies. The small leaves are covered in white felt beneath, and from above appear margined in white, enhancing the wavy edges. The leaf margins of *S. monroi* are more markedly crimped, and its flowers are handsome in the expected bright yellow. Little known until recently, this species seems to have been taken up by garden centres, and deserves to become more popular, though better suited to the milder counties. This is not to say that it is entirely frost-tender; and indeed it is very pretty when the crinkled leaf margins are whitened by hoar frost.

Other members of the genus are, by comparison, scarcely known in British gardens, though a few species with thick, leathery leaves are much used in mild coastal gardens for their resistance to salt gales. *S. reinoldii* is the largest, making a small tree in mild gardens if sheltered, or a dense rounded shrub when seared by salty gales. At Inverewe it revels in exposure right down to the high tide level. In flower it has nothing to recommend it, but the foliage is extremely handsome, rounded (as implied by its former name, *S. rotundifolius*), thick and leather-textured, shining dark green above and white-felted below. If grown as a tree or open-habited shrub it also displays peeling bark, of buff and fawn tints.

Not unlike is *S. elaeagnifolius*, smaller-growing, with narrower leaves buff-felted beneath. It is as wind-resistant as its larger relative. The descriptions of these two species by W. Arnold-Forster, whom we have already met in the chapter on *Olearia*, are worth quoting: *S. reinoldii* has leaves 'polished green above and pale gilt underneath when young'; *S. elaeagnifolius* forms a 'wide pudding of a bush, broader than its height'. He grew both of these, and many other antipodean plants, in full exposure in his garden on the Atlantic coast of Cornwall, where they crouched among granite rocks, lashed by the sou'westerlies. A variant grown at Inverewe is known as 'Joseph Andrews'; it has also been called *S. elaeagnifolius* var. *buchananii*, though the *S. buchananii* of botanists is another plant with thinner leaves, silvery-white beneath.

The pet of this group is *S. bidwillii*, a 'compact alpine' version of *S. reinoldii* with small very thick oblong leaves, as wind-resistant as any in the group.

Linking the two groups already discussed is *S.* 'Leonard Cockayne', a hybrid between *S. greyi* and *S. reinoldii* forming a well-branched shrub, head-high or taller, with leaves white-felted below, shiny green above, and large sprays of flower. With 'Leonard Cockayne' we are entering the realm of very little-known senecios, only to be found – so far at least – in botanic gardens, the National Collection itself and the gardens of one or two enthusiasts for the genus. But among them are some good things. *S. huntii* is one, a Chatham Island native looking, until it flowers, rather more like a shrubby spurge than a senecio. Its foliage is arranged similarly in close formation at the ends of the branches, each leaf narrow and pale shiny green, though felted below when young in an un-spurge-like manner. *S. huntii* may form a rounded man-high shrub, or a little tree of 20 ft or so, and is very free with its yellow flowers. Crosses with the Dunedin hybrids give plants similar to *S. huntii* itself, but greyer of leaf.

Less tall is *S. perdicioides*, a bushy shrub with small oblong, toothed leaves and small yellow flowers in summer. A native of North Island New Zealand, it is very tender. This too has crossed with the ubiquitous – I am tempted to say pervasive – Dunedin hybrids to give a taller plant with rather larger flowers of the same bright yellow.

Not every antipodean senecio has yellow flowers. *S. hectoris*, from the South Island of New Zealand, has proved short-lived at Inverewe, but does well at Brodick, on the Isle of Arran, whence replacement stocks are obtained as necessary. In the wild it forms an evergreen, or partly deciduous, upright and sparsely branched shrub to 12 or 14 ft, the young branches covered with a loose wool and the big, markedly toothed leaves with a 'grey cottony down' beneath. Unlike other senecios, which have entire leaves, *S. hectoris* is distinguished by the pinnate lobing to the base of each leaf. The white flowers, with the yellow disc so common in daisies, are borne in summer in wide heads.

A cross between this and *S. perdicioides*, which arose in a garden in Wellington, New Zealand, is named for the owner, 'Alfred Atkinson'. Inheriting the fully evergreen and much-branched habit of the yellow-flowered parent, it has from *S. hectoris* large leaves which are at first buff-coloured before becoming, in maturity, pale green above, paler and rather downy below, with slightly wavy margins. From its large-leaved parent it inherits also its white flowers, freely borne. For mild gardens it is a handsome foliage shrub of unusual soft pale green tone.

Lastly, there is *S. kirkii*, which occurs in wooded and hilly country on North Island New Zealand at altitudes of no more than 2,500 ft, and can therefore be expected to be tender in Britain. Unlike most it is free of down. The smallish leaves are very variable in shape; the flowers are large in the genus, up to 2 ins across, of pure white with a yellow disc.

It is clearly essential that genera such as *Senecio* and *Olearia*, which include many tender species, should be held as National Collections in gardens with suitable climates. But most senecios are easily raised from cuttings, and a visit to the National Collection may encourage inland gardeners to buy a plant of more than just the familiar 'Sunshine'.

The National Collection

The National Collection of Senecio, shrubby New Zealand species, is held at Inverewe (National Trust for Scotland). Although designated in April 1981, at the same time as Olearia, it is not as yet quite so complete, and not all the plants described in the foregoing chapter are yet represented in the Collection. In particular, it has been extremely difficult to obtain material of true S. greyi, true S. laxifolius, and some of the more obscure and tender species and named hybrids.

Clematis

IF YOU have ever said to yourself, or to a nurseryman who is extolling a clematis to you in the hope that you'll buy it, 'Yes, it's lovely, but I haven't got room for it in my garden', then you should go to Burford House Gardens, at Tenbury Wells in Worcestershire, where the first National Collection of *Clematis* was conceived. Go with a notebook and an open mind. John Treasure, who has created the garden at Burford House since the mid-fifties, has a deep interest in plants, and is imbued with the conviction that they should be grown in ways that enhance their own best attributes, not just treated as collectors' pieces. At Burford there are many lessons to be learned, both in the Clematis Museum and in the garden, in the use of clematis as garden plants. The lesson begins, in fact, in the wild, where they are found, invariably, in close association with other plants. Most – not all – are climbers, and in the wild their stems are supported by neighbouring plants. In the garden this means that any reasonably stalwart shrub, including other climbers, can be a host for a clematis.

Since most people start by thinking of walls for clematis and other climbers, this may as well be our starting point too. Instead of erecting a wooden or plastic-coated wire trellis on your wall, and growing your clematis on it to show its bare legs increasingly over the years as you have less and less time to train its new shoots carefully each year, try a clematis and a climbing rose together, or decorate a wall-trained pyracantha with one. Large-flowered clematis and climbing roses of the HT persuasion combine extremely well, their opulent blooms providing a feast that distracts from the plants' shapelessness. Try the deep blue-violet 'Lasurstern' with a deep red climbing rose such as 'Guinée', or 'Etoile de Hollande', or the paler, prodigiously free-flowering 'Mrs Cholmondeley' with a pink HT like 'Madame Caroline Testout' or 'Lady Waterlow'. Or try a pale blue cultivar with palest shell-pink rose 'New Dawn'. If pink isn't your colour, or clashes with your walls, you may prefer violet-blue and yellow, complementary colours rather than harmonising ones: 'Lasurstern' again, or perhaps 'Lady Northcliffe', with the rich yellow climbing rose 'Lawrence Johnston', named for the creator of the garden at Hidcote. Between yellow and pink lies the splendid rose 'Climbing Mme Edouard Herriot', the Daily Mail rose, salmon and coral-pink, another colour that happily mixes with 'blue'. If you like white, you could blend a white clematis and a white rose, very refined: 'Marie Boisselot', say, with that lovely old climbing rose 'Mme Alfred Carrière'. Clematis and honeysuckles, clematis and wisteria, clematis and jasmine: the possibilities are great and the two climbers need not, of course, coincide in their flowering season; you may prefer to have them consecutively in flower to get a long, if less concentrated, effect from the same bit of wall. The best clematis to use in such combinations are those you cut hard back in January: catalogues give details of pruning requirements for each variety offered, so it is easy to check before you buy. Nor need you confine yourself to the large-flowering clematis in this context. One of the prettiest plantings of this kind I have ever seen brought together *Clematis macropetala* 'Markham's Pink' and *Akebia quinata*, which has cupped, chocolate-maroon flowers in spring among pretty foliage composed of five rounded leaflets to each leaf. 'Markham's Pink' is sometimes described as sugar pink, but I'd call it, rather, dusky mauve.

Shrub roses, and many other shrubs too, also make excellent companions for clematis. For a soft blend of colours, grow a subtly-toned cultivar such as 'Hagley Hybrid', in shades of dusty mauve-pink, with the ineptly named rose 'Magenta', actually a tender greyish-mauve flushed with rose-pink; or try *Clematis* 'Duchess of Albany' with *Rosa rubrifolia* (now correctly *R. glauca*) and a ground planting of *Salvia officinalis* 'Purpurascens', the purple-leaved sage. The clematis is one of the *texensis* hybrids, and bears its sugar-pink flowers upright like little lily-flowered tulips. At Burford House it grows with *Ceanothus* 'Gloire de Versailles', in powder blue. The Duchess is about the most easily obtained of this very desirable group; others that you should snap up if you see them offered are 'Etoile Rose' with open, nodding bells of pale pink deepening to cerise at the centre of each tepal; and 'Gravetye Beauty', with wider-open, starry flowers of ruby red. 'Sir Trevor Lawrence' has upright flowers like 'Duchess of Albany', but in cherry red. Both these last are virtually herbaceous and not vigorous, so a shrub of more modest dimensions would suit them.

These *texensis* hybrids were originally bred by Jackman's of Woking in 1890, by crossing *C. texensis* and 'Star of India', also raised by the firm. The original Wokingensis hybrids, as they were then called, included not only 'Duchess of Albany' and 'Sir Trevor Lawrence', which are still in cultivation, but also 'Countess of Onslow', 'Duchess of York', 'Grace Darling' and 'Admiration', all now thought to be lost. 'Etoile Rose' was bred in France; 'Gravetye Beauty' also, introduced by William Robinson of Gravetye Manor. Raymond Evison, whose brainchild the Clematis Museum at Burford House was, has a horror story to tell of a good *C. texensis* form, which grew for years in a Worcestershire garden. The head gardener tried many times, without success, to propagate it, until finally he lifted the plant, divided it into six, and distributed it among keen and successful clematis growers. Disastrously, all six died, and unless any evidence turns up to the contrary, we must believe that this clone is now extinct.

But I have strayed away from shrubs hosting clematis. If you were to wander around your garden, pen and notebook in hand, critically considering each shrub as a potential support, I think you might be amazed at the scope your garden suddenly offers. When I did this in a former garden of my own, not many years after it had been an entirely bare site, I finished up with a list of fifty-four potential clematis hosts; far more than I could afford to fulfil at the time!

As well as using shrubs for hosts, you can of course hook your more vigorous clematis right up into the trees: the massed white flowers of a *montana*, for example, look dramatic set in a dark pine or cypress. But choose your tree a little carefully. Most smallish garden trees, crabs, cherries, thorns, apples and so on, are safe enough hosts provided you bear in mind the tree's greedy roots, and plant your clematis accordingly. One way is to plant it beneath the outer branches, and provide a stout string to lead the climber into the tree. Choose, too, a tough clematis, not a large-flowered and correspondingly more exacting hybrid. Montanas, yes, and the *orientalis* kinds with thick-petalled yellow lanterns, or the viticellas, which I will describe later. Even so greedy a tree as a birch could be adorned with one of the viticellas, together with a vine for autumn colour, say, provided you keep away from the birch's fibrous mat of roots.

For large-flowered clematis, a more appropriate support than a competing tree would be a pole, pergola or trellised fence. Here will be all sorts of happy possibilities of combining, once more, these and other climbers. Together with roses on pillars they make a fine vertical feature in a mixed border, or indeed in a rose garden, if such you have. Clematis and old roses seem to have an especial affinity, their colours harmonising particularly well, the clematis bringing to the soft bluish crimsons, pinks and creamy whites of the old roses the bluer shades of mauve and violet. If you want to enhance the blue tones of such old roses as 'Reine des Violettes', with its greyish-mauve shadings, don't give it as a companion one of the bluest clematis, however; the rose by contrast will look far pinker. A dusty mauve cultivar, as it might be 'Victoria', will be a kinder match, enhancing the bluish tones of the rose.

The clematis season lasts virtually all year, with careful selection, though the large-flowered kinds which I have chiefly considered so far are basically summer-flowering, from June to September or October depending on the variety. In spring – April and May – those of the Atragene section produce their small nodding lanterns on, typically, plants of fairly moderate vigour. *Clematis alpina*, from Europe, and *C. macropetala* from China, are extremely hardy. They have survived temperatures lower than $-30°C$ without snow cover and still flowered freely the following spring, so they are unquestionably valuable in exposed gardens and ideal for a north-facing exposed wall or a very windy fence, as well as for shrubs that must take a buffeting. *Clematis alpina* itself has blue flowers, and a number of selections have been made; a fine new one is the creamy-white 'Burford White', which, like any white flower, would look superb against dark foliage, or make a striking combination with a coral-scarlet flowering quince, perhaps (the flowering quinces or 'Japonicas', like the clematis, are happy on a northerly exposure). 'Columbine' has long pointed flowers of clear pale blue, and 'Francis Rivis' is the largest in flower of all this group of mid-blue colouring. There is a 'White Columbine', and 'White Moth' is an older white, usually listed under *C. alpina* but now considered a form of *C. macropetala*, as suggested by its pretty, fuller flowers, seeming almost double in effect, appearing in May. *C. alpina* has also given rise to dusky purplish-pink 'Ruby' and the much more appealing 'Willy', pale pink inside and darker on the outside. All these need a moderate-sized host; a tree paeony such as *Paeonia lutea ludlowii* or *P. delavayi* perhaps, or (though not for pink clematis) *Berberis darwinii* or a *Kerria*, preferably the butter-yellow single-flowered 'Guinea Gold' rather than the more orange-yellow shapeless double form all too often grown. I have seen a blue *C. alpina*, probably deep blue 'Pamela Jackman', looking splendid among the bronze-yellow new growths of *Physocarpus opulifolius* 'Luteus', or, as at Great Dixter, with the red spring foliage of a *Pieris*. In all these combinations you would need to keep a careful watch on the clematis to see that it does not choke the host shrub; or give it a pole or tripod to support most of its bulk.

Some new *C. alpina* forms have recently been introduced from Sweden. 'Helsingbord' and 'Tage Lundell' have striking purple-blue flowers and are forms for the future. Another to look out for is the recently-introduced Japanese *C. ochotensis*, closely allied to *C. alpina*, with larger flowers and broader, slate-blue tepals.

I must pause to explain again this word 'tepal', which we have already met in magnolias. Most flowers have petals and sepals, the latter the much smaller, usually green or greenish, more or less petal-shaped parts below

the brightly-coloured petals. In some plants, of which clematis and magnolias are examples, the petals and sepals are not differentiated, and for
these the word 'tepal' was coined by George Johnstone, a magnolia grower
of immense erudition and experience who has already received mention
in the appropriate chapter.

Back to our Atragene group of clematis, however. *C. macropetala*
'Markham's Pink' has already received mention, but even prettier to my
eyes is the type, with its full, double-seeming rich blue flowers enhanced
by creamy staminodes at the centre. Named kinds are 'Lagoon' and
'Maidwell Hall', and in white the enchanting 'Snowbird'. A light blue
form found in China by Professor Harry Smith in 1922 and named 'Harry
Smith' is one to look out for, while 'Ballet Skirt' is a full-flowered pink
form of great promise. A much copied idea of Vita Sackville-West's, seen
by many in her garden at Sissinghurst, is to combine a blue and a pink
form of *C. macropetala* together in an Ali Baba jar, allowing them to
overflow and mingle freely. All the Atragene clematis, incidentally, have
attractive seed heads of old man's beard type, fluffy and whitish, making
a worthwhile extra after the flowers have gone.

The other great group of spring-flowering species is typified by *C.
montana*, much more vigorous climbers than the dainty Atragenes. They
are useful garden plants for covering unsightly outbuildings and large
walls, but look far more natural growing over and through large trees
such as pines. They will grow up to twenty or thirty feet, but are less
hardy than the Atragenes; severe winter weather can cut them right back
to the ground, though only in frosts of freak severity such as those in
1981-2 need we fear to lose them entirely. *C. montana* has white flowers,
C. m. rubens pinkish-mauve, borne in May and early June in great abundance from ripened stems of the previous season; some of the best forms
have a delicious vanilla scent, such as 'Elizabeth' with gappy soft-pink
flowers. In shade this becomes almost white. Much deeper in colour is
'Picton's Variety', with 3 ins wide flowers and very often an extra tepal
or two per flower. Like *C. montana rubens*, from which it derives, it has
purplish-tinted young foliage, the pigment affecting all parts of the plant
and not just the flower. 'Tetrarose' is a tetraploid form with deep rosy-
mauve tepals and attractive bronze-green foliage. A much lighter pink
form is 'Vera', with 3 ins wide strongly scented flowers. Closely related
to *C. montana* is *C. chrysocoma*, lost to cultivation until its recent reintroduction from Yunnan in China by Roy Lancaster. It has very downy
foliage. Its hardiness has yet to be put to the test, but its brilliant white
flowers with yellow anthers make it a must for the warmer garden.
C. chrysocoma sericea (*C. spooneri*) is tougher, with flowers tinged pink,
and less downy foliage. 'Continuity' is an unusual form with deep
pink, yellow-anthered flowers, borne continuously if not very freely

during summer on flowering stems 8-10 ins long. Sadly, it is not winter hardy.

There are other less than hardy clematis that well deserve a space on a sheltered wall or in a conservatory, and since we have wandered onto the subject of tenderness I will consider these now. Natives of the southern hemisphere (except for *C. armandii* from China and the Mediterranean *C. cirrhosa*), they are hardy enough for mild southern gardens, or into the Midlands, if given a sheltered situation and well-drained soil.

One of the hardier evergreens is *C. armandii*, with bold very handsome green foliage and masses of dazzling white 1-2 ins flowers in March and April. The two named kinds that are well worth looking out for, but not at all easy to obtain, are 'Snowdrift', a large-flowered kind with broader leaves than the type, and 'Apple Blossom', deep pink in bud and with dark reddish-pink stems on the new growth. The flowers of *C. armandii* are strongly vanilla-scented. Be warned, some forms are very poor, with squinny off-coloured flowers; and that handsome foliage can look very tatty, especially at the winter's end; while old plants that have not been regularly tidied up (i.e. pruned) can become full of disgraceful dead brown foliage and look, frankly, awful. They need full sun to flower well.

You will need a sunny aspect, too, for *Clematis cirrhosa*, from southern Europe, and its Balearic Island form *C. c. balearica*. The first has pendent greenish-cream bells, freckled inside, mainly produced in winter. The Balearic form has very finely cut foliage, at least in its most appealing variants; hence its 'common name' fern-leaved clematis. The foliage turns bronze-green as winter approaches. This too produces its freckled bells in periods of mild weather from January on. If you grow these in a conservatory, or cut flowering stems and bring them indoors, you will perceive their agreeable lemony fragrance.

The New Zealand species include *C. fosteri*, which has a delicious lemon verbena scent, product not of its bright apple-green leaves as in the plant it mimics but of the creamy-green flowers. It would make an ideal container-grown plant for flowering indoors in April and May. Similar, with smaller starry flowers in great masses, and more finely cut foliage, is *C. australis*. *C. afoliata* is a very different thing, a collector's piece to most of us. Known as the rush-stemmed clematis, it has almost leafless stems and produces its small, creamy yellow, daphne-scented flowers from February to April. *C. paniculata* (which used to be called *C. indivisa*) is the largest-flowered New Zealand species; a magnificent thing when suited, producing quantities of large (1-2 ins) pure white flowers with pink anthers. April is its season when grown outside, and it needs a mild climate and a warm wall, or the protection of a conservatory, to survive and flower freely.

Once you have succumbed to the particular appeal of the species, and of small-flowered clematis in general, you are likely to want to grow a selection at least of the summer-flowering kinds. There is a group known as the Viticella clematis – because a species of that name figures in their parentage – which includes several charming, easy and hardy kinds, not susceptible to the wilt which so often affects the large-flowered kinds. *C. viticella* itself is wild in southern Europe, and has elegantly nodding purple flowers on long stalks; it grows, at Great Dixter, through a large *Hydrangea villosa*, and the big soft leaves and mauve-blue lacecap flowers of the shrub are an ideal foil for the clematis flowers. Closely related to *C. viticella*, the Portuguese *C. campaniflora* has smaller flowers, nodding again, wide-open bell-shaped, and skimmed milk colouring; enchanting, if not showy, and vigorous in growth.

A great advantage of these Viticella types is that you can cut them hard back in January or February (the usual advice) or earlier if you will, from November on, right down to a foot from the ground. Thus they are the perfect companions for shrubs, and for draping over massed winter heathers – a partnership pioneered by John Treasure at Burford House, and successfully copied in many gardens. In summer the clematis trail over the heathers, their flowers held horizontally, facing upwards at you; in late autumn you cut away all the visible disgrace of dying, blackened foliage and tangled stems, and in winter the heathers have things all to themselves. If you add to your heathers, as so many people do, sundry conifers, you will find that the clematis will appreciate these too and scramble up your exclamation-mark junipers or, more attractively, along the slanting branches of the Pfitzer hybrid junipers. *Clematis* 'Etoile Violette' has deep violet flowers and looks well on a yellow-green background such as *Juniperus communis* 'Depressa Aurea' – anything brighter 'gold' than this might look a little hectic. The wine-red 'Abundance' combines startlingly with a golden-foliaged heather such as *Erica × hybrida* 'Jack Brummage'. On a dark ground (*E. carnea* 'Vivellii' perhaps) the pale, indeed virtually white, 'Little Nell' or 'Minuet' would show up well. Both have deeper margins to the flowers; the former light mauve, 'Minuet' a deeper shade of near-purple. 'Alba Luxurians' is sometimes as entirely white as its name implies, but more usually each tepal is stained with green at the tip. You may think this sounds odd or even unhealthy, but many love it, myself and most flower arrangers included. Give it a backing where the green stain will be enhanced, not lost: the near-black of a yew or holly, say, rather than mid to pale green foliage.

Of the bicoloured persuasion again, like 'Minuet' only more so, is 'Venosa Violacea', white veined purple with wholly purple margins. This, or one of the other, deeper-coloured kinds like 'Abundance' or 'Rubra' (a bluish red) looks superb in a shrub such as well-established buddleia.

Both get hard pruned in early spring, but buddleias grow so fast that the climber and its host make pretty good time together.

The darkest of all the Viticellas is 'Royal Velours', deep velvety purple and needing careful placing. Graham Thomas, for many years Gardens Adviser to the National Trust, and author of several well-known books on gardening and plants, admires it in association with the shiny, orange-red fruits, furry red stems and white-backed leaves of the Japanese wine-berry, *Rubus phoeniculasius*. The oddity in the Viticella group is 'Purpurea Plena Elegans', with soft dusty grey-purple, fully double rosette-shaped flowers, freely borne on vigorous growth. It associates ideally with old roses; one of the happiest combinations I've seen had it blending with the like-coloured moss rose 'William Lobb' and feathery, grey-green *Juniperus* 'Grey Owl'. Also in the group were the great skeletal, metallic footballs of *Allium christophii*, and sharp magenta, black-eyed *Geranium psilostemon*: a mix of subfusc colours with a strong leaven to save it from insipidity.

Even such vigorous species as the orange-peel types, *C. orientalis* and its allies, can grow successfully in a host shrub such as a sizeable rose, if you exercise the discipline (on yourself and the clematis alike) of pruning hard back each winter. Try *C. orientalis* itself, or better still the form known under the collectors' number of L & S 13342 (from Ludlow and Sherriff's Himalayan expedition of 1947) through a strong-stemmed shrub rose such as *R. moyesii*, where the yellow lanterns will mingle with the rose's vivid vermilion hips. L & S 13342 has attractive, finely cut green foliage in lacy contrast to its thick-textured tepals; from the colour it should be called lemon peel, not orange. *C. orientalis* 'Burford' is one that cropped up in John Treasure's garden, and this has immense vigour, almost uncon-trollable, with rather stubby yellow lanterns. Another, 'Bill Mackenzie', is a better thing with larger, longer lanterns and the usual mass of fluffy seed heads. I have seen an illustration of a hedge of *C. tangutica*, another in this group, growing in – I think – Poland, all in seed and entirely smothered in its whitish wigs.

What we have all been calling *C. orientalis*, and what the nursery trade will offer you as *C. orientalis*, is apparently not the real thing, which has now been reintroduced from the wild. With its scrolled-back yellow tepals making a turk's-cap effect, it is quite different from the more familiar pointed lanterns. *C. serratifolia*, though not turk's-cap in shape, shares the enhancing purple stamens, set here in pale lemon tepals. A nice lemony scent from this one, and good feathery seed heads again. I liked it growing in a group of sea buckthorn, *Hippophaë rhamnoides*, with willow-slim grey leaves and pale orange berries (on female plants, that is). *C. flammula* would also go well in the sea buckthorn, where its masses of little hawthorn-scented white flowers would appear in August and September. Try it, too, in a shrub rose such as *Rosa sweginzowii*.

Clematis flammula is like a very superior old man's beard, *C. vitalba* – to which it is indeed closely related. Though the old man's beard, our only native British clematis, is much too rampant and coarse a thing to find a place in most gardens, it is one parent of the sprawling, rather than climbing, *C. × jouiniana*. The foliage of the hybrid is also rather unpleasing, but is concealed in its season by such a mass of flower that it hardly matters. The type does not flower until September, but 'Praecox' begins in July and flowers for three months, covered with the same profusion of small, starry blooms of skimmed-milk colouring, borne all along the 10 ft annual growths. 'Mrs Robert Brydon' is similar; but with room for only one, choose 'Praecox' every time.

The other parent of *C. × jouiniana* is *C. heracleifolia*, so called because of its large leaves which recall those of *Heracleum*, a genus including the giant hogweed. This is perhaps the most common of the subshrubby or virtually herbaceous species, somewhat variable but always bearing flowers of some shade of blue, recalling in form those of a hyacinth. 'Cote d'Azur' is a named kind said to have deeper blue flowers. Some forms of *C. heracleifolia* make quite a woody framework, but *C.h.* var. *davidiana* is more truly herbaceous, with spreading underground shoots. Unlike the type it is quite strongly, though not entirely pleasantly, scented. 'Wyevale' is a good named kind of good blue colouring.

Much more discreet, and to some eyes correspondingly more desirable, is the herbaceous *C. integrifolia*. This is rather weak-stemmed and needs support from neighbouring plants, lest its many nodding, deep blue flowers find themselves dashed to the ground by the least wind or summer shower. 'Olgae' is similar, 'Hendersonii' larger in flower with spreading petals. All three are much more manageable, at 3 ft or so, than *C. × eriostemon*, which is a cross between *integrifolia* and *viticella* and bears *integrifolia*-like flowers on semi-woody stems up to 10 ft. If you want a tall plant needing support, you would do much better with *C. × durandii*, which is a hybrid between *integrifolia* and *× jackmanii* and has bolder, indigo-blue flowers with deeply-grooved tepals around a pale central boss of stamens. As it is semi-herbaceous it is well suited to growing over a moderate-sized shrub from which its old stems will be cut away each season.

The ironically-named *C. recta* is not erect at all, but falls about, its densely-growing stems smothering any plant on which it lies. Both the type and 'Purpurea', of which only the young growths are really purple, bear a froth of little white flowers at midsummer. The only way I have seen it satisfactorily grown was on the summit of a steep bank down which it flopped, or in another garden at the top of a retaining wall, adjacent to the similarly sprawling rose 'Raubritter' with whose little cupped pink flowers it looked very pretty. Both the rose and the clematis are of sufficient vigour to cope quite well with each other where they overlap.

A very different herbaceous species is *C. douglasii* var. *scottii*, with rather glaucous foliage and urn-shaped flowers, the four tepals recurved at the tips and downy on their outer surfaces. In colour it is a slightly pinkish lavender, especially where the tepals curl back; 'Rosea' is a good clear pink. Both grow to about 3 ft.

With this little diversion to consider some of the herbaceous species you may encounter, I have strayed away from the fragrant climbers I was considering. Of these, *C. rehderiana* and *C. veitchiana* are always greatly sought after for their cowslip scent. The panicles of little, pale buff-yellow bells appear in August to October among hairy leaves. Even better than these – though I may have had a particularly good form – is *C. connata* with larger, more decidedly primrose-yellow bells. Raymond Evison brought back seed of this from the Kangding Gorge, so we may hope to see more of it about before long. Even more exciting than this is *C. aethusifolia*, a recent reintroduction from China. Very finely-cut leaflets of light grey-green resemble the foliage of carrots, a wonderful foil for the small, tubular, light yellow flowers, which are jasmine-scented. Native to the Great Wall area of China, this was reintroduced by Roy Lancaster in 1980. Raymond Evison has also introduced or reintroduced several clematis from China and Japan, and I should like to end this chapter with an account of his eventful trip to China.

The journey took the party of travellers to Hong Kong, and then by train to Canton (Guangzhou). On arrival in Canton they were told that because of aircraft problems their journey to Chengdu would have to be delayed for two days. This gave them an unexpected opportunity to look at gardens in Canton, and also to visit an outlying botanic garden. Here came the first clue that on this trip delays and transport difficulties were to become an omen for finding a new clematis. In the botanic garden at Canton they found *Clematis chinensis*, not in flower, but certainly the true species, of which the foliage when pressed and preserved as an herbarium specimen turns black along the stem. Similar species, mostly forms of *C. terniflora*, do not. The party's luck was not in, however, when they journeyed to the outlying botanic garden; when they enquired whether *C. armandii* or *C. florida sieboldiana* were to be found in that area the guide pointed to a range of hills about two days' walk away and said 'Yes, over on those hills!'

After a delayed arrival in Chengdu, the capital city of the Sichuan Province, the team set off along the old road to Lhasa in Tibet. The plan was to pass through the famous town of Kangding and on up to 14,500 ft, passing into the old parts of Tibet, now in Sichuan, through the Zheduo Pass. However, even before they reached Kangding they found many clematis. The first was discovered on a hillside early one morning, only because there was a delay of six to seven hours while a landslide, which had blocked the main road, was cleared. Here, *Clematis tangutica* and *orientalis* forms grew through and out of rock and scree, but the most exciting find in this area was a beautiful autumn-flowering species with nodding, thick-tepalled white flowers. Samples of this came back with the team to England, but none survived the following winter, so it remains unidentified.

The next morning, because the engine of one of the minibuses was overheating, the party had an early breakfast while the engine cooled. Here, before breakfast alongside a fast-flowing stream in the Kangding Gorge, five different clematis species were found. Right beside the stream a strange species with a *Thalictrum*-like flower was in full bloom: a possible member of the *C. vitalba* group with creamy-white flowers. The next find was a superb form of *C. connata*. This species has yellow, cowslip-like flowers, and a distinctive very broad base to the petiole; in this particular form the leaf stem base was the largest seen during the expedition and in fact larger than any forms in cultivation. Unfortunately, however, this form seems to be slightly prone to damage by early autumn frosts in Europe, due to its late flowering habit.

The third species they found was again the superb nodding, white-flowered species that is still not in cultivation, nor known to the Chinese botanists in Peking who are making a special study of the genus *Clematis*. The fourth find was a great surprise, a species with nodding flowers resembling the American *c. pitcheri*; again, this has not yet been identified. Seed collected in the Kangding Gorge germinated well and the first plants flowered during the autumn of 1984. The seedlings differ from the plant found on the expedition: they have deep pink tepals rather than the deep reddish pink of the wildling. This too may not prove hardy or garden-worthy due to its late September/October flowering period in Europe. The other species found in this location was a form of the *orientalis/glauca* group with deep yellow-green tepals and fine glaucous foliage.

The next find came on a planned stop well above Kangding, where *C. gracilifolia* was growing. The resulting seedlings produced very finely divided leaflets, somewhat more so than the plant from which the seed was collected. *C. gracilifolia* had previously been introduced by Professor Harry Smith in 1935 from the Sikang Province while on an expedition from Sweden. His form has more broad-based leaflets than the form found above Kangding. This newly-introduced form seems to be the earliest flowering hardy *Clematis* species in cultivation, and its white, montana-like flowers are nicely scented.

The party continued their journey through the Zheduo Pass; leaving the main road to Lhasa behind them, they travelled towards their goal of

Gonga Shan. Regrettably, due to continual problems and illness, they never reached Gonga Shan on this expedition. However, their luck was in again as nightfall approached. The journey was halted as one of the minibuses hit a large boulder in the narrow roadway which lay tightly between the hillside and a great drop into a very swollen river. The driver was persuaded to stop for a rest, and this gave the team time to discover another three clematis species. One was again the unnamed nodding white species, this time at about 12,000 ft; another was a rather strange-flowered form of the *rehderiana/buchananiana* group; the last a superb form of *C. glauca/orientalis*. The *rehderiana* type was in seed, and the resulting seedlings produced their first flowers in the autumn of 1984. The species, still to be named correctly, is probably a form of *C. buchananiana*, but far superior to anything in cultivation. It flowers very freely, producing, on long peduncles (flower stems) usually eight to ten yellow tubular bells resembling the cowslip but with much deeper tepals which are quite strongly scented. This should make a very vigorous climber – a great assest to the autumn garden. The third species was the one that got away. This form of *C. glauca*, or *C. glauca akebioides*, had superb foliage, and its nodding, four-tepalled flowers, yellowish-green on first opening, turned pure yellow and matured to a rich orange-brown; followed by silky seed heads. The seed collected here was too juvenile to germinate. Other similar clematis were found later and brought back to England, but this was the only sighting of this especially fine form.

Altogether, on this trip, about twenty-five different species and forms were found and brought back for Raymond Evison's National Collection. Though not every new introduction may deserve garden-space, even those with insignificant flowers may have value as a parent. Perhaps we may look forward to a new race of hardy and beautiful clematis hybrids?

The National Collections

The National Collections of Clematis are held at Burford House, Tenbury Wells, Worcester (Treasures of Tenbury Ltd), and The Guernsey Clematis Nursery, Domarie Vinery, Les Sauvagées, St Sampson, Guernsey (Mr Raymond Evison).

The Tenbury National Collection was designated in April 1981, when it was already a mature and extensive collection comprising the range of taxa grown in the garden and a great many others, many of them rare or new to cultivation, collected by Raymond Evison. Burford House is the home of John Treasure, who has been collecting plants, and especially clematis, for thirty years or more, using them to great effect in the garden he created. During the late 1950s John Treasure and Eric Evison, who was responsible for starting the nursery at Burford House, began propagating clematis for sale. At this time clematis were thought to be difficult to root and not very profitable. However, under the expert attention of Eric Evison's son Raymond, production increased to 250,000 or 300,000 clematis plants each year. Raymond's involvement grew during the 1960s: by the mid 1970s Treasures of Tenbury had received Gold Medals at several of the Royal Horticultural Society's Chelsea Flower Shows, and the name had come to mean clematis to many gardeners. The late 1970s and early 1980s saw an increase in the number of clematis species and cultivars grown at Burford as Raymond Evison travelled, first into America and Europe and then into China and Japan, meeting other clematis growers and nurserymen. In conjunction with the National Collection visitors may now see an exhibition of the history and development of the genus Clematis in the Clematis Museum in the old stable block at Burford House. Text, coloured photographs and line drawings, many taken from old books on clematis, are complemented by a world map showing the distribution of clematis.

In January 1985 Raymond Evison moved the propagation of clematis from Tenbury Wells to the island of Guernsey to help with the expansion plans of Treasures of Tenbury's nursery. The many clematis species and cultivars in the collection gathered over the years by Raymond were taken to his new nursery for propagation purposes.

Production in Guernsey, after a few initial problems, rapidly increased. However, the Board of Directors of Treasures decided to concentrate on retail sales at Tenbury and Raymond took over the Treasures' wholesale customers in 1987. The Guernsey Clematis Nursery is now one of the largest clematis producers in Europe, with over 500,000 young plants being produced in 1987.

Raymond was also responsible for forming the International Clematis Society, in 1984; there are now some 300 members throughout the world, including China, Japan, Poland, the USA and Canada, New Zealand and Australia. Two Newsletters are produced each year and a seed exchange is held annually.

If you wish to see a selection of clematis imaginatively grown in a garden of great charm maintained to a dauntingly high standard, then a visit to John

Treasure's garden at Tenbury Wells is for you. If, however, you want to study the widest range of clematis species and cultivars to be seen in the British Isles, including much wild-collected material, nowhere will you see more than on the island of Guernsey, at Raymond Evison's young but already thriving clematis nursery. As this is purely a wholesale nursery, you will not be able to place retail orders for clematis; but Raymond will gladly forward details of the International Clematis Society to fellow-enthusiasts.

Perennials
and Rock Plants

Introduction

WHEN I came to consider into what sections of this book my selected genera should fall, there was little difficulty with the trees and shrubs. Separating perennials from alpines and rock plants became a much more subjective matter. Take the groups of plants I want to write about here. Kniphofias (red-hot pokers) and agapanthus, heucheras, *Lychnis*, the yellow daisies in all their diversity, pyrethrums and penstemons, Michaelmas daisies and the tall, brilliantly-coloured lobelias are all what we think of as herbaceous perennials, suitable for borders and beds. Geraniums, thalictrums, euphorbias, foxgloves, campanulas? Well, plenty of geraniums (the real thing, of course, not pelargoniums) are clearly border plants; others fit more easily into a wilder setting, grass, edges of woodland, among shrubs, but they are still recognisably in the same category. Foxgloves, too. A good many geraniums, again, are rock plants, some of them true alpines. There are exquisite little thalictrums for choice peaty corners and big, muscular ones for borders, sun-basking spurges for hot rocks and others for woodland or wetland. *Campanula*, as a genus, is even more polymorphic, varying from the 6 ft *C. lactiflora*, a whopping herbaceous perennial for border or wild garden, down to tiny, tricky alpines such as *C. zoysii*.

Sedums, too: *S. spectabile* and its kin, 'Autumn Joy' and the like, are fine border plants. With 'Vera Jameson' we are on the brink of the rock garden category. No doubt about little *S. spathulifolium* and its variants, you might think: but my sister uses them as ground-cover under her floribunda roses, in great sheets that get walked on and ripped out by handfuls when they encroach too much. Then take primroses. Double and old, named primroses are garden toys that arouse feelings of nostalgia among their devotees, who squeeze them into all sorts of places in their gardens: but scarcely can they be classed as border plants nor as rock plants. Among shrubs, yes, or – cottage-garden style – tucked in among

131

this and that, shaded by cabbages or paeonies or weeds. The forms of *Bellis perennis*, too, are little, cottage-garden plants as much as, or more than, they are good-tempered spring bedding plants. The same people who admire primroses and double daisies often, and for much the same reasons, collect old pinks. All these are cottage-garden plants as we now, I think, all of us understand the term. Their popularity shows no sign of waning as we nostalgically yearn for the days that never were. Nowadays we plant the smaller dianthus, especially the little species and a few choice hybrids, among other rock plants and alpines, including indeed the smaller campanulas, sedums and geraniums. Up a size or two, with old border pinks and the named Allwoodii types, and you have ideal plants for the front of borders, spilling over stone walls or mowing stones, their glaucous foliage unifying a disparate collection of plants perhaps.

The Kabschia saxifrages, then, are the only plants I shall be considering in these pages which are solely rock plants. For this reason, I gave up trying to force the non-woody, non-bulbous plants into neat categories, and propose to treat them all together as one large group, from which you may select according to your own needs.

Display

Perhaps a word or two about display may give you some ideas to adopt, adapt or disagree with. The herbaceous border, which many gardeners think of as the traditional way to display hardy perennials, derives from the dictates of early nineteenth-century gardeners such as Loudon, who recommended grading the plants in borders by height and colour in strict regularity. Later, Gertrude Jekyll, whose early training was as an artist not as a gardener, brought an artist's appreciation of colour and form to the flower border. Her ideas of mixed borders of subtly graded colours are still a model and inspiration to many. At about the same time William Robinson was urging the greater use of old perennial garden plants in place of fashionable carpet bedding. He advocated growing them not only in borders, but also in grass, at woodland edges, and in similar informal settings, which we now class as wild gardening.

The conventional border had the backing of a wall or hedge, as for example Miss Jekyll's borders, or the Long Border at Dixter, with its tall yew hedges; and this remains the model in most gardeners' minds when using the phrase 'herbaceous border'. A rival style is that pioneered by Alan Bloom, who has written much and persuasively about perennials in island beds. The practical results of his theories can be seen in the island beds at Bressingham, a superb piece of design and planting using, predominantly, herbaceous perennials. Where adapted to smaller gardens, this style is less successful; I know of more than one garden where too many island beds have been cut out, in 'informal' shapes with meaningless curves and bulges, destroying the open centre which formerly gave a sense of space to a small area.

Whether in borders or beds, if you want above all masses of colour in your garden, you will have little choice but to go in for spring and summer bedding, for more permanent borders planned to provide a concentrated display over a shortish period, or for a combination of the two. Many herbaceous plants, and among them – of those I shall be treating here – notably the yellow daisies, pyrethrums, penstemons and asters, will indeed provide massed colour in their season. With these groups of plants, as with others that have received the attentions of the breeders, the flower is all; their foliage is often coarse and uninteresting, unobtrusive or at best merely pleasant. To many of us a more satisfactory garden picture is made by foregoing some of the concentrated colour display and choosing plants with good foliage as well as attractive flowers. Such are many of the geraniums, ligularias for moist soils, some red-hot pokers (some are rather coarse but all have sword-shaped leaves contrasting with the rounded forms of so many perennials), and some *Lychnis*, notably the silver woolly *L. coronaria* and *L. flos-jovis*. Most *Heuchera* species have excellent foliage and understated flowers; only the cultivars and hybrid offspring of one species offer bright colour as well as lovely leaves. Many other genera not included in this book could be added to the list of perennials with good foliage.

As for the smaller plants, one thing I want to make clear is that you do not need a rock garden to grow rock plants. By all means, if you garden in an area where natural stone is abundant, use it to build a rock garden: but even then, consider if the stone might not be better used to construct raised beds or retaining walls. Much will depend on your surroundings; a Cotswold village house and a Welsh cottage may both be constructed of local stone, but a rock garden constructed to resemble a natural rock outcrop may look quite out of place in the domesticated setting of the village. Several alpine gardeners I know have no rock garden, but they grow a great selection of alpines and rock plants successfully in settings that fit congruously into their surroundings and please the eye as much as the plants.

Building dry stone walls, either to make a raised bed or to retain a bank of soil, is one of the most therapeutic and satisfying tasks I know, if you have suitable stone. As your wall goes up, so you pack it with soil, and tuck your plants in; within weeks, it seems, the plants will settle and grow and your wall will look as though it has been there for years. If you are building on a fairly generous scale you could plant the more enthusiastic campanulas, such as those two willing and vigorous growers with the impossible names, *C. poscharskyana* and *C. portenschlagiana*, or pinks that will fall in curtains of blue-grey foliage, attractive all year and a feast for the eye and nose when in flower, if you sensibly choose the clove-scented kinds and plant them where you can inhale their warm perfume without bending. Dozens of sedums grow happily in walls, scuttling along cracks which they fill with their succulent leaves, and flowering abundantly. Some of the little geraniums will grow well in walls too, and at the foot of a shady wall you might find choice corners to tuck in a special primrose or two. Among paving stones the little double daisies will find a cool root run, their heads in the sun.

If your taste is for the smaller, trickier alpines, the tiny campanulas or the Kabschia saxifrages perhaps, then trough gardens may be for you. Real stone troughs are hard to get now, and expensive if you do track them down. But white glazed sinks can still be found, and covered with the trough-gardener's ally, hypertufa: a mix of cement, sand and peat, moistened and slapped on to your sink that you will have previously cleaned and coated with unibond glue, dried to tackiness. Gloved hands (rubber heavy-duty gloves for preference) patting the mixture smooth, but not *too* smooth, will make it look almost as if worked with stone-masons' tools. The exact proportions of the recipe vary according to your intended results: the more cement, the more durable but also the harsher in appearance will be your hypertufa trough. Do set the sink in place before you begin: once covered it will be impossibly heavy, and worse still after you have filled it with drainage crocks and a nice open, gritty but humus-rich compost. Some people have successfully covered expanded polystyrene boxes with hypertufa to make a less heavy trough (make friends with your local radio and hi-fi supplier, for example, to get the boxes), or constructed their own wooden formwork and cast a trough, giving the hypertufa strength with a reinforcement of chicken wire. On a larger scale you could build a tank of concrete blocks – remembering to leave drainage holes as always – which you then cover with the mixture. As we shall see in the chapter on campanulas, Peter Lewis has made good use of old asbestos-cement water tanks to grow his plants.

Far more than a conventional rock garden, however well executed, raised beds, retaining walls and troughs lend themselves to the sort of garden most of us have – small and surburban, or perhaps small and cottagey. Perhaps the acme of the alpine gardener's art is to be found in alpine houses, where, for the most part, those exquisite and desirable specimens that win the prizes at Alpine Garden Society shows around the country are grown. Lovingly tended in clay pans, these are no warmth-cossetted tenders (with just a few exceptions): most alpines are grown inside to protect them from our excessively wet winters, and a first requirement is ample ventilation to combat moulds. The protection of an alpine house does enable us to enjoy the very early flowers of the Kabschia saxifrages undamaged by rain or frost, or to grow woolly-leaved plants without fear of intemperate rains, trapped in their insulating fur, inducing foul rots. And then, it must be said, an alpine house is pleasant protection for the gardener also, from too much rain or sleet, or from those biting east winds that plague our gardens in spring as a searing and desiccating alternative to the blustery, wet west winds that blow for most of the rest of the year.

When you consider how different their native conditions are from those in which we grow them, it is amazing how willingly alpines grow in our lowland gardens. The plants from high altitudes are the most resentful of our long growing season which denies them their winter rest, cosily blanketed in snow which keeps them dry and prevents them from freezing; but even these can often by induced to grow with the protection of an alpine house or even a pane of glass, set to keep the winter rains from them without depriving them of air. In summer, plants that need a moist atmosphere, such as primroses or even double daisies, can suffer dreadfully from a few days' drought; and never a summer goes by without a spell of dry weather, hot and sunny or exacerbated by chilly, drying winds. Despite all these problems, alpines and rock plants remain popular, their miniature charm perhaps exercising the fascination of any other small thing – dolls' houses, train sets, models of all kinds. The high alpines, their needs in cultivation challenging the most dedicated grower, have the allure of exclusivity as well.

The Plant Breeders

Many perennials have been extensively hybridised and selected by the plant breeders. Of the plants chosen to feature in this book, hundreds of Michaelmas daisies, pyrethrums and kniphofias, and dozens of penstemons, as well as heleniums and other yellow daisies, have been introduced over the years, with agapanthus, heucheras and lobelias too. Few of these are still available in commerce, and the National Collection holders have long 'wants' lists. Where, now, is *Aster amellus* 'Bessie Chapman', or *Kniphofia* 'Hortulanus Laren'? Both of these, and many more perennials, have been on the NCCPG's search lists for some years, and sooner or later one must assume that plants which are not reported over a period of years have become extinct. Some of these may not have been worth perpetuating; yet who knows what unique combination of genetic material might now be lost that could have produced a new and valuable cultivar? Reading old catalogue descriptions, over and over one thinks, if only we still had that plant; while the older generation of gardeners all have stories to tell of a favourite plant that they have not seen for years, and would love to rediscover. In the past, cottagers may well have helped to preserve, for us to enjoy, some of the old-fashioned plants that were ousted from the gardens of villas and mansions by their fashion-conscious owners, who preferred exotic bedding plants and, thanks to cheap labour and cheap coal, could afford the glasshouses and the workers to produce them. Now the National Collection holders struggle to keep the old varieties of primroses alive, or to make sense out of the 30,000 names in the Dianthus register. The saxifrage collection at Waterperry covers just one section of that great genus, yet runs to over 200 varieties, some old, some new; names of plants that Farrer lovingly described still figure in the list today. Yet just a few hours of scorching sun can parch a Kabschia saxifrage beyond redemption, and if yours is the last remaining plant, a precious cultivar may be lost for ever. Pyrethrums, kniphofias: these are just two groups of plants that have succumbed to their own dread disease, wiping out huge stocks and eliminating for ever, perhaps, certain varieties. Yet if such plants as remain can be found, and grown in the National Collections, they can at least be assessed, and with modern techniques of propagation perhaps kept in cultivation if considered worthy, rather than being allowed to die out through default.

Agapanthus

WE ARE now so used to seeing agapanthus in hardy flower borders that we forget, perhaps, that they quite recently came into their own as hardy perennials. The first species to be introduced, indeed, came to England in the latter part of the seventeenth century, brought by Dutch traders from the Cape: for these are South African plants. By the turn of the century this first introduction, *Agapanthus africanus*, had flowered in the glasshouses at Hampton Court. For the next two centuries it was regarded as a glasshouse plant, and except in mild areas is still best so treated. *Agapanthus* species fall into two broad categories; those from the coastal regions of the Cape, with evergreen leaves, are susceptible to frost, while the species from the inland mountains and high table land are deciduous and well able to withstand frost.

A. africanus must have rapidly earned the English name blue African lily, and this species, together with the plant usually known as 'A. umbellatus', are typically of good deep blue colouring. In a botanically confusing genus such as this it is hard to put definitive names to individual plants, but 'A. umbellatus' seems to have largely usurped the position originally held by *A. africanus* as a fine late summer perennial for mild gardens, or as a noble tub plant trundled under cover in winter for less favoured areas.

Whatever its botanical and taxonomic status, the name 'A. umbellatus' well describes the rounded inflorescence, each small lily-like flower borne on a green spoke to form a more or less spherical head of pale or deep blue, or less commonly white. The colour range of agapanthus is not wide: pure white, opalescent pale blues and greys and warm whites, and deeper blues through to rich ultramarine.

The plant so widely known as 'A. umbellatus' probably belongs not in *A. africanus* but in *A. praecox*, another Cape species introduced about a century later than *A. africanus* itself. Since then both deep blue and white

137

forms have been perpetuated by division, though they are also easy to
raise from seed. Despite the name *A. praecox*, which seems to imply an
early flowering season, the big spheres of trumpet-shaped flowers are
borne late, virtually into early autumn. The broad dark green leaves are
evergreen and reduced by frost to a sorry mush, but in mild gardens this
is a good perennial lasting long with very little attention. Big old clumps
cope, even, with matted grass invading their territory, though eventually
whether in the open ground or in tubs the thick, fleshy roots become
hopelessly congested and the flower heads dwindle in number.

Two subspecies are distinguished in *A. praecox*: subspecies *orientalis*, a
shorter plant, and subspecies *praecox*, very big and handsome, though the
double-flowered form is disappointing. There is also a *minimus* form of
praecox in the National Collection. Some named kinds seem to belong
here, like the Californian-raised 'Albatross', a very fine white. Forms with
variegated leaves probably belong here, too, though the elusive 'Golden
Rule', unlike the older, tender 'Aureovittatus', probably belongs with the
newer, hardier kinds to be described later in this chapter.

Nearly a century later again, *A. campanulatus* was introduced to cultivation in Britain. With fully deciduous leaves, this is a much hardier
plant with rather flatter heads of flower, paler and softer than the deep-
toned *A. praecox*. A dwarf, dark blue form, *A. campanulatus mooreanus*,
was named for Sir Frederick Moore of Glasnevin in the last quarter of the
nineteenth century, and now seems rare, though the name remains familiar; it has yet to be found for the National Collection at Torbay Hospital
in Devon. The much taller *A. campanulatus patens*, however, is represented:
the widely flared flowers create a dense but rather small head. Both have
greyish-green leaves, narrower than the evergreen kinds.

In the early years of this century *A. caulescens* and *A. inapertus* were
introduced. Both are deciduous and hardy, but otherwise very different.
The first, which is seldom seen outside botanic gardens, has very broad,
ribbed green leaves and large, open heads of blue flowers. The leaves of
A. inapertus may be green or glaucous, but it is the flower heads which
are very distinct, the narrow, tubular flowers hanging down in a little
mop-head quite unlike the usual sphere. *A. inapertus* and its variants flower
in early autumn. There is a pretty white form, light or deeper blue forms
of various heights, and the splendid, royal blue *A. inapertus pendulus*.

I have already suggested that agapanthus are easy to raise from seed.
They are also very promiscuous, as the Hon. Lewis Palmer discovered
when, in the 1950s, he sowed seed of 'all the most beautiful wild forms'
of agapanthus growing side by side in Kirstenbosch National Botanic
Gardens, Cape Town. Of the 300 seedlings he raised, every one proved
at first flowering to be a hybrid.

Turning this propensity to advantage, Mr Palmer raised large numbers of agapanthus at his home, Headbourne Worthy near Winchester, finding that they throve on his chalky soil and that a great many of his hybrids were both beautiful and hardy. The flowering season of what came to be known collectively as the Headbourne hybrids extends from midsummer to late October. The foliage varies from narrow and daffodil-like to broad straps, and from glaucous to the more usual bright green. In size there are now hybrids for every garden, from less than 18 ins to 4 ft 6 ins or more, and the full colour range is represented. The flower shape varies from wide hyacinth-like bells that look you in the face to slender hanging tubes.

Just how far the Hon. Lewis Palmer dominated the raising of hardy hybrid agapanthus was demonstrated in the 1971-7 trials at Wisley, when of seventy-two entries, sixty had been raised by Palmer.

As so often, until the National Collection holders have performed their own long-term assessment of their plants, the Wisley trials must prove our best guide to the value of different named clones. A First Class Certificate awarded after trial is a high accolade, and an Award of Merit is valuable also; the lower awards of Highly Commended and Commended are also granted after trial. Five of the seven FCC agapanthus in the trial were Palmer plants, with one from the Crown Estate Commissioners, whose ten entries had all been selected from the original Headbourne hybrids, and one from Hydon Nurseries.

No true white agapanthus gained a First Class Certificate; the nearest was 'Delft', of palest blue tone enhanced by deeper midribs, on tall stems to 4 ft 6 ins. Lesser in size are 'Anthea' in pale blue with deeper margins, and 'Luly', named for the raiser himself and a very handsome light blue. 'Cherry Holley' is a splendid, rather shorter deep blue, notable for fading cleanly without any taint of red-purple. 'Ben Hope' is also deep blue, Hydon's 'Zella Thomas' a mid-sized deep blue, and 'Sybil Hornton' pale violet blue.

With the Award of Merit cultivars the colour range widens to take in the tall, pale grey-white 'Rosemary' and exquisite 'Snowy Owl', which, like 'Sybil Hornton', remains on the search list. Several Award of Merit and Highly Commended cultivars are not yet in the National Collection either, and with so many to choose from I shall mention chiefly those award-winners that are. The light, misty blue 'African Moon' came, like so many others, to the National Collection from the Savill Gardens (Crown Estate Commissioners) where many Palmer and other cultivars are preserved. 'Loch Hope', like 'Ben Hope' already mentioned, was selected from plants growing in the Savill Gardens; the lake, like the mountain, is deep blue. 'Royal Blue', another Crown Estate plant, is aptly named; 'Molly Howick' is paler. From Jackman's Nursery came the sweet little 'Lilliput', a very deep blue not much over a foot in height.

Several aristocratic ladies' names are attached to agapanthus, and of these 'Alice Gloucester', a beautiful white, received a Highly Commended, as did creamy-white 'Victoria'. But the group bearing the names of royal establishments – 'Balmoral', 'Sandringham', 'Windsor Castle', 'Glamis Castle' and several others – must have been named since the Wisley trials, for none features in the list of entries. Other handsome kinds that may still be obtainable, but gained no award, are pale, tall 'Blue Moon' and mid-toned 'Blue Giant', this last from Bressingham whence came also dark blue, nodding 'Bressingham Blue'. 'Isis' is another Bloom plant; 'Midnight Blue' came from Slieve Donard. 'Phantom' is a tall, opalescent cultivar seeming to have much affinity with 'A. umbellatus'; it arose in the garden at Coleton Fishacre, along the coast from Torbay, where agapanthus self-sow. But 'Torbay' came to the National Collection from Dorset, its precise origins obscure. 'Underway' was bred by Norman Hadden who, as we shall see in a later chapter also introduced a kniphofia of that name.

It is time, perhaps, to consider how agapanthus may be grown to best effect in the garden. Their clear colouring looks well with the softer yellows, with apricot (of pale kniphofias or tangerine-juice, bronze-leaved *Crocosmia* 'Solfatare' perhaps) or with pink, and with grey-leaved plants or among lime-yellow foliage. The lighter blues can stand against purple foliage, such as *Cotinus coggygria* 'Royal Purple' – an especially good pairing for the blues that fade towards purple. White agapanthus combine well with claret or burgundy flowers; again, cultivars with purplish buds and pedicels would be a good choice, such as the old 'Ardernei Hybrid'. A very pretty planting in a garden near London has a long, Yorkstone path flanked by narrow beds on either side, each with a single row of roses, 'Ballerina' in pale pink on one side and her carmine counterpart 'Marjorie Fair' on the other, interplanted and surrounded by hundreds of agapanthus. If the roses had matched on both sides of the path, it would have been better still. These agapanthus were, I guess from the variation in size and colour, a seed-raised batch deriving from the Headbourne hybrids. In gardens mild enough to accommodate 'A. umbellatus', coppery-pink tea roses such as 'General Schablikine', or the delicious soft creamy-pink of 'Mme Berkeley' or, among the yellows, primrose-buff 'Anna Olivier' or lemony 'Marie van Houtte' could be substituted for the hardier shrub roses. In a quite different idiom, at both the Savill Gardens and Wisley, where also is a good collection of named agapanthus, they are grown among other monocots, plants with, usually, sword-shaped leaves, parallel-veined, such as kniphofias, daylilies and crocosmias, yuccas; and non-monocots of suitably spiky character such as the steely blue eryngiums which also assort so well in colour. Neil Lucas, whom we have met earlier, in the chapter on *Ceanothus*, sets the strap leaves of agapanthus against the broad, shining, sculptural acanthus leaf, its deep green setting the pale blue agapanthus flower heads in strong relief.

The National Collection

The National Collection of Agapanthus *is one of five held by the Devon Group of the National Council for the Conservation of Plants and Gardens. Whereas some group Collections are dispersed in the gardens of several members, Agapanthus has become largely the responsibility of Neil Lucas, who manages to combine his demanding duties as head of the grounds at Torbay Hospital, Torquay, with the care of this and the* Ceanothus *Collection. Despite a very early plea for information about, and material of,* Agapanthus *in Devon (the Group published a well-researched list of species in 1983) the great majority of the plants in the Collection have come from the Savill Gardens, about forty taxa; another twenty came from Coleton Fishacre garden and nursery, and a few from other sources in and outside Devon. The Collection was designated in September 1983, but work on it scarcely began until 1985.*

Aster

Now that so many people buy their plants from garden centres, our gardens are becoming more and more colourful in spring at the expense of the other seasons; for spring is the peak buying season, and growers and garden centre owners know that a plant in flower sells far faster than one that is not. But if spring is many people's favourite season, some of us prefer autumn, finding its chill mornings, its soft light and the colours of dying foliage not melancholy but refreshing after the dusty langour of summer. To us it comes naturally to think first of autumn; we plan for brilliant autumn colour, knowing that its ephemeral nature will ensure we never have time to tire of it. We love the flowers of September and October: not the lingering relics of summer, but those that must hurry to bud up and open before frost slays them.

It is surprising, in a season which evokes images of flame and scarlet, yellow and crimson in foliage and fruit, just how much pink and mauve there can be in the garden: pink Japanese anemones, the violet-magenta berries and rosemadder foliage of callicarpas, candy-pink *Nerine bowdenii*, the dusty pink duvets of *Sedum spectabile*, with carmine, mauve and lilac Michaelmas daisies.

Michaelmas daisies vary in height from 6 ins or so to 6 ft, and in colour from white through mauve-pink to dark purple and from pale lavender to deep violet. There are no true reds, nor any true blues; the reds lean towards purple and magenta, the blues are all shaded with pink or red – nurseryman's blue perhaps, but true blue, no. In flower size they vary greatly, too, from tiny flowers massed on the stems to daisies 3 ins across. Those with the largest flowers, such as 'Fellowship' in delicate petunia pink with semi-double flowers, or 'Marie Ballard' in powder-blue; white, cream-budded 'Blandie'; bright petunia 'Desert Song' or 'Percy Thrower', violet with a silver sheen: these produce their largest flowers if divided each year, each division limited to a single stem. They are less weatherproof than the kinds with smaller flowers massed on dense and much-branched stems: 'Chequers' is a superb deep violet with golden centres, 'Winston Churchill' is described by Miss Allen – who owns one of the National Collections of Michaelmas daisies – as 'glowing beetroot red'; 'Crimson Brocade' is less red than its name implies, and most of these so-called reds are of bushy habit. A great many of these 'reds' derive from 'Red Rover', a deep rose-crimson, bred by Edwin Beckett, gardener to the Hon. Vicary Gibbs at Aldenham, where there was a great collection of *Aster* species. Beckett raised no fewer than thirty-seven award-winning Michaelmas daisies, including 'Pink Nymph'. 'Alderman Vokes', not I think a Beckett cultivar, has small orchid-pink flowers well spaced, an airy and elegant plant.

Michaelmas daisies were conventionally grown in borders devoted entirely to a range of the large-flowered kinds interspersed perhaps with cultivars of *A. cordifolius* and *A. ericoides* for their light, feathery effect. Their late season means that they can also follow early-flowering herbaceous plants such as lupins or delphiniums, or mingle with daylilies. In more mixed plantings, the bluer Michaelmas daisies can be contrasted with yellow flowers, dwarf *Solidago* 'Cloth of Gold' or the lemony-primrose 'Lemore', or black-eyed *Rudbeckia* 'Goldsturm'. Softer contrasts are made with *Chrysanthemum rubellum* cultivars: deep lilac 'Sarah Ballard' with orange 'Paul Boissier', or 'Marie Ballard' with the gentle apricot 'Mary Stoker'.

For deep, strong colour to contrast with paler shades, try 'My Smokey' in royal purple, large-flowered 'Thundercloud' in deep doge purple, or 'Percy Thrower'. For palest tones, lightening a colour group or making clouds of gentle colour among silvery and grey foliage, you could choose from 'Lassie' in pale phlox pink, or the similar-toned 'Colin Bailey'. There are many paler lavender-blues: one of the most famous of all Michaelmas daisies is 'Climax', a big six-footer with both vigour and elegance, producing great pyramids of clear porcelain-blue single flowers. Mrs Thornely's 'Blue Gown' is similar but flowers two weeks later. It was from the daisy-filled garden of Mrs Thornely, in Devizes, that Miss Allen and her companion Miss Huish first acquired, during the Hitler war, the plants that stimulated their interest in Michaelmas daisies and formed the basis of a collection that now includes over 400 different varieties. Miss Allen is justly proud of her own 'Belmont Blue', with semi-double incurved violet-blue flowers well spaced on heather-like growth.

Of the many raisers of Michaelmas daisies represented by their plants at Belmont House, where Miss Allen has her Collection, and at Temple Newsam Park in Leeds, where another of the National Collections is grown, the best known must be Ernest Ballard. Many of his plants are given family names; 'Marie Ballard' and 'Sarah Ballard' we have already met, and there are several others. He also used 'Colwall', the name of his village, as in 'Pride of Colwall', a fine double violet-purple with silvery sheen. It was Ballard, too, who bred the ecclesiastical range: this included 'The Archbishop' in deep amethyst violet, 'The Sexton', an early, single-flowered violet-blue, and dusky plum-purple 'The Bishop'.

To Ballard's Old Court Nurseries, at Colwall, in 1948, came Percy Picton, to work as nursery manager. To digress for a moment, his previous postion had been that of head gardener at Hagley Court, in Hereford, where he had worked since the early thirties. Before that he had worked under Ernest Markham at Gravetye Manor, home of William Robinson, and the place where many of that irascible writer-gardener's controversial and original ideas were put into effect. So we find a connection with clematis as well as with asters. But to return to Michaelmas daisies, in those days the nursery at Colwall was entirely geared to the production and sale of asters; each year the best seedlings would be selected from acres of plants by Percy Picton, Ernest Ballard himself and the young Paul Picton, who now owns the nursery and holds there another National Collection of Michaelmas daisies. But this Collection has had to be recreated, for at one time stocks were greatly reduced, and cultivars from before 1940 are hard to find. Even the famous ecclesiastical range seems to have vanished.

As well as all these fairly tall Michaelmas daisies, there are several dwarf hybrids deriving partly from *A. dumosus*, and ranging in height from 6-18 ins; ideal plants, therefore, for the front of the border. This dwarf race was developed by H. Victor Vokes for use by the War Graves Commission. Ernest Ballard was more interested in pure *A. novi-belgii* dwarfs, and raised several, including white 'Snowsprite'. Others, some with *A. dumosus* blood, from other raisers include light lavender-blue 'Audrey' and 'Lady in Blue', 'Lilac Time' and 'Court Herald'. Lavender-pink and mauve-pink dwarfs include 'Little Pink Beauty' and 'Margaret Rose', 'Pink Lace' and 'Nancy'. 'Dandy' and 'Starlight' are purple-red. Some smaller Michaelmas daisies, too, are proving hard to find. At Colwall, Paul Picton has been purchasing 'Little Boy Blue' for some years, and now has a large pile of labels to testify to his endeavours: but not one of the plants was rightly named, and 'Little Boy Blue' is still on the search list.

All these, *dumosus* blood or no, are derivatives of *Aster novi-belgii*, which has its origins in the eastern United States. Also from North America is *A. novae-angliae*. A tough plant, this lacks charm; many of the varieties are graceless, and their colouring is often unappealing, an undefined pinkish mauve. 'Harrington's Pink', however, is a good thing for its colour at least, about the only clear pink aster there is. It flowers in September and is marred only by its poor habit. Although given a name that implies it is a garden form, it was apparently found as a wildling in Canada. A much newer *novae-angliae* which has made quite an impact in a short time is 'Alma Potschke', in fierce cerise-magenta. A good new white is 'Herbstschnee' or 'Autumn Snow'.

Miss Allen's, Old Court Nurseries' and the Leeds Michaelmas daisies are not the only National Collections of asters. At Upton, a National Trust property near Banbury, there is a National Collection, not this time of *novi-belgii* and *novae-angliae* Michaelmas daisies, but of the small-flowered kinds derived from *A. cordifolius* and *A. ericoides*, with various other species, and of *A. amellus* cultivars. The small-flowered cultivars, and the cultivars and hybrids of *A. amellus* and *A. thomsonii*, are good garden plants, not suffering from mildew, needing little or no staking and generally of good constitution. Yet they have been curiously neglected lately. We can hardly afford, these days, the luxury of a Jekyllian border, cloudy with Michaelmas daisies and much grey and silver foliage, pale primrose snapdragons and white dahlias, to make its impact in September only and remain in decent obscurity before and after its season. The small-flowered asters, many of which have neat, unobtrusive foliage in place of the often coarse, mildew-stained leaves of the *novi-belgii* kinds, fit more comfortably into the mixed plantings which suit our smaller modern gardens, where every border must look as attractive as possible for as long as possible. At Upton, colour earlier in the year comes from old varieties of phlox and delphiniums, with clumps of pampas grass at intervals to give pattern in a long border, and Hybrid Musk roses giving bulk and scent at the back; bergenias and old beared irises furnish the front of the border, and the asters carry on the season well into autumn. Coinciding with the small-flowered asters in season are Japanese anemones in white, pink and subdued magenta. Late-flowering kniphofias in cream, yellow and pale apricot, and later as we have seen the forms of *Chrysanthemum rubellum* and Korean chrysanthemums, can be used to introduce a different range of colours.

The forms of *Aster ericoides* and *A. cordifolius* are fairly similar in floral effect, with clouds of small, starry flowers in branching sprays on twiggy stems. *A. cordifolius* 'Silver Spray', with arching sprays of glacial palest lilac flowers, is typical, at about 4 ft in height with a September to October season. 'Ideal' is shorter and a little earlier, pale blue in colour. Another with elegant arching sprays is 'Photograph', of similar cool milky blue colouring. 'Aldebaran' is soft violet-blue, enlivened by dark centres. Then there are 'Sweet Lavender' with arching sprays, and the upright, but still graceful, 'Elegans', in soft lilac. Less typical are the *A. cordi-belgii* cultivars (*A. cordifolius* × *A. novi-belgii*) of which 'Little Carlow' is the best surviving cultivar, a compact plant with massed flowers in violet-blue. The charming warm, deep pink 'Little Dorrit' is similar in habit; it appeared at Belmont

House and was recognised as a good new kind by Miss Allen's quick eye. These have more vigorous growth than the pure *cordifolius* types, more upright sprays with large flowers, and lack the typical heart-shaped foliage which gives the species its name.

An aster which is by no means as widely grown as it deserves is *A. lateriflorus* 'Horizontalis'. Here is a plant with some of the poise of a shrub, on account of its horizontal branching which gives it a structure lacking in most asters. The tiny leaves turn to coppery purple in autumn, setting off little pale lilac flowers dominated by their rosemadder stamens. The effect is pleasantly muted. At the famous garden at Great Dixter, home of the Lloyd family, *Aster lateriflorus* 'Horizontalis' is used as a low hedge, flanking the two sides of a paved path; at its feet, excluding all weeds and running forward onto the flags, is *Polygonum vaccinifolium*, neat of leaf, its slender pink spikes coinciding in season with the aster.

The varieties of *Aster ericoides* all have similar tiny leaves – *ericoides* means like *Erica*, the heaths – and twiggy slender stems needing no staking. They will stand drier conditions than most asters, which on the whole need fertile soil that does not dry out. They are all charming, and they add to the colour range, for 'Brimstone' has creamy-yellow flowers. 'Golden Spray' sounds even yellower, but is actually white, with prominent yellow centres. Also white are 'White Heather' and 'Delight', this one also golden-eyed. In blue-lavender there are 'Blue Star' and 'Star Shower', while 'Pink Cloud' is pale lilac-pink and 'Ringdove' rosy-lavender. 'Esther' has larger flowers than most, in light mauve-pink, over pale green foliage. There is also a tall, lilac-flowered *A. ericoides* cultivar called 'Hon. Vicary Gibbs' and another in lavender named 'Hon. Edith Gibbs' – interestingly, the Gibbs family of Aldenham own the estate in which Belmont House, Miss Allen's home, stands. The Gibbs's gardener, Edwin Beckett, who as we have seen raised 'Red Rover', is commemorated in *A. paniculatus* 'Edwin Beckett', a tall plant with off-white daisies. *A. ericoides* 'Vimmer's Delight' is an unusual little cultivar, half the height at 18 ins of most, with stiff spikes of white flowers, rather resembling *A. tradescantii*, but that Tradescant's daisy is 4 ft in height. This last was the first Michaelmas daisy to be introduced, by John Tradescant, gardener to Charles I, in 1633. It appears, in fact, that *A. tradescantii* of gardens may actually be a form or hybrid of *A. paniculatus*, but I think we will all wish to go on using the name that commemorates the Tradescants. A small-flowered aster of which I am very fond is *A. divaricatus* (*A. corymbosus*) with sprays of white stars on slender black stems; naturally of flopping habit, it should not be staked into unnatural rigidity, but allowed to fall forward. Miss Jekyll planted it behind bergenias, so that it could loll onto those big leathery leaves.

In some gardens the varieties of *Aster amellus* may be a little tricky – Miss Allen finds them 'beautiful but temperamental' – but elsewhere they are first-rate garden plants. It is hard to imagine why asters such as *A. amellus* 'Framfieldii' and 'Twilight' are not more often planted; they are among the most rewarding of late-flowering border plants. Though 'Twilight' looks like a small-flowered *A. amellus* cultivar, it has a running root growth with masses of shoots covering quite a wide area. All the *amellus* cultivars have thick, woody clumps with new growth formed at the base of the old flowering stems. 'Twilight' might well, Paul Picton believes, be another *Aster* species crossed with *amellus*. The wild *A. amellus* is a European plant (also found in Asia Minor), short and tough, with coarse leaves and clusters of large flowers on stems that may stand up or flop. Near to the wildling in character is 'Ultramarine'. Later selections are larger in flower and less refined, though more colourful. Many famous names are still absent from the National Collections: not only violet-blue 'Bessie Chapman', but rose-pink 'Mrs Ralph Woods' and pinkish-violet 'Heinrich Siebert' too. But many have been found. Among the pinks are 'Nocturne', 'Sonia' and 'Lady Hindlip'. 'Rudolf Goethe' is pale mauve, 'Rotfeuer' deep reddish-violet; violet-blues include 'Moerheim Gem' and 'Violet Queen'. From the western Himalayas, *Aster thomsonii* is represented in gardens by its form 'Nanus', endlessly in bloom with starry, lilac-blue flowers. Like the *A. amellus* varieties it should be planted in spring, never in autumn. A marriage between *A. amellus* and *A. thomsonii* resulted in the wonderful *A.* × *frikartii*, a plant of great refinement and elegance, with upright, branching sprays of large, clear lavender-blue flowers appearing from July to October. The three seedlings raised by Frikart in Switzerland in 1920 were named for three famous peaks: 'Eiger', 'Jungfrau', and 'Mönch'. Another is 'Wunder von Stäfa', a later and less perfect seedling, less blue than the others. A newer hybrid, dwarfer than *A.* × *frikartii*, is 'Flora's Delight', with greyish leaves and lilac flowers marred only by overlarge yellow centres. Give all these a sunny position and good soil. Their soft clear colouring blends beautifully with the gentler pinks and mauves, with greyish foliage too. Try them with *Sedum spectabile* and some *Anaphalis* perhaps, one of the few greys to appreciate richer living. Paul Picton combines *A.* × *frikartii* 'Mönch' with Japanese anemone 'Profusion' and the huge, wine-purple sprays of *Buddleia* 'Dartmoor'.

Another small flowered aster is *A. acris*, a lovely thing for distant effect with domed clouds of clear lavender-blue. The type has a tendency to fall apart; choose, therefore, the dwarf form 'Nanus' if you are allergic to staking. Close to, the flowers of either are seen to be poorly shaped, but with its long season of flower it is worth growing none the less. Worthier even than this is *A. spectabilis*, a violet-tinted, autumn-flowering daisy somewhat like a good *A. amellus* in effect; a valuable garden plant that deserves to be better known.

The National Collections

The National Collections of Aster are at Belmont House, Tyntesfield, Wraxall, Bristol (Miss I. Allen and Miss J. Huish); at Temple Newsam Park, Leeds (Leeds City Council); at Old Court Nurseries, Colwall, Malvern (Paul Picton); and at Upton House, Edgehill, Warwickshire (The National Trust).

The Collections at Belmont House and Temple Newsam Park are largely confined to Michaelmas daisies. Miss Allen's Collection at Belmont House was designated as a National Collection in March 1983, when it already consisted of over 400 varieties. These had been assembled by the two ladies during and since the Hitler war. The ladies moved from Bristol to Devizes in 1941 to escape the air raids, and frequently visited the flowering garden of Mrs Thornely in Devizes, a mass of daisies of all kinds defying the utilitarian war-time cabbages and potatoes that filled most other gardens. Each year of the war Miss Allen bought a few varieties of Michaelmas daisy. The ladies made a hazardous war-time journey to Colwall near Malvern, to see Ernest Ballard's collection. Mr Ballard grew many hundreds of daisies each year and selected only the very best for naming; the next best were sold unnamed and great bunches were cut to sell as cut flowers. Many of the Ballard daisies still grow at Belmont House.

At Old Court Nurseries, Colwall, are also grown several of the Ballard-raised Aster novi-belgii cultivars and many others from different raisers, with A. novae-angliae and A. amellus cultivars, and a good range of species and small-flowered cultivars of Aster as well. In the days when the nursery specialised in asters, the two acres of the home nursery were devoted to displaying the plants offered for sale; for in those days plants were sold from the open ground. Paul Picton recalls, as a young man working in the nursery, the many weeks spent each spring doubled over setting out line after line of young stock.

During the 1960s, when the trend towards shrubs began to dominate, herbaceous plants became so unfashionable that all but about forty cultivars of aster had to be discarded at Colwall. Paul Picton freely acknowledges the debt he, and many others, owe to Miss Allen who kept so many of the old cultivars going when nurseries were obliged by commercial pressures to discard them. When container-growing, and as a result summer sales of plants in flower, became the usual practice, Old Court Nurseries adapted once again and after a break of fifteen years the Pictons felt able to start rebuilding the Aster collection, with help from Miss Allen, Mr Ronald Watts (another Michaelmas daisy raiser) and assiduous searching in nurseries and garden centres country-wide. The National Collection at Old Court Nurseries was designated in July 1987.

The Michaelmas daisies at Temple Newsam Park, Leeds, grow in raised beds in a new garden constructed to display them. The National Collection was designated in March 1986.

The Collection at Upton House is of the small-flowered asters such as the cultivars of A. cordifolius and A. ericoides, with various other species, and of

A. amellus. *They were chosen for their ease of cultivation, and for their value in prolonging the season of display in a publicly-visited garden. The Upton asters were designated as a National Collection in November 1985.*

Bellis perennis

IT IS hard to realise, as we walk around a late twentieth-century garden, just how many of our common garden plants are introductions of this century or of the latter part of the last. The Tudors and Stuarts knew few of the flowers we now take for granted, and in consequence any unusual forms of native flowers were lovingly cultivated. Primroses, violets and daisies in various colours, or with double flowers, could be tucked in any small corner and must have been cherished in many cottage gardens, perhaps as long ago as mediaeval times.

Bellis perennis is the botanical name of our native daisy, the same little plant that infests our lawns – or decorates them, if you take a more relaxed view of mown grass. This modest flower has given us many garden forms with flowers of pink or red, as well as white, single or double or quilled, or with variegated leaves. We have no record of their first introduction to our gardens, but they were certainly known in the gardens of Europe by the sixteenth century. We learn from the German herbalist Leonard Fuchs (1501-60) that the garden daisy (which he called *Bellis minor hortensis*, distinguishing it in this way from the wild daisy, his *B. minor sylvestris*) was planted 'in almost all gardens' of his southern Germany, and that 'there are many kinds, some double, others single, some white, some blood red'. Fuchs's Herbal, which was issued with the woodcuts already coloured, illustrates a semi-double daisy with deep red ray florets and a small yellow disc, the whole flower head about the same size as the wild daisy.

By this time, too, the Hen and Chickens daisy, *Bellis perennis prolifera*, was grown in gardens. Dodoens, a Flemish herbalist half a generation younger than Fuchs, wrote of these little daisies (the translation is by Henry Lyte, 1578, made from a French translation of Dodoens's native 'Doutche or Almaigre tongue'): 'the small leaves [ray florets] are so thick sette or so double that a man shall perceive very littell of the yellow in the middell, or none at all. And these floures are sometimes white, sometimes very redde, sometimes speckled or partie coloured of white and redde. There grow also sometimes about the compasse of the sayde littell floures, many more as it were small floures growing upon small stemmes out of the knops or cuppes of the sayde floures'. This is, without doubt, the Hen and Chickens daisy.

The much-quoted Gerard, whose Herball dates from 1597, though he referred to 'diverse of the small Daisies differing in colour of the flowers, and in the doubleness thereof', described only two, a double white and a double red. A generation later John Parkinson (*Paradisus*, 1629) describes many more: a single daisy with red rays and a yellow disc, and doubles of various colours. 'Some are wholly of a pure white, some have a little red, either dispersed upon the white leaves [ray florets], or on the edges, and sometimes on the backes of the leaves; some againe seem to be of a whitish red, or more red than white, when as indeede they are white leaves dispersed among the red; others are of a deepe or dark red colour, and some are speckled or striped with white and red through the whole flower: and some the leaves will be red on the upperside, and white underneath.' 'Parkinson's White' is an attractive little daisy so double as to form a dome-shaped head.

None of these variants had flowers bigger than the wild daisy, but they were colourful and easy to grow. At first they must have been passed from garden to garden as they were lifted and divided each year or so. During the seventeenth century nurseries began to appear around London to meet the demand for plants, and the little daisies' popularity must have increased still more as they became more widely available to the population of the fast-expanding city. Where cottagers might have used them to edge a path, London dwellers often used them in window boxes. It is piquant to imagine the balconies and window ledges of London's elegant Georgian squares, now self-consciously decked with helichrysum and geraniums, or with safe, unchanging evergreens, trimly wearing rows of little pink, crimson or white daisies. No doubt they would need frequent replacing, for the conditions in a window box would not be ideal for them. The cool root run of the cottage garden path would suit them better.

The Victorians used daisies to clothe the ground beneath rose bushes. 'Aucubaefolia', with yellow-splashed leaves, was a favourite in this role, and the rich living of a well-fed rose bed would have been much to the daisies' liking. Double daisies, too, had their place in spring bedding, with wallflowers, tulips and hyacinths, lasting until early summer before running to seed.

By the last quarter of the nineteenth century the forms of *Bellis perennis* were apparently no longer so popular, overshadowed by the many exotics, both hardy and half hardy, that were now available to the public. Like so many other plants – the double primroses are another group to be met in this book – they were kept going, no doubt, in cottage gardens and by those who consciously favoured the quaint and old-fashioned or who simply preferred well-loved favourites to modern fads. Yet even as some authors were lamenting the changing fashion that led many people to scorn the double, speckled and striped daisies, commercial growers were breeding *Bellis perennis* for increased size of flower head, achieving – according to Shirley Hibberd, who wrote between 1879 and 1887 – flowers twice or thrice the size of the original. 'The form is that of a hemisphaerical cushion ... white, rose, red, crimson or purple.' Most of these new kinds came from Europe, where no less a nurseryman than Louis van Houtte (1810-76), who grew so many flamboyant tropical plants, was also very fond of the little daisy, listed up to twenty different kinds in his catalogue, and encouraged the raising of new cultivars.

Still others were listed in nursery catalogues of the early years of the present century, until the outbreak of the Hitler war. Among them are names still familiar: 'Dresden China' probably dates from the early twentieth century, but 'Rob Roy' is much older (1818?). Both are among the kinds regarded as permanent plants, and still grown today. In our time it is the Pomponette series in white, rose and red, that seem to lead the field among seed strains. But the tiny pink 'Dresden China' and crimson 'Rob Roy', 'Alice' (the 'pink Rob Roy') and the white counterpart of 'Dresden China' called 'The Pearl' are just a few among the many names listed by Jean Andrews, who holds the National Collection in her cottage garden in Warwickshire. Here, among widely spaced paving stones to give their roots the cool run they thrive on, she grows nearly a score of varieties, these among them. Here too is Dodoens's little Hen and Chickens daisy, kept going as a curiosity for 400 years or more; and almost as ancient, 'Parkinson's White'. 'Staffordshire Pink' is larger than most of these, and more modern kinds include not only the Pomponettes, but also those, such as 'Goliath' or 'Monstrosa', which show by their names how far they have been developed from the single little wildling.

There remain many historically important daisies on the 'wanted' list. Among them is the Victorian 'Aucubaefolia' with double white and crimson flowers over yellow blotched, yellow veined leaves. 'Bon Accord' (a name we meet also among the double primroses) is a sturdy plant with fleshy foliage and deep rose pink flowers; 'Etna' has quilled, brilliant crimson petals. There are several whites on the list, larger than 'The Pearl': long-stemmed 'Snowball', the nineteenth-century 'Snowflake', 'The Bride' (who should have a pink and rose 'Bridegroom'), large-flowered 'Venus' and others. 'Victoria' is very large as daisies go, in red and white stripes. Then there are the other colour variants from the nineteenth century, double purple 'Eliza' and double lilac 'Madame Crousse' (again the link with double primroses is seen in a near duplication of names). 'Helichrysiflora' is said to have small pink everlasting-like flowers, and 'The Crown', again dating from the nineteenth century, was 'mottled'. Sadly, they seem to be lost to cultivation, though Jean Andrews hopes still that they may be growing in a garden somewhere. Certainly she is reasonably confident that 'Aucubaefolia' is still to be found.

Seed strains are many, for the daisy was developed by seedsmen all over Europe, and Jean has raised plants from seed sent from Germany, Hungary, France and Italy, 'ranging in size from 4 ins to over 12 ins in height, in single, semi-double, double and quilled, in white, pink, salmon, cerise and red'.

Grown as part of the permanent planting of a garden, the daisies need moist, rich soil. They are intolerant of summer drought, and quickly shrivel, succumbing to aphis and slugs. On the other hand, if it is too wet, the little plants have evolved a survival mechanism; the leaves lift vertically to protect the crown, just as the petals close in dull or wet weather to protect the pollen. Provided their roots are cool and well-nourished, however, daisies flower best with their faces to the sun. They should be dead-headed, and divided when they become congested. Margery Fish, who in the sixties did so much through her writing and the example of her idiosyncratic garden to stimulate interest in a host of cottage garden plants, wrote in *An All the Year Garden*: 'whenever there is a blank space near the front of the border I stud the ground with divisions of *Bellis* "Rob Roy", and the exquisite little "Dresden China" daisy and its white counterpart "The Pearl".' It is clear that, just as she did her double primroses, she loved to divide these little plants and give them fresh ground, and they thrived on it. Jean Andrews writes 'an occasional spray with pyrethrum will keep the aphis at bay, and a sharp eye for slugs and snails, which also like moist, damp paths, is all that is necessary.... The daisies are underplanted with tiny bulbs, such as snowdrops, chionodoxa, *Iris reticulata*, species crocus, *Anemone blanda*, *Allium coeruleum* and the autumn crocus. This gives a flowering path of many colours for most of the year, for very little cost and upkeep.'

The National Collection

The National Collection of Bellis perennis *cvs.*, the little daisies, is grown in the cottage garden of Mrs Jean Andrews, Shrewley Gardens, Crossways, Shrewley, near Warwick. Jean has always been interested in the older plants, the kinds that would have been grown formerly in the garden of her cottage: useful herbs, and old selected forms of familiar plants. Almost from the moment she began caring for her present garden she had an interest in the daisies, especially the Hen and Chickens daisy which she read about in Margery Fish's book on Cottage Garden Flowers but was unable to find for sale anywhere. It was not until the then General Secretary of the NCCPG gave her the address of a grower in Scotland that she was able to acquire a plant.

Jean writes 'that first purchase paved the way for many more, 'Parkinson's Double White', mentioned in his book Paradisus of 1629, 'Rob Roy' 1918 and 'Alice', his pink counterpart, 'Dresden China', the miniature pink Bellis and 'Robert' her white companion, and 'Staffordshire Pink', the showy larger one'. She goes on to comment on 'the fascinating fact that . . . if Rembert Dodoens who was born in 1517 or John Parkinson in 1567 were to walk around my collection, they would instantly recognise them. Their ancestors have been grown by generations of cottage gardeners and townsfolk, and they are part of our heritage.'

The National Collection of Bellis perennis *cvs.* was designated in March 1985.

Campanula

THE GENUS *Campanula* is large and variable. There are about 300 species, and as most of these come from the north temperate zone, they are not too difficult to grow in this country, at least as regards their climatic needs. There are few truly tender species, especially if we exclude *C. vidalii*, from the Azores: this, in any case, is now residing in another genus, *Azorina*. The few campanulas which come nearest to being tender, like *C. isophylla* and *C. fragilis*, together with the Greek species which often come from near sea level, can take lower temperatures if kept in fairly dry compost and very dry atmosphere under glass, preferably in a conservatory which is near to frost-free. *C. rigidipila*, which comes from the mountains of Ethiopia, and sounds as if it could be tender, is in fact as tough as any, and can be grown outside without damage even when the ground freezes hard to some depth. This is the experience, at least, of Peter Lewis, whose garden in Cambridgeshire where the National Collection is housed is not one of the warmest in Britain.

Although so variable, campanulas fall loosely into two groups, from the gardener's point of view at least: the small species suitable for growing in rock gardens, troughs, or pans in the alpine house; and the larger species and cultivars that are suited to the border or even the wild garden. It is with these that I want to begin. Many are old cottage garden favourites. Among these, and perhaps the best known, is *Campanula persicifolia* the peach leaved bellflower, and its many forms – though probably fewer forms than names. The type is a clear lavender-blue, growing to about 3 ft, with wide open saucers facing you on wiry stems. 'Telham Beauty' is a fine large-flowered kind of this colouring, beautiful with clear pink old roses or with soft yellow. *Campanula persicifolia* also comes in white, charming in a Jekyllian mixture of sweet Cecily, ferns, white foxgloves and white aquilegias. Both blue and white forms come in double and cup-and-saucer variants: 'Dawn Patrol' is a double blue and 'Moerheimii' a double white. I have had unidentified double whites of different styles, one a neat, formal, fully double rosette, the other more ragged and less full. Whether one was 'Fleur de Neige' I know not. The cup-and-saucer types are charming and very cottagey, resembling cup-and-saucer Canterbury Bells – which of course are also campanulas, *C. medium*.

All the forms of *Campanula persicifolia* are easy and long-lived perennials, so long as they are given a little attention every spring, thinning out and replanting in fresh soil. Many campanulas, like this one, are travellers, exhausting the soil in which they grow and moving on to seek fresh nutrients. *C. persicifolia* does not spread invasively; rather does it travel too slowly for its own needs, hence the help it requires from the gardener. In a light soil other species may become quite a nuisance. *C. glomerata* is one – in any case rather a coarse thing, though certainly an eyeful of rich violet purple colour in summer if you choose the selected 'Superba', or deep rich purple var. *davurica*. Dwarfer forms are 'Joan Elliott' and 'Purple Pixie', and these also extend the season early and late. *C. glomerata acaulis* is neat for the front of the border, but even this Peter Lewis plants in a concealed pot in the border to keep it in bounds.

The territorial ambitions of *C. glomerata* are modest, however, compared with those of the beautiful weed *C. rapunculoides*, which not only runs, but also seeds without restraint. You may find yourself unwittingly inviting it into your garden if you acquire a plant labelled *C. bononiensis*: for this name has sometimes become attached to the wicked weed. The true *C. bononiensis* is an elegant and well-behaved plant with slender greyish leaves and tall stems of starry lilac bells. More like *C. rapunculoides* in aspect, though not in behaviour, is another whose name is sometimes taken in vain: *C. trachelium*, the nettle-leaved bellflower or Coventry Bells. Wide-open bells may be lilac or white – 'Bernice' is a double lilac – and there is also a double white form. They increase all too slowly and are charming cottage-garden plants.

Much taller than these is *Campanula lactiflora*, a tough and hardy border plant that will also cope with grass, long lasting in flower and suitable for picking for vases. The type is a pale lilac, and there is also a white and at least two deep violet-blue selections, 'Superba' and 'Prichard's Var.'. Perhaps the most interesting is 'Loddon Anna', a soft pink. These tall forms, like *C. persicifolia*, assort well with generously-proportioned old-fashioned roses, with glaucous foliage of rue or the tall, fluffy pale greeny-yellow flowered *Thalictrum speciosissimum* (*I. glaucum*), the lime-green froth and pleated fans of *Alchemilla mollis*, pale blue *Clematis heracleifolia*, herbaceous in character and with heads of hyacinth-like flowers, and white perennial pea scrambling through. The pale lilac form combines well in colour with the soft primrose daisies of *Anthemis tinctoria* 'E. C. Buxton'. 'Pouffe' is an aptly-named dwarf form of *C. lactiflora* originating from

Bloom's nursery a few years ago; as the name implies, this is a tidy dwarf plant, in colour pale blue and very free-flowering.

C. latifolia is another border favourite, a strong-standing bold plant which is soundly perennial and which sets abundant seed, needing careful gathering before it has its own way. The broad basal leaves are a good feature of this species; they diminish slightly up the stem, which bears long tubular bells of large size and good colour, violet-blue. In an informal, or 'wild', setting where the plants can be allowed to seed freely, as at Hidcote, you could add to this bellflower the meadow cranesbill, *Geranium pratense*, and sweet Cicely with its beautiful, aromatic, fern-like foliage. 'Brantwood' and var. *macrantha* are difficult to distinguish; both are of a deeper purple than the type. 'Gloaming' is a pale lavender-pink, and there is a good white form too, which could join the self-seeding group, or in a more controlled setting be placed in bold contrast with early, bright orange lilies.

Yet another campanula suitable for the border is named in a confusingly similar way to the preceding two. *C. latiloba* is known for the beauty of its winter-persistent rosettes of leaves – a rarity among campanulas – decorative at a time when foliage is appreciated. Erect stems in summer are covered almost throughout their height by wide cups reminiscent of the much smaller *C. carpatica* in its best forms, of lavender blue. 'Highcliffe' is one of the best forms of *C. latiloba*; a sport which originated at Hidcote is 'Hidcote Amethyst', a fine lilac-pink, good with the dusky purple-leaved *Weigela florida* 'Foleis Purpureis' and pineapple-scented, purple-eyed *Philadelphus* 'Belle Etoile'. 'Percy Piper' has a deeper corolla with a pale eye, and also throws side stems from the rosette more than does the type; this may be exploited by cutting back the main stems, thus keeping the plant in flower for a long period.

Other border campanulas are *CC. punctata, takesimana, sarmatica* and *alliariifolia*. These may not be closely related botanically, but for the gardener they have in common a low rosette throwing up stems of large pale bells, mostly one-sided. *C. punctata* is at its best when grown where you may look up into the bell to see more clearly the rich pink and red markings within the creamy, or faintly mauve, bells. The more recently introduced *C. takesimana* is even paler in flower, and extremely attractive. It has been on the NCCPG 'Pink List' of rare plants urgently needing wider distribution, but is so appealing, and so easy of cultivation, that it is spreading around freely. Indeed, in light soils it should be watched for its own invasive tendencies. In the hard clay of Peter Lewis's garden it is well disciplined. If too enthusiastic it is easy to lift and thus restrain the runners, which can be passed on to other keen gardeners to ensure its wider distribution. It is native of Korea and the nearby islands, and is very hardy.

C. sarmatica, from the Caucasus – home of many campanulas – has a basal tuft of hairy leaves; the foot high grey stems bear large lavender-blue bells which are also hairy. A clump of these, set toward the front of a sunny border, forms an attractive patch; it does not do so well in more shady spots, though many of the larger campanulas and some of the lower spreaders are quite shade-tolerant. Certainly *C. alliariifolia* is pretty shade-tolerant, and in a dark corner its nodding, creamy-pale bells show up well over apple-green foliage.

Of the same persuasion as these species are two lovely hybrids with large tubular bells; *C. punctata* may enter into their parentage. 'Burghaltii' has flowers of palest lavender-grey, hardly a colour at all, more a hint of pearl combining to perfection with blue-grey hostas, with silvery foliage perhaps on the sunny side, and the whole thing forming a ground planting around an ethereally pale rose such as 'Penelope' in coral fading to blush-white, or the pale clear pink of 'New Dawn'. *Campanula* 'Van Houttei' has similar long, tubular, down-pointing bells in a deeper shade of greyish violet.

Campanula pyramidalis is the giant of the race, usually treated as a biennial and grown in pots; this because the flowers are not long-lived once they have been pollinated by bees, and so last longer in a conservatory or even indoors. It is a perennial, if not long-lived, and may be grown in the border, but will not give of its best. There are blue and white cultivars of the chimney bellflower, and also a variegated form. Many of the border campanulas can be grown, as the chimney bellflower habitually is, in pots of a suitable size, and used on patios or in conservatories, or even taken into the house when flowering; they will need feeding, and should be kept in their pots for one season only, then divided and set in the open ground for a year to recuperate and recover strength.

Blurring the edges of my arbitrary division between border and rock campanulas come two impossibly-named bellflowers, *C. portenschlagiana* and *C. poscharskyana*. They are widely offered and, in their place, excellent garden plants; but too vigorous for the ordinary rock garden, at least in their typical forms. *C. portenschlagiana* is quite vigorous enough to form good ground-cover for a group of old roses, holding its own even against that other generous weed-smotherer, *Alchemilla mollis*, against the lime-green froth of which its starry lavender-blue flowers look very well. 'Bavarica' ('Major') has slightly larger flowers. It is also a fine wall plant, as suggested by its former name *C. muralis*. Even more vigorous, forming large mats of entangled stems with masses of starry lavender-blue flowers in summer, is *C. poscharskyana*, thriving almost too well even in poor soil or, like the preceding species, on a wall. 'Stella' is a selection that may be less territorial.

Of medium-sized campanulas, suitable for the front of a border or perhaps for the lower areas of a large rock garden, Peter Lewis likes *C. raddeana* from the Caucasus; it is not grown as often as it deserves. About 1 ft in height, it has characteristic rosettes of cordate leaves, markedly veined, with uparching and branched stems ending in a mass of deep violet-blue bells in which the bright orange pollen contrasts sharply. *C. betulaefolia* is so named for the resemblance of its foliage to birch leaves, very unlike that of most campanulas. The stems are thickly borne, and branched, holding upright bells which are reddish outside when in bud; the flower is white or sometimes pale pink. It is usually short-lived except in a scree or alpine house.

Campanula carpatica also falls between two stools, and gets unjustifiably little mention in literature about alpines. It is extremely variable in itself, and is responsible for many hybrids. It can be coarse and straggling, especially when grown too richly, but in some of the more compact forms of delicate colouring it is a charming plant. There are singles and doubles of every shade of campanula blue and white, and is so variable that it is great fun to grow from seed. 'Isobel', an old selection, is a fine coloured one which has kept its popularity – William Robinson thought well of it – and also its vigour, a characteristic of most *C. carpatica* forms though fortunately they are not rampant, merely willing. 'Chewton Joy' is china blue, and flowers later than most. 'White Star' is an old, and good, white form, while 'Blue Moonlight', somewhere between white and blue, is well-named. *C.* × 'Haylodgensis' is really a double *carpatica*; it has the palish foliage which betrays a little lack of vigour, but treated well it can be attractive when well-covered with its flat-faced lavender-blue rosette flowers. Its sport, the white double 'Warleyensis', is much more robust. Both tend to weaken themselves by a too-long flowering period, and the advice given by H. Clifford Crook (*Campanulas*, pub. Country Life, 1951), to give them a northerly exposure, or at any rate a cool one, to ensure winter dormancy, certainly seems to produce the best results. *C. turbinata* is a compact form of *C. carpatica*, some 5 ins in height.

C. cochlearifolia is the well-known and loved fairy bells, very like a miniature of our own dainty harebell – the bluebell of Scotland. 'Miss Willmott' and 'Miranda' are among the best forms; the first is silvery blue, the second silvery mauve, a little taller than the type. Others are the white, *alba*, 'Cambridge Blue', 'Oakington Blue' – an old one from Alan Bloom, of good deep colour – 'Blue Tit' and the double 'Elizabeth Oliver' in a delicate powder blue. Most of these can be invasive, and certainly extract something from the soil which makes them move on to pastures new. Nevertheless, though they can be a nuisance on the rock garden, in a sink or tub they are easily controlled, so long as the compost is reconstituted from time to time. *C. pulla* is another beautiful miniature, with large deep blue-violet bells. It is early, holds itself in flower for about a fortnight, and also likes to have its soil renewed fairly frequently. *C. × pulloides* is a *pulla × turbinata* hybrid, between the two in looks with deep blue, blowsy blooms on a taller stem than those of *pulla*.

To provide the well-drained soils that campanulas prefer, you may need, if you garden on a similar stiff clay to Peter Lewis, to make raised beds, and to use sinks, troughs and tanks, to get the best results. Many of the plants in the National Collection are grown in reject asbestos-cement watertanks, purchased from a second-hand building materials source. These, with hardcore and rubble in the lower half, topped up with a good open compost and surfaced liberally with grit, make an excellent home for campanulas, the more especially as that scourge of campanulas, the slug, seems to dislike the climb up the outside of the rough tank. Quite a lot of tufa is used, both as rock to form suitable habitats for the crevice-growers, and also as dust in the compost. This seems to suit many plants, even some lime-haters, and is especially appreciated by most bellflowers. For the few lime-haters it is a simple matter to fill such beds with gritty siliceous compost.

For the alpine house are some of the most challenging of all alpines, *CC. cenisia, raineri, morettiana, zoysii* and *alpestris*. They are all very beautiful, and *zoysii* with its clear pale narrow bells curiously crimped at the mouth is especially fascinating; all are worth the effort and care needed to keep them. The first is definitely a lime-hater, but the others prefer lime, and grow as well as anywhere in tufa crevices. They need the shelter of the alpine house in winter to save them from the damp and alternating freeze and thaw of the British winter, so alien to their native habitat.

C. formaneckiana, from Greece, is a beautiful small alpine; while it is biennial, if happy it seeds itself, saving you the bother of having to remember to sow it yearly once one has two successive generations established. It forms a handsome rosette, itself a fine decoration over winter. A stem of up to 18 ins bears large Canterbury-bell-like flowers which are usually white, though blue or pink forms occur. It seems quite hardy, but deserves alpine house protection in winter to keep it from damp. Also appreciating such protection, and a gritty soil or crevice, are *CC. atlantis, mollis, cashmiriana* and *arvatica*. This last, from Spanish mountains, forms mats of little leaves in rosettes, from which arise 3 ins stems with upturned starry flowers of rich violet-blue, or pure white. *C. cashmeriana*, like the little Spanish species, is saxatile in nature and grows most happily in narrow crevices. Softly hairy leaves set off large pale blue bells sitting in the saucer of the broad calyx lobes.

There are many other species, especially among the little gems for rock gardens, that would deserve mention if space allowed. However, I will conclude with a plant that is an oddity even in so polymorphic a genus as *Campanula*: *C. thyrsoides*. Here is a plant from subalpine pastures of

Europe, with long, narrow, bristly leaves in a rosette from which arises a fat, erect spike of fragrant, straw-yellow or slightly green-tinged flowers. Its monocarpic nature means that after flowering it dies, but it is fortunately not hard to raise from seed and is attractive as well as curious.

The National Collection

The National Collection of Campanula is held at Padlock Croft, West Wratting, Cambridge (Mr and Mrs Peter Lewis).

The Lewis's campanulas were designated as a National Collection in September 1982, when they grew about seventy different kinds; now there are very many more in the Collection. The Lewis's garden of a little over a half-acre lies just off the low-lying fenland of Cambridgeshire, at the county's highest point, on sticky Suffolk boulder clay. With liberal applications of manure and leafmould it forms a rich mixture for border plants; the smaller campanulas, needing sharp drainage and a more open compost, are grown in raised beds and tanks. A few need the protection of an alpine house to keep winter wet from them. As well as growing the plants, the Lewises are forming a reference herbarium and are studying all the available – and rather out-of-date – documentation on the genus Campanula.

Dianthus

LIKE the primrose and its forms, pinks and carnations have, over the centuries, been immensely fashionable for a period, then sunk in popularity, before emerging once again from obscurity. In the earliest times of which we have any record, pinks were grown, as were virtually all plants, largely for their usefulness rather than their beauty. The strong clove or nutmeg scent of pinks was used to spice wine or ale, hence the old name 'Sops in Wine'; rather as we mull our inferior wines sometimes, helping them along with a dash of spirits and a handful of spices, and heating them carefully, not to volatilise all that good alcohol.

The carnation and the pink are said to derive from *Dianthus caryophyllus* and *D. plumarius*, plants of European origin which may have reached Britain with the Norman monks in the eleventh and twelfth centuries. The name carnation was at first used only for the flesh-coloured form of the clove gilloflower. It is, perhaps, from the same root as the word 'carnal', pertaining to the flesh; but another theory suggests that the root is a form of 'coronation', the flowers having been used for crowns and garlands. Yet again, other authorities suggest that 'by a series of mispronounciations, the word derives from medieval Arabic as used in Turkey and Persia...' The Arabic word would have been *qaranful*. The crimson form was more highly valued, for it had the strongest clove scent. The carnation developed as a florists' flower in the span of a century or so, between 1580 and 1660-80; and as a florists' flower it was not only bred to a range of colour and a perfection of form far distant from its humble beginnings, but was also lovingly documented and portrayed, to our mingled delight and despair as we trace its development through charming descriptions and paintings, but reflect sadly on how many of these old kinds have been lost. By contrast, the pink was considered an inferior flower, suitable for cottagers perhaps but hardly worth describing let alone illustrating, and its past is less well known. Now the position is reversed; few of the old carnations survive (we are not concerned, here, with the great development of modern kinds) while, though many have been lost, the tougher constitution of the old pinks has kept many of them going for today's National Collection holders and other devotees to grow and to attempt to name.

During the sixteenth century then, the carnation eclipsed the pink. It was immensely popular with the Elizabethans, who – as we see with the primroses – loved bizarre colours and aberrant forms: the appearance of the first double carnation in the mid-sixteenth century was the start of the development of the carnation in the hands of the florists. This first break was a semi-double, but by the end of the century, when Gerard's Herball was published, a fully double form had appeared: the 'Great Double Carnation' of unknown origin. By now there were many odd colours: 'Carnation ... Gilloflowers ... Sops in Wine ... Pagiants or Pagion (a kind of purple), Horseflesh, Blunket, purple, white double and single gilloflowers, as also a gilloflower with yellow flowers'. Around this time too, came the first development of strange flakings and streakings of contrasting colour, which by selection gave many strictly defined classes of markings, including the Bizarre which was marked with two or more distinct colours on the ground tone. Another class of carnation that remained a garden flower and never attracted the attention of the florists in the same way, was the 'Painted Lady', of which many kinds were known, perhaps forty or more, some 'painted' on the upper side of the petals, some on the underside. At least one, perhaps more, 'Painted Lady' survives, very distinct in leaf with broad, thick 'grass' and semi-double flowers of white stippled with rose pink on the upper side of the petals. From the seventeenth century, or perhaps earlier, survives 'Fenbow's Nutmeg Clove', a smallish double flower of crimson-scarlet on slender stems over bluish grass. This may even be a double form of Chaucer's Sops in Wine, dating from the fourteenth century. Sophie Hughes has provided me with several scholarly comments on pinks, including this on Sops in Wine. 'The use may not go back to Roman times and to Chaucer as we have all assumed. Hilary Spurling has been writing to me and shed more light on the more recent (i.e. 1604) use of the plants in her manuscript of "Lady Fettiplace's Book" which gives several uses for "red Jillyflowers" which must, I think, have been early carnations. They went in a spiced wine "Claret wine water", and into various conserves, sweet, sour and, she says, delicious. Another ray of light on the phrase "soppes in wine" is that this may have been an actual dish – a recipe she has, originally using ale, if made with red wine comes out looking very much like the "Sops in Wine" grown at Kew and sold by Beth Chatto. Sue Farquhar thinks this plant is "Waithman's Beauty" and I have it listed as such. Her Sops came from [the Rev.] Moreton and is a huge clove-scented white.' The double nutmeg clove was found in the garden of Colonel Fenbow, in whose family papers was found evidence that his ancestor, Julian Fenbow, had planted it in 1652 to spice his wine. It may already then have been an old variety, cherished for its distinctive perfume. But Sophie says that she has seen at least four different plants labelled 'Fenbow's Nutmeg Clove', none with the strong nutmeg scent she expected. Sue, however, believes she has the true Fenbow. It is illustrated in colour in C. Oscar Moreton's book, *Old Carnations and Pinks*.

Old carnations can sometimes be roughly dated by name. 'The Prince of Denmark', for example, dates from the end of the Stuart period (the name commemorates Queen Anne's husband, not Hamlet). This old carnation was rediscovered when a bunch of flowers, of which one or two of this delightful flaked, clove-scented carnation, was brought to a patient in hospital. By good fortune the stems had been cut with some leaves attached; a cutting was rooted, and young plants of 'The Prince of Denmark' were soon distributed among dianthus enthusiasts. It was a further piece of luck that there was someone (whether patient or visitor, I know not) able to recognise that here was a plant worth saving. Other carnations were renamed when found growing in old gardens.

During Stuart times the fashion began of naming carnations after famous people of the day, or after the raiser or his friends, and there were also some bearing robust, even coarse names such as 'The Lust Gallant'. Earlier, just as with primroses, carnations were named by their colours: 'Pale Pageant', 'The Blew Gilloflower' (a deep tawny purple).

By comparison with these old carnations, surviving old pinks are very numerous. Sophie Hughes has over 200 different pinks in her collection but lists only a handful of carnations. The old pinks are distinguished from the carnations by their lower, more matted growth, and their June flowering season (newer pinks have had perpetual carnation blood infused into them to prolong their season). In pinks, too, the colour range is more restricted, to white, pink and purple, with none of the yellow and tawny shades of the carnations. Because they were considered inferior plants they were scarcely documented or illustrated, but we do have some survivals of past centuries that can be reasonably surely dated. 'Caesar's Mantle' is one, probably a sixteenth-century pink, a single 2 ins flower of dusky maroon red with a darker maroon central zone and deeply toothed petals. From the seventeenth-century dates 'Pheasant Eye', a deeply fringed white double with a deep purple eye and a strong perfume. The centre of 'Pheasant Eye' always 'stands up'. 'Queen of Sheba' may date from this time or even earlier; it is a very distinct pink with small single flowers, the sharply serrated petals curiously marked with ivory or magenta. It has a sprawling habit and a strong scent.

The Rev. Oscar Moreton dates 'Fair Folly' too to the seventeenth century. It is a larger-flowered kind than 'Queen of Sheba', single, raspberry-red in colour with two regular white flashes on each petal. Yet another seventeenth century pink that still survives is 'Bridal Veil', a very full double fringed white with a pink and green centre and a strong perfume. Like so many of these very full flowers, it tends to split its calyx so the petals flop over sideways instead of forming a symmetrical bloom.

During the eighteenth century many more pinks were named, and a fair number survive. Among them is the Chelsea Pink or 'Little Old Lady', with small striped reddish flowers. 'Bat's Double Red' is another famous name from about this time, a carmine-red double of repeat-flowering character. Thomas Bat was a nurseryman in Hackney, born in the latter half of the seventeenth century. 'Cockenzie', known as the Montrose Pink, is a sweetly scented double carmine, with deeply fringed petals and what Sophie Hughes describes as 'delicate but sturdy' foliage. 'Musgrave's Pink' (also called 'Charles Musgrave' or 'Old Green Eye') is another of this vintage which is still commercially available – a most charming white single pink with slightly fringed petals and a clear apple-green eye. From the late eighteenth century dates 'Gloriosa', an old Scottish pink which is perhaps a carnation cross, with large rose-pink dark-eyed double flowers. It flowers early and is very fragrant. 'Inchmery' is of very neat habit, with palest pink well-formed double flowers and a sweet scent.

The great contribution of the eighteenth-century raisers of pinks to the development of the flower was the creation of the laced pinks. The most distinct, and the one that set the standard, was 'Lady Stoverdale', produced by a grower named James Major, head gardener to the Dukes of Lancaster, in 1772. The vogue for laced pinks spread, and they were taken up by the Paisley Pinks, although no documentation can be found in Paisley or anywhere else. 'Paisley Gem' still survives; raised by John Macree of Paisley in about 1798, it has large well-laced blooms of purple on white, freely borne. Very similar, with clean maroon lacing on very double white flowers, is 'Dad's Favourite', flowering over a long season and believed to be an old Paisley Pink; it was rediscovered by A.J. Macself and sometimes bears his name. 'William Brownhill' is another of similar colouring, with white flowers laced and zoned with maroon.

From a generation or so later came 'Lady Granville' and 'Murray's Laced Pink'. The first, dated firmly by Moreton to 1840, has crimson lacing on a white ground, and slightly fringed petals; she is rather delicate-looking, with long stems and small grass. 'Murray's Laced Pink' was feared extinct and was thus placed on the NCCPG's search list – it was still about, however, for Sue Farquhar has always grown it; but it is hard to propagate and remains very scarce. It has well-formed flowers, frilled and fully double, laced – when the lacing appears, which is seldom – with rose-madder on white. Sue likes 'Beauty of Healey' very much; raised in the late nineteenth century by G. W. Grindrod of Whitworth, Rochdale, it has semi-double flowers, white with very formal, correct lacing in pale and deep purple. 'John Ball' was raised by a Mr McClean in the mid-nineteenth century and named after John Ball of Turner's nursery in Slough. It has a deep purple central zone on a white ground, with purple-violet lacing; but the plants of this name that Sophie Hughes grows differ from Sue Farquhar's and the naming is not yet entirely clear.

Not all the nineteenth-century pinks are laced. The most famous of all must be 'Mrs Sinkins', grown by a workhouse master in Slough and named for his wife. Though not without faults – notably that regrettable tendency to split its calyx, often a fault with these very full doubles – it is so good-tempered, with such good silvery-blue foliage and such a profusion of heavily clove-scented white flowers, that its popularity never wanes. Not unlike 'Mrs Sinkins' in habit is 'Sam Barlow', a fully double white with a maroon-black eye; indeed, 'Sam Barlow' was sometimes described as 'black and white'. The pink known as 'Paddington' was raised by Thomas Hogg on the side of Paddington Station in 1830; it has very double deeply fringed pale pink flowers, with a deep maroon centre and a strong perfume. 'Rose de Mai' also dates from the early nineteenth century; its large double fringed flowers, pale mauve-pink streaked with white, are borne over strong silver foliage.

A quite different class of pinks originating in the nineteenth century are the mule pinks, bred by André Paré of Orleans and also known as the Orleans pinks. They are sterile hybrids (hence 'mule') with sweet William blood, giving them their green 'grass' and clustered heads of small double flowers, salmon pink in 'Emil Paré' and a rather nasty bluish rose in (the possibly now extinct) 'Napoleon III'. The mule pinks need regular propagation by cuttings and are especially apt to flower themselves to death.

'Camelford A' was the name given to a pink brought by a visitor to Sue Farquhar's garden from the Cornish village of that name; but then came another visitor with photographs of pinks from an old publication, including 'Revel's Lady Warncliffe', with white, jagged plum lacing and plum-purple centre, unmistakably the Camelford pink. Sue Farquhar has been lucky too, in having help from Stanley Webb, who lives in Oxford, ten miles or so from her cottage; he knew Moreton well, indeed lunched with him regularly, and was familiar with many of the pinks and carnations that Moreton grew. So often he has been able to confirm the tentative naming of pinks. But another pink, made famous by Margery Fish, still bears the name she bestowed on it: 'Brympton Red'. A fine single, raspberry-red with darker lacing and eye, it was found in the old garden of a workhouse at Beaminster and grown in the garden at Brympton, whence Margery Fish had it. Its origin remains a mystery.

With the last three groups of pinks, of which both Sue Farquhar and Sophie Hughes grow a selection, we come to the first development of modern hybrid pinks. Those of the raiser C. H. Herbert of Acres Green, Birmingham, were all derived from the old laced pinks, but were selected for a carnation-like habit. Few, if any, now survive but they were used in breeding another line which we shall encounter shortly. Far better known are the Allwoodii pinks, bred by Montagu Allwood in the years just after the Great War, from a cross between 'Old Fringed' and perpetual carnations. The result was and is a race of hardy, perpetual flowering pinks; both Sue Farquhar and Sophie Hughes keep a few of the early Allwoodiis, such as 'Laced Hero', irregularly marked with deep maroon on white; or 'Hope', the first laced Allwoodii, named in 1935. Sophie Hughes thinks highly of this: 'deep maroon marbling and lacing on pale pink, combines best qualities of its parents in strong patterning from Paisley stock and good constitution from the perpetual flowering carnation'. The newer Allwoodiis, including the famous, rather garish salmon pink 'Doris', are grown by Jack Gingell in his National Collection at Colchester. He shows a fine selection at the Royal Horticultural Society's summer shows at Vincent Square, demonstrating the range of bright colours to which these plants have now been developed.

By crossing the Allwoodiis, Herbert's pinks and some older garden pinks, F. R. McQuown raised the London pinks, including 'London Brocade' with neat semi-double blooms formally laced with dark red on pale pink; or 'London Glow', a deep almost black ruby-red with a wire edge of rhodamine pink. Some years ago, I was given cuttings of a pink which I considered to be a deep plum-red with a delicate white wire edge; it was used as an edging in a garden overlooking the Wye, just in Wales. The owner of the garden was one of those keen amateur ladies of uncertain years who, without ever knowing accurately the names of plants, keep some interesting things going and distribute them among their friends: the joy and despair alike of conservationists, who are able to get hold of old cultivars but without a name, or with some such nickname as Mrs Jones's pink. This particular pink was growing in great masses in the Welsh garden whence I had it; the owner had been pulling off pipings, rooting them and popping them in here and there for years. I rooted about a dozen cuttings and gave several to Sophie Hughes, who told me recently that it was a 'rather changed version of "London Glow" ... always unstable according both to its raiser, F. R. McQuown, and a venerable employee of Allwood's whom I met last summer. I like yours better than the original, which was laced in a rather fudged way. I expect you have forgotten it by now – very dark red double, with a delicate white wire edge. Hard to propagate!'

Pinks have traditionally been used, as was this 'London Glow', as a neat edging to flower borders, to which their cushions of silvery or blue-grey foliage make a firm and unifying frame. Sue Farquhar grows her pinks mainly in her sloping front garden, surrounded by paved paths on which they can spill without hindrance, mixed with other plants that enjoy sharp drainage – *Euphorbia myrsinites* was looking particularly good when I visited her one windy January day – and, at the bottom of the slope, in richer soil, old auriculas. Sophie Hughes likes to add campanulas, veronicas, creeping thymes, little violas of the self-sowing kind like 'Bowles's Black' or *V. cornuta* in white, lavender and lilac; and she especially likes the combination of pinks, irises and old roses with the clear pure blue of *Linum perenne*. Jack Gingell, as a specialist not only in pinks but also in grey and silver foliage, sets the bright colours of his Allwoodii pinks among a froth of platinum and steel grey, silver and glaucous blue, where they glow more vividly than ever.

The National Collections

The National Collections of Pinks are grown at Old Inn Cottage, Piddington, Bicester, Oxfordshire (Mr and Mrs Farquhar); at Kingstone Cottages, Weston under Penyard, Ross on Wye, Herefordshire (Mrs Sophie Hughes); and at Ramparts Nursery, Bakers Lane, Colchester, Essex (Mr and Mrs Jack Gingell).

Sue Farquhar's and Sophie Hughes's collections both comprise old garden pinks and carnations. Sue Farquhar's pinks were designated as a National Collection in September 1983; Sophie Hughes's in March 1986. Each had been collecting for several years, and their collections are largely parallel. Sophie Hughes has over 200 different pinks in her collection but only a few carnations – the old border carnations are now much scarcer than old pinks.

The Ramparts collection includes some old garden pinks, and many of the newer border pinks including the popular Allwoodii pinks. They were designated as a National Collection in September 1982.

Digitalis

THERE IS a great deal more to foxgloves than the familiar tall, rose-purple wildling of our woodland and waste ground, or its selected forms offered in the seed catalogues, as it might be the blowsy Excelsior hybrids. This was very apparent when the Warwickshire Group of the NCCPG, holders of one of the National Collections of *Digitalis*, staged its Gold Medal exhibit at the 1986 Royal Show. Here were not only these familiar flowers, but also the exquisite Apricot form, in its selected Inverewe strain, creams and whites and the crushed strawberry hybrid *D. × mertonensis*. Then there were the species, soft yellows and tans and browns, with orchid-like spikes or pouting flowers, and strangest of all a shrubby foxglove from Spain with narrow, glaucous-blue leaves and tawny-orange flowers.

Foxgloves are notoriously promiscuous, and many are biennials needing fresh raising each season. Thus they are ideally suited to a group Collection, as at Warwickshire NCCPG Group, where a participating member may grow only one or two species or varieties to help keep the strain pure. At the other National Collection of *Digitalis*, held by Westfield Botanics in Wiltshire, Terry Baker grows his display foxgloves all together in a garden setting, for visitors to compare and contrast, and a separate set is grown under controlled conditions to ensure seed and named plants that are true to type.

The particular charm of our wild foxglove, *Digitalis purpurea*, lies in its gracefully hanging flowers in one-sided tall spikes. In the Excelsior hybrids, a seed strain widely offered, and awarded a First Class Certificate in 1954, the range of colours runs from white, through cream and lemon to pink, rose and purple; but 'improvement' has created a spike with the flowers set nearly horizontally, staring blatantly at you from all around the stem. This does, true, allow you to see the freckled interior wherever you may be standing. But a good selection such as the Giant Spotted strain is tall enough to allow you to see its magnificent purple blotches without stooping, and bears its flowers in the approved foxglove manner, drooping and one-sided. At the other extreme from these is the little Foxy strain of dwarf foxgloves grown as annuals, if sown in late winter, and reaching a stunted 2½ ft. Most horrible of all among forms of *D. purpurea* is the 'Campanulata Mixed' strain in which the spike is crowned by a huge blob of a floret like a purple Canterbury bell, glaring at you and entirely spoiling the balance of the spike. Strains like Gloxiniaeflora also demonstrate by their name how far the traditional narrow bell has swollen to gape-mouthed monsters.

After these aberrations it is a relief to turn to lovely things such as the white, cream, primrose or apricot forms that retain the elegant spike in a greatly refined colour range. They can be had separately by selection, though 'Sutton's Primrose' is no longer offered commercially. 'Sutton's Apricot' remains available, and whites can be had too. If you save your own seed for next season you can easily rogue out any purple foxgloves before flowering time. Simply pull up ruthlessly any seedling with purple-flushed petioles (leaf stalks): these will have purple flowers.

White foxgloves are a delight in the garden, especially in the dappled shade that so well suits them. Try them among green and white shrubs, the snowball tree – *Viburnum opulus* 'Sterile' – perhaps, and with ferns, white columbines and sweet Cecily in emulation of a Jekyll planting. In more open spots they can combine with Hybrid Musk roses such as creamy 'Moonlight', which has purple young growths to echo the purple blotches in the foxgloves; add *Iris orientalis* (*I. ochroleuca*) to take over when the foxgloves finish. If you can locate, or isolate for yourself, a cream or primrose strain then you have one of the loveliest flowers to use in an early summer border. After the foxgloves have finished you can yank them out, and move in a late-sown annual or a good-tempered perennial that will move cheerfully in full growth. 'Sutton's Apricot', in truth an opalescent creamy peach, is exquisite with the climbing rose known as 'Mrs Honey Dyson', all peaches and cream with honey stirred in. And all these are fine pot plants when well grown in a generously-sized container, to stand by your front door perhaps or on the shady side of a patio.

The common foxglove has a wide distribution in the wild, throughout Europe, and an especially beautiful form is the subspecies *heywoodii* from southern Portugal. Needing rich soil and dappled shade, this choice foxglove has subtly luminous velvety grey foliage and creamy-pink flowers opening from pale lemon-green buds.

As well as mongrel strains of *D. purpurea*, there exist hybrids between different species. The most familiar is *D.* × *mertonensis*, of which the parents are the common foxglove and *D. grandiflora*. The hybrid has inherited in

large part the perennial nature of the second-named parent, and appears –
from its size and ability to breed true from seed – to be a tetraploid. It is
short-growing, at 2 ft or so, and has quite large flowers of a curious
coppery strawberry shade, showy if not particularly refined.

It inherits its short stature also from its perennial parent *D. grandiflora*
(*D. ambigua*). This subalpine species has flowers of typical foxglove shape,
in a delightful shade of soft buff-yellow with tan and bronze freckles and
veining. It forms good clumps of narrow evergreen foliage, and is easily
raised from seed to grow willingly in sun or in light shade. *D. davisiana*,
from Turkey, is similar, with perhaps a shade more lemon in the flower
colour. Try them in an informal setting with blue or white lacecap
hydrangeas, or in sunnier places with the Hybrid Musk rose 'Buff Beauty',
or to contrast with black-crimson moss rose 'Nuits de Young' or the grey-
purple of 'William Lobb'. For smaller groups *D. grandiflora* 'Temple Bells'
is a selection of about 1 ft in height.

From southern Europe and north Africa comes another yellow
foxglove, *Digitalis lutea*, less decidedly perennial than the last two, and
very much smaller in flower, bearing many pale lemon narrow bells on
tall slim spikes over smooth green leaves. With such a wide range it is a
variable species, the Grecian form said to be better than the Italian, and
individual collectors' selections such as that made by Chris Brickell of
the Royal Horticultural Society no doubt offering scope for still more
improvement. It flowers before *D. grandiflora*, in early summer. *D.* 'Glory
of Roundway' is *D. lutea* × *D.* × *mertonensis*, the result 'basically a pink *D.
lutea*'. The Balkan *D. viridiflora* has densely flowered racemes of greenish-
yellow, conspiciously veined small flowers.

Another Greek foxglove is *D. lanata*, known in this country since the
turn of the eighteenth and nineteenth centuries. Also small flowered, with
slender spires, *D. lanata* differs in its odd little creamy-grey tubular flowers
each with a large pouting white or pearly grey lip. *D. l.* subsp. *leucophaea*,
also grown in the National Collections, differs in botanical detail only.
From the Balkan peninsula again, *D. laevigata* has few-flowered spikes,
and is of brownish colouring, with a network of veins and a white lip.

Of similar height, 2–3 ft, is the southern European *D. parviflora*. But
here we have something entirely different, almost orchid-like, for the
many narrow tubes are densely packed to make a slender poker of bizarre
chocolate-brown colouring. *D. ferruginea* is taller – almost twice the
height – and paler, with rusty brown interiors to the buff, lipped flowers.
Either or both could join *Carex comans*, a tawny-haired sedge, some of
the tan and copper flower arrangers' roses such as 'Café' or 'Julia', and
perhaps a creamy-tan kniphofia, against a backdrop of a milk-chocolate-
leaved *Cotinus coggygria* and *Buddleia* × *weyeriana* of the honey-gold
flowers.

Also in this colour range, but a very different plant again in aspect, is the shrubby Spanish *D. obscura*. All the species just described have fairly narrow foliage compared with the common foxglove, but in *D. obscura* it is slenderer still, its glaucous colouring a beautiful contrast to the flared ciliate bells of orange and yellow. This is commonly rather tender in Britain, but Terry Baker has a form collected at higher altitude, which should prove hardier. If so, it would be a plant worth growing in many a garden for its bright but not garish colouring, and the lovely balance between leaf and flower tones. *D. mariana* is another Spanish species of which the name has become confused, in gardens, with *D. obscura*, although as a subspecies of *D. purpurea* it is very different, with white-felted leaves and purple flowers.

In *Digitalis dubia* we have a diminutive creature small enough for the rock garden, with purply-pink flowers on 9 ins stems over downy foliage. It is not very perennial, nor fully hardy, as may be expected from its origins in the Balearic Isles, where it grows on rocky slopes, and in scrub or light woodland. Bigger than this, and tougher, is *D. thapsi* from Spain, which with its mauve and purple spotted flowers is very like *D. purpurea*, bringing us full circle to the familiar foxglove of our woodlands with which we began.

The National Collections

The National Collections of Digitalis, the foxgloves, are held by the War-wickshire Group of the NCCPG and by Westfield Botanics, Rookery Nurseries, Atworth, Melksham, Wiltshire (Mr Terry Baker).

The Warwickshire Group's Collection was designated in November 1985. It is held in the gardens of about ten members, some of whom have only one species or variety, others up to three or four: this deliberate isolation helps to keep strains pure in a genus notorious for its promiscuity, and comprising many biennial members needing regular repropagation from seed. It is also an ideal arrangement for NCCPG members who wish to participate actively in the National Collections movement without feeling able to take on the sole responsibility for a Collection. The Group has slowly been able to increase the number of taxa in the Collection by obtaining seed from Jim and Jenny Archibald's collection in Turkey in 1986 (which added, among others, D. lamarckii and D. schishkinii to the Collection), and by the more usual methods of purchase and exchange. Already they have been able to restore to the garden at Inverewe, where it was thought to be lost, young plants of the Inverewe strain of Apricot foxgloves.

Terry Baker grows his foxgloves, as we have seen, in two ways: in a garden setting, for display, and under controlled conditions of isolation to ensure pure seed strains, from which he raises new plants for the display garden and for sale to help finance the National Collection; he, like other National Collection holders, finds it essential to label the Collection very carefully and this, with the extra costs of its maintenance, represents a financial strain. His Collection was designated in March 1986.

Euphorbia

THE HARDY spurges are at the very opposite pole among (chiefly) non-woody plants from such as Michaelmas daisies or pyrethrums, both highly bred, with a short concentrated season of effect and little beyond sheer colour to commend them. The few cultivars of euphorbia, by contrast, have arisen entirely through selection, not breeding, and those few have retained the qualities of the parent species, losing only the odd defect. Range of flower colour is not theirs: almost all have bracts (for they lack showy petals) of sharp lime-green to acid yellow, just a few running to orange and reddish tints. But many are extremely decorative when displaying these bright bracts, while others are primarily foliage plants, some are valued for their ground-covering properties or for their willingness to thrive in wildish conditions, yet others offer bright spring or autumn colour, a few are small and neat enough for rock gardens, and a few of borderline hardiness are valued by gardeners in mild areas. The succulent species, which are many and diverse, and tropical kinds such as the familiar Poinsettia, do not form part of the National Collection and will receive no further mention here.

To try and simplify the choice of hardy euphorbias from among the many now available, I shall consider them in approximately the categories adumbrated just now, beginning with the largest groups, those grown for floral effect and those for foliage value.

Among foliage plants, a form of one of our British natives, the wood spurge, ranks highly. *Euphorbia amygdaloides* 'Rubra' has red-purple foliage, brighter in some forms than others; for despite the presentation of the name as a cultivar it is habitually raised from seed and somewhat variable. The best are extremely handsome, whether at the woodland edge or in the border. Good light is needed to maintain the best colour. Above the foliage, in spring, come the same columnar, lime-green inflorescences as those of the Wood Spurge itself, reaching no more than knee-

177

high. In later summer the red foliage makes an attractive foil for the fuzzy white flowers of *Eupatorium ageratoides*. The wood spurge also has a variegated form keeping a tenuous hold on cultivation; a pretty, but weakly plant apt to 'miff off' and much disliking chilly winters.

E. × martinii is a hybrid between *E. amygdaloides* and *E. characias*, occurring naturally in France and leaning, depending on which area it comes from, more to one parent or the other. One form is very like the wood spurge, with a flush of red to the young foliage; neat and pleasing without being hugely exciting.

The best forms of the shrubby, evergreen *E. characias*, by contrast, are decidedly exciting. It is a Mediterranean species, *E. c.* subsp. *characias* from the western Mediterranean and Portugal, *E. c.* subsp. *wulfenii* from the eastern. All forms have thickish stems, exuding when cut the usual milky latex – a skin irritant – and dying after bearing flowers, the new stems which will produce next year's flowers pushing up among the exhausted older ones. The foliage is narrow and glaucous, the inflorescence columnar, green to yellow in colour. During winter, and when the plant is undernourished or otherwise stressed, the foliage takes on pleasing tones of reddish purple; stems that will flower turn their heads down, shepherd's crook style, before straightening up as the flowers open. *E. c.* subsp. *characias* has narrow, green inflorescences with red-brown glands giving the appearance of chocolate 'eyes' – or, as E. A. Bowles recounted, of frog spawn. Subsp. *wulfenii* has broader columns of flower of sharper chartreuse, lacking the chocolate eye. Some seedlings have especially wide, open heads and make a very different effect from the tight spikes of *E. c. characias*. 'Lambrook Gold', or 'Lambrook Yellow' (both names appear in literature, but perhaps only one plant exists) is, as its name implies, particularly yellow and must be propagated by cuttings; seedlings are not entitled to the cultivar name. *E. c. sibthorpii* is also yellower than many, and more glaucous than most in leaf: a handsome thing, but tenderish. All the forms of *E. characias*, indeed, are apt to suffer in hard winters.

In their different ways, all make a fine effect through the year, and a startling contribution to the sharp sap-greens and lime-yellows of spring. Try them with Mr Bowles's golden grass, *Milium effusum* 'Aureum', the clear pale yellow-green of emerging daylily foliage, *Helleborus corsicus* perhaps for its jade-green bowls and toothed, greyish leaves, and yellow crown imperials or doronicums. A redder note can be added with flowers of Japanese quince, or a good berberis such as *B. linearifolia* 'Orange King', and red-cupped daffodils. Later, though the euphorbia flowers will have faded and been cut away, the acid-toned theme can be continued with *Philadelphus coronarius* 'Aureus', *Sambucus racemosa* 'Plumosa Aurea' whose bronzed young foliage will earlier have echoed the daffodils' redder tints, and the citron froth of *Alchemilla mollis* at ground level. In a different mood, once more with the emphasis on foliage, the glaucous undertones of *E. characias* are picked up in sunny, warm corners by the strong blue-glaucous leaves of 'Jackman's Blue' rue, paler grey-blue *Romneya coulteri* and white-striped spears of *Iris pallida* 'Variegata'.

Narrow foliage of pale grey-blue is borne by *Euphorbia nicaeensis*, another Mediterranean forming a low mound half the height, at 2 ft, of the shrubby types just described. The flowers appear in summer and autumn over a long season. It is not widely available, but worth seeking out, the ideal plant for a blue and yellow scheme. Better known are two other euphorbias grown chiefly for their metallic blue-grey foliage. The more familiar, and the tougher, is *E. myrsinites*, a trailing plant bearing foliage of glaucous grey, in aspect very much as though someone had dipped a spray of monkey puzzle in aluminium paint. In spring the usual acid flowers, tinged with orange in the form 'Washfield' from the nursery of that name, tip the sprawling stems. Despite its southern European origin it is quite hardy, preferring full sun and a well-drained soil, as it might be to the front of a raised bed or on a rocky bank where its prostrate stems can best be appreciated. It contrasts pleasantly, for year-round foliage effect, with the old-gold whipcord stems of *Hebe ochracea* 'James Stirling'.

Similar, but less hardy, is *Euphorbia rigida* (still sometimes labelled *E. biglandulosa*). The stems, standing nearly erect, are clothed with pointed glaucous grey leaves and crowned in early spring with bright lime-green starry heads. It looks exceptionally well in a hot, dry gravel bed, among other glaucous, silver and grey-leaved plants, little blue-leaved white-flowered *Omphalodes linifolia* seeding around and the pale grey-pink furry caterpillars of *Pennisetum orientale* nearby, in Mr and Mrs Wills's garden in Avon. Theirs is the form, collected by the roadside on one of their Greek holidays, that earned an Award of Merit from the Royal Horticultural Society in March 1984.

Much smaller than either of these is *E. capitulata*. Roger Turner (whose extensive collection of euphorbias formed the basis of the National Collection cared for by Sarah Sage in Herefordshire and added a few taxa to the other National Collection of euphorbias at Oxford Botanic Garden) is rather disparaging about it in his 'Review of Spurges for the Garden' (*The Plantsman*, Dec. 1983). However, having grown *E. capitulata* myself along with virtually all the others I describe in this chapter, I think he underrates it: or else I had a good form. As I knew it, it was a little evergreen creeping plant less than 1 in high, with tiny blunt blue-green leaves and miniature chartreuse heads, delightful in a rocky pocket of a sunny bank intended to remind it of its native Balkans.

Most of the euphorbias I have so far discussed are valued for both flower and foliage. In the foliage department there remains one to be mentioned that is scarcely worth having in flower, except that the little brownish, nondescript things are honey-scented, giving the plant its name: *E. melli-fera*. Sadly, it is tender, as may be expected of a native of the Canary Isles. In mild districts, where it not merely survives – as it may in sheltered inland gardens – but forms a true shrub of 6–8 ft, it is a magnificent foliage plant with ample strong green, lanceolate leaves.

    E. griffithii departs from the euphorbia norm by forsaking lime-green. The good green foliage has pink midribs, the inflorescences vary from coppery red to orange. 'Fireglow' is the form usually encountered, with appropriately hot brick-red flowers. It can be a pest, with its questing roots; red-tinged snouts appear in spring feet away from the original rootstock, so care is needed in placing it. In stodgy clay it may be more restrained. Christopher Lloyd's form 'Dixter', selected from seedlings raised by the late Hilda Davenport Jones of Washfield Nursery, gives no such trouble. It has, in Roger Turner's words, 'dark and sumptuous' red-flushed foliage, greyish pink beneath, and deep orange flowers, a combination that earned it an Award of Merit in 1984. Apparently happy in moist, though emphatically not in soggy, soils, all forms of *E. griffithii* are handsome with ferns and candelabra primulas in the yellow to burnt orange-red range, *P. helodoxa* perhaps and for orange, *P. cockburniana*; or with the yellow honeysuckle azalea.

    With the mention of moist soils, we may fittingly come to the first of my selected spurges where foliage is very much secondary to 'flower'. *E. palustris* indicates by its name that it is, in nature, a marsh plant. In the garden it is a splendid flowering plant, forming bushes topped by vivid lime-yellow heads in late spring, and turning to yellow and orange in autumn before dying down. It can well join other bold, moisture-loving plants such as web-footed rodgersias, ligularias, *Iris pseudacorus* 'Variegata' showing its green and yellow spears at the height of the spurge's season, and forms of *I. sibirica* in blue and purple. Happily for those without a patch of moist soil, it grows perfectly well also in dry places.

    E. palustris is much larger than the most commonly seen spring-flower-ing spurge, *E. polychroma*. This European perennial makes dense clumps giving some of the brightest acid yellow tones of spring, lasting for many weeks, a startling contrast to scarlet *Anemone fulgens* or with orange and yellow Welsh poppies against yellow-variegated foliage of golden privet or *Cornus alba* 'Spaethii'. The plant I and many others have grown incorrectly named as *E. pilosa* 'Major' (a different species altogether) is but a larger and later variant of *E. polychroma* with a repeat, or at least an echo, of its flowering season in late summer. First time round it is still in good colour to accompany the deep velvety red of *Rosa gallica* 'Tuscany', and to contrast in form with the lime froth of *Alchemilla mollis*.

    A central European spurge scarcely known as yet, *E. brittingeri* is a worthwhile plant like a shorter, later, *E. polychroma*. Also resembling *E.*

polychroma, but taller – overtopping even the yard-high *E. palustris* – is *E. villosa*, with an open, bright yellow inflorescence. Now available in commerce is another little-known spurge, this one from the Himalayas, *E. wallichii*. Plantsmen's appetites were whetted by the photograph, in the RHS Journal *The Garden* of November 1977, of this spurge with blue and purple *Iris kumaonensis*, growing in Kashmir, the countless clumps of euphorbia interspersed with the iris in otherwise bare-seeming, rocky ground. Seed became available and a few of us enjoyed the good leafy clumps and, at last, above dark, purple-edged foliage, the broad three-bracted chartreuse inflorescences that lasted long in beauty.

Another species introduced at about the same time is one from east Nepal, discovered by Tony Schilling of Wakehurst Place (the country outpost of the Royal Botanic Gardens, Kew) in 1975. It was at first thought to be a variant of *E. sikkimensis*, which I will describe shortly; the two share a late summer flowering season, and both have the expected vivid lime-green colouring. But they differ in some important ways, both botanically and horticulturally. *E. schillingii*, named for its discoverer, makes a good clump, needs no support, and lacks the red young shoots which are so characteristic of *E. sikkimensis*. At Wakehurst Place it grows with blue lacecap hydrangeas, which appreciate the moisture-retaining soil that suits the euphorbia. But it should be happy in any reasonable soil that does not dry out, and its bold, darkish foliage with white midrib well sets off the strong design and sharp bright colouring of the bracts. It seems to be easy to propagate from basal cuttings taken in spring – which will be the way to increase Tony Schilling's original, wild-collected clone, Schilling 2060 – or from seed.

Very different from these is an annual or biennial, European spurge regarded by many – not by me – as a nuisance in the garden. The Tintern spurge, as its name implies, also occurs in a small area of the Wye valley on the borders of England and Wales near Tintern Abbey. Overwintering plants form neat little clumps of small fresh green leaves; as spring advances into summer they develop their open candelabras, 12–18 ins tall, of coral-red stems bearing masses of tiny citron flowers. The Tintern spurge seeds itself around quite freely but is easily removed and makes a delightful addition to many colour schemes. I used it with jade-green *Galtonia princeps*, the flat heads of *Sedum spectabile* that start life glacier green before opening to subdued pink, and pale pink roses.

Another spurge, from sandy shores of the western Mediterranean but perfectly hardy in Britain, can also be a nuisance because of its wandering roots. *E. pithyusa* is an attractive thing, however, with glaucous foliage and rounded heads of flower.

Native of dry places throughout central Europe and the Mediterranean is *E. seguieriana* subsp. *niciciana*, a little bushy plant with pale glaucous, needle-like leaves, and heads of lime-yellow in summer, a pretty contrast to blue agapanthus or to apricot-orange kniphofias.

Some herbaceous spurges are noted for the colouring, in spring, of their new growths. *E. longifolia*, a Himalayan species, is a compact plant with pink margined leaves, each with a prominent white midrib. As the leaves first emerge the margins are markedly white also, contrasting with the reddish stems. In summer appear the usual heads of yellow-green. Closely related, and much more widely grown, is *E. sikkimensis*, a taller plant, tending to flop when in late summer flower. Its best season is early spring, when it emerges in bright scarlet and pink young growths, likened by Graham Stuart Thomas to 'bright red glass'.

With its mildly wandering roots pushing up gappy shoots, *E. sikkimensis* cannot be considered good ground-cover. A few spurges, however, admirably exclude weeds, and will grow even in dry rooty shade. *E. robbiae*, now regarded as a variety of *E. amygdaloides*, is a dense-growing evergreen from Turkey, forming thickets of stems bearing rosettes of good dark green foliage, topped in spring by peridot-green columnar inflorescences. For a self-sustaining group in woodland conditions, plant *E. robbiae* with Welsh poppies, wood anemones, wood sorrel, bluebells, primroses and ferns; not a group to place too near any choice treasures, but decoratively clothing the ground all year. For more tamed settings, a group of *E. robbiae* with broad leathery paddles of bergenia foliage and white-striped spears of *Iris foetidissima* 'Variegata', and the glossy dark green foliage on horizontal branches of *Prunus lusitanica* 'Zabeliana', would cover the ground all year in a safe but somewhat unchanging blend of foliage with incidents of flower from three of the four components.

Far more insidiously invasive than *E. robbiae* is the cypress spurge, *E. cyparissias*. However pretty this may look in its native European habitats, it is a menace in the garden, with fast-spreading roots that grow unseen in winter, the shoots appearing in spring inextricably tangled with neighbouring plants. Each shoot is like a little feathery conifer, with pale green foliage topped by yellow flowers. If you must grow it, partner it with something equally thuggish such as the old tawny daylily, *Hemerocallis fulva*, or *Alchemilla mollis*, and let them fight it out.

Invasive also, by enthusiastic self-sowing, is the caper spurge, a biennial admired for the geometrical precision of its stiffly arranged leaves, but less acceptable as its explosive seedpods spread youngsters all about the garden. Don't be misled by the English name: the seedpods may look like capers, but the plant is poisonous.

E. dulcis also self-sows, though less aggressively; it is a perennial spurge from Europe preferring moist shade, and barely noticeable until in autumn it adopts livery of red, pink and orange before dying back for the winter. The Irish spurge has similar soil preferences, and may also self-sow freely, but *E. hyberna* is valued for its excellent bright flowers above reddish, almost leafless stems. Not knowing its reputation for enjoying damp shade, I grew it in a rather dry, sunny border where it throve, a happy contrast to purple *Cotinus* and orange Bellingham hybrid lilies.

The Portland spurge, which also in the wild crosses the Channel to France and Spain, is a neat little mound with somewhat blue-green foliage on spiralling stems, often attractively tinged with pink. With *Helleborus lividus* and the painted fern *Athyrium niponicum* 'Pictum' to pick up the pinkish flush in their own greyish foliage, and nodding mauve-pink flowers of *Allium cernuum*, it contributed to a quiet-toned group that gave year-round pleasure.

And this, indeed, is the great value of spurges: whatever the season, there is a euphorbia that will be looking good in the garden.

The National Collections

The National Collections of Euphorbia *are held by Mrs Sarah Sage of Abbeydore Court, near Hereford, and at Oxford Botanic Garden (Superintendent, Mr J. K. Burras). The basis of the Collection at Abbeydore was the extremely complete collection of spurges amassed by Roger Turner and in due course, when the plants completely dominated his small town garden, passed by him to Pershore College of Horticulture, where the National Collection was first designated. After being held for about four years there, the plants were transferred in the main to Sarah Sage, with a few species going to Oxford Botanic Garden to add to the already fairly complete collection growing there. The two new National Collections were formally designated in July 1985.*

The recent cold winters have severely tried some of the more tender species, of which stock must always be kept protected from frost. It is hardly surprising to lose E. dendroides, a more or less woody species rather like a leggy E. characias, or the Canary Isles E. mellifera; but young plants of E. × martinii and E. portlandica, which might have been expected to be quite hardy, also perished. Some young E. characias also died. Ken Burras makes the point, incidentally, that virtually all the plants you might find offered for sale as E. characias, E. wulfenii and E. sibthorpii are seed-raised, the seed itself the result of open pollination, and though excellent plants, are 'hybrid swarm' material; so you should not be too surprised to find you cannot exactly match your plant to the book description.

Geranium

Unlike plants such as asters, with their huge numbers of confusingly similar cultivars, geraniums have not undergone the proliferation of named kinds that marks so many members of the daisy family. Most geraniums have retained the grace and ease of cultivation of the wild species. Several of those we grow in our gardens are indeed British natives and thus can be relied upon to grow willingly in most areas in these islands, even in the cold north-east or sea-swept Western Isles. Most geraniums, or cranesbills, are hardy; they differ also from pelargoniums or storksbills, which are commonly miscalled geraniums, in their five regular petals, while pelargoniums have two petals of different size from the other three to give them the characteristic 'prick-eared' flower.

As we have been considering chiefly plants for the herbaceous or mixed border, I'll stay in this mood and take first those geraniums which are suited to such borders. Foremost perhaps is the splendid G. × *magnificum*, which gives indeed a magnificent and concentrated display of its large, rich violet-purple flowers with deeper veining, over typical geranium foliage which often colours well in autumn. It is a tallish plant, up to $2\frac{1}{2}$ ft or more, and has immense vigour, enabling it equally to cope with border conditions or to make a good showing in part shade among shrubs. Like many geraniums it makes a fine companion for shrub roses and, to match its early summer season, you could follow John Hobson's recommendation and pair it with 'Nevada', that tremendous rose with large, creamy single flowers. (John is in charge of the Parks Department in Cambridge where the Collection of *Geranium* cultivars is grown.)

The parents of G. × *magnificum* are G. *ibericum* (a name you'll find attached to the hybrid itself, in gardens) and G. *platypetalum*, both originating from the Caucasus and north-east Turkey. Both are, of course, represented in the National Collection of *Geranium* species and primary hybrids at the University Botanic Garden in Cambridge, where you can clearly see the superiority of the sterile hybrid as a garden plant.

Another group of border geraniums of similar stature derives from our native meadow cranesbill, *Geranium pratense*. The wildling itself is a beautiful plant, as anyone who has seen it flowering along road verges in limestone areas must agree. Here it associates with, often, meadowsweet and rosebay willow herb, an unbeatable blend of cream, magenta pink and violet blue. The leaves of the meadow cranesbill are finely cut, more so than those of *G.* × *magnificum*, and it has a longer flowering season, from June through till August. It has given rise to several distinct forms, some of which – the doubles especially – are well-loved garden plants of delightfully old-fashioned appearance. The double white is rather small flowered; the two blues are altogether better things. The earlier to come into flower is 'Plenum Caeruleum', with loosely double lavender-blue flowers on branching sprays over a long season. 'Plenum Violaceum' has neater, more rosette-shaped deep violet flowers shading to purple at the centre. They assort best with other plants of the 'cottage garden' persuasion (no-one quite seems to be able to define a cottage garden plant, but I think we all have a nebulous mental image of what is meant), with domesticated plants such as old-fashioned pink, cerise and purple roses and double mock orange, and the pink spires of *Linaria purpurea* 'Canon Went' perhaps, or a penstemon such as wine-red 'Garnet'.

Other forms of *G. pratense* have single flowers, in the same branched sprays. A good white form has been grown for some years now at Cambridge and Dr Peter Yeo, who has been responsible for creating the National Geranium Collection at the University Botanic Garden, proposes the name 'Galactic' for it, to emphasise the milky whiteness of its flowers. 'Mrs Kendall Clarke' as usually labelled in gardens has lavender blue flowers with paler, grey-blue veins; but the true 'Mrs Kendall Clarke', we are told, is 'pearl grey flushed with softest rose'. 'Striatum' in white variably streaked with violet-blue is another named kind, which produces from seed offspring very like itself, and does duty for 'Mrs Kendall Clarke' in most gardens.

The single-flowered meadow cranesbills are all apt to seed themselves freely, and this makes them less than ideal in a disciplined border setting, but adds to their value for naturalising – in grass especially. Here their rather weak stems will be supported by the surrounding vegetation and, if they do flop, they will look acceptably relaxed rather than obtrusively untidy. Because of their late flowering season you will have to keep to a programme of management of your long grass areas which allows them to flower, and preferably to seed, undisturbed; tidy minded gardeners may find that they cannot cope with the hayfield that results from leaving grass uncut until late July at the earliest. Much depends on your temperament here.

Our other sizeable British native cranesbill, *G. sylvaticum*, flowers earlier than *G. pratense*, in May. Like the meadow cranesbill, *G. sylvaticum* is very variable in the wild; pink, white and lavender-blue forms can all be seen growing together, especially in north-eastern Europe. The typical form of these islands has violet-blue, white-eyed flowers; 'Album' is pure white and especially lovely in light shade with blue aquilegias; var. *wanneri* is pink with deeper rose-purple veining; and Graham Stuart Thomas cites a plum-coloured form as well. 'Mayflower' is a richer violet-blue with a smaller white eye, a fine early-flowering border plant, that John Hobson likes to see in association with shrubs such as *Cytisus* × *praecox* or *Potentilla* 'Elizabeth'.

Fairly recently two geraniums of meadow cranesbill type, though lower-growing and more inclined to spread at the root, were introduced to cultivation. They have more finely cut leaves than the meadow cranesbill, and larger, more upright flowers, one in lilac-purple, the other warm white with a network of pastel-violet veins. Originally christened *G. bergianum* and *G. rectum album*, they were subsequently known as *G. pratense* 'Kashmir Purple' and 'Kashmir White'. Dr Yeo now considers them to belong to a distinct species, which he has dubbed *G. clarkei*. Whatever the name by which you acquire them, they are excellent garden plants, delicate in appearance but not lacking in vigour. With their running roots they make fairly good ground-cover, not perhaps quite dense enough to exclude all weeds, but soon producing a carpet of flower. John Hobson likes to grow 'Kashmir White' with a yellow shrubby potentilla such as *P. farreri*.

Of similar running habit and height, not much above a foot, is the exquisite *G. himalayense* (also known as *G. grandiflorum* or, less familiarly, as *G. meeboldii*). Over finely cut leaves dance large, deep violet-blue flowers in early summer. Indeed, this and many other geraniums (but not *G.* × *magnificum* which fires all its guns at once) will, if regularly divided and reset in freshly manured or composted ground, amaze you by the length of their flowering season. In its first year of planting in good soil *G. himalayense* will flower for months, seemingly without intermission. This, and its form 'Gravetye', which has a slightly more pronounced reddish-purple flush at the centre, are equally valuable at the border front, or running back among shrubs where the daintily cut leaves make good cover. Like that of many others the foliage colours brightly in the autumn to russet or even scarlet. These cranesbills' particular quality of blue assort well with light yellow: the old, pale bearded *Iris* × *flavescens* or rose 'Frühlingsgold', are suggested by Graham Stuart Thomas, or they make delightful companions for *Rosa chinensis* 'Mutabilis', with its butterfly-like blooms opening from coppery pink buds to chamois-pale flowers that deepen with age and pollination through pink to crimson. An old double form of *G. himalayense*, 'Plenum', has latterly acquired the name 'Birch Double'. With its light pinky-lilac flowers, it is a pretty thing but needs quite different companions: pink and white double Scotch roses perhaps, or it is exquisite with silver foliage, *Artemisia* 'Powis Castle' or the selected form of *A. absinthium*, 'Lambrook Silver'; there is far too much pink in its make-up to blend happily with yellow flowers.

Not so the admirable 'Johnson's Blue', a superb plant considered by Dr Yeo to be a hybrid between *G. himalayense* and *G. pratense*. It was raised from seed gathered by A. T. Johnson from his finest forms of *G. pratense* and sent to Mr Ruys of Dedemsvaart in Holland. Dr Yeo describes it as a 'fairly exact intermediate between the putative parents'; in garden terms this means that we have a plant with ample, finely cut foliage making dense mounds, surmounted by a long succession of clear lavender-blue flowers on branching stems, taller than those of *G. himalayense*, but less stout and correspondingly more graceful than the meadow cranesbill. Being sterile, it wastes no energies in setting seed but flowers for a long season. When, as inevitably it does, it becomes untidy, it may – as may so many other cranesbills – be cut hard back, almost to ground level, when it will quickly refurnish itself with fresh foliage. Like the geraniums already mentioned, 'Johnson's Blue' is a fine companion for roses, pink or yellow; also for the fragrant, early clear yellow daylily, *Hemerocallis flava*.

That jewel among perennials, *Geranium wallichianum* 'Buxton's Variety', has probably the longest flowering season of any geranium except 'Russell Prichard', for all that it doesn't get going until July. Thenceforward, it produces an unending succession of clear porcelain-blue flowers, enhanced by a large white eye, reminiscent of that beguiling annual *Nemophila* with the repellent English name, baby blue eyes. These wide saucers are borne on leafy stems that weave their way among their neighbours, never more charmingly than when – as in a Welsh garden I know – they appear among the felty grey leaves and pipe-cleaner, bobbled stems of *Ballota pseudodictamnus*, with *Clematis* 'Perle d'Azur' in the identical shade of Spode-blue above and tumbling down to join the geranium. In a different mood, it could be encouraged to scramble through *Cotoneaster horizontalis*, or set against *Berberis thunbergii* 'Atropurpurea' to catch the sun.

G. wlassovianum is similar in habit, but with velvety foliage in place of the lime-green of 'Buxton's Variety', and dusky violet, purple-veined flowers; needing a sunny position and perhaps some grey foliage to show off its sombre colouring, or the subtle grey, mauve and pink variegations of *Fuchsia magellanica* 'Versicolor'.

A unique plant with foliage rather like that of 'Buxton's Variety', but entirely different flowers, has been the subject of more detective work by Dr Yeo. Introduced by Kingdon Ward in 1956 from Burma, and originally believed to be *G. yunnanense*, it has been distributed quite widely in gardens under that name. In part shade it grows easily and produces branching sprays of nodding pink flowers, the petals reflexed like those of a cyclamen or a martagon lily, enlivened by crimson filaments and blue-black anthers. The true *G. yunnanense*, however, has only just been introduced to cultivation and its garden worth remains to be assessed; our plant is *G. pogonanthum*. A pale flowered form of *G. yunnanense* is the same as the botanists' *G. candicans*, but – more confusion – the name *G. candicans* has been incorrectly applied to *G. lambertii*. This is a beautiful geranium with quite large, nodding, deeply cupped white flowers with a crimson stain at the base of each petal, borne late in the season and well into autumn. If you can contrive to grow it on a bank, or in a raised rock pocket perhaps, at or near eye level, you will better appreciate the lovely markings of the flower, the crimson veining and bright green of the sepals revealed between the petals. This form is now to be called 'Swansdown', to distinguish it from *G. lambertii* as originally illustrated, which had pale pink flowers lacking the crimson stain.

None of these geraniums has foliage to be ashamed of but, for quality of leaf above all, I would choose *G. renardii*. Solid, mounded clumps of grey-green foliage with a strong tactile quality, like figured velvet, need no enhancing yet form an ideal setting for the pearly-white, violet-veined flowers, the whole plant a harmony of quiet greyish tones blending with the grey-mauve foliage of *Rosa rubrifolia* (*R. glauca* as we must now call it) and purple sage with its greyish-purple leaves, as a setting for the bright magenta-rose of an admirable hybrid of *G. endressii* called 'Russell Prichard'. From June well into autumn this enthusiastic interweaver shows its brilliant flowers over grey-green, silvery-backed leaves, popping up through the branches of the sage and clambering into the rose. As its other parent is *G. traversii* (of which more later), it needs a sunny position such as will, in any case best suit the sage. If, like me, you care to introduce primrose yellow to relieve sombre colours and offset strong magenta, you could choose sulphur-toned *Achillea × taygetea*, which also brings feathery grey-green foliage to add to the harmonising tones of this group.

A newer plant of similar parentage is 'Mavis Simpson', probably a hybrid between *G. endressii* and *G. traversii* var. *elegans*. The leaves are rather less grey than those of 'Russell Prichard' and are faintly brown-blotched in spring; the flowers are shell pink and appear from early to late summer. If the magenta of 'Russell Prichard' is too much for you, 'Mavis Simpson' would perform a similar role in the group just described. Unfortunately it is not reliably hardy.

If you fear it not, geraniums of all sizes can be had in flaunting magenta; the largest is *G. psilostemon* (formerly *G. armenum* which was not only easier to pronounce but also told us where the plant came from). At 3-4 ft, it is one of the biggest of all geraniums except some members of the *palmatum* group; its brilliant magenta flowers are relieved or enhanced (depending on your attitude towards their colour) by black centres and black veins, and appear in June. For giving piquancy to cool greys and mauves, as in the planting of Rose 'William Lobb' and *Clematis* 'Purpurea Plena Elegans' already described (Clematis chapter); or in Byzantine mixtures with orange alstroemerias and lilies, as proposed by Graham Stuart Thomas, this geranium is unsurpassed. I especially like it with clear pale yellow, as it might be the satiny cups of *Althaea rugosa*, a self-supporting perennial hollyhock native to much the same regions as the geranium itself. Dr Yeo recommends planting *G. psilostemon* 'in broken shade against a dark background; the sunlit flowers will then appear intensely luminous'.

If you find the colour too powerful, *G. psilostemon* has a more discreet form of rich lilac-pink called 'Bressingham Flair'. A newish hybrid of *G. psilostemon* to look out for is 'Ann Folkard', the other parent of which is the monstrously invasive *G. procurrens*. The hybrid has not inherited this characteristic, forming a widespreading plant but not rooting down as it goes. Over foliage that Dr Yeo describes as 'golden green', 'Ann Folkard' bears flowers of velvety magenta purple, black-eyed and dark-veined. Dr Yeo is very enthusiastic about this plant and calls it 'stunning'.

You may wonder what a botanic garden is up to, growing so many hybrids and named forms of geranium. In fact, responsibility for the National Collection of geraniums has been split between the University Botanic Garden, which concerns itself essentially with species and naturally occurring hybrids, and the City of Cambridge Parks Department, where the named cultivars are grown. Here I saw several different forms of the Pyrenean *G. endressii*, that admirable pink-flowered cranesbill that is unsurpassed as evergreen ground-cover among the geranium tribe. *G. endressii* is invaluable in shade, and here the bright mauve-pink flowers (Graham Stuart Thomas, more kindly, calls them chalky pink, and E. A. Bowles likened them to the colour of raspberry ice) appear uninterruptedly all summer and autumn on 15–18 ins stems. Dr Yeo thought, until recently, that 'A. T. Johnson', a lighter, silvery pink, was no longer in cultivation. 'Rose Clair', he thought, might also have disappeared; it was originally described as having clear rose-salmon flowers, faintly veined. However, he now writes that 'although these names are in general circulation they are often borne by plants that have no right to them. For all that, plants bearing these names at Cherry Hinton Hall [Cambridge] do at least differ from one another in the ways implied by the descriptions, so my earlier-expressed fear that "A. T. Johnson" is lost may yet prove to be unfounded'.

John Hobson is more positive: '"A. T. Johnson" does exist!' I drew Dr Yeo's attention to this upon reading his book and we looked at the plants in the cultivar collection at Cherry Hinton. He agreed: 'one for the revised edition' was how he put it. 'I also believe I have "Rose Clair", but have not verified this to my satisfaction yet.' Beth Chatto has a form of G. *endressii* with deeper mauve-pink flowers, a thoroughly good doer highly thought of by John Hobson, whose pleasant task it is to grow and assess these different geranium cultivars; but not an easy colour to use perhaps. Nicest of all to my eye, and the one I chose to grow in my own garden, is 'Wargrave Pink', with light but bright salmon pink flowers over nicely cut foliage and the same dense, weed-proof habit of growth.

A hybrid of G. *endressii* that has vigour enough to colonise large areas, under trees or in the sun, is 'Claridge Druce', with dark foliage and bright petunia pink flowers during a long summer season. Hardly a border plant, this one; it is much too energetic a spreader. With G. *endressii* and its hybrids, indeed, we have come to a range of cranesbills that are well suited to planting among shrubs, or in light woodland. They are admirably designed to perform the combined role of ground-cover and of unifying, in their broad masses, a disparate collection of shrubs and other plants. Into this category, too, comes the strongly aromatic G. *macrorrhizum*, from the leaves of which oil of geranium is extracted commercially. These leaves, rounded in outline and sticky in texture, are evergreen, and take on brilliant autumn and winter tones of salmon, scarlet and apricot. The plant forms dense, entirely dependable ground-cover. The type has flowers in some shade of purplish-pink to near magenta, but like so many other species this one is variable in colour and has produced some splendid forms. 'Album' from Bulgaria, has fairly large white flowers with pink stamens, set in pink calyces; the effect is blush rather than white and it makes a fine ground-cover beneath white or pink flowering cherries, such as pink-flowered *Prunus sargentii*. 'Bevan's Variety' has deep magenta flowers in red calyces, a powerful colour clash which some find offensive (not me). Like 'Album', it was collected in the wild. So, too, was 'Ingwersen's Variety', a pretty pale mauve-pink variant with light green foliage. This and a slightly darker form from Bulgaria make, in a garden I know, an enchanting spring picture beneath a rowan, with the forget-me-not blue sprays of *Brunnera macrophylla*, pink and blue Spanish bluebells, lily of the valley, and plum-red *Dicentra formosa* 'Bountiful', blending in harmonious colours and forming total, weed-suppressing cover. This kind of planting lends itself to almost indefinite expansion; I can imagine adding pale pinky-mauve aquilegias, *Geranium sylvaticum* perhaps for height, the good lavender-blue Jacob's ladder *Polemonium foliosissimum*, Solomon's seal, and the spearing evergreen leaves of *Iris foetidissima* to add a contrast of shape all year.

Another cranesbill that would be well suited to such an informal setting is *G. phaeum* and its variants. The mourning widow grows in damp meadows and woodland edges, and is thus admirably adapted to growing in shade in our gardens. As the English name implies (it is an established alien, incidentally, not – as I thought until Dr Yeo corrected me – a British native) this is by no means a showy plant, but the little, nodding, deep maroon flowers with reflexed petals have their own charm. Slate-coloured forms are known as var. *lividum* and there is an exquisite white. A particularly fetching form with slightly larger lilac-mauve flowers and distinctive light green foliage has been named 'Lily Lovell'. *Geranium phaeum* and *G. macrorrhizum* both have variegated-leaved forms of absolutely no merit at all except in the eyes of those who like all variegations, regardless.

Herb Robert is another native cranesbill that is decidedly a plant for wilder parts of the garden. *G. robertianum* has two albino forms, 'Celtic White' and another whose pure white flowers are set off by red stems. This is sufficiently well thought of to be offered by two or three nurseries in response to a plea from the NCCPG to make it available commercially. It seeds true and, with a tiny root in proportion to its size, is easily removed if it appears where it shouldn't. The white form of *Geranium sanguineum*, the bloody cranesbill (also native to these islands, though the albino is European) is another for wildish places, for it is much larger and floppier in growth than the crimson-magenta type.

For the front of a sunny border, raised beds, or rock gardens if not too small, *G. sanguineum* itself, and many of its forms, are well suited; they form low mounds and freely interweave themselves among their neighbours. The bloody cranesbill (blood was never this blue) flowers freely over a long period, starting in early summer. Several forms have been named and one, 'Jubilee Pink', was thought worthy of the highest award, a First Class Certificate, at the RHS Trials held at Wisley in 1976. It is fairly compact, and has flowers of bright magenta-pink. From the same stable (Jack Drake's nursery at Aviemore) came 'Shepherd's Warning', deeper and redder in colour, which though not so well received at the trial is considered superior by its raiser. 'Glenluce' is an older plant, collected by A. T. Johnson around 1935, and distinguished by wild-rose pink flowers and silky leaves. The smallest of the *sanguineum* forms is var. *lancastriense*, in palest sugar-pink with crimson veins, a honey of a plant for the front of a small border, for raised beds or among rocks.

Geranium sanguineum var. *lancastriense*, indeed, is beginning to lead us firmly towards the rock garden, where *G. traversii* var. *elegans*, a putative parent of 'Mavis Simpson', would be well suited in a warmish, well-drained pocket. Native of the Chatham Islands, it grows wild on coastal cliffs, and in the garden is best displayed at the edge of a raised bed or trailing over a rock face. All who see it fall for its silvered leaves, of notched and rounded outline, and pale shell-pink flowers. *Geranium traversii* itself when first discovered was described as having white flowers, but this form, already believed to be in danger of extinction in our gardens immediately after the Hitler war, now seems to be lost to cultivation. Mr Walter E. Th. Ingwersen, who voiced that fear in his admirable booklet about geraniums, which appeared in 1946, described it as a compact mound of 6 ins or so in Sussex but an invasive, leafy, flowerless mass in a south Devon garden. Let me assure you that the pink var. *elegans*, in the south Devon garden where I grew it, was by no means invasive and flowered copiously. It grew here on a border's edge above a low retaining wall, and seemed indeed to suffer, not from excess wet as in Mr Ingwersen's experience, but from drought; the plants near the edge were apt to shrivel in dry spells. Its companions were *Parahebe* (*Veronica*) *perfoliata*, that curious Australian veronica with eucalyptus-like foliage and sprays of clear lavender flowers and, for later flower, the slightly bluer *Convolvulus mauretanicus*, its satiny cups a happy combination with the opaque pink of the geranium.

Of similar stature and spread is *G. cinereum* and its forms. All have greyish foliage, forming neat clumps, with flowers varying in colour from white to brilliant magenta of *G. cinereum* var. *subcaulescens* and its selected forms. 'Ballerina' is widely available, a dear little plant with subdued, half-mourning-mauve flowers heavily veined in dark red. Very similar, though less seductively named, is 'Laurence Flatman', distinguished by the inverted triangle of darker colour at the apex of each petal. The shocking magenta flowers of *Geranium cinereum* var. *subcaulescens*, like those of the much taller *G. psilostemon* already described, are enhanced by a black central blotch, very dark red veins and black stigmas and stamens. With its form 'Giuseppi' and 'Splendens', it is large enough to find a place at the front of a small border but compact enough for most rock gardens; all prefer to grow in full sun, with good drainage.

Hybrids between *G. cinereum* and its close ally *G. argenteum* are collectively known as *G. × lindavicum*. 'Apple Blossom' is one of them, with silvered leaves and almost white, faintly veined flowers. At Cambridge, in a corner of the nursery ground, I photographed an as yet unnamed × *lindavicum* cultivar with opal-white flowers.

G. argenteum itself is one of the gems of the alpine geraniums. Over small, finely cut and intensely silvered leaves appear, in June and July, flowers of palest pink to white – in Reginald Farrer's words: 'great diaphanous dog-rose blossoms'. This exquisite creature needs no more than grey rock to set it off; and is all the better for short commons, for in rich soil it becomes a bloated version of its true self. At its best it is surpassed only by *G. farreri*, an enchanting but rather tricky customer

from screes and shingle of the Min Shan in Kansu (China). The pale pink
flowers of G. *farreri* are pointed up by dark stamens.

Much easier than this, if less aristocratic, is *Geranium dalmaticum*, in effect
a miniature G. *macrorrhizum* lacking the pungently aromatic foliage and,
like it, variable in colour from mid rose-pink to white. The two are closely
related and have hybridised. G. *dalmaticum* itself is a delightful, easy rock
garden plant for sun or light shade. At Wisley it grows vertically in a
retaining wall with tiny ferns, with which its neat glossy foliage contrasts
charmingly. The hybrids, bearing the group name G. × *cantabrigiense*, are
larger and aromatic. A form produced by deliberate cross-pollination at
Cambridge University Botanic Garden has rosy-purple flowers; 'Biokovo'
is a white-flowered form found growing wild in Yugoslavia. Where G.
macrorrhizum itself might prove too far-spreading, these hybrids could be
a fine substitute.

Despite its running habit I have a soft spot for G. *pylzowianum*; its
thread-like stems, finely divided leaves and little underground tubers can
scarcely harm any but the choicest alpines, and its large rosy-mauve
flowers are enhanced by a greenish centre where the sepals are visible.
Closely related is the plant known to gardeners as G. *stapfianum roseum*.
Dr Yeo's research has tracked this down with reasonable certainty to G.
orientalitibeticum, so the plant has exchanged one cumbersome name for
another. Larger and more inclined to smother its neighbours than G.
pylzowianum, it is a plant for the border front rather than a rock garden.
As a companion for a rose such as 'Little White Pet', it is admirably in
scale.

Invasive for another reason is the little New Zealand geranium with
chocolate-brown leaves, that die off appealingly to shades of apricot and
orange. Be warned; G. *sessiliflorum* 'Nigricans' seeds itself around ardently
and is apt to put its deep taproot straight down the centre of your most
treasured alpines, whence it cannot be extracted without carnage. Where
such nasty habits do not matter it is a dear little plant. I can envisage its
odd-coloured foliage with the coppery-bronze New Zealand sedge, *Carex
buchananii*, with other oddities such as *Corokia cotoneaster*, the wire-netting
bush, or some of the New Zealand coprosmas with similarly wiry stems.
I once raised a big batch, from seed, of *Coprosma rugosa*. As babies they
were irresistible, all shades of olive and copper, chocolate and bronze, and
I grew enthusiastic about just such a grouping; but as the coprosmas grew
up, so they became greener and less seductive.

I have as yet made no mention of a group of geraniums of quite distinct
character, suited in the main to mild, sheltered gardens and well deserving
a place in the conservatory in colder areas. In the 1960s a regular visitor
to Cambridge was Harold Pickering, who lived in Madeira. He produced
for the Botanic Garden what he called 'the Giant Geranium', which was

in cultivation in Madeira and which he had also found growing wild there in a remote spot reached by a tunnel. Major Pickering's giant geranium turned out to be a new species, closely related to another Madeiran endemic, *G. palmatum* (also known as *G. anemonifolium*) and, Dr Yeo tells me, 'was by some dismissed as being that long-known plant. Pickering insisted it was different and I grew it alongside *G. palmatum* and *G. canariense* at Cambridge.' The giant geranium is now called *G. maderense* and, when they are seen growing side by side, small differences between *G. maderense*, *G. palmatum* and *G. canariense* are clearly seen: differences that are hard to detect in dried herbarium specimens. *G. canariense*, unlike the other two, is endemic to the Canary Islands and has a close ally in *G. rubescens* from Madeira, a fairly hardy plant very like a large Herb Robert, with beetroot-red stems and magnificent overwintering rosettes of foliage.

All these big rosette-forming geraniums have handsome deeply cut leaves, those of *G. maderense* the most elegantly fern-like of all. *G. rubescens* is a biennial, but *G. canariense* and *G. palmatum* are both perennial and bear, over their great mounds of foliage (held on a short stem in the former) wide dense sprays of fuchsia pink flowers, up to 4 ft tall in *G. palmatum*. *G. canariense* flowers earlier than *G. palmatum*, and *G. maderense* habitually begins even earlier, in February under glass. It is a gigantic aromatic plant with a distinct stem to the leaf rosette, flowering at anything up to 5 ft with a huge inflorescence of magenta-pink flowers 'surrounded by the purplish-haze of its glandular hairs' (Yeo). A big plant which has developed a tallish stem, propped by its own leaf stalks that bend backwards like the spokes of an umbrella, is a grand sight. Although it looks so lush in leaf, it is extremely resistant to summer drought and does much of its growing in winter. Flowering so early it is a bold and striking plant, whether in flower or only in leaf, for a conservatory. *G. palmatum* and *G. canariense* grow well out of doors in mild areas, and I have succeeded with them in the bone-dry, rooty shade of a big *Pittosporum ralphii*, where their lilac-pink flowers made a charming setting for the purple corduroy petals of *Osteospermum* 'Peggii' sprawling at their feet. They grew equally happily, when not eaten by rabbits, in the same garden in an open border, coinciding in flower over a lengthy season with the pale lilac spires of *Erysimum linifolium* 'Variegatum'.

There are many more geraniums worthy of growing in our gardens, and I am conscious that I have left out several that are not just lurking in botanic gardens and in the National Collections, but can actually be bought quite readily. However, the genus *Geranium* is bidding to take over this section, if not the whole book, and I must therefore direct you, if you are smitten by them, to Dr Yeo's recent book *Hardy Geraniums*, or to Graham Stuart Thomas's *Perennial Garden Plants* where several species are described in his habitual beguiling prose. Read, too, Mr Ingwersen's booklet, and any of Mr A. T. Johnson's books on gardening: it is largely thanks to these two great gardeners of an earlier generation that geraniums came to be appreciated in our gardens.

The National Collections

The National Collections of Geranium *are at the University Botanic Garden, Cambridge, and at Cherry Hinton Hall, Cherry Hinton Road, Cambridge (Cambridge City Council).*

Geranium species and primary hybrids are grown at the University Botanic Garden, where Dr Peter Yeo had assembled a very complete collection of a genus in which he has a great interest (see Bibliography at the end of this book). The collection was designated as a National Collection in October 1981, one of the very early entrants to the scheme. Later it was suggested that the City Council Parks Department should take on the responsibility for Geranium *cultivars, and in March 1984 these were formally adopted as a National Collection. (A similar division has been adopted with* Bergenia *and* Fritillaria *at Cambridge.) Thus the University Botanic Garden can participate in the National Collections scheme without becoming involved in the many garden cultivars which, it is felt, do not properly form part of its main interest, while interested students of the genus* Geranium *can see both species and garden cultivars at nearby sites.*

Heuchera

Heuchera is a genus of plants in the Saxifrage family, originating from the North American continent, and comprising a number of species of quiet charm together with one of brilliant colouring. This one, the coral bells (*H. sanguinea*) has imparted its vivid tones to a range of cultivars falling, as we shall see, into two main groups. Both, in their different ways, have escaped the trend to blowsy vulgarity that all too often afflicts plants once the breeders have bestowed attention upon them. When to such impeccable restraint in *Heuchera* you add foliage that is pleasing at worst, and beautiful at its best, you have a race of plants that should be seen everywhere; and if their cultivation were well understood, probably would be.

As with other National Collections in which both species and cultivars are represented, I will first describe some of the species before turning to the garden varieties deriving from them.

Alphabetically at the head of the list, first to reach Britain – it was probably introduced by John Tradescant the younger, who made several trips to Virginia from 1637 onwards and certainly had it growing in his garden at Lambeth by 1656 – is *H. americana*, the alum root. It is one of the most handsome in foliage, as suggested by its other English name, satin leaf. This well describes the beautiful sheen of the broad, dark green leaves, enhanced in youth by coppery veins. Some forms are suffused with coppery-red, deepening to plum purple on the undersides of the leaves. This fine foliage, whether green or copper, forms good weed–excluding clumps above which the tiny greenish flowers are borne in little spires at the usual heuchera season of early summer. Mary Ramsdale, who holds the National Collection in her Essex garden, writes that 'it is interesting to note the substantial lobed leaf with its faint diffusion of colour along the veins which is typical in the collected plant, and to contrast it with the vine-shaped leaf with its soft suffusion of bronze and satiny texture

198

that characterises the plant available in commerce as *H. americana*'. In old gardens are found intermediates between the two extremes, suggesting that the plant of commerce is the result of conscious or unconscious selection over the years. A plant which some authors give as *H. × grayana*, suggesting that it is a hybrid between *H. richardsonii* and *H. americana*, is considered by others to be the first link in a chain of forms which connect the two species. *H. undulata*, too, with plain green, wavy-edged leaves, may be a child of the alum root.

H. richardsonii is the name borne, in her writings, by a heuchera favoured by Miss Jekyll for its bronze-red foliage, but it does not sound much like *H. richardsonii* in the National Collection, which Mary Ramsdale describes as having short-stemmed heart-shaped leaves, white velvet-downy, and tiny greenish-white flowers. Whatever Miss Jekyll's coppery-leaved heuchera, it must have been handsome in her spring garden combined with red primroses, or with bronze-red and brown wallflowers, and orange and scarlet tulips, giving way to the cold white blooms and green-black foliage of *Iberis sempervirens*. Hortus III, an American publication, gives *H. richardsonii* as a synonym of *H. hispida*, the older name. Here the plant is also given the name satin leaf, and Hortus III notes that it turns crimson in winter, a description which better fits garden forms or hybrids of *H. americana*.

Deepest of all in leaf colour is 'Palace Purple', which occurred at Kew Gardens. Seeking to acquire plants cultivated prior to 1700 for the Queen's Garden behind Kew Palace, Brian Halliwell, Assistant Curator, had seed of *Heuchera americana* from a North American botanic garden. Some seedlings had red foliage, unfading as the season advanced though brightest in spring. Subsequent generations from these red-leaved heucheras revealed that they come virtually true from seed. The plant received an Award of Merit from the Royal Horticultural Society in 1982, and has been identified as a form of *H. micrantha diversifolia*.

With large, somewhat ivy-shaped leaves, 'Palace Purple' is a handsome foliage plant for permanent plantings, whether in conventional borders or island beds, or among shrubs. It is also especially valuable in spring and summer bedding, raised fresh each year for the best colour from young plants. Sown in July for spring bedding, Brian Halliwell recommends it as a companion to the lily-flowered tulip 'White Triumphator', or blue Dutch Iris 'Wedgwood'. Mary Ramsdale likes to use the less well-coloured seedlings from a home-raised batch as a softer contrast to variegated foliage. I should like to see it, for example, with the broad-bladed sedge from Japan, *Carex siderosticta* 'Variegata'.

H. micrantha itself is very beautiful in leaf, with grey marblings to set off tall plumes of countless tiny blush-white flowers on pink stems. It has imparted its airy grace to a range of cultivars, as we shall see. Also airy and elegant in flower is creamy-white *H. villosa*, but this is quite different from other heucheras in its large, maple-like leaves of clear apple-green on long stems, and its late summer flowering season, matching the willow gentian for which it makes a pretty companion. *H. villosa* often colours in autumn, as do *H. pubescens* and *H. glabra*. *H. pubescens* is also attractive in new young leaf, of a delicate bronze. The flowers may be greenish white, suffused with purple, or there is a good albino. *H. glabra* (formerly *Tiarella colorans*) is stoloniferous, making good ground cover, with narrow deeply lobed leaves and open panicles of flower in early summer.

There are two distinct forms of the Californian *H. pilosissima*. The National Collection plant is furred with pale, rusty brown hairs, and has lobed, crenate leaves forming a dense clump, over which on 14 ins stems airy panicles of tiny white flowers with a reddish tinge give, writes Mary Ramsdale, 'the appearance of a delicate pink cloud'. The other form has white velvety hairs and the greyish-blush flowers are borne in plumy sprays; it is not fully hardy.

H. cylindrica forsakes the grace of these species, though still with good, dark green, heart-shaped leaves making solid clumps. The stems are stiffly upright, typically bearing pokery spikes of small brownish flowers. Alan Bloom's Hyperion' is a much better colour, and free-flowering, in deep old-rose pink, with marbled leaves. It is shorter growing than his *H. cylindrica* 'Greenfinch', which is the plant that first aroused Mary Ramsdale's interest in heucheras, and is sought after by flower arrangers and amateurs of green flowers for its 3 ft spikes of creamy jade and silver-marbled leaves. *H. c.* 'Alba' is ivory white; 'Green Ivory' is a seedling of 'Greenfinch', strong and free, with more white in the flower. All the forms of *H. cylindrica* flower a little after the main run of heucheras, in summer, and Mary Ramsdale likes to use 'Greenfinch' with white or yellow daisies, or with gold foliage.

All the heucheras thus far described are of gentle, subfusc or even nondescript colour. For richness and brilliance of tone it is to *H. sanguinea* and its offspring that we must turn. The coral bells is shorter, at 12 ins or so, than the species we have thus far been considering. The leaves are dark and marbled, the large flowers clear coral-scarlet. The first plants of *H. sanguinea* were brought, it seems, from Mexico in an open basket, six roots carefully nurtured through the long sea voyage, by Dr Murray in 1885. By 1887 it had received a First Class Certificate from the Royal Horticultural Society, when shown by Thomas Ware of Tottenham Hall nurseries whence the plant was introduced to general cultivation. Early cultivars or hybrids of *H. sanguinea* such as 'Pluie de Feu' or 'Huntsman' were of good, clear colouring, but not free-flowering; or, like the dull pink 'Pruhonicia', bore large flowers over good foliage but were of dim colouring. From 1920 onwards Mr Bloom senior, Alan Bloom's father, turned his attention to heucheras, Alan himself continuing the work from 1931. Most of today's named kinds are the result of Alan Bloom's work over forty years, developing the plants not for the market but as garden plants. His own favourites include those, such as 'Scintillation' with massed pink bells rimmed with crimson, that received Royal Horticultural Society awards. 'Scintillation' achieved a Highly Commended in 1956, Award of Merit in 1957 and First Class Certificate, the highest accolade, in 1958: perhaps a record achievement for one plant. 'Red Spangles' is of intense blood-red colouring and 'Firebird' (Award of Merit 1960) crimson-scarlet. 'Freedom' (AM 1938) in rose-pink, 'Rhapsody' (AM 1959 – 'the best pink' according to Alan Bloom, writing in 1967), coral-rose 'Oakington Jewel' (AM 1938), pink 'Jubilee' and deeper 'Ibis', and soft-toned 'Apple Blossom', with 'Snowflake', extend the colour range, while 'Shere Variety' – not of Mr Bloom's raising – is a good dwarf scarlet and 'Pretty Polly' a clear pink of similar stature. 'Sunset' is a late-flowering red extending the already quite long season of heucheras. 'Zabeliana', though appearing in the lists as though a species, is according to some authors a child of *H. sanguinea*, with tall pale-pink, long-stalked flowers. The National Collection plant, however, has sober brown-purple spikes.

Many descendants of *H. sanguinea* inherit fine silver-marbled foliage, and all display the larger flower of that parent, but something of its clumsiness too, when seen against the airy elegance of the *H. × brizoides* types. These have from the *H. micrantha* parent their slender sprays of many tiny flowers.

H. micrantha itself received an Award of Merit in 1896, its pink form in 1900, and *H. m.* 'Gracillima' in 1902. This last was one of the heucheras grown by Alan Bloom's father as a cut flower, valued for its 'thin wiry stems branching out to carry scores of tiny pink bells'. 'Rosamunde' is another old *H. × brizoides* type with tiny pink flowers. But once again it is Alan Bloom's work with heucheras that has given us the finest kinds for our gardens. Indeed, the first breakthrough he made with the genus, combining freedom of flower with rich colouring, was 'Bloom's Variety', developed originally as a cut flower for the Bloom family's market-growing business; it received its Award of Merit in 1932 for its coral-red bells on 2 ft stems. 'Splendour' is a later kind (AM 1959), its scarlet flowers tipped salmon, its foliage – a legacy again of *H. micrantha* – especially good. 'Sparkler' in carmine and scarlet, 'Coral Cloud' with shiny, crinkly leaves, intense carmine 'Gloriana' (AM 1957), pink 'Mary Rose', opalescent 'Pearl Drops' and ivory-tinged flesh 'Orphée' all inherit the light, open panicles of *H. × brizoides*.

Heucheras are not, it must be said, plants for the 'stick 'em in and let 'em alone' gardener. They need a well-drained, rich but not heavy soil and a sunny position. On stodgy clay or cold wet soils they do not thrive, but a sandy or thin soil if well laced with rotted manure or compost will grow good heucheras. They tend, on any soil, to grow out of the ground and become woody, so they should be top dressed annually with sifted compost to encourage new fibrous roots. A heuchera that has gone woody is one that will quickly die if you turn your back. Then, every three years or so, you should lift, divide and deeply reset your heucheras, discarding the woody portions and retaining those with some fibrous roots. This operation should be carried out after flowering, from July to September: though some authors suggest October or March, and much depends on the season. Given these attentions, *Heuchera* is a genus of grace and balance, qualities not invariably allied, in other genera, with the range of clear colours offered by the descendants of the coral bells.

The National Collection

Mary Ramsdale's National Collection of Heuchera *was originally intended to be held by the Northern Home Counties Group of the Hardy Plant Society, as a result of a suggestion made by the HPS Conservation Subcommittee, but in the event the Group felt unable to take on the responsibility. Meanwhile, Mary Ramsdale had already begun collecting plants of the genus, in which she had an interest, so it was agreed, in November 1982, that she should take on the Collection. Mary Ramsdale also holds a National Collection of* Sidalcea, *and was responsible for building up the Collection of* Chrysanthemum maximum *(the Shasta daisies) which is now the responsibility of the Ayr and Arran Group of the NCCPG. As an active and knowledgeable member of both the NCCPG and the Hardy Plant Society, Mary Ramsdale exemplifies the close cooperation between the two organisations.*

Kniphofia

MOST people's conception of a kniphofia begins and ends at the common red-hot poker, a rather coarse thing that usually inspires contempt or even active dislike. It is very rewarding, therefore, to hear the reactions of garden visitors who haven't previously encountered anything beyond this despised thing, when they see the collection of kniphofias grouped together, showing their tremendous diversity of colour, size and even shape.

The old red-hot poker, *Kniphofia uvaria*, was one of the first species to be introduced to Britain from their native South Africa, towards the end of the eighteenth century. During the next 100 years other species were introduced, and by the end of the nineteenth century thirty-five species were known in South Africa. At about this time the German nurseryman Max Leichtlin, of Baden Baden, became interested in kniphofias and began importing seeds and plants from South Africa. From these he made some spectacular hybrids, now mostly extinct, but the most famous of all, 'Star of Baden Baden', may have been rediscovered recently in Ireland. It was, or is, typical of the massive, rather tender hybrids he favoured, though its buff-yellow colouring tinged with greenish-bronze is more muted than most.

Several new species were based on Max Leichtlin's introductions, and one was named for him. *Kniphofia leichtlinii* was one of the species grown by Compton Mackenzie, who as well as being a novelist of repute and enormous output, was a passionately keen amateur gardener. When living in Cornwall he turned his attention to kniphofias, growing all the Leichtlin hybrids he could as well as a good many species. Both *K. leichtlinii* and the similiar *K. comosa*, the first with almost erect light canary-yellow flowers enhanced by protruding crimson stamens, the second much smaller with yellow stamens, are now considered to fall within *K. pumila*, so Herr Leichtlin's work with the genus must live on in our memories, and perhaps in the plants of 'Star of Baden Baden' in the National Collection.

We are perhaps apt to think that all early kniphofias were of the 'Star of Baden Baden' persuasion. However, a note in the *Gardeners' Chronicle* in 1906 suggests that there was already a great range of colours and sizes of poker available: 'Kniphofias ... can now be had in many fascinating shades of colour, ranging from creamy-white through all shades of yellow, apricot, coral, red and crimson, either self-coloured or in the two or three contrasting shades peculiar to the group.... They vary from slender, multi-flowered, grassy tufts a foot in height ... to noble plants ... which have a grand effect in large borders and in the garden landscape.'

As we will see with other groups of plants described in this book, some cultivars are undoubtedly considerably more robust than the norm and survive for decades where others seem to die out in a few short years. Both 'Gold Else' and 'Chrysantha', dating from the earliest years of this century and belonging to the 'slender, multi-flowered' type, are still grown, and the former is readily available in commerce. Slim and grassy-leaved, it has neat, clear lemon-yellow pokers appearing in June. It combines delightfully with *Achillea clypeolata* in similar colouring but with flat plates of flower among grey foliage, and the soft scarlet *Penstemon* 'Firebird' in a mixed group with the Old Velvet rose, deep maroon *Rosa gallica* 'Tuscany'.

There were several breeders of kniphofias around the time of the 1914–18 war, Prichards of Christchurch among them. Their catalogues of the years before and after the Great War list dozens of varieties, many of their own raising. One such was the famous 'C. M. Prichard', whose name has become attached for some reason to *K. rooperi*. (I will examine some of the difficulties of naming kniphofias later in this chapter.) *K. rooperi* is a massive autumn-flowering poker with fat goose-egg heads of orange and yellow, a robust and handsome thing to set among tall, azure-blue *Salvia uliginosa*, which can be allowed to loll into the stiff, upstanding pokers. At the other extreme in size and shape is *K. galpinii* (of gardens), also autumn-flowering, with grass-fine leaves and slender flames of red-orange flowers opening from green buds. Try it set about with masses of grey foliage, for in autumn the silvers acquire a special tender luminosity that suits the cool, misty atmosphere and enhances the slim coral spears of the kniphofia.

Few kniphofias enjoy cold, wet winters, but the grassy-leaved kinds such as *K. triangularis*, in which *K. galpinii*, *K. macowanii* and *K. nelsonii* are now considered to reside, are among the hardiest. But in mild climates such as suit the greatest range of pokers, you can use a supporting cast of plants like the Mexican salvias, which combine well with the pokers in colour and have an immensely long flowering season. This helps to pull together a collection of which different members flower in every month of the year. Gazanias need bedding out each year, but 'Silver Beauty', 'Cream Beauty' and others are worth the little trouble; their prostrate growth and silver foliage are a perfect complement to the spiky pokers, and their bright lemon or soft cream daisies are just right for matching flower colour with contrasting shape. The NCCPG's new gazania, the double 'Yellow Buttons', would be a splendid poker companion. Like the kniphofias, they are South African in origin, and so are osteospermums (which used to be called *Dimorphotheca* and are still more familiar under that name). The white and the blue-flushed osteospermums, like 'Blue Streak', and the pale yellow, bronze-backed 'Buttermilk', again mix well; daisies once more but very superior ones to assort with the choicest, tenderest kniphofias – if you can get them.

All the spreaders, plants of low growth with insinuating arms, suit pokers well, weaving among the clumps. With the salmon and coral-pink pokers, little pale 'Modesta', deeper 'Timothy', 'Sunset', long-spiked 'Dawn Sunkissed' and the stouter 'Severn Salmon', *Sphaeralcea munroana* and the energetic *Malvastrum lateritium* look very well. Both are spreading, semi-woody mallows, the first with little coral-pink cups and the mal-vastrum with larger flowers, warm apricot-buff with bright terracotta centres.

Kniphofia 'Chrysantha', as we have seen, is an old hybrid, a seedling of the species *K. citrina*, which dates from before 1906. It quickly increases and produces masses of its neat, green-budded tapering spikes opening to clear yellow, beautifully framed by the little orange-scarlet trumpets of *Zauschneria* 'Dublin'.

Needing a warm spot at the foot of a south-facing wall is 'Zululandii', a very early-flowering vermilion-scarlet poker. Here too if you can obtain it you should plant *K. ichopensis*, a most beautiful species with widely-spaced curving tubes in sharp yellow, just touched with orange in the bud, growing from a tuft of leaves that look most un-poker-like, more like a Spanish iris perhaps. Another rather tender oddity is *K. isoetifolia*, an Abyssinian species which flowers in autumn, in light orange-apricot, opening from the top downwards to produce a delightful mopheaded effect.

One of the oddest of all pokers, loved by some and loathed by others, is 'Erecta'. This very old named cultivar starts by looking like any other poker in a good clear scarlet, but soon the conventionally down-facing florets begin to turn, to a point first straight out at right angles to the stem, and finally vertically upward, clasping the stem so that the flower spike looks immaculately upside-down. I like it because of its colour, its willingness to grow, and the fact that its weird behaviour keeps the spike clean for much longer than many pokers; too many have that tendency to die off at the base before they have properly opened at the apex.

Some of the most striking hybrid pokers have very long, narrow spikes. 'Samuel's Sensation' is one of them, a beautiful shade of coral-scarlet paling to creamy-buff at the base. Mr Watkin Samuel (better known for his delphiniums) bred a great many pokers between the wars, striving always for quality of flower spike and especially to eliminate the tendency to go off at the base before the top of the spike properly opens. Sadly, very few of his pokers still seem to exist; 'Wrexham Buttercup' is one of his, a fine yellow that is highly thought of (and won an award, like 'Samuel's Sensation', at the recent Wisley kniphofia trials). All pokers grow very easily from seed, and you can get some fine things if you don't mind their having no name. At Threave in Scotland, one September, I saw a fair-sized bed of mixed pokers growing from knee-high to well over my head, in every colour a poker can adopt: near-white and cream, through all the buffs and yellows from primrose to canary, apricot, near-pink, coral and salmon, tawny gold, amber and orange, vermilion, scarlet and dusky crimson, as well as green. All these had been raised from one head of 'Samuel's Sensation'.

All this makes identification a very hazardous business. The best description you are likely to find, unless of an award-winning poker, is something like 'red, 3ft, August' in an old catalogue. This would fit probably sixty or seventy pokers, even among the named kinds; and unnamed seedlings, some excellent, in gardens throughout the country add to the confusion. Really the only way to be sure of correctly naming a cultivar is to have it from an impeccable source, but even this is far from straightforward, as two of the pokers in the Collection demonstrate. One is 'Underway', bred by that famous amateur gardener Norman Hadden, of Porlock. This came to the National Collection from two sources: one was the Savill Gardens (Crown Estate Commissioners), the other an amateur gardener who knew Norman Hadden well and had his plant of 'Underway' from Mr Hadden himself. When they flowered they were quite different, one much paler and with a more cylindrical spike than the other. On the face of it, the plant that came at only one remove from the raiser should be the right thing; but so eminent an authority as Graham Thomas maintains that the Savill plant is the true 'Underway', received by him from Mr Hadden and donated to the Savill Gardens. The donor of the other is certain that there could have been no muddle in his hands. Which one *is* 'Underway'?

The classic muddle over poker names is one I have already alluded to, 'C. M. Prichard'. This name is now firmly attached to *K. rooperi*, which I have already described as having large, goose-egg-shaped heads of orange and yellow in autumn. Go back to the original description in the catalogue of the breeders of 'C. M. Prichard', Messrs Prichard of Christchurch, of 1910 (the year they introduced 'C. M. Prichard') and you find 'self yellow, massive spike, 4–5 ft, August–September'. In 1922 the plant won an Award of Merit at the RHS, and was described as a bright yellow variety 'of tall and stately habit'. By the late fifties, however, the name seems to have got itself attached to *K. rooperi* in the nursery of the Prichard brothers themselves, perhaps due to a mix-up in the nursery rows (by this time the brothers were advanced in years and the nursery was declining). Understandable enough, however, to accept a plant that comes from the raisers themselves as the correct thing. Meanwhile, the real 'C. M. Prichard' seems to be lost for good. To add piquancy to the search, however, you should know that the plant believed to be 'Star of Baden Baden' came to the National Collection in Cheshire under the name 'C. M. Prichard' – and though the first is of more muted colouring, both can fittingly be described as 'tall and stately yellow' kniphofias.

But to return to the different shades and shapes of pokers, the near-whites and creams are often tinged chartreuse or lime-green in bud, and they come in all sizes. 'Little Maid' is a superb small, slim poker, no more than 18 ins high of which at least half is flower, not stem. This is one of several good pokers, now mostly lost, bred in the seventies by Beth Chatto. It is alarming just how quickly distinct kinds of pokers can disappear from cultivation, and it emphasises how important the National Collections movement is in conserving garden plants. Much bigger than 'Little Maid' is 'Maid of Orleans', an American cultivar from the fifties, once widely offered by the nursery trade but now only around in private gardens and no longer, I believe, in commerce. 'Torchbearer' is a selection from a strain known as Lemon Cream, of which 'Maid of Orleans' is one parent (the other is the massive crimson-red 'Prince Igor'), and another poker of the same parentage, with more green in the bud, is 'Mermaiden'. Greener still is one of Beth Chatto's pokers that seems imperturbably hardy and robust, the aptly-named 'Green Jade'. Its true green spikes, appearing in August, blend well with galtonias in white (*G. candicans*) or green (*G. princeps*), their large bells forming spires on 3 ft stems, and with a late, pale yellow daylily, or the lemon yellow *Crocosmia* 'Citronella' perhaps. But names can be misleading: 'Limelight', which you might expect to be quite green, is a canary yellow poker with cylindrical spikes appearing in mid-autumn, green only in bud.

Most of these hybrid pokers have closely packed heads of flower. Another quite different style of poker takes after species like *K. snowdenii* (properly *K. thomsonii* subsp. *snowdenii*) with its widely-spaced curving florets, somewhat reminiscent of a lachenalia. 'Zeal Primrose' is a very nice example of this type, with pale primrose flowers widely spaced on shortish stems.

So far I have mentioned chiefly the smaller pokers, short in growth, slender in flower spike: very suitable for small-scale planting and intimate border groups. There is a whole range of big, bold pokers, however, which lend themselves to the sort of landscape effects described by William Robinson and Gertrude Jekyll in their writings. They both liked to see large groups of red-hot pokers with bamboos, pampas grass and even the big Japanese polygonums, which we now find such a menace for their spreading ways. There is no need to include such invasive weeds in our landscape schemes, but large groups of orange and vermilion pokers in a wide setting can still look very fine, with plenty of good green foliage around, and perhaps the creamy plumes of *Holodiscus* or *Sorbaria*, the weird spiky green heads of the hardy papyrus, *Cyperus vegetus*, or perhaps with *Hydrangea arborescens* 'Grandiflora' which has no pink at all in its make-up, just creamy-green and white. One of the best pokers of this kind was received as 'Hidcote Seedling', a giant of a thing on stout 6 ft stems; 'Mount Etna' is another big robust poker of similar vermilion and orange colouring, shorter at about 4 ft. Many species of wild origin are of this type: *K. tysonii* subsp. *tysonii* and *K. praecox*, for example. Then there is the massive 'Nobilis' which, like *K. praecox*, has won awards at Royal Horticultural Society shows and trials.

The original National Collection was first formed in Gloucestershire and moved with its owners to Coleton Fishacre on the south Devon coast. Here there was space to plan for big bold groups of pokers to be seen against the sea and sky. Probably the most famous poker for seaside gardens, growing happily almost in sand-dunes, is 'Atlanta'. This big, glaucous-blue-leaved poker produces its stout red and yellow flowers very early, in April or May, and gets its name from the hotel garden where it was found growing in Cornwall; but it originated in Surrey, not by the sea at all.

Another way to use the big, bold pokers, if you have not the space for landscape schemes, is in a late summer border group where – emulating Graham Thomas – you could plant them with *Ligularia* 'Desdemona' which has large, kidney-shaped purple-backed leaves, *Crocosmia* 'Lucifer', *Hypericum* 'Hidcote' (or 'Rowallane' perhaps in milder gardens) and a golden-leaved shrub such as *Cornus alba* 'Aurea' (all lime yellow) or 'Spaethii' (green and gold), or *Philadelphus coronarius* 'Aureus', which has the bonus of sweet scent from its early summer flowers. Another group I once saw, and liked very much, had big pokers with the hardy, lime yellow-leaved *Fuchsia* 'Genii' and *Lobelia laxiflora*. This, unlike bedding lobelias, is a more or less hardy perennial with narrow leaves and slim, red and yellow trumpets in summer.

At Wisley and also at the Savill Gardens kniphofias are grown with other monocots, all plants having sword-shaped or spiky leaves: agapan-

thus, yuccas and crocosmias, daylilies and galtonias. Agapanthus in blue
and white look particularly good with yellow and apricot pokers. In the
south Devon garden where the National Collection was formerly housed,
this idea was adapted for a milder climate, with the addition of hedychiums
(half-hardy members of the ginger family), cannas, and watsonias (South
African plants related to, and rather resembling very refined gladioli). An
amusing group was composed of *K.* 'Royal Standard', an old Prichard
cultivar with fairly short stems topped with nicely-shaped two tone spikes
of clear vermilion-scarlet and sharp yellow, behind a hardy aloe which,
when it flowered, produced a closely similar flower spike over its narrowly
triangular, saw-edged leaves. Kniphofias were originally considered to be
aloes (Linnaeus described the first species to be introduced, *K. uvaria*, as
Aloe uvaria, following earlier authors), and seeing these two flowering
together it was easy to see why the two groups might have been considered
to be one.

Most of the groups I have been describing are for summer and autumn,
from the early June flowers of 'Gold Else' to *K. rooperi*'s big October
flower heads. You can have flowers all the year on your pokers, given a
fairly open winter, if you plant *K. sarmentosa*. This is a true species, related
to *K. caulescens* and echoing, rather less dramatically, that species' bold
blue-grey foliage. In summer, *K. sarmentosa* produces fairly ordinary
flower spikes, reddish coral from glaucous-green buds, but as the weather
cools so do the colours of its flowers, until in late autumn they are the
palest jade green just touched with coral, elegantly tapering to the apex
of the spike when in tight bud, with the lower flowers just opening,
standing out horizontally. These delicious confections (for yes, they do
look almost edible) continue to appear all through winter, not just in a
mild climate like that of south Devon but also, I read in an old *Gardeners'
Chronicle*, in chilly Ledbury in the West Midlands.

Both *K. sarmentosa* and *K. caulescens*, bolder and bluer in foliage and
with fatter, cylindrical spikes of coral pink and creamy lemon enhanced
by a fuzz of protruding stamens, look superb in a sea of grey-felted
Helichrysum petiolare, with the clear blue-lilac cups of *Convolvulus mauretanicus* and the strange, hooded, dove-mauve and greenish-cream flowers
of *Gladiolus papilio*. The convolvulus comes, as its name implies, from
North Africa, but the other components of this group, like the pokers,
are from South Africa. It is fun to mix plants according to their geographical origins as well as their cultural requirements; it adds greatly to
their interest and brings a decided congruity to the garden scene. I think
this is especially important if you tend to be a collector rather than a
selector; you have to exercise some form of restraint to avoid a total
muddle, and this is one discipline you could choose.

As *K. sarmentosa* finishes, in March, for a brief rest before launching on

Acer palmatum 'Senkaki' at Hergest Croft   R. A. & W. L. BANKS

Betula jacquemontii and *B.* 'Jermyns' at Hergest Croft   R. A. & W. L. BANKS

Malus 'Oporto' (red), 'Chilko' (pink), and 'Excellenz Thiel' (white) at Hyde Hall   HARRY SMITH HOR-
TICULTURAL LIBRARY

General view of the *Sorbus* Collection at Winkworth Arboretum   ERIC BARRS

Ceanothus at Cannington: *C. incanus* (left) *C.* 'Edinburgh' (centre) and *C. dentatus* (right)

Cistus palhinhae   JANE TAYLOR

Olearia ilicifolia   JANE TAYLOR

Rhododendron rex subsp. *arizelum* with *Acer japonicum* 'Aureum' in the Valley Gardens

JANE TAYLOR

Aster ericoides 'Blue Star' at Upton (National Trust)   W. A. LORD

Campanula pulloides at Padlock Croft   PETER LEWIS

Euphorbias at Abbey Dore   SARAH SAGE

Geranium cataractarum ssp. *pitardii* at University Botanic Garden, Cambridge   DR P. F. YEO

Kniphofia 'Sunningdale Yellow' at Coleton Fishacre   JANE TAYLOR
Lobelia splendens 'Blinkferia' at Ivy Cottage, Ansty   ANNE STEVENS

Penstemon 'Garnet' at Rowallane   W. A. LORD

Primula vulgaris 'Lilacina Plena'   MRS P. GOSSAGE

Saxifraga 'Primrose Dame'   ADRIAN YOUNG

Galanthus 'Magnet' at Wisley   W. HALLIDAY

The *Narcissus* Collection at Coleraine   H. WRIGHT

Nerine humilis in the wild   A. NORRIS

Tulipa marjolettii at University Botanic Garden, Cambridge   DR P. F. YEO

its brighter summer flowering, 'Zululandii' begins, or may already have started to flower as far back as January. 'Zululandii' too is variable in colour; I have seen it deep dusky vermilion, or quite pale and wan. It doesn't seem to be much known, and perhaps is not too hardy. It used to grow in the half-hardy house at Wisley, where it was exceedingly happy and increased abundantly, but now I know of only three gardens where it grows (the others are Sharpitor at Salcombe (National Trust) and Barton Manor, on the Isle of Wight, the home of one of the National Collections).

At least 'Zululandii' still exists. One of the most striking of all pokers ever to be introduced to cultivation in this country must have been *K. multiflora*, which I have never seen except in illustrations. A giant of a plant, it bears its short, stubby, creamy-white flowers in narrow tapering spires on 10 ft stems over a great mass of long leaves. The effect, to judge from photographs and the comments of earlier gardeners who were fortunate enough to grow it, was a huge eremurus. It was introduced, from its native Natal, around the turn of the century and soon flowered in captivity.

Compton Mackenzie grew it in his Cornish garden before the Great War. It flowered for him at the same time as *Buddleia auriculata*, in winter, and in much the same soft buff-cream colouring. Meanwhile it was being distributed in the trade as well. Before the Great War, it was offered by one nursery at the then huge sum of 10/6 d a plant, but by the thirties the same nursery could offer it wholesale at 20/- a dozen (or 1/6 d each retail). Other nurseries offered it too at this time (though they may have bought in stocks from the 20/- wholesaler). It appears to have faded from cultivation during the Hitler war, and I have found no further reference to it in horticultural literature or trade catalogues since the thirties. Perhaps someone will reintroduce it from the wild, together with other species which were once introduced and then lost.

The National Collections

The National Collections of Kniphofia are grown at Barton Manor, Whippingham, East Cowes, Isle of Wight (Mr and Mrs Anthony Goddard), and at Bridgemere Nurseries, near Nantwich in Cheshire (Mr C. R. Sanders is the Director responsible for the Collections held there).

Designated in September 1982, the first Kniphofia Collection is one that has had a change of both location and owner since its inception. It was formed by Jane and Dick Taylor and originally grown at The Level, Pillowell, near Lydney in the Forest of Dean, Gloucestershire. When they moved to south Devon to restore the garden at Coleton Fishacre on behalf of The National Trust the kniphofias were moved too, and over the next two years the Collection increased to over 100 species and cultivars. Research revealed references to about 600 named kinds in old catalogues and botanical works, but it seems likely that very many of these are extinct. Even 100 kinds present quite a problem in a garden, though by associating similar kinds so that they appear to be all one group (though this called for very careful labelling) it was possible to pack quite a few into a small space at Coleton Fishacre, where they could not be allowed to dominate the eighteen-acre site. After Dick Taylor's death the Collection was transferred to Mr and Mrs Anthony Goddard and the plants were moved to the Isle of Wight in the spring of 1986.

Although much newer (it was designated in October 1986) the Collection at Bridgemere already includes about forty species and hybrids, chiefly but not solely duplicated in both Collections. It is especially valuable with a slightly tender genus to have Collections in areas with different climates, both to safeguard the less hardy species and to test their comparative resistance to cold and wet.

Lobelia

THE TALL, perennial, moisture-loving lobelias are some of the most exciting plants to bring rich, refulgent colour to late summer borders wherever the soil is reasonably moist. They are about as unlike the popular conception of a lobelia as can be, unless you have the sort of eye and mind that can dissociate size and colour from form, when you will detect similarities in the shape of the flower.

These lobelias are mostly a little tender, by repute at least, though hardier kinds are being raised in Canada and tried out in England. It is the stop-go English winter they resent, as do so many other plants from more rational climates. Perhaps even more than this, I believe, they fall victim to slugs or leatherjackets in spring as the new growths appear; for the heavy, rich, moist soils that best suit lobelias also harbour the greediest gastropods. A thick winter mulch is helpful in keeping soil temperatures reasonably constant through alternating cold and mild spells, and vigilance, plus slug bait if you have no environmental objection to it, will help to combat the slug menace in spring. But leatherjackets are harder to cope with in the years when, as happens from time to time in some gardens – happily not in the National Collection in Dorset – they reach plague proportions. If you are thus affected, a few divisions of your plants kept as insurance in a frame over winter are thus always worth the little effort they demand.

As well as brilliant flower, some lobelias have richly coloured foliage also. Let us consider whence these derive. The species that have given rise to our garden cultivars are three, or perhaps four, all from North America: *L. cardinalis*, *L. fulgens* from Mexico and the Texan *L. splendens*, which some authors consider should be included in *L. fulgens*, and lastly the eastern *L. syphilitica*. *L. cardinalis* is the cardinal flower, grown in Britain since the seventeenth century, the species to which many cultivars are often, but erroneously, ascribed. It has green foliage, where so many of the hybrids are coppery or purple in leaf. A yard-high spike of vivid pillar-box scarlet flowers tops the basal leaves in late summer. It is variously stated, by different growers, to be either more, or less, hardy than the purple-leaved kinds. Anne Stevens in Dorset, grower of one of the National Collections, has found that all of hers, purple or green, under a 3 ins mulch, came through a severe winter unharmed. The conclusion to be drawn is that if you like the look of the plant, give it a try in your garden.

The Mexican *L. fulgens* is suffused with reddish-purple in stem and leaf, and bears similar scarlet flowers on stems of similar height to the cardinal flower. From this and *L. splendens* derives the beetroot colouring in the foliage of several cultivars. *L. syphilitica*, from the eastern USA, was also known in Britain in the seventeenth century, and seems clearly much hardier than the cardinal flower or the Mexicans. Relishing the same heavy, moist soils, this is a leafy plant – too leafy perhaps for perfect balance – valued for its clear blue flowers appearing rather earlier than the scarlet kinds. There is a white form, 'Alba', a dwarf variant 'Nana' and the compact 'Blue Peter', selected by Alan Bloom. The cool blues look well with *Primula florindae*, the Himalayan cowslip with fragrant bells of white-dusted primrose on tall stems.

Lobelia syphilitica is a parent of *L. × vedrariensis*, and some of its blue colouring has bled into the flower of the hybrid offspring to produce good purple blooms. Purple is a tricky colour-word to use; if it is accepted as including the range from a tone bluer than crimson to one redder than violet, then this is just the range in which *L. × vedrariensis* falls. Seedlings come fairly true. 'Tania' is also a child of *L. syphilitica*, with good spikes of garnet purple on brown stems.

Mr Gordon Pugsley, a skilled plant breeder, turned his attention to lobelias and using *L. cardinalis* × *L. syphilitica* produced a range of colours from crimson to mauve, as well as nearly pure blue and clear red. 'Old Port' is one of his, a deep crimson in colour.

Hybrids other than *L. × vedrariensis* are sometimes grouped as *L. × speciosa*, but in catalogues and gardening literature are more usually listed simply by their cultivar names, or under *L. cardinalis*. Of these, 'Queen Victoria' is widespread and widely known, often indeed referred to as '*L. cardinalis*'. As more and more people visit the National Collections and see the true cardinal flower, let us hope this misattribution will slowly fade from use. 'Bees' Flame' is another of this persuasion but less familiar as a name, nor perhaps so widely available though possibly not so old as 'Queen Victoria', which was certainly around in the twenties. Strangely, neither has received an award from the Royal Horticultural Society, though others now scarcely known have done so. But 'Queen Victoria Improved' received an Award of Merit in 1938, and one cannot help wondering if this is the plant we still grow. A priority for National Collections is to seek out plants of their chosen genus which have received awards, and thus it is that plants such as 'Carmine Gem', which received its award in 1896, remain on the search list though probably long since extinct. The next round of awards to hybrids of this type came in 1910, when scarlet-crimson 'Gloire de St Anne's' and bright carmine 'Sam Barlow' received Awards of Merit. In 1918 it was the turn of 'Mrs Humbert', which was mentioned wistfully by Margery Fish in her book *Gardening in the Shade* (1964) as a pink cultivar she had read of but never seen. Mrs Fish generally obtained a plant she had set her heart on, so it is strange to read in Alan Bloom's *Hardy Perennials* of 1957 of this 'salmon pink' cultivar, with no suggestion that it was hard to acquire. Much later Mr Graham Stuart Thomas, in *Perennial Garden Plants* (1982, 2nd ed.) also refers to it, as 'rose pink', without qualification. Is it, or is it not, still about? It certainly has not found its way to the National Collections as I write.

'Huntsman' received an Award of Merit in 1927 for its large, brilliant scarlet blooms, and in the same year an AM went to 'Shirley Crimson'. 'Anne' gained its AM in 1932, and out of thirty-six cultivars entered in the Wisley Trials in 1938 another two received awards: carmine rose 'Flamingo' and 'Queen Victoria Improved', already mentioned. Since then there have been no awards other than the Highly Commended for 'Tania' in 1976.

Other cultivars that were certainly around in the fifties and sixties, when Margery Fish and Alan Bloom were in their different ways doing so much to promote interest in hardy plants, include 'Russian Princess' and 'Jack MacMasters'. The first, said to be a cultivar of *L. cardinalis*, has pale pink flowers with a white spot on each, and green foliage. 'Jack MacMasters', said to be *L. fulgens* × *L. syphilitica*, has violet-blue flowers over green foliage. Anne Stevens grows it in Dorset and finds it as hardy as the others.

The Canadian breeding programme, aiming for greater hardiness and fuller, richer spikes of larger flowers, used *L. syphilitica* var. *syphilitica*, *L. cardinalis* subsp. *cardinalis*, and the cultivars 'Queen Victoria' and 'Illumination'. From these have resulted a host of fine new tetraploid cultivars such as 'Cherry Ripe', garnet-crimson 'Dark Crusader' and 'Will Scarlett'. The colours range from blood-red, cardinal and scarlet through every shade of cherry and rose red to rich crimson, beetroot and regal purple.

Lobelias with colouring nearest to violet, whether of this breeding or from other stables, make glowing Byzantine combinations with yellow daylilies or with ligularias, their big, often purple-backed leaves and chrome or saffron-yellow daisies in broad heads contrasting with the upward-reaching spikes of the lobelias. Or you could use in place of the

ligularias another daisy, the black-eyed Susan, *Rudbeckia* 'Goldsturm' –
both enjoy the same moist soils that suit the lobelias. The scarlet kinds
with purple leaves assort well with the bold jagged leaves of *Rheum
palmatum* 'Atrosanguineum', and coppery-toned *Rodgersia podophylla* of
the web-footed leaves, with cooling shades of lemon and white from *Iris
orientalis* (*I. ochroleuca*), pale daylilies and the fresh, cream and white broad
blades of *Carex siderosticta* 'Variegata'.

All these associations so far suggested are for moist soils as part of a
permanent planting. But lobelias are easy-tempered plants, and can be
used in other, entirely different ways. Their willingness to move when
well advanced in growth – even in July or early August when about to
flower – means that you can use them as replacements for an earlier-
flowering component of your border. This may be another perennial that,
having flowered, can be moved without setback, or an early annual that
has had its fling. When moving any plant at this season, of course, you
must water thoroughly both before and after the move unless the season
is very wet, even puddling it in to its new quarters if need be.

The lobelia is used in this way at Great Dixter, where 'Queen Victoria'
combines with the silver, fine-cut foliage of *Senecio leucostachys*, and purple
castor-oil plant behind, with the blue haze of *Caryopteris* × *clandonensis*.
'Dark Crusader' mixes happily with a bedding verbena such as 'Silver
Ann' or 'Pink Bouquet', both of spreading habit, with scented sugar-pink
flowers over which the ruby-crimson lobelia takes on added richness.

Using lobelias in this way another problem in their cultivation is
automatically overcome. They have a tendency to grow bare at the centre
and if not frequently divided may die out altogether. Division is best
carried out in the spring if the lobelias are to be left in the ground for
winter. The divisions can then be lined out to grow fat until July when
you move them across to their new quarters. Some gardeners prefer to
lift divisions in autumn and hold them, potted, in a frame for the winter.
Either way, they are pretty quick to bulk up, but if still more plants are
wanted, peg the stems onto moist, gritty compost, when plantlets will
develop along the stems and can be separated once rooted.

The National Collection holders both grow some of the species which
had no part in the breeding of these hybrids, and as such do not strictly
form part of the National Collection as defined. For all that, I want to
mention two that are uncommon, none too hardy, and in their different
ways highly desirable. *Lobelia laxiflora* has narrow green leaves and mildly
wandering roots; the slender stems are topped by slim red and yellow
tubular flowers for weeks in summer. I have seen it looking wonderful
with the fat orange goose-egg heads of *Kniphofia rooperi*, a late-flowering
red-hot poker, and lime-yellow-leaved, red-stemmed *Fuchsia* 'Genii'. This
lobelia is, though not fully hardy, tougher than the Chilean *L. tupa*. Here

is a noble plant with large, soft green leaves – grey-downy in the best forms – and stout stems bearing claw-like flowers of dull rusty-orange to deep crimson red. The cultivar 'Brilliant' is of this latter colouring. Try it in rich, moist soils with maximum shelter, when you may see its spires reach above your head.

The National Collection

The National Collection of Lobelia, *tall moisture-loving types, is held at Ivy Cottage, Ansty, Dorchester (Mrs Anne Stevens). It was designated in November 1985 as a result of Anne Stevens's wish to participate in the National Collections Scheme with a genus or group of plants suited to her rich, boggy soil. Here Asiatic primulas, many iris and* Trollius *thrive, with hostas and rodgersias for bolder foliage, and the lobelias for later and more brilliant colour. Like other Collection holders, Anne Stevens adds to her plants by exchange, purchase and from seed and cuttings, and enjoys the business of tracking down elusive plants and in the process meeting other horticulturists with shared interests. A second National Collection of these lobelias was designated in March 1986, to be grown at Lancashire College of Agriculture & Horticulture, Myerscough Hall, Bilsborrow, Preston; as yet it is in its infancy.*

Lychnis

INCLUDED in this genus, which is a member of the Pink family, are some favourite cottage garden plants, with cosy cottage nicknames – Dusty Miller or Rose Campion, Catchfly or Sticky Nellie, Ragged Robin, Maltese Cross etc.

Lychnis coronaria, the dusty miller, has been growing in our gardens since 1593, introduced from its stony haunts in southern Europe (it also extends into western Asia). Woolly silvery-white leaves and stems give it its nickname; they beautifully offset the brilliant plum-magenta rounded flowers from which the timid alternative epithet rose campion derives. It is well adapted to dry, poor soils, and can happily be teamed with silver or grey foliage or set with stunning effect against the strong blue of *Veronica teucrium* 'Crater Lake Blue'. The dusty miller has a white, cerise-eyed form, 'Oculata', and a clear white which combines delightfully with blue-grey foliage, of rue perhaps or of grasses such as the little *Festuca glauca* or taller, elegantly arching *Helictotrichon sempervirens*. Any or all of the forms of the rose campion could team with the softening lavender blue and greyish-green foliage of *Nepeta* × *faassenii*, the familiar garden catmint. The dusty miller seeds itself around freely, but is easy to remove, its rosette of woolly leaves anchored by the least tenacious of rootstocks; so with minimal effort you can remove surplus seedlings and leave only those that will look, with care, like happy accidents.

'Abbotswood Rose' may, it seems, be a hybrid; it has similar very grey foliage and flowers of brilliant crimson pink. The other putative parent of 'Abbotswood Rose' is *Lychnis flos-jovis*, the flower of Jove, smaller than the rose campion, and native of rocky places and screes in the central Alps. It has tufts of grey woolly leaves topped with many heads of deep rose-pink flowers of varying tints. 'Hort's Variety' is a pretty clear pink and there is a charming white form. All are ideal front of the border plants that blend well with soft or pale blues.

219

The showiest of the catchflies is *Lychnis viscaria* 'Splendens Plena', with eye-catching cerise double flowers rather like tiny carnations over dark green foliage, a little like that of a thrift. The catchfly, so called for its sticky stems, enjoys a slightly less arid soil than its grey-leaved cousins but, like the flower of Jove, makes a charming front of the border plant. Again, there is a nice little white form, while the species itself, with frilly bright pink-magenta flowers, is not to be despised.

Small enough for a rock garden, or even a trough, is the alpine and subarctic *Lychnis alpina*, forming tuffets of dark green or purplish foliage topped with short spikes of deep rosy-pink flowers. When I grew this on a rock garden of which the underlying soil was coal-mine waste it found conditions entirely to its liking and seeded around abundantly, but several gardening friends who admired it and went away with a seedling or two found it less easy to please. One opined that it might have rather particular trace-element requirements. Be that as it may, one year I noticed I had it no longer; could it have exhausted whatever trace-element it was that at first suited it so well in the coal dust?

These species of *Lychnis* all incline to shades of magenta, chalky pink, cerise: colours that blend well with each other as well as with the suggested greys and silvers or soft lavenders and pure pale blues. At the other end of the red range of the spectrum is *Lychnis chalcedonica*, the Maltese cross or Jerusalem cross, so called from the shape of the flowers. The Maltese cross needs richer conditions than the dusty miller, and its uncompromising vermilion needs to be kept away from any pinks or crimsons with blue in their make-up. Powerful combinations almost impose themselves with this plant; its own colour scheme, the pillar-box-red flowers set in bright green leaves, admits of no emollient tones. Try it with the strong purple-violet of *Salvia nemorosa* 'Superba', or the assertive yellow of *Oenothera tetragona*. The white *Lychnis chalcedonica* 'Alba' on the other hand is rather insipid, not a good clean white; nor does the pink 'Rosea', politely likened to washed-out salmon and less flatteringly to dirty pink washing, seem to blend with any other plant. There is a sumptuous double in the same brilliant red as the type, and a double white was grown in 1772. Tantalisingly, this is reported from time to time, but no-one ever seems actually to have seen the plant, and as I write it still remains on the search list.

Another *Lychnis* in the same colour range of hot reds is the hybrid *L.* × *haageana*, which comes in orange, white or red; a brilliant thing but short-lived and regularly devoured by slugs. The hybrid has itself crossed with *L. chalcedonica* to produce *L.* × *arkwrightii*, a plant dating from the early years of this century, its flowers vivid orange-red in colour. The selected form 'Vesuvius' seems more perennial and has good dark maroon-brown leaves contrasting with the clear, strong orange-red of the flowers.

Plants such as these are typical of the garden plants the National Collections seek to conserve; without regular attention and re-propagation, they can so easily slip away from cultivation and be lost forever.

The National Collection

The National Collection of Lychnis is grown at Hinchley Wood Middle School, Surrey, under the guidance of Mrs Jean Sambrook.

The collection owes much to Jean Sambrook's determination to involve the children in a project that would help to further the aims of the NCCPG, teach the children gardening skills and instil in them a respect for their garden heritage. She chose Lychnis for its ease of cultivation, brightly coloured flowers and because she already grew, in her own garden, the nucleus of a collection. The Hinchley Wood project was accepted into the National Collections scheme in October 1983, and work began immediately on cultivating a suitable plot of ground, sowing seeds, acquiring plants and teaching the children, not only basic horticultural skills, but also about the NCCPG and the need for such details as labelling, record-keeping and accurate nomenclature. The children soon took to their new project and now undertake all the tasks that adult gardeners might do, including mixing their own composts, sowing seeds, pricking out seedlings, potting and planting. Seeds are collected each year by the children, to raise young plants for the following year. A particular achievement was to show some of the Collection at the Royal Horticultural Society's Show at Vincent Square, in July 1987. The children put the stand together and were in attendance to speak to the public about their National Collection.

Penstemon

To JUDGE from the lengthy lists of named penstemons submitted to the Royal Horticultural Society for trial in 1861, 1904, 1909, 1914 and 1930, Britain's herbaceous borders must have been jewelled with the colours of these long-flowering, near-hardy flowers; 190 varieties were sent for trial in 1909, 136 in 1914, 103 in 1930. It would be hard, now, to assemble more than about half the number sent in 1930. Once again, then, we find that a group of plants once valued, and therefore plentiful, has dwindled to a handful of surviving kinds.

The genus *Penstemon* contains many species, ranging from alpine shrublets to perennial or short-lived species with large, showy flowers. From these last has been bred a range of named cultivars which are the subject of three National Collections, one in Scotland, one in southern England, and one in Northern Ireland. It says much for their versatility as garden plants that in all three locations penstemons had already formed a feature of the gardens where the National Collections are now housed.

The large-flowered penstemons, of opalescent or gem-stone colouring, that can be raised from seedsmen's strains are generally referred to the species *P. cobaea* and its hybrids. They are somewhat tender, but may survive mild winters in much of the country. Named kinds, perpetuated by cuttings, may derive from *P. cobaea* and *P hartwegii*, with contributions from other species, notably the hardy *P. campanulatus*. A few perennial species are grown in their own right as border plants, in addition to the many cultivars of mixed blood.

The fact that many border penstemons are not entirely hardy can be turned to advantage, for the small discipline of taking cuttings each autumn ensures a supply of young plants, which flower for much longer than older ones. It also gives the provident gardener a supply of fillers to plug gaps where the winter, or old age, have killed the previous occupant. One of the reasons that Margery Fish's borders always looked so well filled, if to some eyes a little chaotic, is that she was always dabbing in young plants of this and that in any small gap – double daisies, penstemons, primroses etc.

The names of gemstones come naturally when describing the colours of penstemons, and one or two have been given jewel names: 'Garnet', 'Ruby', 'Mother of Pearl', or simply the word 'gem' with a distinguishing epithet, such as Mr Bowles's carmine, white-throated 'Myddelton Gem', granted an Award of Merit in 1909 and still grown today. It is a mystery why the name 'Opal', which would so well describe a certain colouring among penstemons, seems never to have been used.

Penstemons belong to the foxglove family, and the flower shape reveals the relationship, varying from the narrow tubes of pale rose-pink 'Evelyn' to the big flared bells of cherry-red and white 'Rubicunda'. These two cultivars can be taken as representative of the two extremes of hardiness within the group. Narrow, evergreen leaves characterise the species *P. campanulatus*, of which 'Evelyn' is a hybrid, or perhaps a selection. Forming bushy plants 18 ins high and wide, 'Evelyn' is hardy in southern Britain at least. Cultivars that make plenty of basal growth of narrow leaves can usually be regarded as hardier than the bare-stemmed, larger-leafed kinds. They can be cut hard back in spring, and will last for several years, though after their first year or perhaps two their floral efforts will be concentrated into a big display in mid-summer with not much to follow. Young plants, on the other hand, will go on into autumn. 'Pink Endurance' is like a slightly larger 'Evelyn'. Margery Fish grew a plant she knew as *P. campanulatus* 'Rose Queen', smaller than 'Evelyn', with rosy-crimson flowers. This tended to sow itself around her garden, a trait not usually thought of as characteristic of penstemons.

'Garnet', another hardy penstemon, is well described by its name, the rather larger bells of deep wine-crimson borne over good leafy clumps of narrow clear green foliage. Its colour is just right with the dove-grey, purple-flushed foliage of *Rosa glauca* (formerly *R. rubrifolia*) and a ground planting of sombre-leaved *Sedum telephium* 'Munstead Red', with the egg-shaped burgundy-red heads of *Allium sphaerocephalum* and rosetted double *Geranium pratense* 'Plenum Violaceum', and some silver foliage to lighten a subfusc group. 'Rich Ruby' has quite large, deep red flowers brighter than 'Garnet'.

'Ruby' itself, however, appears synonymous with 'Firebird', which is also burdened with the name 'Schoenholzeri'. This cherry-scarlet penstemon, amply set with medium-sized bells, clearly has blood of the skinny-limbed, tubular-flowered scarlet *P. hartwegii*, a native of Mexico. (The genus as a whole belongs to the north American continent.) Though of vivid colouring, 'Firebird' is of that rare scarlet that mixes equally well with the yellow or with the blue half of the spectrum. It is a delight with small yellow kniphofias such as 'Gold Else', with the deep velvet crimson of *Rosa gallica* 'Tuscany' also in the picture. In an all-red border, such as Peter Healing's at The Priory, Kemerton, it adds brilliance to a tapestry of purple foliage and red flowers: bronze-leaved dahlias such as the old 'Bishop of Llandaff', purple beet and purple cannas and *Lobelia* 'Queen Victoria', scarlet in flower and beetroot-red in leaf, and crimson nicotianas adding a more subdued tone leading into the dusky foliage of *Sedum* 'Vera Jameson'.

Other good red penstemons are 'Southgate Gem', of intense scarlet – selected as one of the best in 1914 and still worth growing despite a rather untidy habit – and little crimson-red 'Newbury Gem', etched with deeper red in the throat. Also, like these two, one of the older kinds is fat-belled 'Castle Forbes', red with a white throat. 'George Home' is another large-flowered, white-throated kind of brighter scarlet; 'King George' is speckled in the throat, of rosy-red colouring. 'Chester Scarlet' is another good red penstemon still to be found in commerce. Flowers of such clear red colouring, without the vermilion harshness of annual salvias yet rivalling them in length of season, are not common and deserve every care to preserve them for our own and future gardens.

'Evelyn', though probably the best known, is not the only pink penstemon still grown. 'Hidcote Pink' is of clear colouring with deeper freckling in the throat, and 'Hewell's Pink Bedder' is of branching habit, with medium-sized shrimp pink bells. A taller plant, with small pale pink flowers, is 'Pennington Gem', a pretty companion for *Aster × frikartii*. 'Apple Blossom' is a delightful creamy blush, tipped with deeper pink, and even wide-belled 'White Bedder' has blush-pink tips. 'Snowstorm' is pure white.

At the other extreme of the colour range are the deep purples, 'Purple Bedder', 'Burgundy', and 'Port Wine', and, paler than these, soft iridescent purple-blue 'Sour Grapes'. This is a name more often met than the plant to which it properly belongs, for the name has become wrongly attached to 'Stapleford Gem'. Here is one of several penstemons to which the adjective 'opalescent' can be aptly ascribed, for it has smallish flowers of cream and blue-lilac, soft and gentle tones which Margery Fish liked to combine with dark-leaved, currant-red rose 'Rosemary Rose' and the dark fox-brushes of bronze fennel. 'Alice Hindley' is another of similar lilac colouring that could be used here, or allowed to weave its long arms through the branches of a rosy-pink tree mallow. 'Alice Hindley' is sometimes called 'Gentianoides', but the real *P. gentianoides* is blue-purple in colour, not the true blue its name implies. *P. hirsutus* is another species of lavender colouring, but *P. ovatus*, a hardy species, has pure blue flowers. It is short-lived and needs regularly to be raised from seed.

Though of shrubby habit, presumably with blood of *Penstemon het-*

erophyllus, 'Katherine de la Mare' is the only penstemon regarded as reliably hardy at Threave in south-western Scotland. It is a pretty plant with lilac-blue flowers. *P. heterophyllus* itself forms a low, wide mound decked with small tubular flowers of clear blue flushed with pink and mauve. It has a far tougher constitution than its exquisite pure blue selections 'True Blue', 'Blue Gem' and 'Blue Springs', all of which ally spikes of gentian-blue slender bells to the type plant's narrow glaucous or purple-flushed foliage. They need, and deserve, annual re-propagation to ensure their survival.

Needing a warm position is the Mexican *Penstemon isophyllus*, with lanky stems bearing grey-green foliage and coral-scarlet flowers. A plant I received as *P. taosensis*, with narrow, very glaucous foliage and coral tubular bells, may belong here. Either combines charmingly with the lavender-blue sprays of *Hebe hulkeana*, or interweaving with the silvery comb-like leaves and creamy flowers of *Senecio leucostachys*, another long-limbed creature deserving a warm corner.

Of similar colouring, but generally hardy throughout the British Isles, is *Penstemon barbatus* (*Chelone barbata*), the bearded penstemon, so called because of its hairy throat. This is a plant forming tufty basal growth of grey-green leaves; it can be pulled apart into divisions. Branching stems bear many little foxgloves of scarlet, coral or pink ('Carnea').

Like other species, *Penstemon barbatus* can be raised from seed as well as being increased by vegetative means. Named cultivars, of course, must always be propagated vegetatively, and in the genus *Penstemon* as in others treated in these pages, we find that several of the surviving cultivars are of some antiquity – 'Rubicunda' for example dates from 1906, and we have already seen that others I have described are of similar age – implying that they are of stronger constitution than the many others formerly listed and now no longer to be found. Part of the long-term task of all the National Collections will be to determine which cultivars, new or old, are robust and sturdy plants able, perhaps, to transmit this characteristic to their offspring.

The National Collections

The National Collections of Penstemon at Threave, Castle Douglas (National Trust for Scotland) and Kingston Maurward in Dorset were both designated in October 1984. Kingston Maurward House is a Georgian house which, in the early years of this century, belonged to Sir Cecil and Lady Hanbury, relations of Sir Thomas Hanbury who gave Wisley to the Royal Horticultural Society. The gardens they laid out included a penstemon border, which was restored when, following the war years of neglect, the County Council took over the property. It is now a College of Agriculture and Horticulture. The penstemon border remained a feature for many years before a combination of changes in the garden and a hard winter caused it to be scrapped. In 1983 the Head of Horticulture, Ray Adams, decided to reintroduce a penstemon border. By coincidence at about the same time the Dorset Group of the NCCPG approached the College asking if the Principal would consider holding the National Collection of penstemons there, and offering a number of cultivars and species already collected by the Group.

Threave also houses a School of Gardening, where also for many years penstemons have been grown, providing much-needed colour in the borders from August to October. Bill Hean, the Principal, finds that in that harsher climate even the so-called hardy penstemons can succumb to the winter at any time, so cuttings are taken each year as a matter of routine.

At Rowallane in Co. Down, N. Ireland (National Trust) is a National Collection of penstemons designated in November 1985. The basis of this Collection was the penstemons introduced by The National Trust to fill the late summer colour gap in the walled garden display. Penstemons had originally been grown at Rowallane by Mr H. Armitage-Moore, creator of the garden, so as at Kingston Maurward the plants fulfil a historical role in the garden. Despite his extremely busy schedule as head gardener of a fifty-two acre garden open to the public from 9 a.m. to 9 p.m. seven days a week, Mike Snowden manages to find time not only to compare and attempt to verify the naming of his penstemons, but also to run long-term trials to determine their hardiness, longevity and durability. There are many examples of confused naming; both at Rowallane and at Kingston Maurward the plants grown as 'Evelyn' appear identical to others received as 'Phyllis'.

Primroses

PRIMROSES are just one group in the large and variable genus *Primula*. I think most of us understand by 'primroses' not only the forms and variants of our wild primrose, including double-flowered kinds, but also the forms of *Primula juliae*, a wild species from the Caucasus, showing obvious affinities with our own wild primrose. The best known *juliae* type must be 'Wanda', that neat, willing, brilliant magenta-flowered primrose that still seems to thrive in almost any conditions.

The double primroses especially have for many years had something of a cult following, but they have never been widely available in our time. In the fifties my father-in-law grew them commercially, and had fifty-yard rows, three or four plants deep, of 'Double White' and 'Double Lilac', yet he wrote, even then, that supplies of 'nearly all varieties of double primroses are extremely limited – dangerously limited'. He did, for all that, grow a great many different kinds: something over thirty old doubles, and several of the anomalous forms, about which more later. During the fifties and sixties there were half a dozen nurseries in England, Scotland and Ireland specialising in single and double primroses: today only one of them is still in business. One of these nurseries listed over 200 different named kinds. Yet today probably none of the old *Primula vulgaris* named singles exist; and the old doubles that survive today are a tiny proportion of the vast number that have arisen over the years.

These primroses are simply not long-lived plants. Even wild *Primula vulgaris* is not long-lived. Patches of wild primroses seem to shift several yards over a few years, as the original plants die, and new seedlings spring up. It is the constant renewal of plants in the wild that gives the impression of longevity. Clearly, it is no use expecting cultivated forms of our wild primrose to behave any differently. In the garden, named primroses with *vulgaris*-type foliage need careful division at the right time if they are to be kept going, and are exceedingly tricky when conditions are not ideal.

228

So what are ideal conditions? And when is the right time to divide these plants? To try and answer these questions, I'd like to go back to my father-in-law and his rows of 'Double White' and 'Double Lilac'. After all, anyone who grew these allegedly difficult plants in such quantities that he could pick and bunch the flowers to sell them to the wholesale flower markets must have been fairly successful in his methods. He took his guidance, originally, from early gardening manuals such as '"Eden", or a compleat Body of Gardening' (1758), where you are instructed to 'plant them in fresh Pasture Ground, enriched by the addition of a little Wood-Pile Earth and Cow-dung'. My father-in-law's method was to cultivate the soil very thoroughly indeed, digging in large volumes of well rotted manure, garden compost, leaf mould – any good humus, in fact – to a depth of about 9 ins or so, to make a rich, friable, moisture-retaining medium of uniform texture. He held very firmly that the plants did not make roots to any greater depth than 9 ins, so burying manure or compost in trenches below this level was a complete waste, at least on his clay soil.

Some shade is essential, and a mulch of leaf mould or peat will help to keep the soil from drying out in summer: primroses are distressingly liable to die out in times of drought. The other essential attention primroses need is frequent division, and this of course is the only way (outside laboratory techniques) to propagate them. In Shropshire, where my father-in-law grew his primroses, he considered them fit to divide from the end of April onwards, just as they are going out of flower, and up to the end of June. At this time, when you lift your plant, you will see new white roots growing from the base of the shoots, just above the old rootstock. Cut the old rootstock away below these emerging roots, and cut the leaves back by a half or two-thirds, before replanting in the rich mixture you will have previously made ready for them. Water in very thoroughly, and provide shade and shelter from drying winds. (My father-in-law used hessian screening for his rows in the field, but admitted that it was too unsightly for the garden; here he recommended annuals, or even weeds, to provide shade as a 'cover-crop'.)

Not all the primroses in the National Collections are really old. Indeed, though they have been called Elizabethan plants, and a double white primrose was described by Gerard in 1597, John Martin, whose National Collection of primroses is grown in Shropshire, doubts if any we now grow are older than 'Lilacina Plena', the double lilac, which he allows to date from the eighteenth century. He maintains that today's double white is not the same as Gerard's plant, if his illustration is anything to go by; 'Alba Plena', or 'Double White', is *acaulis*, that is with the flowers on individual stalks like the wild primrose, whereas Gerard's plant was of polyanthus habit. 'Marie Crousse', another famous name still sometimes encountered commercially, is not the same as the original, and some growers have another 'Marie Crousse' which may or may not be the true thing. Old double primroses in early gardening literature were simply described by their colours – lilac, burgundy, sulphur – and were perhaps selections that may have been made again and again from fresh seedling stocks. From time to time, strains of primroses crop up which are very prone to throw double seedlings, and my father-in-law's Glazeley strain was apparently one of these. The plants were collected from a cottage garden so derelict that it had reverted to meadow turf, after fifty years' neglect, and they had every appearance of being vigorous young plants, not woody, stunted survivors – even supposing individual plants could survive long without attention. These, again, were described by their colours, Glazeley Peach, Glazeley Silver and so on; so far as I know, only these two are still extant.

I've mentioned chiefly the old doubles so far, but another kind of primrose that was greatly valued by early gardeners were the anomalous forms such as hose-in-hose (one flower growing within another) or Jack in the Green, with its collar of green below the petals. Jackanapes primroses have the same ruff, but it is partly green and partly in the same colour as the petals; Pantaloon primroses are similar with a funnel-shaped ruff, green on the ribs of the segments and coloured like the petals between. Like the doubles, these anomalous forms arise spontaneously among seedling primroses. Probably none of the *P. vulgaris* old named hose-in-hose and Jack in the Green are still about. The National Collection holders aim to keep as many old named plants as they can, and also to keep all the forms in cultivation, by raising new plants if necessary. Primroses are unique in producing so many anomalous forms, and though individual named kinds may die out, the forms seem to reappear generation after generation.

For example, the gold and silver laced polyanthus, as available (quite widely) now, are a recreation of the old kinds. These delightful plants have quite small flowers, each dark crimson to near-black petal outlined with a wire-fine edging of gold or silver which sometimes extends down the centre of the petals, giving the flower the look of having ten petals. They do not seem long-lived, but are easy from seed.

John Martin raises quite a number of anomalous and double primroses each year from seed, and he does not find these long-lived either, indeed almost biennial. Raising is easy; keeping them is the difficulty. They flower well the second year and then fade out. In this, they behave just like the big, bright polyanthus that are bought by the thousand each year for spring bedding, and have to be renewed each year.

The era of colour-described double primroses, which may be said to have begun with Gerard's plate of the double white in 1597, drew to a close in about 1880. By this time numerous different forms had been described in the literature, and the colours included the white, lilac and sulphur of the seventeenth century, double red and crimson, double pink and (in Curtis's Botanical Magazine for 1794) 'a variety with blossoms of a dingy yellow inclining to red'. In the early nineteenth century colour descriptions became more varied, with straw colour, rose, buff, copper, flesh colour, flush, salmon, dingy and carmine joining the more mundane purple, violet, deep yellow and crimson-purple. But by 1880 their popularity had dwindled, in the face of the thrilling new exotics that were so easily and cheaply raised in Victorian glasshouses.

Even at this time, however, there were a few devotees, some of whom began breeding new double primroses and naming them, not just with a colour description but actually with a proper name. The Dean brothers bred several kinds, including the famous award-winning 'Harbinger' of 1882. Messrs Cocker of Aberdeen raised the fifteen named Bon Accord doubles, and Murray Thompson produced the Downshill group. My father-in-law only ever managed to acquire 'Downshill Ensign', a polyanthus type with large bright purple flowers appearing rather late. All his collection was lost, but John Martin has rediscovered 'Downshill Ensign'. He exchanged some plants with a couple in Hereford, who gave him some plants they had been told were doubles; they had not yet flowered in Hereford, but were so vigorous that their new owners felt they could not be doubles. They were, however, and proved identical to a photograph in one of Roy Genders's books; the naming was confirmed for John by someone who used to grow it. The donors from Hereford had it from an old lady near Malvern in Worcestershire. Although John Martin has been collecting primroses for many years, this is the only old named kind that he has acquired unnamed that he has later been able to identify with any certainty.

'Downshill Ensign' seems to have the blood of *P. juliae* in it, and most growers find this type of primrose, the Julianas, easier to grow than the old *vulgaris* kinds; far more tolerant of less than ideal soil conditions, and not so insistent on shade. There seems, indeed, no reason why more of the Juliana singles should not be offered commercially, except that only the dedicated nurseryman is likely to touch them because of their vulnerability to drought. Even so, as better growers than the *vulgaris* kinds, they can be left to form showy clumps in the general border. Most primrose growers regard the *vulgaris* kinds, by contrast, as hardly more than museum pieces. Half a century ago or so, the old nurserymen must have welcomed 'Wanda' and the other Julianas with relief, after struggling with 'Harbinger', 'Miss Massey' and the like.

Even quite recent Julianas present problems of naming, and sorting out nomenclature is of course an important facet of a National Collection holder's responsibilities, so that gardeners can be sure of getting the right plant. This is especially important when buying by mail order, which is how you are likely to have to acquire any named or double primroses you may want to grow. Some are straightforward enough: 'Wanda', of course, and the violet-blue double 'Our Pat' with plum-toned foliage; the violet Jack in the Green 'Tipperary Purple'; and a few others. John Martin takes the view that if a plant comes with two or more names from various sources, and another plant comes with only one, consistently, the latter must be regarded as true. The example he gives is 'Gloriosa' and 'Lingwood Beauty'. All the plants he purchased, from several sources, bearing these two names proved to be identical. Another, similar but not identical, from another source came to the National Collection as 'Lingwood Beauty' and had never been known as anything else. So, arbitrarily perhaps, the batch of identical plants are considered to be 'Gloriosa' and the odd one out 'Lingwood Beauty'. This plant has intense crimson flowers, freely borne.

There are persistent rumours that Irish gardens are still full of old primroses, but so many requests for primroses come from Ireland that this is probably no longer true, if it ever was. Some named kinds, certainly, originated in Ireland, including the Garryarde forms with their bronzed foliage. Several Garryardes were named, but only 'Guinevere' seems still to be grown in any quantity, a fine pale pink primrose with deep plum-bronze foliage. 'Garryarde Sir Galahad' with pale pink flowers streaked in deeper tones is still extant, and a white (simply called 'Garryarde White') has pale pink buds opening to white flowers over lighter bronze leaves. The Garryardes tend to hybridise with our wild primrose to produce some very pretty offspring: I have had creamy-primrose seedlings with typical Garryarde foliage, many whites, and an enchanting pale grey with bronze leaves. I wonder if 'Garryarde the Grail', with brick-red flowers, still exists?

A much newer primrose is 'Tomato Red', with small flowers of exactly the colour you'd expect from the name; not too easy to place, but very showy and neat. Other small-flowered primroses, older than this one, that seem to be good and willing doers, not demanding division every year, are the very similar 'Dorothy' and 'Lady Greer', and 'Kinlough Beauty'. Both the first two are miniature polyanthus types, their tiny flowers in bunches on short stems. 'Lady Greer' is pale creamy primrose, and 'Dorothy' has the faintest flush of pink on a similar creamy ground colour. 'McWatt's Cream' is another tiny, creamy-yellow polyanthus-stemmed kind with the same neat foliage. 'Kinlough Beauty' is a miniature again, its small pink flowers with a distinct white candy-stripe down the centre of each petal. Distinct as it is, it has none the less acquired another, quite incorrect name, that of 'E. R. Janes', which is probably no longer extant; it had brick-red flowers. 'Tawny Port' is a charming deep claret red with very dark, indeed almost black, shiny foliage.

Margery Fish, whose garden at East Lambrook Manor has remained almost a place of pilgrimage thanks to her many books, was a great admirer of old primroses. She exchanged voluminous correspondence with my father-in-law about them, with requests such as 'have you 6 plants of your bronze oxlip hose-in-hose to spare?' She grew many primroses and, unlike my father-in-law, she seemed to divide them whenever the mood was upon her; but I think that applied mainly to the Julianas. Several primroses are still in cultivation with the prefix Lambrook; like my father-in-law and his Glazeley primroses, she merely gave them colour names. 'Lambrook Peach' in pale pink is enhanced by red calyx and stems. All the Lambrooks are singles and are now, twenty or more years after she named them, as much collectors' pieces as the Garryardes. A modern, or at least recently introduced, double primrose that seems (so far) to be an easy grower is 'Sue Jervis' in palest peachy pink, a very pretty primrose indeed with enough vigour to grow in a border.

Most people find, I think, that the easiest primrose of all is 'Wanda', which Margery Fish liked to grow in virtually full shade, finding the plants more luxuriant and the flower colour less harsh than in part or full sun – but some of us revel in that potent magenta and don't particularly want it toned down. There is a white 'Wanda', and 'Wanda's Rival', which is deep lilac rather than magenta. Rarer than these is the hose-in-hose form of 'Wanda' in the same brilliant shade as the original. 'Purple Splendour' is like an improved 'Wanda', while 'Wanda Improved' is freer flowering and of more intense colour than 'Wanda'.

If magenta doesn't appeal to everyone, few people fail to be attracted by blue primroses. Modern breeders of huge polyanthus realise this, but there are also blue primroses more in accord with the plants we are considering here. 'Blue Riband' is a deep smoky blue with a yellow eye, and I have grown two or three good blue doubles in this colour or a paler, almost sky-blue; but they didn't last. A legendary blue double was 'Buxton's Blue', in pure blue. Mr E. Hugh Buxton wrote to my father-in-law 'The history of the plant is this. A great uncle of mine, who lived at Bettws-y-Coed, was planting out a bed of single light-blue primroses. He had a few plants over and told his wife to throw them away. Instead she planted them in the kitchen garden and next year, walking round together, they found one was a double which flourished. When he died she sent me a plant of it as his nearest relation and young friend, and when she died it was named after her (its original name was 'Mrs E. C. Buxton'). It is a pure turquoise blue.' My father-in-law worked his stock up to forty plants before, through a series of mishaps, virtually his entire collection died out, and so far as I know 'Buxton's Blue' has not been seen since. But meantime, thanks to the enthusiasm of those who have grown double primroses, something akin to a mythology has grown up around them;

their memory is kept alive even when the plants themselves have disappeared, and their devotees continue to search for them against lengthening odds.

The National Collections

The National Collections of Primula, *section Vernales cultivars — forms of primrose — are held at Oakenlea, West Coker Hill, Yeovil, Somerset (Mrs Pam Gossage); The Orchard, Longford, Market Drayton, Shropshire (Mr John Martin): and Tan Cottage, West Lane, Cononley, nr. Keighley (Mrs D. L. Shaw).*

Pam Gossage began collecting primroses about fifteen years ago; by 1976 she had thirty-four different kinds. At the end of that long drought summer she had only seven primroses left. However, she persevered and built up her collection again, though several named kinds were apparently lost to cultivation entirely in 1976, as other growers experienced the same difficulties. She offered her primroses as a National Collection in March 1983, and has had to cope with two more drought summers since they were designated, in 1983 and 1984. It has been difficult to keep the collection flourishing, but she persists, and has learnt some valuable lessons about the cultivation of the trickier kinds.

John Martin began collecting more recently, about seven years ago, and already has an impressive collection and a network of other enthusiasts with whom he exchanges plants. His primroses were designated as a National Collection in March 1984. As well as collecting old primroses, and verifying their naming whenever possible, John Martin is raising many new kinds from seed each year, retaining only the best; but he finds them short-lived, needing to be raised afresh almost each year just as modern polyanthus.

Barbara Shaw has also been collecting primroses for some years and exchanging with other enthusiasts. Her primroses were designated as a National Collection in November 1985.

Pyrethrums

When the National Council for the Conservation of Plants and Gardens were carrying out a close study of certain genera or groups of garden plants, to determine the rarity status of the individual varieties in each group, *Pyrethrum* was one of the initial one hundred groups selected. After research revealed references to 293 cultivars it was dropped as it threatened to monopolise the scant resources available. The NCCPG list of pyrethrums now commercially available, by contrast, gives only twenty-one cultivars: a measure of how far the popularity of these plants, once so highly valued as cut flowers as well as in the border, has declined.

There seem to be two reasons for their decline. Prior to 1939 there were hundreds of acres of pyrethrums grown in England, especially in Cambridgeshire, for the cut flower market. In the early thirties Alan Bloom, until then with his father one of the growers supplying this market, switched to plant production, and as there was still a strong demand for pyrethrums, he set out to grow as many named cultivars as he could obtain. By 1939 he had acquired over thirty kinds, doubles and singles. Stocks were cut back during the war when everything had to take second place to food production, but Alan Bloom was certain the demand would pick up again as Britain's economy recovered. In the early fifties, therefore, he bought a lorry load of pyrethrums, including some very old cultivars, from a nursery in Dover that was closing down. His objective was to build up stocks of 150,000 plants in a wide range of cultivars, and by 1953 he was two-thirds of the way there, with 100,000 plants in forty cultivars. In that year, too, 'Evenglow' was introduced in Denmark; Alan Bloom made a special trip there to secure distribution rights in the UK, and despite its weak stem which made it a poor cut flower the new, shrimp pink pyrethrum sold well. However, just as Alan Bloom reached his target of 150,000 plants a very wet winter damaged some of the stock, and, around the same time in the mid-fifties, demand declined as market growers found rising labour costs eroding their profit margins, and rumours spread of sickness in the stock.

Alan Bloom persisted none the less, raising some seedlings from 'Evenglow' crossed with deeper coloured doubles. As saleable stocks of the best were built up, by the late fifties, they were named and introduced: 'Ariel', 'Prospero', 'Taurus', 'Inferno', 'Vanessa', 'Venus' and 'Bellarion'. But then the sickness struck. It is not a killer; it simply undermines the plant's constitution. The disease has affected all growers, though every so often a nurseryman, growing plants on fresh soil perhaps, manages to produce healthy vigorous stocks for a while; and, as we shall see, Alan Bloom believes he may have found a way to overcome the sickness.

It is time, perhaps, before mentioning some of the players in the pyrethrum scene, to say what pyrethrums are. They are members of the daisy family, typically pink, white or red leaning towards crimson and magenta. Originally placed in the genus *Pyrethrum*, a name they have adopted for their own until it has in effect become their 'common name', they were then considered to be part of the big *Chrysanthemum* genus, with the specific name *coccineum* which they still retain after their latest move at the hands of the taxonomists, to the genus *Tanacetum*. In their heyday as cut flowers they were valued for their form, the pure daisy shape of the large single flower or the rosetted double, for their usually stiff stems and lasting qualities in water, their colours, and their early summer season, conveniently ahead of such other classic cut flowers as *Chrysanthemum maximum*, the Shasta daisy.

Neither of the National Collections of Pyrethrum holds more than a fraction of the many cultivars that have been raised over the years. But Mr Goddard, who grows his pyrethrums in his garden in East London, has been attracted to them and has collected them since the sixties, when living in Padstow, Cornwall. Here the crimson cultivars in particular were much in demand to decorate the church at Whitsuntide. Mr Goddard grew them then, as he still does, in rows in the vegetable garden, for cutting.

This was the time when Alan Bloom's new cultivars were appearing. Both Mr Goddard and Alan Bloom have lost most of them except 'Vanessa', a double rosy-carmine to which Alan Bloom ascribes an 'orange flush'. As well as from Bressingham, Mr Goddard acquired pyrethrums from Kelways of Langport, Somerset (a nursery long renowned for this group of plants) and from Carliles at Twyford, Berks, a famous herbaceous plant nursery. Mr Goddard recalls being very impressed while living in Cornwall, by Kelways' exhibit at the Royal Show at Wadebridge: it included some very well grown cultivars of pyrethrum.

In 1968 Mr Goddard moved himself and his pyrethrum collection to the suburb of Chingford, where the plants now grow on a much stiffer soil. A few more cultivars were obtained from Kelways and from Carliles, and also from Gayborder Nurseries, now closed down, where Michaelmas daisies were also grown and raised.

The great names in pyrethrums, however, were Kelways and Robinson. For almost one hundred years Kelways specialised in pyrethrums, together with a few other groups of showy border flowers. Old catalogues list dozens of cultivars, but today Kelways offer none: a few survived until the 1985-6 winter but many stock plants were then destroyed by adverse weather.

By the early 1930s, when the Royal Horticultural Society held a trial of pyrethrums at Wisley, Mr H. Robinson of Burbage, Hinchley, had become well known for his pyrethrums. Of ninety-two cultivars entered in the trial, twenty-nine gained awards, and no fewer than eight of these were raised by him. He must, indeed, have had an exceptional eye for a pyrethrum, and the ability to distinguish geese from swans, for only one of his pyrethrums failed to gain an award. Several of his cultivars that received awards after trial had been previously honoured when seen on the showbench: they include such well-known, and still surviving, cultivars as china-pink 'Eileen May Robinson', deeper rose-pink 'Marjorie Robinson' and 'Scarlet Glow'.

But although Kelways' pyrethrums did not do so well as Robinson's in the trials, they had had their day of glory. None, indeed, can match the longevity of 'Aphrodite', Kelways' pure white, early-flowering double pyrethrum which won a First Class Certificate in 1887. For two decades the awards to pyrethrums were dominated by Kelway cultivars, and to this day several surviving pyrethrums bear the family name: 'Kelway's Glorious' in glowing crimson-scarlet and deep blood-red 'James Kelway' are grown in the National Collection. Another Kelway cultivar still grown is 'Silver Challenge', a single with an extra row of petals, white flushed with pink.

During the war, as we have seen, pyrethrums were largely a casualty of the need to grow food before flowers, but in the fifties and sixties there was a resurgence of interest, no doubt chiefly due to Alan Bloom's efforts. In 1957 he could write (in *Hardy Perennials*) that 'at least fifty named varieties of pyrethrum are still in cultivation, some having been introduced more than fifty years ago'. This renewed popularity brought another handful of awards, including a First Class Certificate to the famous, vivid magenta-pink single 'Brenda', some more Kelway cultivars and a couple more of Mr Robinson's raising.

Other pink singles are the clean-toned 'Salmon Beauty', and deep pink 'Sam Robinson'. Among doubles there are peach-pink 'Queen Mary', white 'Lady Randolph Churchill' (from the Kelway stable) and lilac-pink

'Madeleine'. 'J. N. Twerdy' is a double magenta-crimson and 'Yvonne Cayeux', also double, a delicious deep ivory-cream. One or two anemone-centred pyrethrums survive, too: rosy 'Beauty of Stapleford', and the vigorous half-height, newish 'Red Dwarf', which has a pink flush in its anemone centre. Single-flowered 'Bressingham Red' was raised by Alan Bloom and was listed by Bressingham Nurseries until 1981-2. By the following year, however, the Bressingham catalogue was bereft of pyrethrums, although 'Progression', a double pink, featured in the spring 1983 list.

However, a couple of years later Alan Bloom was able to write in the Hardy Plant Society's Bulletin 'in recent years I believe I have learned how to overcome [the] baffling sickness in Pyrethrums.... Pathologists had no clue except to say it was a virus, and advised destruction of all infected plants. This I could not bear to do and when varieties were down to about a dozen and stocks worse than decimated, I began to experiment. At first I tried soot and then lime, but neither showed marked results. Then came sharp sand as well as dipping or dusting divisions in captan or Benlate before planting. But it was where I also used farm manure that results were quite spectacular.

'All this was spread over at least four seasons. I kept no records but went merely on guesswork, trial and error. Now, I would say the soot and lime made no difference because the soil lacked porosity and was too con-gealed until the sharp sand opened it. But with muck, all soil requirements appeared to be met.... So hopefully, a range of Pyrethrums is on the way back but only two or three of my new ones have survived. The best, "Venus" and "Inferno", have not. Now I will try to raise some more ...'

Certainly the results have been sufficiently encouraging for Bressingham Nurseries to list a few pyrethrum cultivars once more, including the apparently indomitable 'Brenda' and 'Eileen May Robinson', 'Bres-singham Red' and 'Evenglow'. Alan Bloom also has stocks of two more dwarf pyrethrums, 'Pink Petite', like a rather less than half-height 'Eileen May Robinson', and single red 'Laurin'.

Although they are often described as border plants, Mr Goddard con-siders pyrethrums better suited to growing in rows in the vegetable garden, where their cultivation can be more conveniently carried out than in the more competitive conditions of the border, and their flowers can be cut for the house without a qualm. Pyrethrums are susceptible to winter damage if disturbed in autumn, and should thus always be planted in spring, or immediately after flowering in summer so they have time to become established before the winter. They prefer a soil that does not dry out in the growing season, but are intolerant of winter wet even when established.

The National Collection

The National Collection of Pyrethrums at Chingford (Mr G. W. Goddard) was designated in November 1986, after his display of several vases of different cultivars at a Royal Horticultural Show brought his collection to the notice of the NCCPG. At that time he was growing sixteen cultivars – eight singles, seven doubles and one anemone-centred. Having collected them since the 1960s, he was well aware that they were disappearing from nurserymen's catalogues, and thought to draw the attention of the public to their beauty, by exhibiting vases of eight of his sixteen cultivars before the Royal Horticultural Society's Floral Committee A in June 1986. Since joining the ranks of National Collection holders he has added a further eight singles, three doubles and one more anemone-centred cultivar to the collection. Now, however, Mr Goddard fears that further cultivars will be very hard to obtain.

The other National Collection of Pyrethrums is held at Lamport Hall, Northampton (Lamport Hall Trust – Head Gardener Mr Mike Coote). Also designated in November 1986, this is a new collection being built up from scratch and as yet consists of few varieties, though more are being sought to augment the collection, which will in time be planted in the part of the gardens open to the public. The gardens, including herbaceous borders, a rose garden and a unique miniature rockwork landscape, are being restored and the pyrethrums will be an appropriate addition to a nineteenth-century landscape.

Saxifraga

SAXIFRAGA is an enormous genus, containing some of the loveliest alpines we can grow. To make classification easier in a genus which includes such widely different plants as London Pride and the minute lichen-like crusts of silvery foliage of *S. caesia*, the genus has been divided into fifteen sections. Waterperry, where the National Collection of one of these sections is grown, has for many years specialised in the cultivation and distribution of section 12, the Kabschia saxifrages. 'Under this repulsive and irrelevant name lie the dearest (in every sense) jewels of the family.' Thus Reginald Farrer, whose prose is irresistibly quotable whether he is enthusing over a beloved plant or scathing about some dingy horror.

The Kabschia section was split by botanists into seven subsections; the first was called Mediae, but quickly became known as Engleria by alpine gardeners. These seven subsections are retained in section Porophyllum, the name we are now to use; but I suspect many alpine gardeners will stick to the familiar name Kabschia, and continue to speak of the Englerias, to define these exquisite and precious plants.

Bear with me a little longer while I go a little further into this question of naming. There are about fifty species in this section in cultivation – all high alpines – and 400 or more hybrids. Most of these were raised before the Hitler war, or even before the Great War, by such people as Dr Boyd in Scotland, Russell Prichard in England (Prichard is a name that has cropped up in this book already, with geraniums and kniphofias) and Herr F. Sündermann in Bavaria. Since their day, confusion has crept into the nomenclature of the hybrids. To bring order into the naming, a system of binomial classification for cultivars of hybrid origin was published (by Drs Horny, Sojak and Webr in the Czech bulletin *Salnicky* in 1974). The system works by giving a binomial name to all cultivars of the same pair of parents: thus *S.* × *boydii* covers all the cultivars resulting from the cross

241

between *S. aretioides* and *S. burseriana*. One practical effect has been some name changes: for example *S. × elizabethae* is now the binomial name for all cultivars from *S. burseriana × S. sancta*. Thus the plant Farrer describes as 'one of the most precious of the early spring jewels', which we have all been calling *S. × elizabethae*, is just one of the offspring of this cross and is now *S.* 'Carmen'. Why Carmen? Because (Farrer again) 'Elizabeth, in this case, is the late Dowager of Roumania, Carmen Sylva'.

Enough about name changes; these few words should suffice to show that the collector of Kabschias will need his wits about him when ordering from catalogues. Those of us who are content to grow just a few of these delights in a trough, rock garden or alpine house will do well to choose them in flower at a specialist grower's nursery, as it might be Waterperry indeed.

The Kabschia Collection at Waterperry owes its existence to Valerie Finnis, now Lady Scott. She told me that when she first went to Waterperry as a student in 1942, she found in a yard behind the house a box frame containing a few cuttings of Kabschia saxifrages. She wondered what they were; found out; and began to grow and study them. From studying to collecting is a short and necessary step, and in this she was helped by Wilhelm Schacht of Munich, who still grew some of Sündermann's hybrids.

It wasn't long before Valerie Finnis had a large collection of Kabschias. She told me that at one time she could recognise about 200 different kinds of their foliage alone and that she expected, most years, to have about that number in flower at one time (their season extends from late winter through to mid or late spring). She showed her saxifrages regularly at the Royal Horticultural Society's shows at Vincent Square, sometimes staging the plants in little rock gardens built on a table for the two-day show, sometimes displaying them in pans. The peak of her achievement must have been the year when she showed 210 distinct varieties in pans at once.

After her marriage Valerie Finnis left Waterperry and the staff there admit that the collection became a little neglected for a while, missing her expert knowledge; but the plants were maintained, and were eventually taken over by Edward Urand and Adrian Young. The Collection now includes well over 250 distinct kinds and new ones are being introduced, as well as old kinds nurtured, and some, believed lost, rediscovered. Adrian Young rediscovered 'Mrs Gertrude Prichard', with grey foliage and large pink reflexed flowers. The wrong plant has been sold under this name for thirty years, but Waterperry have now introduced the correct plant as sold by Prichards in the thirties.

The Kabschias are, on the whole, reasonably easy to grow despite their high alpine origins. They dislike our soggy winters, so drainage is important, but as much at least do they loathe being scorched. Injudicious exposure to a mere hour or two of hot sun in summer can reduce them to a wan shadow of their former healthy selves. Farrer again: 'The thing to remember with the general run of these lovely things is that, while they love light and air, they usually detest being parboiled nearly as much as they would detest being waterlogged. They are plants of the rocks and screes and shingles, and some of them, even in nature, turn towards the cooler aspects, but however fiercely the sun may kiss the Italian and Levantine alps, it is never the same fury in that mountain air; with the melting snow percolating far beneath, and filling all the upper air with a soft veil through which the darts of Apollo can never smite with such lethal ferocity as down on the unprotected sands of Surrey or Kent.' More prosaically, Waterperry's recommendation is that 'raised beds or troughs with a well-drained limey compost are the most suitable means for growing these fascinating plants. They are all hardy but some prefer a little shade in midsummer'.

The Kabschia saxifrages are neat plants with hardy and horny, almost spiky foliage making dense little domes of grey, green or silver. They produce a mass of large flowers on slender stems, seldom more than 3 ins high, in almost every colour except blue. The Engleria saxifrages may have dense horny foliage, but more often they form thick silvery rosettes with taller and stouter spires of small flowers in fluffy calyces on brightly coloured, leafy stems in every shade of scarlet, crimson or purple. The Englerias are not so inclined to suffer from sunscorch or dryness at the roots in summer as the Kabschias.

One of the easiest of the Kabschias is *S.* × *apiculata* (now *S.* × *apiculata* 'Gregor Mendel'), making wide hard mats of bright pale green foliage and flowering early, in February and March, with loose heads of large primrose-yellow flowers on pinkish stems. There is a white form which has not the charm of the yellow, but is just as easy. The great name in the section is *S. burseriana*, the earliest and largest-flowered of the Kabschias, making mats of spiny blue-grey foliage hidden, in February, by big wide-open pure white flowers on slender red stems. Several selections have been made from *S. burseriana*, including Reginald Farrer's wonderful 'Gloria' with huge, solid flowers.

'Faldonside' is an old and famous Kabschia, raised by Dr Boyd and bearing 'great overlapping-petalled splendid flowers of pure citron yellow, well worthy of playing pale suns to even such unrivalled white moons as those of *S. burseriana magna* and *S. b.* 'Gloria''. The original *S.* × *boydii* (now to be distinguished by the cultivar name 'Old Britain'), however, raised in 1890, is now weakened with age and years of vegetative propagation, and needs great care, though it is still represented in the National Collection. It is probably a hybrid of *S. aretioides*, with yellow flowers over hard, tight little hummocks of foliage. *S. burseriana* 'Buttercup', with dark green foliage, is another yellow that has 'Faldonside' as one parent. The other is 'Haagii', an old but still easy yellow-flowered saxifraga, itself a hybrid: *S. ferdinandi-coburgii* × *S. sancta*, from which it inherits its green foliage. *S. ferdinandi-coburgii* crops up again as a parent of the lovely 'Borisii' with bright, clear citron yellow flowers on reddish stems over spiky blue-grey leaves.

Already it must be apparent that many of the 400 or more hybrids in the Kabschia section still survive in cultivation. They are unusual in the world of cultivated plants in retaining the qualities of the wild parent: a neatness in proportion and a wide variety of form in their rosettes, coupled with a purity of colour in their flowers. Newer yellow-flowered hybrids that are highly thought of at Waterperry include 'Sandpiper', which was noticed there. It has large, rich yellow flowers that are unusually reflexed. 'Millstream Queen' is an outstanding hybrid of American origin with large yellow flowers enhanced by an orange nectary ring. Then there is 'Valerie Finnis', a fine yellow with large clear-toned flowers (synonymous with 'Aretiastrum', an earlier (1920) introduction).

White is a common colour among the Kabschias — we have already met *S. burseriana* and its forms. Then there is the charming and easy *S. caesia*, with blue-green foliage sometimes silvered with lime, and loose sprays of milk-white, rounded flowers late in the season. *S. marginata* is a variable and a valuable species with greenish foliage and large, solid pure white flowers. *S.* 'Obristii' is a hybrid between *S. marginata* and *S. burseriana*, with white flowers from red buds, and 'Salomonii' has similar red-budded white flowers over silvery-grey rosettes. It is sparing with its flowers, but its sport 'Joy', spotted a few years ago at Waterperry, is very floriferous and has bright silver foliage. *S. diapensioides* is a tricky customer, and I cannot resist once again quoting Farrer: 'I have seen whole gardensful miff off upon no discoverable cause.' It is rare in nature, forming hard dense cushions: 'to the touch those unyielding elastic masses give a living, pulsing, yet cold-blooded feeling, as if one were caressing the wrinkled and warted skin of some aged and venerable toad'. After that, to say that *S. diapensioides* has milk-white flowers in late spring seems dully prosaic. New white cultivars from America include 'Falstaff' and 'White Imp', soon to be introduced by Waterperry.

Most of the Kabschias love lime, and thrive in a compost heavily laced with lime chippings. Exceptionally, *S. lilacina* is reputed to loathe a limey soil, though still demanding a gritty compost, and needs more shade than most. At Waterperry, however, it grows well in a limey mixture but needs a more water-retentive compost than most. It has solitary flowers of pure lilac to amethyst tones, from which derive most of the red and pink-flowered hybrids. The foliage of *S. lilacina* is 'as close and scabbed in growth as a lichen', and this close, flat growth is also inherited by some of its offspring. Such are 'Irvingii' and 'Jenkinsae', both with pale pink flowers. 'Arcovalleyi' has *S. marginata* as its other parent and bears almost stemless pink flowers over crowded rosettes of foliage. 'Cranbourne' is an easy Prichard hybrid with large rose-pink flowers and grey-green foliage. The Prichard nurseries at Christchurch were named Riverslea, and the saxifrage of this name is a delightful small hybrid with quite large rose-purple flowers and silvery foliage.

'Cerise Queen', also called 'Christine', has cherry-red flowers over dark green, silver-edged rosettes. Perhaps the darkest colour among the older hybrids belongs to 'Myra', a bright deep cherry red. 'Chetwynd' has several pink flowers to a stem and was introduced very recently by Waterperry. An old hybrid between *S. stribrnyi* and a form of *S. marginata*, 'Bridget' has silvery foliage in close rosettes, and mauve-pink flowers; Waterperry gave the name *S. × edithae* 'Jubilee' to a similar hybrid raised by Peter Barrow, which is much more vigorous.

With *S. stribryni* we come to a member of the Engleria subsection, a handsome plant forming silvery rosettes and bearing sprays of pink flowers in fluffy, baggy purple calyces. *S. media* is another typical Engleria with narrow silvery leaves and pink flowers hiding in furry red calyces. Herr Sündermann bred many hybrids in which *S. media* is dominant, making fair-sized rosettes and 'blossoms in loose and showering spikes, with the fading Water Avens tones ... inclining to old-rose and mud colour and sad worn salmon and crushed bad strawberries' (Farrer). The Sündermann hybrids in which *S. aretioides*, of the Kabschia section, predominates are cleaner in colour, 'Water Avens shades of apricot, orange and terracotta'. We meet these offbeat colours also in such as 'Iris Prichard', which is one-quarter Engleria and has flowers of pale buff-apricot. 'Lady Beatrix Stanley' is of the same parentage, *S. × godroniana* (a named form of *S. × luteopurpurea*) × *S. lilacina*. Newer than these are 'Boughton Orange' ('Edgar Irmscher') from Valerie Finnis, a very attractive plant with orange flowers, and *S. × boydililacina* 'Penelope', which is pure Kabschia, raised from *S.* 'Jenkinsae' seed by Rob Dunford of Ripley, Surrey. He did not like the unusual colouring, straw yellow with a flush of pink; 'Penelope' has proved to be the most popular of the new Porophyllum cultivars at Waterperry.

The Engleria saxifrage that most people first encounter is *S. grisebachii* probably in its form 'Wisley Var.', which was first seen at the RHS Garden at Wisley and later found in the wild in Albania. Over wide rosettes, heavily crusted with lime, are borne tall arching sprays of little pink flowers all but hidden in baggy calyces, which, like the stems, are pelted over with crimson-purple fur. Farrer likens it to 'some fine and monstrous *Ajuga* dipped in blood and wine', but to me it has an almost animal appearance. The plant variously known as *S. frederici augustii*

(Farrer), *S.* × *frederici-augustii* (Anna Griffiths) or *S.* 'Frederici Augustii' (Waterperry), is another typical Engleria, a hybrid or perhaps a form of *S. sempervivum* (*S. porophylla* var. *thessalica*) with rosettes of small leaves and arching stems of small pink bells in large fluffy wine-red calyces. *S.* × *biasoletti* 'Crystalie' is a fine hybrid between *S. sempervivum* and *S. grisebachii*, with superb furry crimson sprays arching over rosettes of sharply pointed silvery leaves. A rather tricky old Sündermann Engleria hybrid between *S. sempervivum* and *S. luteoviridis* is *S.* × *gusmussii*, with silvery rosettes and light orange-red flowers.

Evidently, with over 400 hybrids to choose from, and well over half of them represented in the National Collection, I cannot describe them all. You must visit Waterperry yourself, at any time from February onwards, preferably on a Saturday when Adrian Young will be there, and see if you too will succumb to these entrancing little saxifrages, the quintessential alpine plant of high places.

The National Collection

The National Collection of Kabschia *saxifrages is held at Waterperry Horticultural Centre, near Wheatley, Oxford.*

The saxifrages that became, in September 1983, the National Collection of Kabschia *saxifrages were collected initially by one person, Valerie Finnis, who became interested in them when she was a student at Waterperry in 1942. Before long she was able to recognise over 200 different kinds by their foliage alone, and expected, most years, to have about that number in flower at one time. After her marriage Valerie Finnis left Waterperry, and the collection became a little neglected for a while; but the plants were maintained, and were eventually taken over by Edward Urand and Adrian Young. The National Collection now includes well over 250 distinct kinds, and new ones are being introduced as well as old kinds rediscovered – some in Eastern Europe.*

Sedum

THERE IS tremendous variety within the genus *Sedum*: low-growing mat-forming plants, herbaceous kinds typified by the old 'ice plant', and the fascinating Rhodiola section. The best-known of the border sedums is the old ice plant, *Sedum spectabile*. As well as for its thick, fleshy, pale glaucous green leaves and flat heads in late summer of pinkish flowers that glow at dusk, it is valued in many gardens for its appeal to butterflies and bees. The great eiderdown-like masses of the ice plant in late summer are always covered with tortoiseshells, peacocks and commas, their warm coppery-orange colouring clashing unassertively with the tiny mauve-pink starry flowers of the sedum. Forms of *S. spectabile* with brighter colouring have been selected: of these 'Brilliant' and 'Meteor' should not be too hard to obtain. There is also a form with variegated foliage. But perhaps the best variegated sedum of sufficient size to grow in a border is *S. alboroseum* 'Variegatum' ('Foliis Mediovariegatis') in which the grey-green leaves of the type are heavily splashed with creamy yellow. It is a floppy plant with white, pink-eyed flowers in flat heads. Be sure to pull out forthwith any green shoots; with their much greater vigour they will otherwise swamp the creamy-gold in no time.

'Autumn Joy' is a bigger, stronger-coloured hybrid of *S. spectabile*, with wide heads of flowers, green like the ice plant's in bud and opening to deep, clean pink that ages to a rich coppery red and then to its winter livery of sienna-brown. Curiously, this one does not seem to attract butterflies, though it is thick with bees once the flowers are fully open. 'Autumn Joy' has the same good foliage as *S. spectabile*, on taller stems that flop outwards on old congested clumps; divide it regularly, for young plants are the best. Of much the same stature as 'Autumn Joy' is *Sedum maximum*, with similar succulent leaves but flat heads of minute starry pale yellow flowers. It is rather a shame that 'Atropurpureum', with rich beetroot-maroon foliage and stems, does not have the same pale flowers;

instead, the purple colouring has bled into the flowers as well, so they too are reddish. If this is too muscular a plant for you, at 2 ft high and wide, you could choose 'Vera Jameson', a neat little plant of under 1 ft in height with bloomy purple foliage and sombre pink flowers, charming with low silvery foliage, of the feathery *Artemisia lanata* perhaps, frothing about it. A bit smaller again is 'Ruby Glow', with foliage of more glaucous than purple tones, and richer pink flowers almost justifying the epithet 'ruby'. All these sedums flower in late summer and early autumn, with 'Autumn Joy', as its name implies, the latest. The yellow-flowered *S. aizoon* is out by summer; the flat heads of yellow starry flowers top stems bearing green, toothed leaves of the usual fleshy texture. It is a pleasant enough thing, but eclipsed by its form 'Aurantiacum', with darker foliage and reddish stems, and dark yellow flowers at the same rather earlier season. Dark foliage appears again in 'Munstead Red', a selected form of a British wild plant, *Sedum telephium* or orpine. The wildling is scarcely a garden plant, but Miss Jekyll's is a fine thing, as one might expect from that discerning gardener. It is somewhat sprawling in habit, but she no doubt valued it for its subtle colouring, of dark green leaves flushed with purple, and flat heads of muted maroon-red flowers, appearing in late summer. Sedums almost without exception enjoy full sun and well-drained, even hungry soils, so you could set this one with silver foliage, always at its most appealing as summer turns to autumn. Still less common than 'Munstead Red', which is now scarcely offered commercially, is *S. telephium* subsp. *ruprechtii*, of tender and unusual colouring, buff-yellow in flower with pink stems and pale glaucous leaves, and imperturbable good manners. *S. telephium* also has a pretty variegated form, 'Roseovariegatum', pinkish as the leaves emerge in spring but turning to green later; and there is 'Borderi', grey in leaf with coppery pink flowers.

One of the oddest sedums is the sub-shrubby, foot-high *S. populifolium*, with thinner-textured leaves supposedly shaped like those of a poplar or aspen, squarish at the base and coarsely toothed. Pinkish-white flowers appear in summer. Still less like the popular idea of a sedum is *S. rosea*, the only member of the Rhodiola section that is at all well known. With its tight rosettes of very glaucous, toothed leaves, it is often mistaken for a kind of *Euphorbia*, and when the deep pink flowerbuds open, in spring, to yellow flowers the colour-scheme is indeed much like a spurge's. The whole of this section comprises about thirty species, some of which are now very rare and not yet known to many gardeners.

It is hard to pick out just one or two from the Rhodiola section. The very grey-glaucous *S. heterodontum* is a charming, compact border plant, fairly well-known but rather hard to increase, as unlike most sedums cuttings are reluctant to strike. It flowers quite early, in April and May, the red-purple flowers nicely set against the bloomy grey foliage. Several other members of section Rhodiola are border plants of more or less merit, but two at least make charming occupants of the rock garden. *S. hobsonii* is tap-rooted and should not be disturbed until about a year old, for the frail long roots of seedlings are easily damaged. The cluster of basal leaves grows directly from the caudex (the thick stem-like upper portion of the rootstock) and around them radiate the reddish flowering stems, lying flat on the ground and closely set with small bright green leaves; the stems are tipped with little pink flowers. The elegant little *S. primuloides* is also low-growing, with rooting shaggy stems from which arise short branchlets, each ending in a flat rosette of fleshy almost circular green leaves. The little cup-shaped flowers, borne singly rather than in clustered heads, are white.

In other sections of the genus are many other good-tempered rock plants. Some are almost too easy-going, with take-over tendencies; for *Sedum acre*, the common wall pepper, *S. album* and others are easily broken, the little fat leaves falling off the stems at a touch and rolling away to root down and form new plants all too readily. Both these species, however, have variants which are less invasive. The golden form of *S. acre*, 'Aureum', has yellow-tipped stems, 'Elegans' is white-tipped, and 'Majus', which is larger than the type, is not correspondingly more invasive: on the contrary, it has good garden manners. Forms of *S. album* such as *murale*, with pinkish flowers, or 'Coral Carpet' with white flowers and leaves bright red in colour so long as it is grown in austere conditions, are worth admitting. Of similar character is *S. dasyphyllum*, for which I have long had a fondness, on account of its very thick, clustered blue-grey leaves and little pink flowers. It will scuttle along rock crevices very nicely.

Several species in the same section as the border plants, such as *S. telephium*, are extremely pretty plants for rock gardens, to spread forwards over flat stones, or even for the front of small borders. *S. sieboldii* is probably the best known, a plant with trailing stems bearing stalkless, fleshy round leaves of fresh green, edged with red, set in clusters of two or three. The stems bear terminal clusters of starry pink flowers in October, when there is not much else in flower in the rock garden. Its variegated form, 'Foliis Mediovariegatus', with paler glaucous leaves centrally splashed with creamy-yellow, is a little tender, and distressingly apt to revert to green. Scarcely a garden plant, it is popular as a pot plant and delightful in a hanging basket, its stems trailing over the edge. Similar to *S. sieboldii* are *S. cauticola* and *S. ewersii*. The first has glaucous-blue leaves on very short stalks, borne along trailing stems ending in heads of bright purple-rose flowers in autumn, before those of *S. sieboldii*. *S ewersii* flowers earlier, in August or September, and has similar glaucous-grey leaves, but that they are stalkless and clasp the sprawling stems. *Var. homophyllum* is very dwarf and compact; it seldom flowers but is a charming foliage plant.

Related to *S. aizoon*, which we met as a border plant, are several familiar rock garden sedums with rosettes of fleshy leaves, varying in shape, and clusters of yellow flowers. *S. kamtschaticum*, in its variegated form, sells on sight, its oval leaves broadly edged in cream, a colourful setting for the orange-centred yellow flowers. Less bright than this, but a nice thing still, is *S. ellacombianum*, named for Canon Ellacombe who did so much, two or three generations ago, to distribute good and unusual plants, to his friend. E. A. Bowles and many others. The Canon's sedum is fresh green in leaf, compact of habit, and has vivid yellow flowers. Much narrower in leaf is *S. middendorfianum*, more compact than *S. kamtschaticum* and a pleasing, if unspectacular, little plant.

Sedum spurium is a coarse thing, but very common, for it is so easy to grow that it gets handed on to new gardeners, or thrown onto rubbish heaps (which it will quickly cover given the least start). Selected forms are quite worth growing as less aggressive ground cover, however; such as 'Dragon's Blood' ('Schorbusser Blut') which has purplish-bronze foliage and deep red flowers. 'Green Mantle' and 'Ruby Mantle' are described in colour and characteristics by their names. Far better than these is *S. oreganum*, which will also form a dense green carpet if happy. Yellow flowers in clusters appear in summer, above the fleshy, crowded leaves. *S. spathulifolium*, with flattish rosettes of stubby leaves, is deservedly popular and has several variants. Some forms have pinkish or reddish foliage; always more marked if you keep them on short commons, or in very hot weather; *purpureum* has purple leaves and 'Cape Blanco' (often seen labelled 'Capa Blanca') is a much smaller plant with silver-grey mealy leaves, a dear little plant and very good-tempered.

Exceptionally, *S. obtusatum* prefers' shade, but hates being too wet in winter. Its glaucous-green leaves are held in loose rosettes; pale yellow to light orange flowers open in June. *S. pulchellum* is another that is unhappy in the dry, austere conditions that suit most sedums; it actually prefers moist or even damp soil. It is a very pretty plant with fresh green foliage, often pink-tipped, and large starfish flower-heads of many rosy purple flowers. If mistakenly planted in hot, dry soils it will often behave like an annual, and thus may fittingly introduce the last few sedums I want to describe.

Sedum coeruleum is a true annual, with sky-blue flowers contrasting with reddish foliage, very pretty and not difficult to raise from seed; indeed it often self-sows, in suitable gritty sandy soil. By contrast you would do well to save, and carefully sow, the seed of two desirable biennial sedums, *S. pilosum* and *S. sempervivoides*. This last is well described by its name, for it is indeed very like a houseleek or sempervivum, with a crowded rosette of leaves and broad heads of showy carmine-red flowers. *S. pilosum* has densely packed hairy leaves forming tight rosettes, and conspicuous pink flowers in more open sprays. It is an attractive trough plant, preferring well-drained soil especially in winter.

The National Collection

The National Collection of Sedum *is held at Abbeydore Court Gardens, Hereford (Mrs Sarah Sage).*

Sarah Sage, whose sedums were designated as a National Collection in September 1983, is one of the younger National Collection holders and has many calls on her time apart from sedums, yet she has amassed about 240 species and cultivars so far. She grows them at Abbeydore Court Gardens, which belongs to her mother, Charis Ward, who started the garden in 1976 and works it with help from Sarah. Her enthusiasm for the genus began when she was given a plant of 'Munstead Red' from a Gloucestershire garden and, from a Herefordshire garden, Sedum telephium *subsp.* ruprechtii. *Her favourite sedums are those of the Rhodiola section, which she believes are unjustly neglected in our gardens.*

Thalictrum

AMONG the meadow rues, a group of plants that have escaped the attentions of the breeders, are some good things for borders and peat gardens and some weedy rubbish fit only for the wild garden. But the best thalictrums are very good indeed, with beautiful foliage and flowers borne in elegant sprays or composed of a foam of stamens.

Because so many are scarcely garden-worthy, you are unlikely to find more than a handful of species offered by nurserymen. One that you should have no difficulty acquiring is *Thalictrum aquilegiifolium*, its name describing the lovely columbine-like, pale grey-green leaves. A slender plant, it needs close planting to allow the wide heads of flowers to form a cloud of fluffy stamens. These, the showy part of the flower, are commonly warm lilac or amethyst; there is a pleasant creamy-white form, and sombre purple 'Thundercloud'. A native of moist alpine meadows, in the garden it can fittingly join other moisture-lovers, the pale lemon globe flower and *Iris sibirica* perhaps. But it is happy in any good soil. Try it with white foxgloves, vinous-mauve aquilegias, lilac-blue *Polemonium foliosissimum* – a superior Jacob's Ladder – and aromatic *Geranium macrorrhizum* 'Ingwersen's Variety' in mauve pink or magenta-purple 'Bevan's Variety'.

Thalictrum aquilegiifolium is the first of the meadow rues to flower, and has a short season in early summer. Happily, it is sufficiently good tempered to be moved without harm, immediately after flowering, into a spare plot, if you have it in a border where its pleasant seed-heads would not meet your demands for colour in summer. Following it, at midsummer, are the yellow-flowered species. If space is short you should limit yourself to *T. speciosissimum*, tall and lovely with glaucous, divided leaves. The flowers are of the same powder-puff style as *T. aquilegiifolium*, but in unripe-lemon yellow. If to some gardeners its colouring seems rather indeterminate, others appreciate its self-contained colour scheme, easy growth and generous stature. At Hidcote it is associated with *Alchemilla mollis* in Mrs Winthrop's blue and yellow garden. It has enough presence to hold its own against strong yellow ligularias and the green-and-white-striped *Miscanthus sinensis* 'Variegatus', or the big satiny lemon hollyhock, *Althaea rugosa*.

Other yellow thalictrums are less good. *T. flavum* has plain green foliage, missing more than half the point of its better cousin, and 'Illuminator' with leaves tinged yellow is duller still. The green leaves of *T. lucidum* differ in their narrow leaflets, from which it had its earlier name *T. angustifolium*.

The smallest forms of *T. minus*, a British and European native, are delightful in leaf, like tiny maidenhairs often turning gold in autumn. The flowers are greenish and unremarkable. Larger forms exist, and some can be invasive; names like *T. foetidum* may belong here, but this is a muddled group. The Royal Horticultural Society's Dictionary acidly observes that 'botanic gardens distribute more forms of *T. minus* than of any other species, frequently under names which are incorrect'. One which is offered as *T. minus arenarium* is a neat little carpeting plant, rapidly spreading in sandy soils to form a mat of maidenhair foliage, topped by flowers of creamy-green. Another species of variable dimensions, *T. tuberosum* from Spain and the Pyrenees, can in its smallest forms be welcomed to the rock garden for its attractive foliage and sprays of little white flowers.

So far we have encountered only European thalictrums, though *T. speciosissimum* does extend into North Africa. North America is the home of several species, mostly with columbine or maidenhair foliage and insignificant flowers. In the National Collection grows *T. polygamum*, which rejoices in the common names of king of the meadow, or more prosaically, muskrat weed. A tall plant, reaching 8 ft, it has white flowers in large panicles.

The best thalictrums, however, are those which grow wild in Asia, from the Himalayas across to Japan. The Chelidonian group derive their name from *T. chelidonii*, a Himalayan species easier to grow in the cooler north of Britain, where the National Collection is situated, than in the south. Reaching 5-6 ft, it has elegant small, divided leaves over which the flowering stems are decked with open spires of rosy-lilac flowers. Unlike the powder-puff kinds so far described, the Chelidonian group has flowers like miniature clematis, with coloured sepals around a little fluff of stamens. Both meadow rue and clematis belong to the family Ranunculaceae, the buttercup family, but in *Thalictrum* the epithet 'large', used to describe the flowers, means up to one inch across at most, as in *T. chelidonii* itself. The Tibetan *T. diffusiflorum* also has large, lilac flowers with citron stamens, wide bells hanging in loose sprays of about 2-3 ft in height. The blue-green leaves are tiny. Like *T. chelidonii* it prefers cool, moist shade and a peaty soil, where if induced to do well it is of exquisite beauty.

By comparison with these, *T. rochebrunnianum* is almost coarse, and seems no easier to grow. Better concentrate on two western Chinese species, *T. delavayi* and *T. dipterocarpum*. The two are much confused; the name more often encountered is *T. dipterocarpum*, but it is probably attached more often than not to *T. delavayi*. Both have sparse but pretty, wiry bluish maidenhair foliage, and airy wide sprays of lilac flowers with creamy stamens, larger in *T. delavayi* than in *T. dipterocarpum*, which, if indeed it is a separate species, is probably not in cultivation in Britain. There is a white *T. delavayi* also. The covetable 'Hewitt's Double', which lacks the contrasting stamens in each tiny lilac rosette, is shorter-growing than the singles. It is tricky to propagate in any reasonable quantity – cuttings should be tried in preference to division, which is apt to be frustrated by the plant's obdurately slow increase – and likely always to be in demand. Whether *T. delavayi* or *T. dipterocarpum*, these lovely and graceful plants need cossetting in well-nourished, deep soil, with shelter from wind. Plant them deeply, in a hollow, drawing the soil towards the stems as the season advances. They are beautiful with *Dierama pulcherrimum*, the angel's fishing rod, which bears on arching, swaying stems hanging bells in shades of pink, lilac and purple, moving in every breeze.

Yet to be represented in the National Collections are the smaller thalictrums, those that would be selected by devotees of the peat bed. The Japanese *T. kiusianum* has slowly creeping roots and dainty foliage of the usual maidenhair style, underpinning loose clusters of tiny, fluffy purple flowers. The mysterious and desirable *T. orientale*, which Farrer says comes from the Caucasus, has similar foliage and larger, rich pink flowers, borne on branching stems in early summer. Sampson Clay, whose book *The Present-Day Rock Garden* aimed to update and amplify Farrer's monumental *English Rock Garden*, says that Farrer's *T. orientale* is *Isopyrum thalictroides*; *Flora Europaea* describes *T. orientale* as white-flowered and native of Greece and Asia Minor. Rather taller is *T. coreanum*, with leaves like a little green epimedium and lilac flowers.

The National Collection

The National Collection of Thalictrum *at Broughton Place, Biggar, Lanark-shire, arose out of Mr and Mrs Buchanan-Dunlop's interest in the genus, stimulated by their discovery of several* Thalictrum *species in the garden of Broughton Place where they moved in the mid 1970s. The garden had been laid out in the late 1930s and planted with a wide variety of unusual species. First to come to their notice were the elegant* T. aquilegiifolium *and* T. speciosissimum; *further exploration revealed other species 'of quieter character', writes Mrs Buchanan-Dunlop, 'but always rescued from dullness by the intricate delicacy of their foliage'. The Collection has increased to over twenty species, thanks to gifts and acquisitions from international seed exchanges. 'A number of these are young and have still to prove that they are garden-worthy; I feel that the principle aim of the NCCPG should be to protect plants that fall into this admittedly arbitrary category and to protect the many named cultivars that may succumb to the whims of fashion.' Later in her letter, Mrs Buchanan-Dunlop writes that 'chance has given me my favourite* Thalictrum *planting – a kind wind blew a seed of* T. aquilegiifolium *into the middle of a clump of sibirica irises. The result seems to me a perfect balance of form and colour'. The Broughton Place Collection of* Thalictrum *was designated in July 1983. More recently, in November 1986, a second* Thalictrum *Collection was designated at Bridgemere Nurseries in Cheshire, but this as yet includes very few species.*

Yellow Daisies

YELLOW is one of the commonest colours in nature, second perhaps only to purplish pink. You could fill a summer garden with bright yellow flowers, with brassy and mustardy golds and a few precious cooling citron and primrose tones, almost without trying, and a lot of those flowers would come from the group of hardy perennials lumped together as the yellow daisies.

Poor things, they are not a fashionable crowd at the moment. Many are rather coarse plants; on the whole their foliage leaves much to be desired; in colour many are brash: in short, they lack charm. But they are indisputably easy to grow, and are typical of the sort of hardy herbaceous plant that for many years was the mainstay of the English flower border where colour was the first consideration. They are part of our gardening heritage, to use the word so fashionable these days, and as such should not be allowed to die out.

As here defined, the yellow daisies include the genera *Coreopsis, Helenium, Helianthus, Helianthella,* and *Heliopsis*; discerning gardeners may be prepared to allow some virtues to the first two genera, but the others are almost universally derided at present. I hope, however, to show that some are garden-worthy plants, quoting well-known gardeners past and present in support of my comments.

Yellow daisies were first introduced to this country from North America between 1506 and 1617. *Helianthus annuus*, the sunflower, is still a popular annual, especially with children. Commercially, sunflowers are an important crop, grown almost world-wide, producing a high-quality oil with health-giving properties now widely used in cooking, as well as deliciously nutty seeds. Experiments have been carried out showing that sunflowers as a farm crop can even help to make the farmer independent of the oil-producing cartel, for sunflower oil can run machines as well as feeding mankind and his domesticated animals. Another close relative of

258

great food value is *Helianthus tuberosus*, the Jerusalem artichoke, introduced as a regular vegetable crop in the walled gardens of past centuries.

Neither of these species is at present at the slightest risk of disappearing from cultivation, but others, in all the five genera covered by the National Collection, have proved hard to acquire, and the cultivars are even more elusive. A perennial sunflower that is still available, *Helianthus salicifolius*, has never become anything like as popular as its annual cousins, yet both Gertrude Jekyll and, in our time, Christopher Lloyd, have enthused over it. Indeed, only days before writing these lines I was standing with Christopher Lloyd looking at *Helianthus salicifolius* growing in his Long Border, still full of interest in late October. He was just back from the States, where this tall perennial is native, and had greatly admired it there, grown as a hedge 150 yards long. It was a solid wall of small, bright yellow daisies from top to bottom all along both sides. 'But, not being a wall, it grew in sprays, some upright, some oblique, some reaching sideways at ground level, and it was magic in the autumn sun.' Here we could not manage the 'floppy Monarch butterflies, orange-brown with darker veins' that were feeding on it – how good they must have looked against the yellow, and the black disc – but we could all enjoy its splendid leafage for weeks before it begins to think of flowering. *Helianthus salicifolius* is one of the exceptions to the general coarseness of leaf that the yellow daisies bore us with. Instead, it looks like a lush clump of lilies, its stout stems set with many narrow, drooping leaves of a healthy deep green.

I am sure Christopher Lloyd won't mind my saying he was wrong to suggest that if we could grow this sunflower as they do in its native country, we should have heard of it in Gertrude Jekyll's day. She not only knew it (as *H. orgyalis*) she used it for one of her favourite contrivances. It was one of the plants she used to mask an earlier group, gone over and needing some disguise. She had it behind a group of *Achillea filipendulina*, which bears its bright yellow plate-like flowers in high summer, and the fine steely-blue *Eryngium amethystinum*. 'When the bloom of these is done the tall sunflower is trained down on them – this pulling down, as in the case of so many plants, causing it to throw up flower-stalks from the axils of every pair of leaves; so that in September the whole thing is a sheet of bloom.' Something like Christopher Lloyd's hedge, in fact.

Let us stay for a moment with Miss Jekyll, because this group leads, in her border, to a patch of brilliant colour from red hollyhocks and dahlias, scarlet penstemons, gladioli and salvias, and scarlet and orange dwarf nasturtiums. With all these hot colours she did not despise *Helenium pumilum* and *Coreopsis lanceolata*, bearing a long succession of deep yellow flowers. The helenium is not, despite the name she gives it, a species, but a garden form of *H. autumnale*, the North American sneezeweed (why sneezeweed, I wonder?). Heleniums are quite a cut above the coarser sunflower tribe; their foliage is as boring as any, it is true, but their daisy flowers have more quality, with fringed silky petals and velvety brown or yellow central knobs. They also run to sumptuous shades of coppery-tan, deep mahogany and bronze, as well as clear bright yellow. Some people are put off by their down-drooping petals, which make them look as if they are going over before they quite begin. Keep them well away from the pinks or reds with any blue in them; such rich, autumnal colours deserve better.

'Pumilum' is shortish, deep yellow; 'Butterpat' is taller and 'Bressingham Gold' a good newer kind. As a rule of thumb the taller kinds are later-flowering. Thus 'The Bishop', which gained an Award of Merit at the Royal Horticultural Society's Trials at Wisley in 1961, is a mere 2-3 ft in height, and starts to show its pure bright yellow flowers from June, continuing if deadheaded until autumn. The newly opened blooms are much enhanced by their deep brown discs which, as the flower ages and the pollen develops, fade to dull yellow. Almost as early is the foot-taller 'Moerheim Beauty', which – again if deadheaded – will flower from mid-June to late October. Its good temper and fine colouring, dark red-tan with a deep brown disc, earned it an Award of Garden Merit from the Royal Horticultural Society as early as 1934, barely half a decade after it was raised in Holland by Ruys. At the time of the 1960-2 Trials it still outshone its rivals and earned the only First Class Certificate, in 1962.

Though of much the same height at 3½-4 ft, 'Bruno' starts to flower much later than 'Moerheim Beauty', in September, when its large, deep mahogany-red flowers are suitably autumnal. Taller still at 5 ft or more in height are 'Riverton Beauty' in yellow with maroon centre, and 'Riverton Gem' in rich coppery-red. These received Dutch Awards of Merit as long ago as 1909 and 1914 respectively. Like all heleniums they grow in almost any soil, but prefer fairly rich living; these taller cultivars especially are apt to look very sad in prolonged drought if grown in thin soils, their lower leaves withering on the stem.

More recent kinds of coppery-bronze or red-gold colouring are 'Coppelia' and 'July Sun', while 'Spätrot' leans more to red-tan and brown; 'Baudirektor Linne' is deeper still in orange and mahogany-red. One cultivar has appropriated the colour-word 'mahogany' as its name, and 'Crimson Beauty' is another of this shade, not crimson at all but rich red-brown. 'Wyndley' is a warm shade of orange-yellow streaked with chestnut, and the award-winning 'Waltraud', a three-footer flowering from June to September, opens yellow; the underside of the petals are streaked with chestnut red, spreading and suffusing the upper surface to golden brown.

A selection from many that have been introduced over the years, these names will indicate that *Helenium autumnale* has had its days of glory, even if not very popular at present. Nurserymen have to live like anyone else, and don't go in for breeding masses of cultivars of an unpopular genus, so the existence in gardening literature of many cultivar names always shows that a plant has at one time been admired.

These daisies look well not only in the rich mixtures of Miss Jekyll, but also as a deep note among plenty of cream and green, with good bold foliage about them to divert the eye from their own shortcomings in this department. For a strong colour contrast you could set 'Moerheim Beauty' with violet-purple *Salvia nemorosa*; flowers from early July would be deadheaded in August for a second, September season. E. A. Bowles liked to set the coppery-red forms among 'the lilacs of Erigerons, the light yellows of Anthemis, and ... orange shades'. For earlier flower, there is *Helenium hoopesii*, a pleasant thing with warm yellow flowers in June over a big rosette of grey-green leaves.

Taller than the heleniums are the hybrid sunflowers chiefly derived from *Helianthus decapetalus*, such as 'Loddon Gold', a double-flowered five-footer, or the older 'Miss Mellish' or 'Soleil d'Or'. 'Capenoch Star', about 1 ft shorter, is a cooler lemon yellow, flowering from early August till autumn. Miss Jekyll refers, without naming it, to a useful pale form that provided late colour in her borders. Whether or not this was *H. doronicoides*, with typically coarse leaves and small pale yellow sunflowers in late summer, I cannot say. William Robinson would relegate this one to the woodland, where indeed its clear pale colouring could look well and its running, invasive roots be no disadvantage. Another pale sunflower earns a paragraph from E. A. Bowles (*My Garden in Autumn and Winter*), and I wonder if this plant, which he received as *Helianthus laetiflorus* and was subsequently told was a form of *H. tuberosus*, the Jerusalem artichoke, is still grown. It sounds good: 'The plant itself makes a handsome tall specimen, if thinned out or replanted, reaching some 8 ft in height, and in October and sometimes right on into November, bears abundance of pale, clear yellow flowers, large enough to be showy, yet small enough to be graceful. The greatest of its charms, however, is due to the deep black of the stems. They are as dark as the ebony handle of a sable paintbrush, and the contrast with the rich green leaves and daffodil-yellow flowers is delightful.'

Many other perennial sunflowers have running roots and can become a nuisance unless confined, following William Robinson's advice, to wilder parts of the garden, or to the woodland. *Helianthus atrorubens*, for example – not dark red, as its name might imply, but of the usual strong yellow – is quite a weed; but 'Monarch', a garden selection, has large, brilliant yellow flowers with extra, quilled petals around a black eye. It is said to be rather tender. In open settings, even in grass, the more vigorous sunflowers and the common red-hot pokers could be combined in a splash of autumn colour, reds and yellows anticipating or echoing the turning leaves of trees and shrubs.

Heliopsis are mainly of warm shades of yellow, hinting at orange; they too may be single, semi-double or fully double, garish and rather charmless but undeniably easy to grow and vivid in colour. 'Light of Loddon' is from the same stable as 'Loddon Gold'; a single, this one. 'Golden Plume' is a fine large double, and so is 'Goldgreenheart', which is of a more appealing citron yellow with lime-green centre. 'Orange King' goes the other way, almost to true orange; and the old 'Incomparabilis' is a double orange-yellow with zinnia-like flowers. For a blatantly obvious colour contrast, set the yellow with blue, say of eryngiums, if you must. *Heliopsis* have the great virtue of seldom needing division, which may earn them a place in the gardens of those too busy, infirm or lazy to fiddle around with regular replanting.

After the unloved *Heliopsis* it is a relief to turn to *Coreopsis*, a genus of more quality altogether. For a start, *Coreopsis verticillata* has thread-fine foliage to set off its bright (Graham Thomas has 'brassy') yellow daisies, at their largest, and warmest yellow, in the form 'Grandiflora'. *C. verticillata* grows nice and dense and needs no staking, which even the stout-stemmed heleniums are apt to do because of the weight of their flowers. A new introduction among coreopsis, and a genuine colour-break to be wel-comed to our gardens, is *C. verticillata* 'Moonbeam'. Over the same needle leaves of fresh green as the type appear a mass of lazy-daisies of primrose yellow. Each petal has something of the sheen enhancing the pale-flowered celandine, and like that little spring flower this child of summer fades gracefully from citron to cream. There are all too few summer flowers of this emollient colour, and we may be grateful to the Bloom family of Bressingham for introducing it to British gardens from America.

Names of other coreopsis that you may encounter are 'Badengold', 'Sunburst' (double-flowered) and the nice little 'Goldfink', a useful splash of bright yellow for the front of a border. These are all varieties of *C. grandiflora*. They last well when cut, even if rather a bother to pick as their thin stems get tangled, and patience runs out before you have unwoven them. The vivid yellow of *C. auriculata* 'Superba' is enlivened by a central maroon splash. William Robinson suggests that this and the nearly allied *C. lanceolata*, with abundant rich yellow daisies in autumn, enjoy a rich damp soil. They look entirely adapted to sunny conditions, which indeed they need; we forget, perhaps, that a plant liking the sun on its face may not necessarily perform as well as it could if its roots are in hot, dry, starved soil. Annual coreopsis, too, do best in a fairly rich soil, though certainly not in a bog.

Though these genera of composites are loosely spoken of as 'yellow daisies', there are of course many other members of the daisy family that have yellow flowers, yet are very different in character from the sunflower tribe. One such genus is *Ligularia*, genuinely bog-loving plants mostly of statuesque, bold appearance. These form a separate National Collection from the preceding group. *Ligularia* is botanically very close to *Senecio* and most species have sojourned in that genus also. From the gardener's point of view, separating them out distinguishes them from all the other familiar garden senecios, of which the shrubby New Zealanders have already received mention in these pages.

Heavy, wet soil, then, suits ligularias well. The most familiar is *L. dentata* (*L. clivorum*) with bold rounded or kidney-shaped leaves and stout-stemmed loose heads of orange-yellow daisies in high summer. Its most exciting manifestations have leaves brownish above, mahogany-purple beneath, and brighter flowers in a larger inflorescence. 'Othello' and 'Desdemona' – who curiously is as dark as her husband – are well-known; the even darker 'Moorblut' more elusive. All ligularias are attractive to butterflies; among the dusky leaves and rich orange flowers of this trio the coppery tones of tortoiseshells and commas are seen to better advantage than when clashing with the mauve or purple of buddleias or the sad pink of *Sedum spectabile*.

With green, not mahogany foliage, and of rampant habit, *L. dentata* 'Orange Queen' is a selection with large, vivid flower heads. Resembling a small version of *L. dentata*, which is a native of west and central China, the Japanese *L. hodgsonii* has proved hard to obtain. Commercial stock of this name has turned out to be something else. It seems to be a variable plant, ranging from yellow-flowered, green-leaved forms to forms with orange flowers and purplish foliage. This may be no more than a manifestation of the natural variability of the genus or, quite possibly, evidence of its promiscuity. Seed for the National Collection has had to be obtained from Botanic Gardens where the plants are likely to be grown all together in order beds.

In place of the flattish heads of these species, others have tall spires of flower. Linking the two groups are the hybrids between *L. dentata* and *L. wilsoniana* or *L. veitchiana*. Both these latter species were introduced around 1904 from China by E. H. Wilson, who was at the time collecting for the great nursery firm of Veitch. Both have big, broad basal leaves topped by bright yellow flowers in broad green bracts, on spikes reaching to 6 ft in rich moist soil. *L.* × *hessei* is a three-way cross, *L. dentata* × *L. wilsoniana* × *L. veitchiana*, and looks indeed as a cross between the two groups should, with heart-shaped leaves and conical spires of yolk-yellow flowers. Similar is the magnificent Welsh-raised 'Gregynog Gold'. 'Sungold' is another garden hybrid, long-flowering and fairly compact.

The ligularia season opens with *L. sibirica*, a plant with a wide distribution from France to Japan by way of Siberia and the Himalayas. In May and June appear its thin spikes of clear yellow, black-anthered flowers over rounded leaves. The variety *racemosa* has leaves which slowly flush with purple, echoing the maroon puffs of seed. *L. stenocephala* is also early to flower, with large rounded leaves jaggedly toothed, and tall spires of orange yellow.

Yet others in the genus ally to tall, slender spikes of flower a different style of foliage, deeply cut into fingered segments. With *Ligularia japonica* the leaves are the thing, the orange flowers rather sparse. This species is another that has proved elusive. A cross with *L. dentata* has given *L. × palmatiloba*, which joins to the Japanese parent's noble jagged foliage the broad clusters of orange-yellow daisies of the other. *L. przewalskii* is even more striking, the deeply cut leaves of triangular outline ascending the black stems in ever-diminishing size, and topped with slender spires of clear yellow flowers. 'The Rocket' is a selection, or perhaps a hybrid of *L. przewalskii* and *L. stenocephala*. Fluffy seed-heads prolong the season into winter.

Entirely different again in leaf is *L. macrophylla*. The foliage resembles that of some great horseradish, each leaf up to a yard long, of glaucous green. The flower stems may reach as much as 10 ft in rich, wet soil, and bear at their apex foot-long columns of bright yellow flowers.

As well as hosting butterflies, ligularias assort nobly with other hot-coloured, moisture-loving flowers of high summer: *Curtonus paniculatus*, *Lysimachia ciliata* with cooling lemon flowers over chocolate foliage, robust primulas such as yellow *P. helodoxa* or orange *P. bulleyana*, and the reddest manifestations of tall moisture-loving lobelias, 'Queen Victoria' in scarlet with plum-red leaves, or 'Bees Flame'. Yellow-variegated foliage of *Cornus alba* 'Spaethii' would emphasise the rich golds, or the fresh green-and-white *Scrophularia aquatica* 'Variegata' cool down the fiery scheme, with *Thalictrum speciosissimum* adding emollient tones of pale citron fluffy flowers and glaucous foliage. The clearer yellow ligularias can take the purple of *Lobelia × vedrariensis*, or join purple phlox to make great billows of high summer colour in soil that does not dry out. An anti-slug treatment in spring will ensure that the ligularias' noble foliage is not spoiled.

The National Collection

The National Collection of 'Yellow Daisies' – Coreopsis, Helenium, Helianthus, Helianthella, and Heliopsis – is grown at Wollaton Hall, Nottingham, under the care of the Nottingham Group of the Hardy Plant Society.

The Hardy Plant Society members in Nottingham were persuaded to adopt this unfashionable group of plants in February 1983. Wollaton Hall, currently the home of the Natural History and Industrial Museums of the Nottingham City Corporation, and the centre of a public deer park, had a derelict walled garden which was offered to the Nottingham Branch of the Hardy Plant Society in 1981. Help from young people employed under the Youth Training Scheme enabled the members to clear the site, and it was decided to create a formal botanic garden of hardy perennial plants, with family beds extending as far as space and financial resources would allow.

It has not been easy for the Hardy Plant Society members to assemble the National Collection of Yellow Daisies: comparatively few, even of such once popular genera as Helenium and Heliopsis, seem now to be offered commercially either in Britain or in Europe, while even the United States, the botanical home of these genera, has provided few sources of seed.

The National Collection of Ligularia is held by the North Western Group of the Hardy Plant Society. The main part of the Collection grows on the banks of the River Darwen in Samlesbury, near Preston, but plants are also spread among other Hardy Plant Society members' gardens in Yorkshire and Lancashire.

Bulbs

Introduction

WHEN we talk about spring flowers, surely it is bulbs that first come to mind: daffodils and tulips, grape hyacinths and crocuses, with snowdrops and aconites as a foretaste in the short winter days. When those clasped leaves of snowdrops first appear, their tips white and toughened to force their way up through still cold soil, or the little humped shoulders of aconites uncurl with amazing rapidity to display the yellow cups in their green ruffs, then the year seems truly on the turn and spirits lift. All spring and summer there are bulbs to fill our gardens, fritillaries and alliums, irises and lilies, and in autumn crocuses again and colchicums, nerines and amaryllis, and so much else besides.

Bulbs – and here I must make the usual observation that the term includes, for my purposes, corms, tubers and most other underground storage-organs – bulbs are found, in the wild, almost throughout the world but especially in regions which have rather cold winters and hot, dry summers that follow a short spring. Bulbs evolved, indeed, to exploit this type of climate, growing rapidly from stored reserves as soon as spring arrives. Those that are hardy in the open garden in this country come chiefly from regions with a Mediterranean climate of cool, wet winters and hot, dry summers: not just the Mediterranean area itself, but also Central Asia, California, the more southerly parts of Chile, parts of South Africa and of Australia. Other hardy bulbs come from areas where some rain falls in summer: the Himalayas, China and Japan, the Drakensburg Mountains in Natal. Between the two, climatically, are areas such as north-west Spain and south-west France, with a maritime Mediterranean climate. Of the bulbs I shall be writing about here, many narcissi originate in such areas, and are well adapted to our climate. Snowdrops grow in Europe, the Middle East and the Mediterranean; tulips are chiefly Central Asian in origin; and the weird arisaemas grow in Japan, China and the Himalayas. *Nerine* is a South African genus, native to a wide area and containing

269

some hardy and some decidedly tender species. Daffodils, tulips and nerines have all been extensively hybridised, especially the first two, of which thousands of varieties have been named. Snowdrop buffs collect minute variants but their numbers are very small by comparison; and *Arisaema* is entirely unspoiled, with no garden mutants or hybrids that I know of.

There are bulbs for every situation; no garden exists where at least a few bulbs could not be grown. Most snowdrops will grow in light shade and like an open woodland site, a cool and not too dry spot among shrubs, or, if grown in grass, a fairly stiff soil. A great many daffodils, too, grow and look well in grass, where their dying foliage can be partly masked by the lengthening grass; and there are even tulips suited to growing in grass, our native (and European) *T. sylvestris*, and *T. sprengeri* which does not flower until June. There is no need to confine your meadow gardening to bulbs; add cranesbills and meadowsweet, tufted vetch and moon daisies, and much else besides, to make a tapestry of wild and introduced plants in grass that you will not cut until late July or early August.

Other tulips are happier with a summer baking and, depending on size, will be best suited to a raised bed or rock garden, or to a border, where they may open the season among young spring foliage. But if your border is regularly dug over the bulbs will hardly thrive; your fork will spear them, or they will be disturbed at the wrong time in their growth cycles. This sort of frenetic annual activity is less frequent nowadays among shrubs or under trees, and here you may successfully grow many bulbs; the rooty soil promotes better drainage and this will benefit most bulbs.

In more formal settings the show daffodils could be grown; in grass the smaller, less highly-bred daffodils, or wild *Narcissus* species, seem more appropriate. Our native Lent Lily, *N. pseudonarcissus*, is a plant of deciduous woodland, but other species need more open situations, though few tolerate very dry conditions in summer. Tiny narcissi are exquisite in raised beds and alpine gardens, or in pans in the alpine house, where the smaller tulips may also be grown. Bulb frames are increasingly popular with enthusiasts and are ideal for bulbs needing a thorough baking in summer. Larger bulbs, like nerines, which need warm growing conditions, may find a home in a narrow border backed by a wall – the house wall, perhaps – or a fence, in full sun.

Most bulbs are planted when dormant, because that is when the nurseryman can most conveniently send them out. Exceptionally, snowdrops are sent, by specialist growers at least, 'in the green', immediately after flowering. In the garden you can move any spring bulb at this time, and with the leaves still visible you can more readily imagine next year's effect, and get your spacings right. It is not easy to plant a drift of bulbs to give the impression that they have naturalised themselves, but slightly less tricky if you can see what you are doing, while the leaves are still on them.

I've mentioned gardening in layers several times already in this book; in this style of planting, bulbs are the gardener's allies, taking up little space and adding colour and interest at almost any season we may choose. Spring bulbs which make all their growth early in the year will grow among deciduous shrubs, among ferns whose new fronds will hide the bulbs' shabby dying foliage, or between clumps of herbaceous plants. *Hosta sieboldiana*, and other large-growing sorts, will mask the dying foliage of daffodils or colchicums as its own great ribbed leaves unfurl from purple shoots, spearing up like shell-cases in spring. Snowdrops can be tucked in almost anywhere; if galanthophiles are apt to concentrate on their beloved, and often very beautiful, oddities, and give them the choicest positions, the less dedicated can have fun simply spreading their single and double common snowdrops, or broad-leaved *Galanthus elwesii* perhaps, as they finish flowering, until every little corner of the garden has its clump. The same technique works with aconites, if they love your garden: but they will not grow everywhere, even planted green and growing.

Bulbs that need a thorough summer baking require a little more forethought; but there are those corners under house eaves, facing south or perhaps west, where rain seldom reaches the soil in summer and annuals would merely gasp for water in the heat. With bulbs, as with climbers, indeed, it is often just a question of re-adjusting your mind to the possibilities of your garden, when you may be surprised at the number of bulbs it will accommodate.

Arisaema

MOST OF the plants I write about in this book have an obvious appeal: clematis, Japanese maples, geraniums; even the poor disdained yellow daisies are loved by some, and those who dislike them can hardly deny the immediacy of their impact.

The attractions of arisaemas are much more subtle, even insidious. Unless you are already attuned to green or dull purple-brown flowers, to foliage spotted and mottled, to bizarrely-shaped flowers, you may dismiss them as grotesque or weird. Once disengage your mind from a preconception that flowers are bright and round-faced, presenting themselves as colours in the gardener's palette, and the fascination of the arisaemas may begin to exert its pull on you.

What, then, are these curious plants like? They are herbaceous plants, dying back in late summer or early autumn to a corm or tuber for, usually, a long resting season. Most species do not reappear until May or June, perhaps even later, when the inflorescence and the handsome foliage emerge, often with astonishing speed. Every species has leaves of compound structure, differing in this from the simple, spear-head shaped leaves of arum: our native lords and ladies or cuckoo-pint is the best known of these. Like cuckoo-pint, arisaemas have an inflorescence formed of the hooded spathe and club-shaped spadix; the actual flowers are tiny and are clustered at the base of the spadix, hidden by the enfolding spathe tube. The shape of the inflorescence of arisaemas varies considerably on this basic theme, and in this and their strange, sometimes weird colouring, as well as their handsome foliage lies much of their fascination.

Unlike many of the plants in this book, arisaemas have been ignored by the breeders, so that all the plants in the National Collection are wild species. Thus Roger Hammond, who owns the Collection, was able slowly to add to his range of species by writing to botanic gardens worldwide. The response was patchy, but he has built up a small circle of other enthusiasts, who increase their collections by exchanging seed and offsets. The National Collection now includes about thirty-five species, in contrast to the one or two species, or none at all, grown in most of the botanic gardens that responded to Roger Hammond's approach.

The ordinary gardener who succumbs to the lure of these plants can, for all that, obtain and grow half a dozen or more different arisaemas with a little diligence in the search. Before I launch into descriptions with which I hope to tempt you to share my fascination with arisaemas, I will briefly comment on where they grow in the wild and what conditions they need to grow successfully in our gardens. Arisaemas come from subtropical and temperate regions of the world, chiefly in the Northern Hemisphere. Those from Japan, China, the Himalayan region and eastern North America are generally likely to be hardy in the southern half of the British Isles. Arisaemas from tropical south-east Asia, the mountains of East Africa, or peninsular India, need to be grown in a warm greenhouse and I shall describe none of these.

Arisaemas grow in areas where there is no hot, dry season, and they are on the whole woodland plants. They thus need, in our gardens, a cool, leafy soil, moist and retentive but not waterlogged, in part shade; a few are happy in full sun. They do not as a rule do well in pots; probably they dislike the fluctuating temperatures and restricted root run. But you can compromise by growing them in lattice, rather than solid-sided pots, plunged outside in summer and brought into a frost-free environment for the winter. Those you plant out permanently should be mature tubers, planted deeply and marked carefully, with a short cane or a label. Thus there should be no risk of digging them up inadvertently or planting something else in that tempting empty space which the arisaemas apparently leave for eight or nine months of the year. I myself only ever grew three or four different arisaemas, and am no sort of expert on them, but I achieved considerable success with *A. candidissimum* by following these precepts; it flowered freely year after year and the original single, marble-like corm increased to twenty-five in three years. It grew in a slightly raised bed in light shade, in a made-up soil – roughly equal quantities of old, peaty potting compost, well-rotted garden compost, Cornish grit (any good horticultural grit would have done) and the natural sandy loam of that corner of my garden. In similar soils other gardeners' *A. candidissimum* have, I believe, even seeded themselves.

As this Chinese species is one of the easiest to grow and to obtain, I will describe it first. It is also one of the most beautiful, with quite large hooded spathes, pure white exquisitely striped with pale pink inside and pale green outside. These inflorescences appear with startling speed in June or even later, just as you will probably have decided that your *A. candidissimum* is dead. Shortly after them come the handsome leaves, big, broad, three-lobed and rich green. In late summer orange seeds are formed. There is a pure white form, but it seems a pity to forego the pink candy-stripes. A scented, pink-striped form was reported from America some years back and this has been on the search lists put out by the NCCPG for several years. So far as I know it has not been reported again; though some forms have a very faint scent. Perhaps the scented form that was described was one of these, encountered by someone with an exceptionally strong sense of smell.

Also easy to obtain and to grow is *Arisaema triphyllum*, Jack in the Pulpit, from eastern North America. This too has, usually, three-lobed leaves, with the stalk sometimes purple-blotched, and arching spathes which are variable in colour. The least interesting are green, somewhat striped with white; I have seen alluring forms with sombre black-purple spathes striped inside with white.

Arisaema speciosum, from subtropical forests in the Himalayas, will need a more sheltered spot than these to grow and flower successfully. Its foliage is handsome, with brown-mottled stems and three-lobed leaves of rich green edged with tawny-red; they stand well above the inflorescence. The spathe, of characteristic arching hooded shape, is deep purple-maroon with white striping outside; the spadix is creamy-white and is drawn out to a long purple string that dangles from its tip to trail on the ground.

One of the most striking of the genus is *A. sikokianum*. The inflorescence often appears before the leaves, or stands clear of them, so the deep purple spathe, striped with greenish white and drawn out into a long narrow tip, is clearly seen, shielding the brilliant white spadix which ends in a broad knob emerging from the spathe tube. This dramatic Japanese species is rarely seen, but should be hardy in a well-drained leafy soil, at least in southern England.

In some species the spathe arches and curves forward so much that it curls up in mimicry of a snail, or a helmet. Thus *A. ringens* from Japan, Korea and China, which unlike those I have so far described emerges, in some forms at least, very early in the year, in February or March, and needs protection from frost. The tube is green, striped with white, and terminates in a tightly-curled green and white or purple-black spathe, and the leaves are also characteristic, three-lobed, bright shining green, with short pointed tips.

Also curled in this curious fashion is *A. griffithii*, a Himalayan species that grows in forests and rhododendron woodland. The spathe of *A. griffithii* varies from green to chocolate-purple, frilled at the edges and decorated with a network of white veins. This strange confection sits close to the ground beneath bold leaves, deeply veined, with the underside of the network picked out in purple.

The smallest arisaema grows in the wild in open, rocky places in quite dry soils, over a wide area from western China right across to the Yemen. It is hardy and needs to be grown in a more open spot than most. Its little spathes are yellow, veering more or less to green, giving its name of *A. flavum*.

The elusive *A. jacquemontii*, a name all too often applied to quite different species in commerce, also inhabits, in the wild, rather drier places than many, in Afghanistan and the Himalayas. It has firm-textured leaves, all-green, and green spathes, barely striped in white, curving well forward and drawn out into a long thread-like tail.

A few species have spectacular finely-divided leaves. The single leaf of *A. consanguineum*, an Asiatic species, is divided into eleven to twenty narrow leaflets each terminating in a thread-like tip, on brown-mottled stems, the whole thing reaching 3 ft or so. By comparison the inflorescence is quite tame, green or brownish without definite stripes and drawn out at the tip into a long thread. However, this is often followed by bright scarlet, glossy berries, even in cultivation. So, too, with the orange-fruited dragonroot or green dragon, *A. dracontium*, from eastern North America, which has a very long yellow spadix projecting from the green spathe. The leaves are borne above the inflorescence and are much divided.

In fruit arisaemas are not unlike our native cuckoo-pint, with clusters of orange or scarlet berries borne along the spadix. They do not always set seed in cultivation, however, and indeed their sexual behaviour can be distinctly strange. The majority of *Arisaema* species are single-sexed at any one flowering, but the sex of individual plants is not consistent. Having grown as an immature plant for some years the first inflorescence produced will bear male flowers. If the plant is growing strongly it may subsequently produce female flowers. If these are sucessfully pollinated, and seed produced, this may so exhaust the plant that it reverts to a male state. In extreme cases, if say the plant is broken or eaten off, it may revert to a vegetative state for a year or two. Fertilisation is infrequent even when both sexes are growing in close proximity, and it is best to pollinate the female flowers artificially if you want seed.

Seed collected in the wild usually germinates freely if sown promptly, and Roger Hammond hopes to add to his collection in this way. Members of a recent botanising tour to Nepal were asked to look out for arisaemas in fruit, and from eighteen collections as many as fourteen different species may result, to judge from early germination. Perhaps among them will be species new to the National Collection.

The National Collection

The National Collection of Arisaema *is held at The Magnolias, St Johns Avenue, Brentwood, Essex (Mr Roger Hammond).*

Roger Hammond's arisaemas were designated as a National Collection in August 1983. When he began to collect them about twelve years ago he found that very few species were to be had from nurserymen. A high percentage of the bulbs he bought from different bulb growers have been supplied with the wrong names, and some even arrived dead. Arisaema jacquemontii, ordered about ten times from various suppliers, arrived in the guise of A. consanguineum, A. tortuosum, A. concinnum and A. nepenthoides; finally an order of A. tortuosum produced the elusive A. jacquemontii. The response from botanic gardens was patchy too; few had more than one or two, but by writing to botanic gardens world-wide Roger Hammond has painstakingly increased his collection to about thirty-five species, and has built up a small circle of other enthusiasts, who increase their collections by exchanging seed and offsets.

Galanthus

COLLECTING snowdrops is a pastime that can easily develop into a passion: the condition known as galanthomania. True galanthomaniacs are not numerous, but their enthusiasm is contagious, and you begin to realise, in their company, that snowdrops are not just single or double. You learn about the different species, and the sections of the genus *Galanthus* into which they fall; and you become fascinated by the named forms, differentiated by the shape and extent of their inner green markings and their leaves, the breadth and poise of the outer petals, their time of flowering with which you may extend the season of snowdrops in your garden by weeks or months.

This is not the place for a botanical treatise on the genus *Galanthus*, but I will, for all that, just briefly indicate the sections within the genus and how they are differentiated. The common snowdrop, *Galanthus nivalis*, belongs in section Nivales, in which the leaves are applanate in vernation: that is, they lie flat against each other, with the flowering stem held between them, thus:

Section Plicati derives its name from the manner in which the leaf margins are folded back – explicate or plicate; the leaves also lie flat against each other, so that in section we have this:

Finally, there is section Latifolii, with broad leaves supervolute or con-

volute in vernation: wrapped around each other and the flowering stem,
that is:

The common snowdrop is often thought of as a British native, but it
may be nothing of the kind, though extensively naturalised in this country.
It grows in woods and by streams, often forming great masses of its
characteristic clumps of glaucous leaves and nodding white flowers, which
may emerge as early as January or as late as March. In gardens some people
find that the ordinary, rather ragged double-flowered snowdrop increases
even faster than the single; both can be spread around to make new clumps
with great ease, by lifting and dividing them just after flowering and
immediately replanting them in their new positions, in light shade. Almost
any soil suits the common snowdrop, except perhaps a hot, dry, sandy
one; but heavier, cooler soils seem most to its liking. Some of the other
species prefer a sunnier position with free drainage, and I will note these
in turn.

Some galanthophiles maintain that snowdrops – whether the common
G. nivalis or any of the rarer kinds – should be moved regularly, in an
attempt to foil the snowdrop fungus which can cause your *Galanthus* to
dwindle and die with appalling rapidity. Other safeguards are to make
sure you have two or three clumps of each kind in different parts of the
garden, and to give away bulbs as soon as you can spare any, by way of
'banking' them against future losses. Snowdrops have several enemies,
among them the snowdrop fungus (*Botrytis galanthina*) already mentioned,
and narcissus fly (*Merodon equestre*), but the greatest enemy of all is Man.
At Wisley, where the National Collection is grown, snowdrops are not
difficult to cultivate, but the rarer ones are exceedingly difficult to keep;
whole colonies of many of the rarities have been dug up and this sort of
wanton theft, by greedy galanthomaniacs who clearly know what they
are after, is extremely hard to fight. The only remedy, perhaps, is not to
display the Collection; but this goes contrary to the spirit of the National
Collections, which exist as much to show the gardening public the range
of plants they could grow within each genus as to conserve and study
them.

The Wisley Collection at one time amounted to 307 different kinds of
snowdrop, some named garden forms, some species collected in the wild
in Turkey and elsewhere, others unnamed from collections of the past.
One of the difficulties in putting names to snowdrop variants is that

few were accurately described or illustrated, and consequently every knowledgeable galanthophile has his own view about virtually every plant, which rarely seems to result in agreement. I propose only to mention a few of the most distinct kinds, to give an idea of the range of variation.

A distinct species, closely related to the common snowdrop, is *Galanthus reginae-olgae*, which is found wild in the mountains of southern Greece, Sicily, southern Yugoslavia and western Turkey, and flowers in October before the leaves appear. It prefers a more open, sunny position, drier in summer, than ordinary *G. nivalis*, and has distinctive foliage with a prominent glaucous band along the centre. Another autumn-flowering snowdrop, coming a little later, is *G. corcyrensis*, by some authorities considered synonymous with *reginae-olgae*: but they seem to be distinct plants from the gardener's point of view, with subspecies *vernalis* flowering as late as February.

The common snowdrop has given rise to very many garden forms, single and double. Some are robust and easy, others are decidedly miffy. One such is the yellow snowdrop, 'Lutescens'. It is not yellow all over; only the markings, and the ovary, which are normally green in snowdrops, are a washed-out yellow-green, indicating perhaps a lack of vigour. The double yellow snowdrop, 'Lady Elphinstone', is a better grower but with the panic-making habit of reverting to green in the year after a move, so when you buy or swap her you may think you have been supplied with the wrong thing. Another *nivalis* variant which I have never found easy is 'Scharlokii', with twin spathes sticking up above the flower like asses' ears. The outer segments are marked with green at the tip, and this is a marking that appears fairly frequently, as it might be in 'Viridapicis', 'Warei', or the double 'Pusey Green Tips'. At the other extreme from the forms with extra green markings is the entirely white 'Poculiformis'.

There have been many famous snowdrop growers and raisers, and several are commemorated in the names of the surviving snowdrops. Two of the greatest were E. A. Bowles, whose *In My Garden* trilogy contains, in the spring volume, a long chapter on snowdrops that reveals his deep knowledge and love of the genus *Galanthus*; and Sir Frederick Stern, who wrote the standard work, *Snowdrops and Snowflakes*. Stern's criteria for a good garden snowdrop were that it should have a robust constitution; represent a distinct improvement in size or beauty; increase rapidly; and extend, by flowering either before or after *G. nivalis*, the usual snowdrop season. On this basis the best of all, he considered, was 'Atkinsii', received from a friend by James Atkins of Painswick in the 1860s. Another great galanthophile, James Allen of Shepton Mallet, gave it the name 'Atkinsii', and all the bulbs of this variety now in cultivation derive from the generosity of Canon Ellacombe, who freely distributed them from a long line that grew at the foot of a south wall in his garden at Bitton. 'Atkinsii' has large elongated flowers appearing in January, marred only by their tendency to display one or occasionally more malformed segments.

Another fine snowdrop, but not so readily available as 'Atkinsii', is 'Neill Fraser', from the eponymous owner of Murrayfield, Edinburgh. This flowers in February, with fine rounded blooms. You should not have too much difficulty buying a bulb of 'S. Arnott', named for the Provost of Dumfries, who introduced it into cultivation. This splendid, large, perfectly formed snowdrop is sometimes, but quite wrongly, called 'Sam Arnott'. Mr Arnott, whose first name was indeed Samuel, was apparently a gentleman of very formal manners to whom the abbreviation 'Sam' would have seemed an insult. 'S. Arnott', the snowdrop, throve under Walter Butt's care at Chalford; Mrs Matthias who owned Hyde Lodge after Walter Butt showed it as 'S. Arnott' in 1951, when it gained an Award of Merit from the Royal Horticultural Society.

The Straffan Snowdrop is another superb variant, late flowering and very vigorous, with large and beautiful flowers, two in succession from each strong bulb. 'Magnet' has very large flowers, well rounded, on extra long pedicels, so that it moves in the lightest breeze. This graceful snowdrop was raised by James Allen, who also introduced a great many more named kinds, most of which now seem to be extinct. 'Brenda Troyle' is a honey-scented snowdrop with good dark green markings, available – at a price – from specialists.

A dear little snowdrop that I have always known as *G. graecus*, correctly *G. gracilis*, from Greece, Turkey and the Balkans, is another for open, sunny spots. It flowers early, in January, and has narrow, very glaucous leaves with a characteristic twist. Much more muscular than this, and more commonly seen, *G. elwesii* is named for Henry Elwes of Colesbourne, to whom 'S. Arnott' was originally sent. It is characterised by its broad glaucous leaves, folded one inside the other, and large flowers with a broad dark green mark at the base of each inner segment. Because snowdrops hang their heads, incidentally, the base is above the tip of the petals. A dwarfish form or hybrid (perhaps with *G. caucasicus*) of *G. elwesii* is named 'Colesbourne'; it was found by Henry Elwes in grass in about 1911. The tall 'Merlin' may have *G. plicatus* blood in it; it is a James Allen snowdrop, distinguished by the entirely green inner segments. *G. caucasicus*, in the same section Latifolii as *G. elwesii*, is characterised by broad glaucous leaves; it has early and late flowering forms extending its season from early January to late February. Sun or shade seem to suit it equally. 'Lady Beatrix Stanley' is a fine double *caucasicus* × *nivalis*. *G. allenii*, with large, rather green leaves, is by no means so good-tempered, a slow-increasing snowdrop which was spotted by James Allen in a consignment of bulbs from the Caucasus, perhaps a hybrid between *G. caucasicus* and *G. ikariae*. *G. ikariae* itself, still in section Latifolii, has broad green (not glaucous) leaves and green markings only at the tips of the inner segments. It flowers in March.

The section Plicati contains two species, G. *byzantinus* and G. *plicatus*; or perhaps just one, G. *plicatus* and G. *p.* subsp. *byzantinus*. The Byzantine snowdrop is very variable, early flowering and free to increase by bulb division or seed. It has broad glaucous leaves and is distinguished from G. *plicatus* by the deep green markings at the *base* of the inner segments of the flowers; its larger forms are very fine. Sun or shade will suit it equally. G. *plicatus* has large, solid flowers with prominent green markings on the inner segments; it flowers later than G. *byzantinus* and seems happiest in open woodland or similar lightly shaded conditions. Its fine form 'Warham' was collected during the Crimean war and later honoured by a First Class Certificate from the Royal Horticultural Society.

Double G. *plicatus* hybrids can also be fine things. One of the most noted breeders of double snowdrops was H. A. Greatorex of Norwich, who used the viable pollen occasionally produced by double snowdrops on good forms of G. *plicatus* to produce many seedlings of lovely proportions and symmetrical form: 'Ophelia', 'Desdemona', 'Cordelia', 'Hippolyta' and several others. They have full, tightly double flowers not usually marred by the stray ragged central petals of the common double *nivalis*, and are collectors' pieces deserving the greatest care.

As a collector of unusual snowdrops you will be at pains to find them each a home where they will be safe, tucked away in odd corners of the garden between shrubs, or in a sunny sheltered spot, with other garden treasures. The easier snowdrops, on the other hand, can play their part in broader schemes, making their effect, as you divide and increase them, by weight of numbers as well as in their individual beauty. They assort well with good evergreen foliage, such as named ivies – the coppery bronzed 'Brokamp', perhaps, or finely crimped green 'Ivalace'; with *Helleborus niger* in shade or with crimson-leaved bergenias in the sun. Add them to a group of *Ribes laurifolium*, a discreet little winter-flowering evergreen shrub with creamy-green sprays. Spread them in great sheets with winter aconites or *Cyclamen coum*. Or you may wish to emulate one of today's great snowdrop growers by setting them among the best hybrid hellebores in slate blue, maroon black, and primrose, with the first fat crimson shoots of paeonies spearing through, and named forms of celandine appearing here and there.

The National Collection

The National Collection of Galanthus, *the snowdrops, is held at the Royal Horticultural Society's garden at Wisley, Woking, Surrey.*

The former Director of Wisley Garden, Chris Brickell (now Director General of the Royal Horticultural Society) is a galanthophile of immense erudition, and as a result of his enthusiasm for the genus the Wisley snowdrops were designated as a National Collection in April 1981. The Collection at one time amounted to 307 different kinds of snowdrop, wild and garden forms and many unnamed, from collections of the past. Some were lost through theft, but thanks to exchanges and donations from other snowdrop growers the Collection is now one of the most complete in the National Collections scheme.

Narcissus

THOUSANDS upon thousands of different daffodils have been bred and named over the years; so many that to try and assemble them all – or even all those still to be found – in one garden would be a daunting task. Thus it is that in the garden at Coleraine where the first National *Narcissus* Collection is grown, the intention is to concentrate on Irish-bred daffodils.

White daffodils are especially associated with Ireland; they first arrived there with the monks from Spain and Portugal. In these countries the greatest numbers of wild species of narcissus are found and, among them, several exquisite palest sulphur and pure white forms that were introduced to cultivation, and survived in the gentler climate of Ireland when all too often they died out in English gardens.

Encouraged by F. W. Burbidge, an authority on daffodils who was appointed curator of Trinity College Botanic Garden in Dublin in 1879, an Irish nurseryman named William Baylor Hartland devoted nearly thirty years to searching out the daffodils surviving in old Irish gardens and ecclesiastical settlements, selecting and improving them and finally breeding from them many important new daffodils. Names like 'Ard Righ', which flowered exceptionally early, 'Colleen Bawn' and others have become familiar, at least to NCCPG devotees, as these old kinds are now once again being sought. Hartland became famous especially for his white daffodils, selected from the surviviors he rediscovered: 'Colleen Bawn' was one, and others were 'Bishop Mann' and 'Leda'. This last was thought to be extinct as long ago as 1934; but perhaps there is the slenderest chance it may still live undiscovered in some remote garden. These white daffodils were to prove a lasting influence upon a later daffodil enthusiast, Guy Wilson of Broughshane, Co. Antrim. As we'll see, his devotion to daffodils, and especially to the then unfashionable whites, was to enhance Ireland's pre-eminence as the breeding ground of the finest white daffodils.

In 1974, twelve years after G. L. Wilson's death, the Guy L. Wilson Daffodil Garden was formally opened by his nephew, Professor Fergus Wilson, in the grounds of the New University of Ulster at Coleraine. The garden's beginnings were modest: about 160 varieties of daffodil planted among shrubs then constituted the entire Guy Wilson memorial, the bulbs donated by active daffodil growers in Ireland: Sir Frank Harrison, Mrs Kate Reade, Willie Dunlop, Billy Toal, Tom Bloomer and Brian Duncan. Nell Richardson, widow of Lionel Richardson whose work will receive mention later in this chapter, also contributed bulbs to the garden, but never visited it; she died in December 1978. Guy Wilson's gardener for forty years, John Shaw, was consulted on the names of the Wilson daffodils. Among those present was Matthew Zandbergen, a daffodil grower from the Netherlands, a very close friend of Guy Wilson; he paid a moving tribute to him. He too contributed bulbs to the garden.

Despite this, a guest at the opening ceremony was concerned that so few of the daffodils bred by the very person for whom the garden was named were actually growing there. David Willis, Superintendent of the University grounds, found that very few of the Wilson daffodils were available commercially, even so recently after their raiser's death, and he began to track them down. Finally he located more than 200 of the 650 or more that G. L. Wilson registered. In the process he acquired not only many bulbs, but also an unparalleled knowledge of the history of daffodils in Ireland, which led to a doctorate on the subject: in 1980 David Willis became 'Dr Daffodil'. It was Dr Willis, too, who proposed that the National *Narcissus* Collection should be established and maintained at Coleraine, with the Guy Wilson Daffodil Garden as its core. Much of the information on the development of daffodils in Ireland which appears in the following pages I owe to the kindness of Dr Willis in allowing me to plunder his writings in various journals (details of which are noted in the Bibliography at the end of this book).

Daffodils new to the Guy Wilson Daffodil Garden, many of them of great antiquity, reached Coleraine from a variety of sources, thanks to Willis's patient research and pleas for information. First to respond to his request was the Ministry of Agriculture, in the shape of the Experimental Horticulture Station at Rosewarne in Cornwall, who sent bulbs they had had on trial. A large collection of bulbs originally amassed by a New Zealand grower, Clarrie Andrews, reached Coleraine after many delays at the hands of officialdom, understandably concerned about plant health problems. This collection turned out to include many old kinds of daffodil that were no longer to be found in British gardens, including dozens of Guy Wilson's raising. (Rose enthusiasts have had similar lucky finds from New Zealand gardens, and I wonder what other treasures are still growing there, unrecognised perhaps?) The daffodil garden at Coleraine was also given the late Cyril Coleman's collection, containing many historic daffodils till then believed to be extinct, as well as Coleman's own seedlings. He bred, among others, the lovely 'half height' daffodils with *N. cyclamineus* blood: 'Dove Wings', 'Charity May', 'Jenny' and 'Andalusia', still available commercially and among the best of all daffodils as garden, rather than exhibition, flowers.

The National Collection at Coleraine now includes about 1,000 different daffodils, not all of Irish origin; but several great Irish daffodil breeders other than Guy Wilson himself are now represented. Among them are Lionel Richardson (who died in 1961, the year before his friend and rival Wilson) and W.J. Dunlop, Wilson's neighbour at Broughshane, who began raising daffodils from 1937 onwards.

Because of Ireland's pre-eminence, and Guy Wilson's own especial success, in growing white daffodils, I will consider these first, but must not allow them to overshadow the other achievements of Wilson, Richardson and Dunlop and their precursors and successors. The white daffodils go back past Hartland's selections to the subspecies of our own Lent lily, a white Spanish wildling known as *Narcissus pseudonarcissus* subsp. *moschatus*. Hartland's 'Colleen Bawn' and 'Bishop Mann' are said to be improved forms of *moschatus*; indeed the Rev. Engleheart, another (English) daffodil breeder who was to influence Guy Wilson, wrote to Wilson once that he considered 'the form "Colleen Bawn" from old Irish gardens is exactly a magnified Pyrenean Moschatus, whiter than Albicans and of the Moschatus texture'. Wilson himself considered that *moschatus*, a strongly dominant parent, was the original ancester of all the white trumpets (Hartland's 'Leda', incidentally, is considered to have been a form of *N. pseudonarcissus* subsp. *tortuosus*). A characteristic of *moschatus* and its early progeny was the 'swan neck' which gave it its alternative name of *cernuus*, the graceful one, in allusion to its drooping flower. 'Whatever name we may use it will always be one of the most beautiful plants for a cool corner, preferably among small rocks where moss and slender ferns like Oakfern will grow.' ((E. A. Bowles, *The Narcissus*). Already by the 1930s many of these old white daffodils had become rare: 'It is interesting to look at the lists of the eighties [1880s] and to notice how many white Daffodils then listed have disappeared: such as "William Goldring", described as snow white and dog eared, 1 s.6 d. each; "Colleen Bawn", twisted, propeller-like perianth segments and long, cylinder-like trumpet, 2 s.6 d.; "Leda", perfumed like old oak timber; "Gladys Hartland", Cowslip scented, 10 s.6 d. "Bishop Mann" was a vigorous early variety that might repay reintroduction from some Irish garden.' (E. A. Bowles, *The Narcissus*).

One of the most famous of the early whites was just one generation removed from *moschatus*. 'Mme de Graaff' (which in fact had a pale primrose, not white trumpet), raised in 1887 in Leiden, was much used by Guy Wilson in his search for the perfect white trumpet. He found her to be 'a free and reliable seeder' and, using pollen of 'King Alfred' and others, over the years and the generations of daffodils, he raised such famous white trumpet daffodils as 'Cantatrice' (1936), 'Broughshane' (1938) and 'Empress of Ireland' (1952). His lovely 'Vigil', too, is still offered by bulb merchants. By no means all his white daffodils were of the trumpet division; he also introduced among others the large-cupped 'Eastern Morn' with its green-lit centre, and satin-textured 'Desdemona', and the exquisite small-cupped 'Chinese White' (1937). An earlier white was the fascinating 'Cushendall', much admired by E. A. Bowles: '"Cushendall", raised by Mr. Guy Wilson, has the best green eye of any variety. He is right in calling it moss green, for it is a rich and dark green with no cold blue tone about it. The corona has a slight shade of yellow at its edge that gives a wonderful finish to this lovely but expensive flower.'

By the time 'Empress of Ireland' and his other great white daffodil of 1952, 'Rashee', made their debut Guy Wilson had been on the track of his ideal white daffodil for over fifty years. As a schoolboy he loved the yellow daffodils of his mother's garden, the old Lent lilies and Tenby daffodils, 'Telamonius Plenus' and the double *incomparabilis* 'Butter and Eggs', the pheasant-eye (*N. poeticus recurvus*) and the double gardenia-flowered *N. poeticus*, and an old yellow single *incomparabilis* he called the 'Yellow Narciss'. He asked his mother if white daffodils existed, and fortunately for our gardens today she was able not only to affirm that they did, but also to direct him to Hartland's book of 1888, which was rebarbatively entitled 'Ye Original Little Booke of Daffodils'. Here, Guy Wilson found described and illustrated not only Ireland's white daffodils, but also such famous old kinds as 'Horsfieldii' (1845), 'Empress' and 'Emperor' (both from Mr W. Backhouse, 1865★) and 'Grandis'. He began to collect all the Hartland daffodils that he could acquire, and learned the techniques of hybridisation and cultivation probably from James Coey, a very successful grower. Coey was familiar with the daffodils being raised in England at the time by such breeders as Engleheart, whose 'Beersheba' (1923) was for long one of the most admired white trumpets. (Engleheart, incidentally, did not agree with the older Hartland about the classification of daffodils, still today an area of contention, and criticised the 'Little Booke', in which appeared such eccentric divisions of daffodils as 'Tea Cup', 'Coffee Cup', and 'Tea Saucer'.) 'Beersheba' was to be one of the parents of Wilson's 'Cantatrice', which is a flower of perfect form and waxy texture, for long a winner on the show bench.

★ Several members of the Backhouse family were involved in raising daffodils: W. Backhouse (1807–69) of Durham, H. Backhouse (1856–1936) of Darlington and later of Dorset, and Mr and Mrs R. O. Backhouse (1854–1940 and 1857–1921 respectively) of Herefordshire.

The year 1923 also saw the introduction of the first 'pink' daffodil to impose itself upon the consciousness of the general gardening public, 'Mrs R. O. Backhouse'. This is probably still the most readily available of the pink daffodils, and has been much used in hybridising, but Guy Wilson and Lionel Richardson in Ireland, in common with other hybridisers, disliked the poorly-formed perianth of 'Mrs R. O. Backhouse' and other early pinks, and followed another line to achieve the pink colouration. The culmination of Wilson's hybridising for pink colouring was 'Passionale' (1956), a lovely soft-toned thing of large-cupped form, much nearer to true pink than 'Mrs R. O. Backhouse'. Lionel Richardson, Wilson's near contemporary, raised a greater number of pink daffodils than Guy Wilson himself, using his own lines of breeding but also some of Wilson's pinks. To Richardson we owe such famous pink daffodils as 'Salmon Trout' (1948), deep coral pink 'Débutante' (1956) and the outstanding 'Romance' of 1959. These are just three of fifty-six pink daffodils he raised. Many of the modern, clearer pinks are rather expensive; the older, paler apricot pinks still have their place in the garden, if not on the show bench. They combine delightfully with the young, pinkish foliage of some of the epimediums, or the bronze-pink unfolding leaves of the shrubby horse chestnut or buckeye, *Aesculus parviflora*.

There are still comparatively few reverse bicolour daffodils about, and some of the loveliest are very expensive. Two that are quite well known and reasonably priced we owe, directly or indirectly, to Guy Wilson. One of the earliest to be named was 'Binkie', raised in Tasmania from seed sent by Wilson and introduced in 1938. 'Binkie' is a cool, even chilly flower of lunar green paling to icy lemon with white cup, exquisite as a garden plant among the glaucous-pink young leaves of *Paeonia wittmanniana*, itself bearing evanescent flowers of palest moonlight yellow. In 1942 Wilson first flowered 'Spellbinder', a large trumpet daffodil with great presence, fascinating as its lime-yellow colouring fades to contrast the cool white trumpet, still edged in pale lime yellow, with the sulphur perianth.

From the same parents as those which produced 'Spellbinder', Guy Wilson raised some pale lemon or lime-yellow trumpets, notably 'Moonstruck', which fades from a green-shaded citrus tone to near-white. The more conventional bicolour trumpets received Wilson's attention too, and his 'Preamble' and paler 'Trostan' were outstanding in their day. 'Foresight', in milky white with lemon trumpet, is still offered by bulb merchants. His great achievement here was to eliminate the tendency of the yellow colouring of the trumpet to 'bleed' into the white perianth, which spoiled the clear contrast of colours.

Wilson's yellow trumpets, though a few were very fine indeed, were somewhat overshadowed by his friend Richardson's achievements in this division – yet Richardson himself only came to them quite late, after the appearance of 'Goldcourt' and 'Kingscourt' among his seedlings. Dr Willis tells the story of Guy Wilson and Richardson's superb 'King's Ransom'. On a visit to Prospect House, where Lionel Richardson lived, Wilson failed to appear for tea. He was found sitting on a path, his eyes fixed on 'King's Ransom', and when called replied 'bring my tea out here, I can't take my eyes off that flower. It is the most perfect yellow trumpet I've seen'. For all that, Wilson's 'Goldbeater' was a fine early yellow trumpet, while his very late-flowering 'Counsellor' is still in at least one bulb merchant's list.

It is much the same story with the daffodils with red in them, whether yellow and red or white and red. Richardson's earliest and most significant successes were with red and yellow daffodils, such as the sun-proof 'Ceylon'; and with white and reds such as 'Kilworth'. Both these, and others of Richardson's raising, are still available in commerce today. But so, too, is Wilson's 'Home Fires', in orange-scarlet and yellow. Of his fine large-cupped yellow and orange 'Armada', David Willis recounts another Wilson story which typifies his kindness and generosity: Wilson gave the entire stock of 'Armada' to his Dutch friend Matthew Zandbergen at the end of the Hitler war, to give him a new start.

Though the gaudy reds may not have been among Wilson's greatest successes he was effectively the creator of the kinds with white perianth and small cup edged with red or orange. They included cultivars with such enticing names as 'Dreamlight', and 'Misty Moon'. Paler than these is 'Carnmoon', of perfect circular shape, all white but for a green eye and a rim of sharp lemon to the shallow cup.

It is tempting to write endlessly of these enchanting daffodils, and I am conscious that the varieties raised by Richardson have received scant mention, those of other Irish daffodil breeders none at all. Yet the garden at Coleraine is after all the Guy Wilson Daffodil Garden, although the National Collection extends to include many other raisers. This achievement was recognised about five years ago by the International Council on Monuments and Sites, by whom the garden was named as a Heritage Garden 'not because it contains any outstanding artefacts or design features, but because it is a garden devoted in itself to the conservation of garden plants'.

The National Collection

The National Collection of Narcissus described here is held at the University of Ulster, Coleraine, Co. Londonderry, Northern Ireland.

The coleraine daffodils were designated as a national collection in june 1982. The emphasis is on cultivars raised in Ireland, and especially those raised by Guy Wilson and his friend and rival Lionel Richardson. The nucleus of the Collection was the planting of daffodils in the Guy L. Wilson Daffodil Garden, formally opened in the grounds of the New University of Ulster at Coleraine in 1974, twelve years after Guy Wilson's death. Since then many varieties have been added to the Collection, largely thanks to the painstaking work of Dr David Willis, who tracked down many Wilson cultivars. At one time the Collection amounted to about 1,700 different kinds, and although disease reduced the numbers, there are still well over 1,000 different daffodils in the Collection at Coleraine.

With so large a genus as Narcissus, which has received the attentions of many eminent breeders over the years, it would be beyond the scope of any one organisation to grow a full collection, and so the intention is to designate other National Collections elsewhere in Britain, centred on the daffodils of a particular breeder. Recently the miniature daffodils bred by Alec Gray, of which a wide selection is grown at Broadleigh Gardens, Somerset (Lady Skelmersdale), have there been designated as a National Collection. At Brodie (National Trust for Scotland), the cultivars bred by The Brodie of Brodie between 1899 and 1942, the year before his death, are being assembled and have been designated as a National Collection. The Brodie said of Guy Wilson that he knew more of the parentage of The Brodie's daffodils than he did himself; this despite the careful notes and records kept by The Brodie. Recently a more broadly-based National Collection of Narcissus has also been designated, grown by a private collector in Surrey.

Nerine

THE *NERINE* that everyone knows is *N. bowdenii*, hardy outside in much of Britain. It was first introduced to cultivation in this country around 1900, by Mrs Cornish Bowden, of Newton Abbot in Devon; she had received the bulbs from her son, who had collected them in Cape Colony. Other introductions have been made from the wild since then. This familiar *N. bowdenii* has crimped, sugar-pink petals with the characteristic nerine sheen, appearing in September, October, and even November. The form known as 'Fenwick's Variety' is larger in flower, deeper in colour, more vigorous, and more readily available. *N. bowdenii* 'Quinton Wells', which was collected in the wild in the Natal National Park below Mont aux Sources, at about 10,000 ft, by the eponymous Dr A. Q. Wells, is said to be hardier still than the type. A reintroduction from the original site, collected by Tony Norris who holds the National Collection at his Nerine Nursery near Malvern, enabled him to compare the plants with 'Quinton Wells' in cultivation in England, about which some doubts had been entertained. The plants were found to match, with large leaves, flower stems twice the height of the ordinary *N. bowdenii*, and small, very crinkled flowers of rose-pink with paler centres.

Other hardy hybrids or forms of *N. bowdenii* are not lacking, at least for gardeners in the milder parts of the country. They are all best grown in places sheltered by a sunny wall. There is a good white form, 'Alba', and the palest pink *N. b. manina*, described as 'very tough, free-flowering and elegant', with long narrow petals. For richer colouring, you could plant in a warm spot the large-flowered hybrid 'Hera', or its sister seedling 'Aurora', dating from the early 1920s. A note of caution should be sounded here: 'Hera' has been banished from the National Collection as it is badly affected by virus. Clean stocks are needed to save this famous old cultivar. A later hybrid of unknown parentage is 'Paula Knight', with deep rose-pink flowers, the segments each marked with a broad central streak of silvery mauve.

These nerines are most rewarding plants in the autumn garden, adding to the rich pinkness which I have already extolled in writing of asters and sedums. With silvery foliage among the nerines you can achieve an ethereal effect, enhancing the glistening surface of the nerine flowers; or you could boldly mix their vivid candy-pinks with the richer coloured Michaelmas daisies, deep purples and violet blues, and even the assertive magenta-rose of 'Alma Potschke'. Beth Chatto daringly sets *Nerine bowdenii* with the bright gentian-blue three-cornered flowers of *Commelina coelestis*, against a backdrop of the quiet purple, white-dusted foliage of the claret vine.

If *Nerine bowdenii*, at least in its cheaper manifestations, is a plant for massing in bold effects, several other hardy nerines are smaller and daintier, as well as more expensive, and deserve the positions you reserve for other sun-loving garden toys, where they can be appreciated as individuals. The one you are most likely to find offered is *N. flexuosa* 'Alba'; the type has pale pink, much crinkled flowers and is very uncommon; the white is a beauty, with no trace of pink. It tends to be evergreen; the leaves are often turned to mush by winter frosts, but the bulb seems resistant and puts out new leaves and flowers in due season.

A miniature species, *N. humilis*, seems as hardy as *N. bowdenii* in some gardens, though not at the National Collection where it is treated as a summer-dormant species for the greenhouse. It is variable in colour, from pale pink to rose madder, with a deeper central line running the length of each petal. Another small species, of greater hardiness, is *N. undulata*, very free-flowering and fast to increase. The very crimpled petals are pink. *N. masonorum* is a pet, no more than 8 or 9 ins tall, with crisped petals of rose-pink.

Among several other uncommon species is the scarce, and correspondingly somewhat pricey, *N. laticoma*. This is the largest of all the species: the flower heads may be composed of up to forty individual florets. It is 'unique in that the flowers – in some populations only – have a sweet fragrance variously described as similar to vanilla – or almonds', writes Tony Norris.

All the nerines so far mentioned are pink, in varying shades, or white; but Tony Norris hopes to introduce the brighter, sharper colours of tender nerines into the hybrids he is breeding for hardiness outdoors. One such is 'Susan Norris', soft orange in colour, its hardiness proved by surviving the winter of 1981-2 outside. For the really brilliant colours, however, it is still to the greenhouse nerines that we must turn, and here we are faced with a bewildering variety.

For most of us the Guernsey lily, *Nerine sarniensis*, typifies the greenhouse nerines. The Guernsey lily is so called, not because it is a native of that island – like all other nerines, it comes from South Africa – but because, in some way that is not clear despite much scholarly research, it found its way to Guernsey and there flourished and increased. One story tells how the crew of a ship wrecked on the coast of Guernsey were given shelter by the islanders, and how their hospitality was repaid by a gift of six bulbs of *Nerine sarniensis*. However it may be, the first *N. sarniensis* to reach Guernsey was a crimson form, and its descendants can still be seen growing in sheltered gardens there. In the National Collection is an orange-scarlet form, progeny of bulbs collected by Tony Norris under licence in South Africa. The plants we know as *N.* 'Fothergillii Major' and *N.* 'Corusca Major', derivations of *N. sarniensis*, are quite close to the original. 'Fothergillii Major', winner of a Royal Horticultural Society Award of Merit, is usually the first nerine to flower, and remains one of the best, a strong grower with brilliant vermilion flowers. A characteristic of many nerines is the glistening surface of the flowers, adding further sparkle to their beautiful colours. If you examine the flower closely, with a good hand-lens, you will see that the surface is composed of myriads of tiny pearl-like cells which reflect the light. This gives to the scarlet of 'Corusca Major' the quality that earned it the epithet 'Corusca'; it gained an RHS First Class Certificate in 1964 and has remained understandably popular. Indeed, it is the cultivar most used for the cut-flower trade.

N. 'Fothergillii' crops up often as a parent: crossed with *N. flexuosa* it produced the old hybrid 'Mansellii' which some growers feel has had its day; but others feel it still worthwhile for its free-flowering ways, fine rose-carmine colouring and especially for its season, late November and December. With *N. bowdenii* as the other parent, *N.* 'Fothergillii' produced 'Hera' and 'Aurora', already encountered among the hardy nerines.

Many famous names in horticulture have succumbed to the spell of nerines and indulged in breeding their own hybrids. The work was begun by Dean Herbert of Spofforth, gathering information for his treatise *Amaryllidaceae*. His hybrids, which include the blood of many different species, form the basis of several later collections. Henry Elwes, who was also a snowdrop enthusiast as we have seen (and much else besides) continued breeding nerines around the turn of the century: some of his hybrids are still grown today. After his death half his collection went to Borde Hill, Colonel Stephenson Clarke's garden in Sussex, where further crosses were made. Sir Frederick Stern, another galanthophile like Elwes, received bulbs too from his collection, and bred many good things, including the pink, November-flowering 'Cranfield' and salmon-cerise 'Gloaming'. 'Grilse', aptly named for its pale salmon-pink flower with deeper salmon shading to the centre of each petal, is another Stern cultivar.

The great name in the breeding of nerines, however, was Exbury in Hampshire. Many of the famous varieties in the National Collection were raised at Exbury, better known to most of us perhaps for its rhododendrons and azaleas. It was at Exbury that the spectacular 'Inchmery Kate' was raised, the first tetraploid nerine and an important parent. Also significant in producing many superlative nerine hybrids were 'Joan', a fine plant itself with pale salmon-pink flowers, and 'Carmenita', a pale pink flushed with mauve. Their progeny include the wonderful white 'Solent Swan' with pink stamens, and bright rose-pink 'Margaret Rose'; 'Mrs Eddy' in white edged with salmon, and a fine red, 'Lady Louise Loder'. Also raised at Exbury are others that are highly rated by Tony Norris: 'Lady Cynthia Colville', white with a pink-tinged central streak, and the exquisite and elegant white 'Vestal'. 'Mertoun' is an Exbury seedling that has not received the recognition Tony Norris feels it deserves: 'a singularly charming and quite unique flower; the well rounded full head over 5 ins in diameter makes a neat ball of brilliant deep pink, almost cerise, flowers'.

A fairly recent hybrid, 'Rushmere Star' (Award of Merit, 1966) resulted from a cross between N. *bowdenii* and N. 'Fothergillii Major', and inherits the vigour of both, with a large flower of deep rose-mauve. This is the same cross as produced 'Hera' and 'Aurora', but I do not know if anyone has tried 'Rushmere Star' for hardiness in gardens where these two grow outside. Mr Stanley Smee, a successful grower and raiser whose results are much admired by Tony Norris, did however find it undamaged by the severe winter of 1981-2 in an unheated frame, with N. *flexuosa* 'Alba' and 'Bennett Poë' (a bright cerise, very late-flowering hybrid). Most of the foliage was frosted, but the bulbs of all three kinds were firm when the thaw came, and flowered normally the following autumn.

Whether hardy or greenhouse nerines are your choice, Tony Norris insists that the bulbs should be planted with the top of the neck just above soil level, in a well-drained, gritty or sandy soil, and no nitrogenous fertilisers, which will merely encourage leaf. The lesson was learned in the wild, where nerines grow in poor soil. If the compost or soil you give them is open enough so that you can give the bulbs ample moisture without risk of waterlogging, they will also be able to ripen satisfactorily, without the baking often thought necessary. This, all too often, literally bakes or roasts the bulbs in an almost culinary sense, to a point well beyond what they need to ripen and flower flower-buds for next year.

In nature nerines from the extreme south of South Africa receive most of their annual watering in the winter months; the summers are fairly dry and it is then that the bulbs enter their dormant period before putting out leaves again following the rains of autumn. In more northerly areas the rain falls chiefly in summer, so species from these areas are dormant in winter, when they can survive much colder temperatures than the winter-growing species from further south. Between the two areas are species which experience intermediate climatic conditions, and may well remain in active growth, or at least bear their foliage, for much of the year. In effect this means that nerines from further north are hardier in British gardens than those from the south.

Nerines are best not disturbed too often. If you can, leave them undisturbed in the garden for at least five years. If you are growing them in too rich a soil, they will not only fail to flower well until they have increased almost to the point of congestion, half-starved from the competition; they will also, by then, be half out of the ground and much more liable to get frosted. Re-set them in soil into which you have incorporated plenty of sharp sand or grit, then leave well alone. When re-potting your greenhouse nerines, do so carefully, so that you do not damage the roots.

The National Collection

The National Collection of Nerine is held at Nerine Nurseries, Welland, near Malvern, Worcestershire (Mr C. A. Norris).

Mr Norris has lived with nerines all his life: his grandfather started to collect them in 1919. However, it was not until the early 1960s that he began to increase the family collection, which was unlabelled when he took it over. Thus it was that he was compelled to confront the problems of identification right away, and he decided that his best course was to collect named plants to compare them with those he had inherited. By the time he entered into correspondence with the NCCPG – his collection was designated as a National Collection in March 1983 – he had about 750 named varieties, out of a probable 1,000 or more. His collection included nearly all those to which awards have been given. He also had thousands of unnamed crosses being developed and held for future multiplication. Mr Norris also grows all but one of the thirty Nerine species that have been described, with another five awaiting description.

Mr Norris raises an average of 6,000 seedling nerines a year, and considers that over the next twenty years nerines in cultivation will change dramatically as the leap forward in colour range, size, form and stamina becomes established.

Tulipa

THE TULIP Collection at the University Botanic Garden in Cambridge differs from the Daffodil Collection at Coleraine in two important ways. First, it is not a new collection; indeed, it is a survivor, probably the only one, of the Ministry of Agriculture's scheme to establish National Species Collections of various horticulturally important genera, proposed immediately after the Hitler war. The scheme never really got going, but it is good that this one collection remains as a link to the NCCPG National Collections, which already have reached such impressive numbers. Second, the Cambridge collection is confined to species, and includes none of the many thousands of named tulips that have been bred over the centuries.

The tulips often referred to in bulb catalogues as 'botanical tulips' have become increasingly popular in recent years, and even these little wildlings are being bred for bigger and brighter flowers. *T. kaufmanniana*, for example, the waterlily tulip, now exists in dozens of differently coloured variants, many called after composers – e.g. 'Chopin', 'Gluck'. Let us hope that these selections will not be allowed to overshadow the charm and brilliance of the wild tulips.

There are very many species of tulip, native to the Mediterranean regions, the Caucasus, Asia Minor, and extending east as far as China. Of the known species comparatively few are widely grown outside specialist collections. Many new introductions have been made in recent years from Asia; the earliest introductions are thought to have been made around the middle of the sixteenth century, from Turkey. Most of the species we now grow were brought to Europe by the Dutch firm of van Tubergen and the Hoog family, who employed collectors to seek out the species described in the late nineteenth century by the Russian botanist Regel.

The core of the Cambridge Collection came from Sir Daniel Hall's collection at the John Innes Horticultural Institute. Several of the displayed

296

stocks are therefore clones which have been in cultivation for about forty years, such as *T. greigii* and *T. praestans* received from John Innes in 1948. They could probably be traced much further back in the John Innes records, some to W. R. Dykes's collections in the 1920s. Others came to Cambridge from Wisley at about the same time; *T. hageri*, for example, was also received in 1948. Other donors also contributed bulbs, including several collections from the wild. One of the most recent additions to the National Collection is a red and yellow striped, highly scented tulip sent by a lady who has evidence, in correspondence of the seventeenth or eighteenth century, that this may be a tulip of this date from Turkey. It has still to be identified, and may well not figure in the main reference work on tulips, which is still Sir Daniel Hall's 'The Genus *Tulipa*', published in 1940 and now much out of date. However, when it flowered the staff at Cambridge concluded that it must be a garden form, though of ancient lineage, and therefore not appropriate to the National Collection.

The Cambridge tulips are lifted each year, by late July, and replanted, not too early in autumn, in a new site, as in this way the disease tulip fire (*Botrytis tulipae*) is more easily controlled. In practice a 'new' site is one that has not grown tulips the previous year: to find a completely virgin site would be quite impractical. At the same time the bulbs can be cleaned and diseased ones destroyed; the healthy bulbs are spread out to dry and ripen in the sun, shaded only on exceptionally bright days. This artificial ripening is important in all but light, dry soils in this country, for in the wild tulips experience a cold winter followed by a brief spring, when they grow and flower, and a hot dry summer when the bulbs are thoroughly baked. Given suitable soils, however, most tulips will flower for several years if left in the ground, and some, like *T. sprengeri*, will even behave like this in cold, wet clay, as in Terry Jones's garden in Devon where it has become almost a pest, though one that many would envy him. Tulips should be planted fairly deep: 3 ins is about right for the little species, and a depth of 9 ins is not too much for the taller kinds. The recommendation from Cambridge is to plant each bulb in a trowelful of sharp sand, which not only helps the drainage but also ensures that the bulb comes up nice and clean when you lift it as the leaves begin to wither.

Probably the best known of the species tulips is the waterlily tulip, *T. kaufmanniana*, so called because on sunny days the narrow, creamy-primrose petals reflex widely like a *Nymphaea*. When the flowers close the soft crimson or pink markings on the outside of the petals are delightfully set against the rosette of broad grey leaves.

A similar crimson-pink stain marks the outside of the petals of the lady tulip, *T. clusiana*, named for the botanist Clusius (Charles de L'Ecluse) who lived around the time of the earliest tulip introductions to Europe in the sixteenth century. The lady tulip is a charming slender creature, as her name suggests, her slim petals creamy-white flushed pink; she grows to about 1 ft in height. A variety called *chrysantha* (sometimes also referred to as *T. stellata*) is clear yellow, stained with red.

One of the easiest tulip species to grow is the modest *T. turkestanica*, which bears several quite small, starry flowers to a stem. In colour it is white, with a bronze-green exterior and yellow centre, not showy, but with a quiet charm of its own. It flowers very early and increases well without annual lifting; a plant to study closely, for at a distance it is lost.

For a real eyeful of colour you could turn to the gaudy scarlet or crimson species such as *T. fosteriana*, *T. gesneriana* or the slightly less assertive *T. praestans*, or to *T.greigii* which has leaves of glaucous-grey striped and streaked with purple and maroon, a feast in themselves even without the strident flowers, which may vary from a powerful vermilion or crimson-scarlet to rich yellow. This, like the waterlily tulip, has given rise to many named kinds which you will find temptingly described in the catalogues. So too with *T. fosteriana*, a tallish glossy scarlet tulip with, in some forms, enormous flowers. Both these species are best lifted and dried off each year whatever your soil, but *T. gesneriana* will generally go on year after year without disturbance. This satiny scarlet tulip is widely distributed and is now thought perhaps to be of an ancient garden race, naturalised long since in Asia Minor and parts of the Mediterranean. *T. eichleri* is another easy crimson-scarlet tulip that increases well. All these red tulips are best set in plenty of spring foliage, waking up a sunny border where the main season comes later, perhaps. These complementary colours of red and green make a more satisfying garden picture than the slap in the eye you get from all the primary colours warring with each other: red tulips, bright yellow trumpet daffodils, blue grape hyacinths or, earlier, chionodoxas.

Tulipa praestans is smaller in flower than these, but each stem bears several vermilion-orange, pointy-petalled flowers. It is another easy-going tulip that will carry on year after year without lifting. Though often recommended for the rock garden, I find it just too big to be in scale in a small rock garden; in a more expansive setting it looks splendid among grey rocks. My first choice for a small rock garden or raised bed would be little *Tulipa linifolia*, with narrow crinkly blue-grey leaves that lie flat to the ground, and neat, vivid scarlet flowers on short stems. Similar in foliage but much quieter in colour is *T. batalinii*, an enchanting buff-yellow tulip with an olive-green central blotch; named hybrids vary to tender apricot and bronze-toned flowers and are all highly desirable. Both these little tulips are the better for lifting and drying off each year. One year I experimented with *T. batalinii* near the buff-apricot double alyssum, 'Dudley Neville', and silvery foliage of *Artemisia schmidtii* 'Nana' – a pretty combination that I always meant to repeat.

Tulipa tarda is another small species, this one of easy-going temperament, well suited to planting and leaving alone in the rock garden. It has closely packed starry flowers, several to a stem, white with a broad yellow centre, appearing quite late in April or even May. It increases rapidly. I only wish the same were true of two other alluring small species. *T. urumiensis* is a tiny yellow tulip with olive and bronze markings on the exterior; the starry flowers sit in rosettes of narrow grey leaves. *T. aucheriana* has similar starry flowers, but of clear pink with yellow centres and a bronze-green streak on the outside of the petals; set in similar glaucous foliage. This last species is now classed with the variable *T. humilis*, flowering in rose-pink to magenta and even violet. The name *T. pulchella violacea* in catalogues generally refers to a violet-purple form, with a black or a yellow centre (some catalogues offer the yellow-centred one as a distinct form). One of the most exquisite of all tulips is the rare albino, *T. pulchella albo-caerulea oculata*, with translucent white petals and a slate-blue centre: a perfect gem calling for, and deserving, alpine house treatment to protect its fragile flowers.

One of the oddest coloured tulips is *T. orphanidea*, a fetching warm bronze with a green centre. *T. hageri* leans more to copper and *T. whittallii* to orange with tawny-buff exterior. These all grow wild in the eastern Mediterranean, while the big red chaps are central Asian in origin. Though offbeat in colour, these Mediterraneans are of conventional tulip shape, but one of the most bizarre of all so-called species tulips is in fact unknown in the wild and may be an ancient hybrid. This, *T. acuminata*, is fairly tall and has long spidery petals tapering to a point, in a weird blend of yellow and sharp red. Another doubtfully wild species is *T. marjolettii*, but this is a more conventional thing again of graceful habit and gentle colouring, primrose-yellow lightly stained with red on the outside.

The island of Crete boasts three endemic tulip species, *T. cretica*, *T. bakeri* and *T. saxatilis*; the last has long been cultivated. With its running roots it can be reluctant to flower, expending instead all its energies in conquering new territory; at Cambridge it is kept in check, and encouraged to flower, by confining it between slates set vertically in the soil. Once it has filled its allotted area with bulbs it will begin producing its bright pinky-lilac, yellow-eyed flowers. In a garden I once cared for it had thus filled an entire raised bed of 10 ft or so each way, under a *Viburnum carlesii*, in keen competition with thousands of bulbs of a powerfully fragrant *Narcissus tazetta* form. For two or three weeks in April this corner of the garden had as strong an attraction for the visitors as the great banks of early rhododendrons or magnolias. *T. bakeri* is purple with a large yellow inner blotch and green streaking on the outside of the petals, and *T. cretica*, much smaller in stature, is purplish and green again, with touches of pink and crimson, and a nearly white inner surface.

Britain has its own naturalised, if not native, tulip, the rare *T. sylvestris*; rare, at least, in the wild in these islands: it is widespread in Europe and Asia. It will even naturalise in grass or light woodland, where its smallish yellow flowers, marked with green outside, look entirely appropriate. The most successful tulip of all for naturalising, but still unaccountably hard to acquire and absurdly expensive, is *T. sprengeri*, the last of all to flower, in June. Aptly described as satin inside and calico out, it has vermilion-scarlet flowers with dull orange-buff exterior on tallish stems. If you can obtain seed, it will give you flowers in as little as three years from sowing, quicker than any other. Semi-shade and a peaty soil will suit it as well as sun and stodgy clay, or thin grass beneath trees: it is a most accommodating plant.

And with the last of the tulips to flower I must bring to a close this chapter on the genus *Tulipa*, though I have omitted many species that clamour for inclusion.

The National Collection

The National Collection of Tulipa *species and primary hybrids is held at University Botanic Garden, Cambridge.*

The tulip collection at Cambridge Botanic Garden, a survivor of the Ministry of Agriculture's National Species Collections, was designated as a National Collection under the auspices of the NCCPG in November 1981. The basis of the Cambridge collection was the collection assembled by Sir Daniel Hall at the John Innes Horticultural Institute and at Wisley. Many additions have since been made, including several collections from the wild, as new species were introduced to cultivation from central Asia and elsewhere.

Tender Plants

Introduction

So FAR I have been considering only plants that are hardy outside in British gardens – not everywhere in the country, to be sure, but in at least some gardens, in most years. This reflects a bias of the NCCPG, which is primarily concentrating its endeavours on conserving, through the National Collections scheme, garden rather than glasshouse plants. This bias towards hardy plants is imposed more by the limited resources of a new charity than a belief that glasshouse plants are less deserving of conservation; though it does, too, derive from the nature of British gardening, as we shall see. But when, as happens from time to time, the NCCPG has an offer from a grower who already has an established collection of glasshouse or tender plants to bring his chosen genus into the ambit of the National Collections scheme, these offers have been gladly accepted.

Here I have chosen to write chiefly about just one of these National Collections of tender plants, with a passing reference to another. Both begonias and hoyas, especially the first, are plants that are seen in countless living rooms, conservatories and glasshouses throughout the country. Yet their diversity is far greater than most people realise. Indeed, plants are not readily categorised, so that we find, among the begonias, one species that is hardy outside in the south of Britain at least, and many hybrids and strains that are bedded out for the warmer months. Hardiness in plants depends on many factors: not just temperature – maximum as well as minimum – but also when, and for how long, those maxima and minima occur, the range between them, the amount and seasonal distribution of annual rainfall, prevailing winds and much else. You can shiver in a warm pullover among the date palms of San Francisco, in May; or feel colder in balmy coastal south Devon, in January, than in lakeside Switzerland where the *bise* blows out of the north; but pomegranates grow in that lakeside garden, because they get the summer ripening they miss in Britain.

305

The British climate does have a tendency to interrupt, with a drizzly day, a cricket match at the crucial point, so a certain win turns into a disappointing draw; or to catch us out with a vicious winter every few years that wipes out our hebes and cistus. But for all its failings, among which we have now learned to number drought in spring and summer, our climate enables us to grow a wider range of plants outside than in almost any other country. Even if we do have to keep our begonias and hoyas in a protected environment for much or all of their lives, we are still, as gardeners, immensely privileged in our island climate.

Begonia

PEOPLE become gardeners, and plant collectors, for the oddest reasons. Mr M. L. MacIntyre was a keen fisherman who acquired, for its name, the trout begonia; and found himself another hobby breeding miniature begonias in his small greenhouse. Mr MacIntyre's links with the Botanic Garden at Glasgow lasted for twelve years or more, and now continues after his death, for the National Collection of begonias which is grown there was not only formed around his own collection of miniatures, but is supported by a Trust established by his widow. The Trust aims to promote begonias and their research. The Glasgow collection was formally designated as the National Collection in March 1983, the first National Collection of a group of mainly tropical, rather than hardy, plants.

Such a huge genus as *Begonia* – there are about 1,000 species and innumerable hybrids – is far too big to be included in any one collection, and so the Glasgow collection specifically excludes the tuberous and winter-flowering hybrids. This still leaves a tremendous task: the objectives of the Trust include the stated aim to maintain as complete a collection of species as possible, preferably of known wild origin, as well as helping to conserve the well-documented cultivars from pre-1940, and a representative selection of post-1940 cultivars. Fortunately Glasgow Botanic Garden has skilled and experienced staff, numbers of whom are involved in the maintenance of the begonias, with the greatest day to day responsibility falling on Derek Kane, foreman of the supply houses. At least one of every species or cultivar is retained in the separate range of supply houses, with a few growing under different climate conditions. The difficult *B. prismatocarpa*, for example, is now thriving in the Filmy Fern House.

The begonias at Glasgow form one of the long-established special collections. From the 1950s onwards it was built up through the interest of Mr L. Maurice Mason and the stimulus of plants received from other sources, including Rudolph Ziesenhenne of California and the Dutch connection at Wageningen, and in particular M. L. MacIntyre's plants. Ziesenhenne was responsible for introducing and naming the small Mexican species *Begonia bowerae*, which MacIntyre used as a parent of many of his hybrids. They are small and compact, have pretty leaves and are easy to grow, ideal for small greenhouses or as house plants. *B. bowerae* itself, the eyelash begonia, has little hairs along the margins of the light green, chocolate-blotched leaves. The species MacIntyre used to cross with *B. bowerae* were *B. mazae* and *B. pustulata*, also from Mexico; the first has red and green blotches on the upper surface of its crimson-backed leaves, while the other has Nile-green leaves with silver markings. To these he added the central American *B. conchifolia*, in its form (sometimes called var. *rubrimacula*) which has a distinctive red mark where the leaf-blade joins the stalk. Among MacIntyre's hybrids are 'Red Planet', 'English Knight', 'Scottish Knight', and 'Ministar'.

A very popular group of begonias derives from *B. rex*, discovered in London in 1856 among a consignment of orchids from Assam. Crossed with other species from the Himalayan foothills it gave rise to the Rex Cultorum group, with their big multicoloured leaves which almost everyone, at some time, must have pegged down flat on a pan of compost, the veins cut through, to watch the baby plants growing at each cut. Shade and moisture-loving, these begonias do very well under the benches of a warm greenhouse. The Iron Cross begonia, *B. masoniana*, is very like a rex begonia, its big asymmetrical crinkled leaves marked with a ray-like star of chocolate brown. It was introduced from a garden in Singapore by Maurice Mason, who introduced many glasshouse plants and whose begonias also contributed largely to the Glasgow collection. *B. masoniana* is a rhizomatous species; some begonias with these thickened stems, which normally are on or below soil level, have curious 'upright rhizomes'. *Begonia manicata*, discovered in Mexico in 1842, is one of these. The upright rhizome is thicker than the stems of other begonias, and the leaves are arranged in a one-sided manner, giving the effect of a plant which has been growing along the ground before being pulled upright. The fleshy leaves are glossy green above and red beneath, and the small flowers are pink, borne in elegant, tall sprays.

Other begonias are cane-stemmed, and more or less shrubby. MacIntyre's trout begonia, *B.* '*Argenteo-guttata*', is one; other silver-spotted begonias, raised in the nineteenth century and still popular today, include 'President Carnot' and 'Lucerna'. The first silver-spotted begonia in cultivation was discovered in Brazil in 1820 and named *B. maculata*: another tall begonia with those familiar stems, almost like fleshy bamboo canes, and the usual asymmetrical leaves. The pale pink or white flowers are borne in large drooping heads, making this a fine begonia for both flowers and foliage. Quite different from these is *B. luxurians* from Brazil, which has large horse-chestnut-like leaves, reddish above and green beneath. Another with this palmate leaf arrangement is the rhizomatous *B. mac-dougallii*, named by Rudolph Ziesenhenne in 1957. The leaves are especially striking in its coloured form *purpurea*. Of the shrubby species, quite the most astonishing specimen at Glasgow is the Colombian *Begonia foliosa* var. *amplifolia*. It was received in 1969 and later planted out in one of the display houses. This plant must surely qualify for the Guinness Book of Records. Before it was recently replanted, when the display collection was moved to a larger house, it extended over 30 ft, and had produced flowers every day of the year for ten years. It has the general aspect of a woody *Polygonum baldschuanicum*, the Russian vine, in flower. One of the smaller shrubby begonias which is, in its more modest way, very striking is *B. listada*, which has bold dark leaves with bright stripes along the main axes. The leaves come in two distinct shapes on the one plant: the typical asymmetrical form, and a triangular outline.

In a genus so large and varied it is hard to pick out oddities and plants of special interest: almost every species is worth mention, if only space allowed. Although the Glasgow Collection excludes winter-flowering hybrids, I feel I must mention *B. socotrana*, an important parent of the group, which was found growing, in the shade of granite boulders, on the island of Socotra. It was discovered by Sir Isaac Bailey Balfour in 1880, shortly after his appointment to the Regius Chair of Botany at Glasgow University. He described Socotra as 'one of the last places in the world in which a begonia could have been expected to occur'. During the hot dry season *B. socotrana* survives as small bulb-like buds; in the growing season it produces bright green peltate leaves and rose-pink flowers. Soon it was crossed with one of the Tuberhybrida group and, a few years later, with the South African species *B. dregei*, to produce one of the most famous of all begonia hybrids, the first of the fibrous-rooted Cheimantha group: 'Gloire de Lorraine'.

Most begonias are native to tropical and subtropical areas, and need the protection of a glasshouse, or a warm room, but there is one species that is hardy enough to grow outside in the south of England without winter protection. This is *Begonia grandis* subsp. *evansiana*, introduced from China in 1804. *B. grandis* has typical begonia leaves, asymmetrical, green with red-tinted veining, borne on fleshy, succulent, reddish stems. In the axils of the leaves little bulbils form; they drop to the ground to form new plants, or you can rescue them and increase your plantings yourself in a more controlled manner. In flower *B. grandis* is very pretty, with light magenta-pink flowers; or white in the rarer form 'Alba', in which the nodding flowers are set off by pink pedicels and calyces. To give of its best, *B. grandis* needs warm, moist shade; the leaves are thin-textured and burn easily in sun or wind. In winter it dies down to tuberous roots, disappearing completely: another of those plants you need to mark carefully, lest you inadvertently plant something in what looks like an empty space. For a tropical look, set *B. grandis* among ferns, and with – if your climate permits – the great sword-blades of *Iris wattii*, which bears its leaf fans on bamboo-like stems.

The MacIntyre Trust will be used to improve the scientific base of the National *Begonia* Collection at Glasgow, and the facilities for growing them in the gardens. To help publicise the diversity of the genus, and the Collection at Glasgow, an exhibition will be mounted, in photographic form. This will be used as a travelling exhibition, available through organisations such as the American Begonia Society and the NCCPG.

Although the National Collections scheme is concentrating its efforts on plants that can be grown outside somewhere, if not everywhere, in the British Isles, *Begonia* is now not the only genus of greenhouse plants in the scheme. At the Welsh Mountain Zoo in Colwyn Bay, Tony Jackson's remarkable collection of hoyas is also designated as a National Collection. As with the begonias, Maurice Mason had much to do with the formation of the collection, for in about 1982 Mr Mason donated his entire collection of about thirty different species and cultivars to the Zoo. It has grown remarkably since then, through further help from various botanic gardens and private collectors as far afield as Hawaii. The Collection has great potential zoologically, as well as horticulturally and botanically, as a tropical exhibit in conjunction with butterflies, hummingbirds and other delicate nectar-feeding creatures. It is good to be reminded that the National Collections need not, and should not, exist in isolation from the many other faces of conservation.

The National Collection

The National Collection of Begonia *is grown at Glasgow Botanic Garden.*

Based upon the begonias bred and collected by Mr M. L. MacIntyre, the Glasgow begonias were designated as a National Collection in March 1983. Plants were also received from Rudolph Ziesenhenne of California, from Wageningen, and from Maurice Mason. The National Collection of begonias excludes tuberous and winter-flowering hybrids, in an attempt to reduce the genus to manageable proportions.

The National Collection of Hoya *is held at the Welsh Mountain Zoo and Botanic Garden, Colwyn Bay, Clwyd, N. Wales.*

Tony Jackson was given the hoyas which, in March 1984, were designated as a National Collection, by Maurice Mason in the early 1980s. It then comprised about thirty different species and cultivars. It has since grown to much larger proportions thanks to help from botanic gardens and private collectors as far afield as Hawaii.

General Bibliography

ARNOLD-FORSTER, W.: *Shrubs for the Milder Counties* Country Life, 1948

BEAN, W.J.: *Trees & Shrubs Hardy in the British Isles* 4 vols, 8th (revised) edition. John Murray, 1976–80

BLOOM, ALAN: *Hardy Perennials* Faber & Faber, 1957
Hardy Plants of Distinction Collingridge, 1965
Perennials for Trouble-Free Gardening Faber & Faber, 1960
Plantsman's Progress Terence Dalton, 1976

BOWLES, E. A.: *My Garden in Spring* T. C. & E. C. Jack, 1914
My Garden in Summer T. C. & E. C. Jack, 1914
My Garden in Autumn and Winter T. C. & E. C. Jack, 1915

CLAY, SAMPSON: *The Present Day Rock Garden* T. C. & E. C. Jack, 1937

COX, E. H. M. & P. A.: *Modern Trees* Thomas Nelson & Sons, 1961

FARRER, R.: *My Rock Garden* Edward Arnold, 1907
The English Rock Garden T. C. & E. C. Jack, 1918

FISH, M.: *An All-the-Year Garden* David & Charles (reprint), 1971
Cottage Garden Flowers Collingridge, 1961
A Flower for Every Day David & Charles (reprint), 1973
Gardening in the Shade Collingridge, 1964

GRIFFITH, A.: *Guide to Alpines & Rock Garden Plants* Collins, 1964

HEATH, R.: *Collectors' Alpines* Collingridge, 1964

Hillier's Manual of Trees & Shrubs David & Charles, 1972

HYAMS, E.: *Ornamental Shrubs for Temperate Zone Gardens* 6 vols, Macdonald, 1965

INGWERSEN, W.: *Manual of Alpine Plants*, 1978

JEKYLL, G.: *A Gardener's Testament* Country Life, 1937
Colour Schemes for the Flower Garden Country Life, 1936
Wood and Garden Longman Green, 1899

LLOYD, C.: *Clematis* Collins, 1977
Foliage Plants Collins, 1973
Hardy Perennials Studio Vista, 1967
'Mixed Borders' *Journal of the Royal Horticultural Society* Vol. 84, 411–18 (1959)
The Adventurous Gardener Allen Lane, 1983
The Well Chosen Garden Elm Tree Books, 1984
The Well Tempered Garden Collins, 1970

MATHEW, B.: *Dwarf Bulbs* Batsford/RHS, 1973
   The Larger Bulbs Batsford/RHS, 1978
PAGE, R.: *The Education of a Gardener* Collins, 1962
PERRY, F.: *Guide to Border Plants* Collins, 1957
RIX, M. AND PHILLIPS, R.: *The Bulb Book* Pan, 1981
ROBINSON, W.: *The English Flower Garden* 8th ed. John Murray, 1900, and Revised
   Amaryllis Press USA, 1984
SANDERS, T. W.: *Popular Hardy Perennials* Collingridge, 1928
SYNGE, P. M.: *Guide to Bulbs* Collins, 1961
THOMAS, G. S.: *Perennial Garden Plants* 2nd ed. J. M. Dent, 1982
   Plants for Ground Cover rev. ed. J. M. Dent, 1977
   The Art of Planting J. M. Dent, 1984
   'The Artistry of Planting' *Journal of the Royal Horticultural Society* Vol. 95, 390–409
   (1970)
WARD, F. KINGDON: *Berried Treasure* Ward Lock, 1954
WRIGHT, D.: 'Colour Groupings for the Smaller Modern Garden' *Journal of the Royal
   Horticultural Society* Vol. 88, 300–7 (1963)
   'Colour Schemes for Small Gardens' *Journal of the Royal Horticultural Society* Vol. 86,
   215–22, 270–6, 309–18 (1961)

Bibliography by Genus

Acer

HARRIS, J. G. S.: 'An Account of Maples in Cultivation', *The Plantsman*, Vol. 5, 35–8 (1983)
  'Japanese Maples', *The Plantsman*, Vol. 3, 234–50 (1982)
  'Maples from Japan', *Journal of the Royal Horticultural Society* Vol 99, 394–9 (1974)
KRÜSSMAN, GERD: *Manual of Cultivated Broad-leaved Trees and Shrubs* Vol. 1, A–D. Trans. Michael E. Epp. Batsford, 1984.
Bibliography by Genus
Bibliography by Genus
LANCASTER, C. R.: 'Autumn Colour from Maples', *Country Life*, 2.9.1982
  'Maples of the Himalaya', *The Garden* (Journal of the Royal Horticultural Society) Vol. 101, 589–93 (1976)
MITCHELL, A. F.: 'Maples at Westonbirt', *Journal of the Royal Horticultural Society* Vol. 92, 430–5 (1967)
MURRAY, A. E.: *A Monograph of the Aceraceae*, D. Phil. thesis from Pennsylvania State University Graduate School, Dept. of Horticulture (1970)
VERTREES, J. D.: *Japanese Maples* Timber Press, Oregon, 1978

Betula

ASHBURNER, KENNETH: '*Betula* – a Survey', *The Plantsman*, Vol. 2, 31–53 (1980)
ASHBURNER, KENNETH AND SCHILLING, TONY: 'A note on *Betula utilis* and its varieties', *The Garden* (Journal of the Royal Horticultural Society) Vol. 110, 523–5 (1985)
  '*Betula utilis* and its varieties' *The Plantsman* Vol. 7, 116–25 (1985)
JØRGENSEN, PER M.: 'Ornäs Birch, a misunderstood tree' *The Plantsman* Vol. 1, 253–5 (1980)
KRÜSSMAN, GERD: *Manual of Cultivated Broad-leaved Trees and Shrubs* Vol. 1, A–D. Trans. Michael E. Epp. Batsford, 1984

Magnolia

ABERCONWAY, LORD: 'Magnolias at Bodnant' *Journal of the Royal Horticultural Society* Vol. 65, 71–4 (1940)

FINDLAY, T. H.: 'Notes on certain Magnolias planted in Windsor Great Park' *Journal of the Royal Horticultural Society* Vol. 77, 43–6 (1952)
LLOYD, CHRISTOPHER: 'In the spring a gardener's fancy' *Country Life*, 17.3.1977
PEARCE, S. A.: 'Magnolias at Kew' *Journal of the Royal Horticultural Society* Vol. 84, 418–25 (1959)
TRESEDER, NEIL G.: *Magnolias* Faber & Faber, 1978
  'Magnolias and their cultivation' *Journal of the Royal Horticultural Society* Vol. 97, 336–46 (1972)
WILLIAMS, F. JULIAN: 'The Garden at Caerhays' *Journal of the Royal Horticultural Society* Vol. 91, 279–86 (1966)

Malus

CRANE, H. S.J.: *'Malus' Journal of the Royal Horticultural Society* Vol. 86, 160–7 (1961)

Sorbus

FOX, WILFRID: 'Winkworth Arboretum' *Journal of the Royal Horticultural Society* Vol. 74, 80–92 (1954)
FULCHER, R.: 'Further notes on *Sorbus vilmorinii*' *The Plantsman* Vol. 3, 254 (1982)
KNEES, SABINA: 'Some Notes on the Service Tree, *Sorbus domestica* L.' *The Plantsman* Vol. 7, 65–7 (1985)
LANCASTER, C. R.: 'More on *Sorbus*' *The Plantsman* Vol. 3, 255 (1982)
MCALLISTER, DR H.: 'The Aucuparia section of *Sorbus*' *The Plantsman* Vol. 6, 248–55 (1985)
WRIGHT, DAVID: 'Mountain Ashes for Reliable Autumn Effects' *Journal of the Royal Horticultural Society* Vol. 90, 510–12 (1965)
  'Notes on Whitebeams' *Journal of the Royal Horticultural Society* Vol. 90, 256–60 (1965)
  '*Sorbus* – a Gardener's Evaluation' *The Plantsman* Vol. 3, 65–98 (1981)

Ceanothus

ARNOLD-FORSTER, W.: *Shrubs for the Milder Counties*, Country Life, *1948*
LUCAS, N.: 'The National *Ceanothus* Collection' NCCPG Devon Group Newsletter, Autumn 1984
VAN RENSSELAER, M. AND MCMINN, PROF. H. E.: *Ceanothus* California, 1942

Cistus

SWEET, R.: *Cistineae* London, 1825–1830
WARBURG, SIR OSCAR: 'Cistus' *Journal of the Royal Horticultural Society* Vol. 55, 1–52 (1930)

Dwarf Conifers

BLOOM, ADRIAN: *Conifers for Your Garden* Floraprint, n.d.
HARRISON, CHARLES R.: *Ornamental Conifers* Hafner Press, New York, 1975
HORNIBROOK, MURRAY: *Dwarf and Slow-Growing Conifers* Country Life, 1938
WELCH, HUMPHREY: *Dwarf Conifers – A Complete Handbook* Faber & Faber, 1966

Olearia

HOBHOUSE, P.: 'Olearias' *The Garden* (Journal of the Royal Horticultural Society) Vol. 103, 229–34 (1978)

LORD, E. E.: *Shrubs & Trees for Australian Gardens* Lothian, 1956

TALBOT DE MALAHIDE, LORD: 'The Genus Olearia' *Journal of the Royal Horticultural Society* Vol. 90, 207–17, 245–9 (1965)

Pieris

BOND, J. D.: '*Pieris*, a Survey' *The Plantsman* Vol. 4, 65–75 (1982)

HUNT, D. R. AND SCHILLING, A. D.: '*Pieris formosa* 'Henry Price'' *The Plantsman* Vol. 3, 189–91 (1981)

PHAIR, G.: 'Notes on *Pieris*' *The Plantsman* Vol. 5, 63 (1983)

Rhododendron

COX, P. A.: *The Larger Species of Rhododendron* Batsford, 1979
The Smaller Rhododendrons Batsford, 1985

CULLEN, J. AND CHAMBERLAIN, D. F.: *Revision of Rhododendron. Notes from the Royal Botanic Garden Edinburgh* Vol. 39, 1 & 2 (1980 and 1982)

THE ROYAL HORTICULTURAL SOCIETY: *The Rhododendron Handbook – Rhododendron Species in Cultivation*, RHS, 1980.

Clematis

LLOYD, CHRISTOPHER: *Clematis* Collins, 1977

Agapanthus

BOND, J. D.: 'Notes from Wisley: *Agapanthus* Trials' *The Garden* (Journal of the Royal Horticultural Society) Vol. 103, 315–18 (1978)

PALMER, HON. LEWIS: 'Agapanthus' *Journal of the Royal Horticultural Society* Vol. 81, 163–6 (1956)
'Hardy Agapanthus as a Plant for the Outdoor Garden' *Journal of the Royal Horticultural Society* Vol. 92, 336–41 (1967)

Aster

RANSON, E. R.: *Michaelmas Daisies and Other Garden Asters* John Gifford, 1946

Campanula

CROOK, H. CLIFFORD: *Campanulas*, Country Life, 1951

JOHNSON, A. T.: 'Campanulas for Rock Garden & Border' *My Garden* 1947

Dianthus

ALLWOOD, M. C.: *Carnations and All Dianthus* London, 1926

INGWERSEN, W.: *The Dianthus* London, 1949

McQUOWN, F. R.: *Pinks, Selection and Cultivation* London, 1955

MORETON, REV. C. OSCAR: *Old Carnations and Pinks* London, 1955

Euphorbia

RADCLIFFE-SMITH, A, AND TURNER, R.: 'Key to Non-succulent Hardy and Half-Hardy *Euphorbia* species commonly in cultivation' *The Plantsman* Vol. 5, 157–61 (1983)

TURNER, R.: 'A Review of Spurges for the Garden' *The Plantsman* Vol. 5, 129–56 (1983)

Geranium

CLIFTON, R.: *Hardy Geraniums (Cranesbills) Today* British Pelargonium & Geranium Society, 1979

FORTY, JOY: 'A Survey of Hardy Geraniums in Cultivation' *The Plantsman* Vol. 2, 67–78 (1980)

'Further Notes on Hardy Geraniums' *The Plantsman*, Vol. 3, 127–8 (1981)

INGWERSEN, W.: *The Genus Geranium* 1946

YEO, DR P.: '*Geranium candicans* and *G. yunnanense* of Gardens' *The Garden* (Journal of the Royal Horticultural Society) Vol. 109, 36–7 (1983)

Hardy Geraniums Croome Helm, 1985

'The *Geranium palmatum* Group in Madeira and the Canary Isles' *Journal of the Royal Horticultural Society* Vol. 95, 410–14 (1970) and Vol. 96, 44 (1971)

Heuchera

BLOOM, ALAN: 'Heucheras' *Hardy Plant Society Tenth Anniversary Handbook* 23–5

'Heucheras' *The Garden* (Journal of the Royal Horticultural Society) Vol. 102, 58–9 (1977)

'Thoughts while Propagating' *Hardy Plant Society Bulletin* December 1985, 51–2

HALLIWELL, B.: '*Heuchera* 'Palace Purple'' *Hardy Plant Society Bulletin* June 1986, 4–5

RAMSDALE, M.: '*Heuchera*' *Hardy Plant Society Bulletin* June 1986, 25–9

ROSENDAHL, C. A., BUTTERS, F. K. AND LAKELA, O.: 'A Monograph on the Genus *Heuchera*' *Minnesota Studies in Plant Science*, 1936

Kniphofia

BERGER, ALWIN: in Engler, *Das Pflanzenreich* Vol. 4, 38 (1908)

CODD, L. E.: 'The South African Species of *Kniphofia*' *Bothalia* Vol. 9, 367–513 (1968)

JANAKI AMMAL, E. K.: 'A Triploid Kniphofia' *Journal of The Royal Horticultural Society* Vol. 75, 23 (1950)

MACKENZIE, COMPTON: *My Life & Times Octave Four, 1907–1914* Chatto & Windus, 1965

MARAIS, W.: 'Tropical Species of *Kniphofia*' *Kew Bulletin* Vol. 28, 1973

TAYLOR, J.: '*Kniphofia*, a Survey' *The Plantsman* Vol. 7, 129–60 (1985)

THISTLETON-DYER, W.: (Ed.) *Flora Capensis* Vol. VI, London, 1896–7

Flora of Tropical Africa Vol. VII, London, 1897–8

Lobelia

BOWDEN, W.: 'Perennial Tetraploid Lobelia Hybrids' *The Garden* (Journal of the Royal Horticultural Society) Vol. 109, 55–7 (1984)

PUGSLEY, H. C.: '*Lobelia cardinalis* and Hybrids' *Hardy Plant Society Bulletin*, 1966, 131–3

Primroses

GENDERS, R. AND TAYLOR, H. C.: *Primroses and Polyanthus* Faber & Faber, 1954
TAYLOR, H. C. AND C. M.: *A Book about Double Primroses* n.d.

Saxifraga

KÖHLEIN, FRITZ: *Saxifrages and related genera* 1984

Sedum

EVANS, R. L.: *Handbook of Cultivated Sedums* Science Reviews, 1983
HENSEN, KAREL J. W. AND GROENDIJK-WILDERS, NYNKE: 'An Account of some Sedums Cultivated in Europe' *The Plantsman* Vol. 8, 1–20 (1986)

Thalictrum

BLOOM, ALAN: 'Meadow Rue' *The Garden* (Journal of the Royal Horticultural Society) Vol. 103, 200–1 (1978)

Yellow Daisies

BARKER, D.: 'The Heleniums' *Hardy Plant Society Bulletin* 1965, 112–14
BECKETT, K.: 'Ligularia' *The Garden* (Journal of the Royal Horticultural Society) Vol. 106, 122–5 (1981)

Arisaema

BESANT, J. W.: 'Hardy Aroids' *Journal of the Royal Horticultural Society*, Vol. 64, 128–32 (1939)
HENDERSON, A.: 'Dragon Plants and Mousetails' *The Garden* (Journal of the Royal Horticultural Society) Vol. 106, 13–17 (1981)
LANCASTER, ROY: 'Arisaemas in the Wild' *The Garden* (Journal of the Royal Horticultural Society) Vol. 108, 36–7 (1983)
MAYO, S. J.: 'A Survey of Cultivated Species of *Arisaema*' *The Plantsman* Vol. 3, 193–209 (1982)
STEPHENS, J.: 'Arisaemas I have Known' *Journal of the Royal Horticultural Society* Vol. 93, 259–63 (1968)

Galanthus

BOWLES, E. A.: *My Garden in Spring* T. C. & E. C. Jack, 1914
STERN, SIR F.: *Snowdrops and Snowflakes* RHS, 1956
SYNGE, P. M.: *Flowers and Colour in Winter* Readers Union reprint, 1974
THOMAS, G. S.: *Colour in the Winter Garden* Dent, 1977

Narcissus

BOWLES, E. A.: *The Narcissus* Martin Hopkinson, 1934
MORRIS, MEGAN: 'The Hartlands of Cork' *Moorea* Vol. 4, 27–41 (1985)

WILLIS, D.: 'Correspondence to Frederick Burbidge (Trinity College Dublin) on Daffo-
dils' *Moorea* Vol. 2, 45–52 (1983)
'The Development of Daffodil Cultivars in Ireland' *Glasra*, Vol. 5, 21–31 (1981)
'The Origins of Pink Daffodil Cultivars' *The Plantsman* Vol. 3, 51–9 (1981)
WILSON, G. L.: 'Among My Seedlings' *Daffodil Year Book*, 1915
'White Daffodils' *Daffodil Year Book*, 1934

Nerine

ANDERSON, E. B.: '*Nerine bowdenii* 'Quinton Wells'' *Journal of the Royal Horticultural
Society* Vol. 86, 122–3 (1961)
Seven Gardens Michael Joseph, 1973
GALLAGHER, J. T.: 'Greenhouse Nerines' *Journal of the Royal Horticultural Society*, Vol.
91, 205–9 (1966)
HANGER, FRANCIS: 'Nerines' *Journal of the Royal Horticultural Society*, Vol. 71, 254–8
(1946)
NORRIS, C. A.: 'Greenhouse Nerine Cultivation' *Journal of the Royal Horticultural Society*,
Vol. 91, 248–50 (1966)
'Towards Better Nerines' *Journal of the Royal Horticultural Society*, Vol, 100, 486–91
(1975)
SMEE, STANLEY: 'Growing and Breeding Nerines' *The Garden* (Journal of the Royal
Horticultural Society) Vol. 109, 408–13 (1984)

Tulipa

HALL, SIR A. D.: *The Genus Tulipa* London, 1940

List of National Collections

The following collections have been designated as National Collections by mutual agreement between the NCCPG and the organisations/individuals concerned:

Abelia Borough of Torbay, Parks and Recreation Section, Tor Hill House, Castle Circus, Torquay, Devon TQ2 5QN.

Abies Mr J. Noble, Ardkinglas Estate, Cairndow, Argyll PA26 8BH.

Abutilon, spp. and cvs. Somerset College of Agriculture and Horticulture, Cannington, Bridgwater, Somerset TA5 2LS.

bell-flowered Mr N. C. Sayers, 105 Nutleigh Crescent, Goring-by-Sea, Worthing, W. Sussex BN12 4LB.

Acacia Tresco Abbey Gardens, Isles of Scilly, Cornwall TR24 0QQ.

Acanthus Mr L. Butler, Wagtail Cottage, 3 Woolley Green, Near Bradford-on-Avon, Wiltshire BA15 1TY.

Acer, japonicum and *palmatum* cvs. The Forestry Commission, Westonbirt Aboretum, Westonbirt, Tetbury, Gloucestershire GL8 8QS.

except *japonicum* and *palmatum* cvs. Mr R. and W. L. Banks, Hergest Croft Gardens, Kington, Herefordshire HR5 3EG.

The Lord Ridley, Blagdon, Seaton Burn, Newcastle upon Tyne, Tyne and Wear NE13 6DD.

Achillea 'Gardening from Which?' Trials Garden, Capel Manor, Waltham Cross, Hertfordshire, (Diana Rendell, 2 Marylebone Street, London NW1 4DK)

Aconitum University of Aberdeen, Cruickshank Botanical Garden, St Machar Drive, Aberdeen AB9 2UD.

Actinidia, climbing Bristol Clifton and West of England Zoological Society, Bristol, Avon BS8 3HA.

Adiantum The National Trust, Tatton Park, Knutsford, Cheshire WA16 6QN.

Aechmea Department of Recreation and Open Spaces, Liverpool City Council, The Mansion House, Calderstone Park, Liverpool L18 3JD.

Aesculus Mr R. Hicks, The Edward James Foundation, West Dean Estate, Chichester, W. Sussex PO18 0QZ.

Lancashire College of Agriculture and Horticulture, Myerscough Hall, Bilsborrow, Preston, Lancashire PR3 0RY.

Agapanthus NCCPG Devonshire Group, Torbay Health Authority, Torbay Hospital, Lawes Bridge, Torquay, Devon TQ2 7AA.

Ajuga Mr N. B. Junker, Junker's Tree & Landscape Services, Lower Mead, West Hatch, Taunton, Somerset.

Alchemilla University Botanic Garden, Cambridge CB2 1JF.

Allium Mrs P. K. Davies, 6 Blenheim Road, Caversham, Reading, Berkshire RG4 7RS.

Alnus The Lord Ridley, Blagdon, Seaton Burn, Newcastle upon Tyne, Tyne and Wear NE13 6DD.

Amelanchier Mr P. J. Beard, 14 Grays Terrace, Redhills, Durham DH1 4AV.

Amorphophallus Mrs E. Honnor, 14 Homefield Close, Creech St Michael, Taunton, Somerset TA3 5QR.

Ampelopsis/Parthenocissus University of Strathclyde, Education & Recreational Centre, Ross Priory, Gartocharn, Dumbartonshire GB3 8NL.

Anemone, Japanese Anemones Hadlow College of Agriculture & Horticulture, Hadlow, Tonbridge, Kent TN11 0AL.
Mr D. G. Barker, Stone Pine, Hyde Lane, Chelmsford, Essex CM3 4LJ.
Dr J. R. Burwell, 47 Locks Road, Locks Heath, Southampton, Hampshire SO3 6NS.
nemorosa cvs The National Trust, Cliveden, Taplow, Maidenhead, Berkshire.

Anthericum Mr R. Grounds & Mrs D. Grenfell, Apple Court, Hordle Lane, Lymington, Hampshire SO41 0HU.

Aquilegia Mr J. Drake, Hardwick House, Fen Ditton, Cambridge CB5 8TF.

Arabis Luton Parks Division, Wardown Park Offices, Old Bedford Road, Luton, Bedfordshire LU2 7HA.

Araceae, except *Arisaema* and *Zantedeschia* Mrs. E. Honnor, 14 Homefield Close, Creech St Michael, Taunton, Somerset TA3 5QR.

Arbutus unedo cvs Mr T. La Dell, Cattamount, Grafty Green, Maidstone, Kent ME17 2AP.

Arisaema Mr R. A. Hammond, The Magnolias, 18 St Johns Avenue, Brentwood, Essex CM14 5DF.

Artemisia Mr C. C. Williams, Emmings Farm Herbs, Elton, Newnham-on-Severn, Gloucestershire GL14 1JL.

Arundinaria The National Trust for Scotland, Lochalsh Woodland Gardens, Balmacara, Kyle of Lochalsh, Ross-shire IV40 8DN.
Mr D. A. Crampton, Drysdale Nurseries, 96 Drysdale Avenue, Chingford, London E4 7PE.

Asphodelus/Asphodeline Mr R. J. A. Leeds, East Anglian Garden Society, 'Chestnuts', Whelp Street, Preston St Mary, Sudbury, Suffolk CO10 9NL.

Asplenium scolopendrium The National Trust, Sizergh Castle, Kendal, Cumbria LA8 8AE.
Wigan College Horticulture Centre, Christopher Park, Wigan, Greater Manchester WN1 1PR.

Aster novi-belgii Miss I. Allen & Miss J.

Huish, Belmont House, Tyntesfield, Wraxall, Bristol, Avon BS19 1NR.

Leeds City Council, Temple Newsam Park, Leeds, W. Yorkshire LS15 0AD.

novi-belgii, dumosus, cordifolius, ericoides and *novae-angliae* Mr P. Picton, Old Court Nurseries Ltd, Colwall, Near Malvern, Worcestershire WR13 6QE.

ericoides and *amellus* cvs. and hybrids The National Trust, Upton House, Edgehill, Banbury, Oxfordshire OX15 6HT.

Astilbe Lord Harewood, Harewood House Gardens, Harewood, Leeds, W. Yorkshire LS17 9LF.

Mr H. Noblett, Lakeland Horticultural Society, Riseholm, Stainton, Penrith, Cumbria CA11 0ET.

Astrantia Mrs S. Bond, Goldbrook Plants, Hoxne, Eye, Suffolk IP21 5AN.

Athyrium Crown Estate Commissioners, The Great Park, Windsor, Berkshire SL4 2HT.

Aubrieta University of Leicester, Department of Botany, University Road, Leicester LE1 7RH.

Luton Parks Division, Wardown Park Offices, Old Bedford Road, Luton, Bedfordshire LU2 7HA.

Azaleodendron, see *Rhododendron*

Azara University of Exeter, Northcote House, The Queens Drive, Exeter, Devon EX4 4QJ.

Bambusa Mr D. A. Crampton, Drysdale Nurseries, 96 Drysdale Avenue, Chingford, London E4 7PE.

except *Phyllostachys* and *Sasa* Oxford Botanic Garden, Nuneham Courtenay Arboretum, Oxfordshire.

Begonia, except winter-flowering and tuberous Glasgow Botanic Gardens, Glasgow G12 0EU.

Bellis perennis cvs. Mrs J. Andrews, Crossways, Shrewley, Near Warwick.

Berberis Broxtowe Borough Council, Leisure Services, Coventry Lane, Bramcote, Nottingham NG9 3GJ.

Bergenia, except cvs. University Botanic Garden, Cambridge CB2 1JF.

cvs. Cambridge City Council. Mandela House, 4 Regent Street, Cambridge CB2 1BY.

Mr C. D. Hallsworth, 21 Mount Pleasant Road, South Woodham Ferrers, Essex CM3 5PA.

Betula Mr R. and Mr W. L. Banks, Hergest Croft Gardens, Kington, Herefordshire HR5 3EG.

The Lord Ridley, Blagdon, Seaton Burn, Newcastle upon Tyne, Tyne and Wear NE13 6DD.

Buddleia, species The Paignton Zoological and Botanic Gardens, 187 Totnes Road, Paignton, Devon TQ4 7EU.

davidii cvs. & hybrids Dr A. Plack, 'Rhus', Bridford, Exeter, Devon EX6 7LD.

Buxus The National Trust, Ickworth Park, Bury St Edmunds, Suffolk IP29 5QE.

Calamintha Mrs L. Williams, Marle Place Plants, Marle Place, Brenchley, Tonbridge, Kent TN12 7HS.

Calathea Liverpool City Council, Department of Recreation and Open Spaces, The Mansion House, Calderstone Park, Liverpool L18 3JD.

Calceolaria Luton Parks Division, Wardown Park Offices, Old Bedford Road, Luton, Bedfordshire LU2 7HA.

Callistemon Mr R. Sturdy, Rik Sturdy Associates, Middle Copse, Carey, Wareham, Dorset BH20 7PB.

Calluna vulgaris cvs. The Northern Horticultural Society, Harlow Car Gardens, Harrogate, N. Yorkshire, HG3 1QB.
Royal Horticultural Society RHS Gardens, Wisley, Woking, Surrey GU23 6QB.
City of Plymouth, Royal Building, St Andrews Cross, Plymouth, Devon.

Caltha Mr and Mrs J. E. Hudson, The Mill, 21 Mill Lane, Cannington, Bridgwater, Somerset TA5 2HB.

Camassia Mr R. Grounds and Mrs D. Grenfell, Apple Court, Hordle Lane, Lymington, Hampshire SO41 0HU.

Camellia City of Plymouth, Royal Building, St Andrews Cross, Plymouth, Devon.

Campanula Mr P. Lewis, 19 Padlock Road, West Wratting, Cambridge CB1 5LS.

Carpinus The Hillier Arboretum, Jermyns Lane, Ampfield, Near Romsey, Hampshire.
betulus cvs. Mr T. E. Beale, West Lodge Park, Cockfosters Road, Hadley Wood, Hertfordshire EN4 0PY.

Carya Borough of Torbay, Tor Hill House, Castle Circus, Torquay, Devon TQ2 5QN.

Caryopteris Bristol Clifton and West of England Zoological Society, Bristol, Avon BS8 3HA.

Cassiope The National Trust for Scotland, Branklyn, Dundee Road, Perth, Tayside PH2 7BB.

Castanea Viscount Devonport, Ray Demesne, Kirkwhelpington, Northumberland NE19 2RG.

Catalpa The National Trust, Cliveden, Taplow, Maidenhead, Berkshire.

Cautleya Mr E. Needham, Derow, Kelliwith, Feock, Truro, Cornwall TR3 6QZ.

Ceanothus Somerset College of Agriculture and Horticulture, Cannington, Bridgwater, Somerset TA5 2LS.
Torbay Health Authority, Torbay Hospital, Lawes Bridge, Torquay, Devon TQ2 7AA.

Centaurea Mrs H. Hiley, 25 Little Woodcote Estate, Wallington, Surrey SM5 4AU.

Cercidiphyllum Mr T. Hooker, Canford School, Wimborne, Dorset BH21 3AD.

Chamaecyparis lawsoniana cvs. University of Leicester, Department of Botany, University Road, Leicester LE1 7RH.

Chrysanthemum, Korean and Pompom Mr M. Stone, Little Mynthurst Farm, Norwood Hill, Near Horley, Surrey RH16 0HR.
maximum and *leucanthemum* cvs. Lady Hagart-Alexander, NCCPG. Ayrshire and Arran Group, Kingencleuch House, Mauchline, Ayrshire KA5 5JL.
rubellum cvs. Mr B. Wallis 3 Church St, Buckden, Huntingdon, Cambridgeshire PE18 9TE.

Chusquea Mr D. A. Crampton, Drysdale Nurseries, 96 Drysdale Avenue, Chingford, London E4 7PE.

Cimicifuga Bridgemere Garden World,

Bridgemere Nurseries Ltd, Bridgemere, Near Nantwich, Cheshire CW5 7QB.

Cistus Chelsea Physic Garden, 66 Royal Hospital Road, London SW3 4HS.

Clematis Treasures of Tenbury Ltd, Burford House, Tenbury Wells, Worcestershire WR15 8HQ.

Mr R. Evison, The Guernsey Clematis Nursery Ltd, Dormarie Vineries, Les Sauvagees, St Sampson, Guernsey, Channel Islands.

Colchicum The National Trust, Felbrigg Hall, Cromer, Norfolk NR11 8PR.

The Royal Horticultural Society, RHS Garden, Wisley, Woking, Surrey GU23 6QB.

Colutea Cadogan Estates, The Cadogan Office, 18 Cadogan Gardens, London SW3 2RP.

Conifers, dwarf Crown Estate Commissioners, The Great Park, Windsor, Berkshire SL4 2HT.

Convallaria The National Trust, Cliveden, Maidenhead, Berkshire.

Coprosma Mr G. Hutchins, County Park Nursery, Hornchurch, Essex RM11 3BU.

Ventnor Botanic Garden, The Winter Gardens, Ventnor, Isle of Wight PO38 1SZ.

Cordyline Somerset College of Agriculture and Horticulture, Cannington, Bridgwater, Somerset TA5 2LS.

Coreopsis The Hardy Plant Society, 17 Stanley Drive, Bramcote, Nottingham.

Cornus The Hillier Arboretum, Jermyns Lane, Ampfield, Near Romsey, Hampshire.

except *C. florida* cvs. The Lady Anne Palmer, Rosemoor Garden Trust, Torrington, Devon EX38 7EG.

Correa Mrs M. Miles, Trewollack, St Mawes, Truro, Cornwall TR2 5AD.

Cortaderia Luton Parks Division, Wardown Park Offices, Old Bedford Road, Luton, Bedfordshire LU2 7HA.

Corylopsis Dr P. Dykes, Chadwich Manor, Redhill Lane, Bromsgrove, Worcestershire B61 0QF.

Corylus The Hillier Arboretum, Jermyns Lane, Ampfield, Near Romsey, Hampshire.

Cotinus Dr A. Plack, 'Rhus', Bridford, Exeter, Devon EX6 7LD.

Cotoneaster The Hillier Arboretum, Jermyns Lane, Ampfield, Near Romsey, Hampshire.

dwarf/prostrate type Merrist Wood Agricultural College, Worplesdon, Near Guildford, Surrey GU3 3PE.

Crataegus Metropolitan Borough of Sandwell, Recreation and Amenities Department, Hales Lane, Smethwick, Warley, Sandwell, West Midlands B67 6RS.

Crocosmia The National Trust, Lanhydrock, Bodmin, Cornwall PL30 5AD.

Crocus The Royal Horticultural Society, RHS Garden, Wisley, Woking, Surrey GU23 6QB.

except *vernus* and *chrysanthus* cvs. Mr R. Cobb, Aurelia, 188 Bramcote Lane, Wollaton, Nottingham NG8 2QN.

chrysanthus cvs. Mr & Mrs Grout, 5 Rockley Avenue, Radcliffe-on-Trent, Nottinghamshire.

Cyclamen Mr A. Aird, The Cyclamen Society, 134 Lots Road, London SW10 0RJ.

coum cvs Mr R. Poulett, Nurses Cottage, North Mundham, Chichester, Sussex PO20 6JY.

Cystopteris The National Trust, Sizergh Castle, Kendal, Cumbria LA8 8AE.

Cytisus The North of Scotland College of Agriculture, Horticultural Division, 581 King Street, Aberdeen AB1 1UD.

Mr R. Sturdy, Rik Sturdy Associates, Middle Copse, Carey, Wareham, Dorset BH20 7PB.

Daboecia City of Plymouth, Royal Building, St Andrews Cross, Plymouth, Devon.

The Royal Horticultural Society, RHS Garden, Wisley, Woking, Surrey GU23 6QB.

Daphne The Royal Horticultural Society, RHS Garden, Wisley, Woking, Surrey GU23 6QB.

Mrs J. Lloyd, Rookwood, Lustleigh, Devon TQ13 9TG.

Delphinium Leeds City Council, Temple Newsam Park, Leeds W. Yorkshire LS15 0AD.

elatum and *belladonna* cvs. Mr G. Alway, The Coach House, The Old Vicarage, Hillsley, Wotton-under-Edge, Gloucestershire.

Dendrobium Liverpool City Council Department of Recreation & Open Spaces, The Mansion House, Calderstones Park, Liverpool L18 3JD.

Deutzia Leeds City Council, 19 Wellington Street, Leeds, W. Yorkshire LS1 4DG.

Dianella Mr and Mrs H.F.J. Read, Vicar's Mead, East Budleigh, Devon EX9 7DA.

Dianthus, border pinks Mr J.R. Gingell, Ramparts Nurseries,

Bakers Lane, Braiswick, Colchester, Essex CO4 5BD.

Mr and Mrs S. Farquhar, Old Inn Cottage, Piddington, Bicester, Oxfordshire.

old garden pinks Mrs S. Hughes, Kingstone Cottage, Weston under Penyard, Ross-on-Wye, Herefordshire HR9 7NX.

Malmaison carnations The National Trust for Scotland, Crathes Castle, Banchory, Kincardineshire AB3 3QJ.

Dicentra Mr R.A. Brook, Betula, Marsh Lane, Bolton Percy, York YO5 7BA.

Diervilla City of Sheffield Botanic Gardens, Chalkhouse Road, Sheffield, Yorkshire S10 2LN.

Digitalis Mr J. Williams, Foxbrook Bungalow, Rowington, Near Warwick CV35 7AA.

Mr T.A. Baker, The Botanic Nursery, Rookery Nurseries, Atworth, Melksham, Wiltshire.

Dimorphotheca Somerset College of Agriculture and Horticulture, Cannington, Bridgwater, Somerset TA5 2LS.

Dodecatheon Mr & Mrs S.M. Wills, The Manor House, Walton in Gordano, Clevedon, Avon BS21 7AN.

Mr T. Wiltshire, Pencarn, Gonvena, Wadebridge, Cornwall PL27 6DL.

Doronicum Seamill Teachers Centre, West Kilbride, Ayrshire KA23 9NJ.

Dryopteris The Northern Horticultural Society, Harlow Car Gardens, Harrogate, N. Yorkshire HG3 1QB.

The National Trust, Sizergh Castle, Kendal, Cumbria LA8 8AE.

Echeveria Mr H.R. Jeffs, Nutfield Nursery, Crab Hill Lane, South Nutfield, Redhill, Surrey RH1 5PG.

Echinops Cambridge College of Agriculture and Horticulture, Newcommon Bridge, Wisbech, Cambridgeshire PE13 2SJ.

Elaeagnus Mr D.K. Reade, Wyevale Nurseries (Holdings) Ltd, King Acre, Hereford HR4 0SE.

Embothrium The National Trust, Bodnant Garden, Tal-y-Cafn, Colwyn Bay, Clwyd LL28 5RE.

Enkianthus Hadlow College of Agriculture and Horticulture, Hadlow, Tonbridge, Kent TN11 0AL.
Mr P. Cox, Glendoick Gardens Ltd, Glencarse, Perth, Tayside P42 7NS.

Epimedium The Royal Horticultural Society, RHS Garden, Wisley, Woking, Surrey GU23 6QB.
Mrs M. Owen, Parsons Pleasure, Acton Burnell, Shrewsbury, Shropshire SY5 7HQ.
Mr D.G. Barker, 'Stone Pine', Hyde Lane, Chelmsford, Essex CM3 4LJ.

Erica The Royal Horticultural Society, RHS Garden, Wisley, Woking, Surrey GU23 6QB.
City of Plymouth, Royal Building, St Andrews Cross, Plymouth, Devon.

Erigeron Mr P. Heaton, Brackenbury, Coombe, Wotton-under-Edge, Gloucestershire GL12 7NF.

Erodium Mrs M. Addyman, Rivendell, Porters Headland, Pickering, N. Yorkshire YO18 8AG.

Eryngium Lancashire College of Agriculture and Horticulture, Myerscough Hall, Bilsborrow, Preston, Lancashire PR3 0RY.

Erythronium Suntrap Horticultural and Gardening Advice Centre, (Oatridge Agricultural College), 43 Gogarbank, Edinburgh EH12 9BY.

Escallonia Plymouth Polytechnic, Rumleigh Experimental Station, Bere Alston, Yelverton, Devon PL20 7HN.

Eucalyptus Abbotsbury Gardens, Abbotsbury, Near Dorchester, Dorset.

Eucryphia Tal-y-Cafn, The National Trust, Bodnant Garden, Colwyn Bay, Clwyd LL28 5RE.
Mr P. Forde, Seaford Gardens, Seaford, Near Newcastle, County Down, Northern Ireland.

Euonymus, fortunei and *japonicus* cvs. Merrist Wood Agricultural College, Worplesdon, Near Guildford, Surrey GU3 3PE.
except *fortunei* and *japonicus* cvs. Lady Anne Cowdray, Broadleas, Devizes, Wiltshire SN10 5JQ.

Euphorbia Mrs S. Sage, Abbey Dore Court Gardens, Near Hereford HR2 0AD.
University Botanic Garden, Nuneham Courtenay Arboretum, Oxfordshire.

Fagus Northumberland County Council College of Agriculture, Kirkley Hall, Ponteland, Newcastle upon Tyne, Tyne & Wear NE20 0AQ.

Ferns, hardy Crown Estate Commissioners, The Great Park, Windsor, Berkshire SL4 2HT.

Forsythia Mr W.R.B. Webb, Webbs Garden Centres Ltd, The Nurseries, Wychbold, Droitwich, Worcestershire WR9 0DG.

Fraxinus excelsior cvs. Prof. & Mrs P. Laybourn, Ashgrove, Waterfoot

Row, Thorntonhall, Glasgow G74 5AD.

Fritillaria, spp. University Botanic Garden, Cambridge CB2 1JF.

imperialis cvs. Cambridge City Council, Mandela House, 4 Regent Street, Cambridge CB2 1BY.

Fuchsia, hardy types Croxteth Country Park, Croxteth Hall Lane, Liverpool L12 0IIB.

University of Leicester, Department of Botany, University Road, Leicester LE1 7RH.

Galanthus The Royal Horticultural Society, RHS Garden, Wisley, Woking, Surrey GU23 6QB.

Garrya National Botanic Gardens, Glasnevin, Dublin 9, Ireland.

Genista The North of Scotland College of Agriculture, Horticultural Division, 581 King Street, Aberdeen AB9 1UD.

Mr R. Sturdy, Rik Sturdy Associates, Middle Copse, Carey, Wareham, Dorset BH20 7PB.

Gentiana University of Aberdeen, Cruickshank Botanic Garden, St Machar Drive, Aberdeen AB9 2UD.

Geranium, spp. and primary hybrids University Botanic Garden, Cambridge CB2 1JF.

cvs. Cambridge City Council, Mandela House, 4 Regent Street, Cambridge CB2 1BY.

Geum Mrs Alison Mallett, Lurley Manor, Tiverton, Devon EX16 9QS.

Gooseberry cvs. University of Manchester, Department of Environmental Biology, Williamson Building, Oxford Road, Manchester M13 9PL.

Grevillea Mrs S. Clemo, Pine Lodge, Cuddra, St Austell, Cornwall PL25 3RQ.

Hamamelis Mrs P. Edwards, Swallow Hayes, Rectory Road, Albrighton, Wolverhampton, W. Midlands WV7 3EP.

Heathers City of Plymouth, Parks Department, Mount Edgcumbe Country Park, Plymouth, Devon. The Royal Horticultural Society, RHS Garden, Wisley, Woking, Surrey GU23 6QB.

see also *Calluna vulgaris* cvs.

Hedera The National Trust, Erddig, Near Wrexham, Clwyd.

Northumberland County Council College of Agriculture, Kirkley Hall, Ponteland, Newcastle upon Tyne, Tyne and Wear NE20 0AQ.

Hedychium Mr E. Needham, Derow, Killiwich, Feock, Truro, Cornwall TR3 6QZ.

Helenium Mr A. R. Busby, 16 Kirkby Corner Road, Canley, Coventry, W. Midlands CV7 86D.

The Hardy Plant Society, 17 Stanley Drive, Bramcote, Nottingham.

Helianthella The Hardy Plant Society, 17 Stanley Drive, Bramcote, Nottingham.

Helianthemum nummularium cvs. Hampshire College of Agriculture, Sparsholt, Winchester SO21 2NF.

Helianthus The Hardy Plant Society, 17 Stanley Drive, Bramcote, Nottingham.

Helichrysum, alpine Mr R. Stuckey, 38 Phillips Avenue, Exmouth, Devon.

Helicodiceros Mrs E. Honnor, 14 Homefield Close, Creech St Michael, Taunton, Somerset TA3 5QR.

Heliopsis The Hardy Plant Society, 17 Stanley Drive, Bramcote, Nottingham.

Helleborus NCCPG Hampshire Group, Lower House, Whiteparish, Salisbury SP5 2SL.

Suntrap Horticultural and Gardening Advice Centre, (Oatridge Agricultural College), 43 Gogarbank, Edinburgh EH12 9BY.

Hemerocallis The National Trust Antony House, Torpoint, Cornwall.

Borough of Epsom and Ewell, Parks Department, Ewell Court House, Ewell Court Avenue, Ewell, Epsom, Surrey KT19 0DZ.

Leeds City Council, 19 Wellington Street, Leeds, W. Yorkshire LSI 4DG.

Hepatica Mr M. Bishop, Somerset College of Agriculture and Horticulture, Cannington, Bridgwater, Somerset TA5 2LS.

Mr M. D. Myers, Fairview, Smelthouses, Summerbridge, Near Harrogate, N. Yorkshire HG3 4DH.

Hesperis University of Leicester, Department of Botany, University Road, Leicester LE1 7RH.

Heuchera Mrs M. Ramsdale, Walters Gift, Start Hill, Gt Hallingbury, Bishops Stortford, Hertfordshire CM22 7TF.

Hibiscus Notcutts Nurseries Ltd, Woodbridge, Suffolk IP12 4AF.

Hoheria Dr H. K. N. Lister, Chapel Knap, Porlock Weir, Somerset TA24 8PA.

Hosta The Royal Horticultural Society, RHS Garden, Wisley, Woking, Surrey GU23 6QB.

Lord Harewood, Harewood House Gardens, Harewood, Leeds, W. Yorkshire LS17 9LF.

Lt Col and Mrs H. Jordan, Kittoch Mill, Carmunnock, Lanarkshire G76 9BJ.

large leaved Leeds City Council, Department of Leisure Services, 19 Wellington Street, Leeds W. Yorkshire LS1 4DG.

Hoya Mr A. A. Jackson, The Welsh Mountain Zoo, Colwyn Bay, Clwyd LL28 5UY.

Hydrangea Derby City Council, Leisure Services, Roman House, Friar Gate, Derby DE1 1XD.

Hypericum The Northern Horticultural Society, Harlow Car Gardens, Harrogate, N. Yorkshire HG3 1QB.

Ilex Crown Estate Commissioners, The Great Park, Windsor, Berkshire SL4 2HT.

Iris University of Reading, Department of Botany, Plant Science Laboratories, Whiteknights, P.O. Box 221, Reading, Berkshire RG6 2AS.

sibirica cvs. NCCPG Salop Group, Haygarth, Cleeton-St Mary, Cleobury Mortimer, Kidderminster, Worcestershire DY14 0QU.

Bearded & A.M. cvs. Lee Valley Regional Park Authority, Myddelton House, Bulls Cross, Enfield, Middlesex EN2 9HG.

unguicularis cvs. Mr R. D. Nutt, Great Barfield, Bradenham, High Wycombe, Buckinghamshire HP14 4HG.

(section Apogon series spuriae) Mr S. Anderton, Stable Cottage, Belsay Hall, Belsay, Newcastle upon Tyne, Tyne and Wear NE20 0DX.

(series laevigatae not *I. ensata*) Mrs S. Bond, Goldbrook Plants, Hoxne, Eye, Suffolk.

Jasminum Borough of Torbay, Tor Hill House, Castle Circus, Torquay, Devon TQ2 5QN.

Juglans Mr T. Hooker, Canford School, Wimborne, Dorset BH21 3AD.

Juniperus × *media* Cunningham District Council, Moorpark House, School Road, Kilbirnie, Ayrshire KA25 7LD.

Kalmia Mr P. A. Cox, Glendoick Gardens Ltd, Glencarse, Perth, Tayside PH12 7NS.

Kniphofia Mr A. Goddard, Barton Manor, Whippingham, East Cowes, Isle of Wight PO32 6LB.
Bridgemere Nurseries Ltd, Bridgemere, Near Nantwich, Cheshire.

Laburnum Cambridge College of Agriculture & Horticulture, Newcommon Bridge, Wisbech, Cambridgeshire PE13 2SJ.
Mr J. Makepeace, Parnham House, Beaminster, Dorset DT8 3NA.

Lamiastrum and *Lamium* Mr J. Sharman, Church Lane Farm, Cottenham, Cambridge CB4 4SN.

Lavandula Norfolk Lavender Ltd, Caley Mill, Heacham, King's Lynn, Norfolk PE31 7JE.

Leptospermum Mr M. Drummond, The Manor of Cadland, Cadland House, Fawley, Southampton, Hampshire SO4 1AA.
  scoparium cvs. Mrs M. Miles, Trewollack, St Mawes, Truro, Cornwall TR2 5AD.

Leucojum Mr R. D. Nutt, Great Barfield, Bradenham, High Wycombe, Buckinghamshire HP14 4HD.

Lewisia National Trust for Scotland, Branklyn Garden, Dundee Road, Perth, Tayside PH2 7BB.

Libertia Mr & Mrs H. F. J. Read, Vicar's Mead, East Budleigh, Devon EX9 7DA.

Ligularia Hardy Plant Society, The Old Sawmill, Castle Woods, Skipton, N. Yorkshire.

Ligustrum The Hillier Arboretum, Jermyns Lane, Ampfield, Near Romsey, Hampshire.

Linum Mrs P. Taylor, 17 Bartelotts Road, Slough, Berkshire.

Liriodendron Mr I. Hicks, The Edward James Foundation, West Dean Estate, Chichester, W. Sussex PO48 0QZ.

Liriope Mr & Mrs H. F. J. Read, Vicar's Mead, East Budleigh, Devon EX9 7DA.

Lithocarpus The Hillier Arboretum, Jermyns Lane, Ampfield, Near Romsey, Hampshire.

Lobelia cardinalis and *fulgens* cvs. Mrs A. Stevens, Ivy Cottage, Ansty, Dorchester, Dorset DT2 7PX.

Lonicera, spp. and primary hybrids not cvs. University Botanic Garden, Cambridge CB2 1JF.
  climbing spp. and cvs. Mr D. Bradshaw, J. Bradshaw & Sons, Busheyfields Nursery, Herne Common, Herne Bay, Kent CT6 7LJ.

Lupinus, Russell Lupins Mrs P. Edwards, Swallow Hayes, Rectory Road, Albrighton, Wolverhampton, W. Midlands WV7 3EP.

Lychnis Mr R. Sargent, Hinchley Wood First and Middle School, Claygate Lane, Esher, Surrey KT10 0AQ.

Magnolia The National Trust, Bodnant Garden, Tay-y-Cafn, Colwyn Bay, Clwyd LL8 5RE.
Crown Estate Commissioners,

The Great Park, Windsor, Berkshire SL4 2HT.

Mahonia Mr J. May, Wimborne Gardens, Stapehill Road, Stapehill, Wimborne, Dorset BH21 7ND.

Crown Estate Commissioners, The Great Park, Windsor, Berkshire SL4 2HT.

Malus University of Manchester, Department of Environmental Biology, Williamson Building, Oxford Rd, Manchester M13 3PL.

Dr R. Robinson, Hyde Hall Garden Trust, Hyde Hall, Rettendon, Chelmsford, Essex CM3 5ET.

Meconopsis Durham Agricultural College, Houghall, Durham DH1 3SG.

Mentha, culinary mints Mr R. Lunn, Herbs In Stock, Whites Hill, Stock, Ingatestone, Essex.

Mertensia University of Aberdeen, Cruickshank Botanic Garden, St Machar Drive, Aberdeen AB9 2UD.

Monarda Leeds Castle Foundation, Leeds Castle, Maidstone, Kent ME17 1PL.

Muscari Miss J. Robinson, Chequers, Boxford, Suffolk CO6 5DT.

Narcissus University of Ulster, Cromore Road, Coleraine, Co. Londonderry, Northern Ireland BT52 1SA.

Mr M. Harwood, Hope Cottage, Halebourne Lane, Chobam, Surrey GU24 8SL.

Alec Gray miniatures Broadleigh Gardens, Bishops Hull, Taunton, Somerset TA4 1AE.

Brodie cvs. The National Trust for Scotland, Brodie Castle, Invernesshire.

Nepeta Leeds Castle Foundation, Leeds Castle, Maidstone, Kent ME17 1PL.

Nerine Mr C. A. Norris, Nerine Nurseries, Welland, Near Malvern, Worcestershire WR13 6LN.

Nerium oleander Mrs N. Macmillan, Woodhouse, Lower End, Swaffham Prior, Cambridge CB5 0HT.

Nothofagus Tavistock Woodlands Estate Office, Gulworthy, Tavistock, Devon PL19 8JE.

Oenothera Mr J. N. D'Arcy, The Old Vicarage, Edington, Westbury, Wiltshire.

Olearia The National Trust for Scotland, Inverewe Garden, Poolewe, Achnasheen, Ross-shire IV22 2LQ.

Omphalodes University of Aberdeen, Cruickshank Botanic Garden, St Machar Drive, Aberdeen AB9 2UD.

Ophiopogon Mr & Mrs H. F. J. Read, Vicar's Mead, East Budleigh, Devon EX9 7DA.

Origanum Mr & Mrs Titterington, Iden Croft Herbs, Frittenden Road, Staplehurst, Kent TN12 0DH.

Osmunda The National Trust, Sizergh Castle, Kendal, Cumbria LA8 8AE.

Mr A. R. Busby, 16 Kirby Corner Road, Canley, Coventry, W. Midlands CV4 8GD.

Osteospermum Somerset College of Agriculture and Horticulture, Cannington, Bridgwater, Somerset TA5 2LS.

Ourisia The National Trust for Scotland, Inverewe Garden, Poolewe, Achnasheen, Ross-shire IV22 2LQ.

Ozothamnus Mr S. Benham, Gardens

Cottage, Knightshayes Court, Tiverton, Devon.

Paeonia, spp and primary hybrids The National Trust, Hidcote Manor Garden, Hidcote Bartrim, Chipping Campden, Gloucestershire.

cvs. pre 1900 NCCPG Gloucestershire Group, Green Cottage, Redhill Lane, Lydney, Gloucestershire GL15 6BS.

Papaver orientale cvs. West of Scotland Agricultural College, Horticulture and Beekeeping Department, Auchincruive, Ayr KA6 5AE.

annuals Thompson and Morgan (Ipswich) Ltd, London Road, Ipswich, Suffolk IP2 0BA.

Paphiopedilum Liverpool City Council, Department of Recreation and Open Spaces, The Mansion House, Calderstone Park, Liverpool L18 3JD.

Paradisea Mr R. Grounds & Mrs D. Grenfell, Apple Court, Hordle Lane, Lymington, Hampshire SO41 0HU.

Parahebe Mr G. Hutchins, County Park Nursery, Essex Gardens, Hornchurch, Essex RM11 3BU.

Parthenocissus University of Strathclyde, Staff Educational & Recreational Centre, Ross Priory, Gartocharn, Dumbartonshire G33 8NL.

Passiflora Mr R.J.R. Vanderplank, Greenholm Nurseries Ltd, Langley Road, Kingston Seymour, Clevedon, Avon BS21 6XS.

Pelargonium Fibrex Nurseries, Honeybourne Road, Pebworth, Stratford-upon-Avon, Warwickshire CV37 8XT.

Penstemon Dorset College of Agriculture, Kingston Maurward, Dorchester, Dorset DT2 8PY.

The National Trust for Scotland, Threave School of Gardening, Castle Douglas, Dumfries DG7 1RX.

large-flowered cvs. The National Trust, Rowallane House, Saintfield, Ballynaminch, Co. Down, Northern Ireland BT24 7LH.

Pernettya Hadlow College of Agriculture and Horticulture, Hadlow, Tonbridge, Kent TN11 0AL.

Philadelphus Leeds City Council, Department of Leisure Services, 19 Wellington Street, Leeds, W. Yorkshire LS1 4DG.

Phlox, herbaceous perennials Leeds City Council, Department of Leisure Services, 19 Wellington Street, Leeds, W. Yorkshire LS1 4DG.

Phormium Somerset College of Agriculture and Horticulture, Cannington, Bridgwater, Somerset TA5 2LS.

Photinia The Hillier Arboretum, Jermyns Lane, Ampfield, Near Romsey, Hampshire.

Phyllodoce Mr P.A. Cox, Glendoick Gardens Ltd, Glencarse, Perth, Tayside PH2 7NS.

Phyllostachys Mr P. Addington, Stream Cottage, Churchwood, Fittleworth, Pulborough, West Sussex RH20 1HP.

Mr D.A. Crampton, Drysdale Nurseries, 96 Drysdale Avenue, Chingford, London E4 7PE.

Picea Mr. J. Noble, Ardkinglas Estate, Cairndow, Argyll PA26 8B.

Crown Estate Commissioners, The Great Park, Windsor, Berkshire SL4 2HT.

Pinellia Mrs E. Honnor, 14 Homefield

Close, Creech St Michael, Taunton, Somerset TA3 5QR.

Pinus, except dwarf cvs. The Hillier Arboretum, Jermyns Lane, Ampfield, Near Romsey, Hampshire.

Pittosporum Bicton College of Agriculture, East Budleigh, Budleigh Salterton, Devon EX9 7BY.

Platanus The National Trust, Mottisfont Abbey, Near Romsey, Hampshire.

Platycodon Hoo House, Gloucester Road, Tewkesbury, Gloucestershire GL20 7DA.

Pleione Mr I. Butterfield, Butterfields Nursery, Harvest Hill, Bourne End, Buckinghamshire SL8 5JJ.

Polygonatum Hardy Plant Society, The Old Sawmill, Castle Woods, Skipton, N. Yorkshire.
Mr and Mrs K. Beckett, Branley Cottage, Stanhoe, King's Lynn, Norfolk PE31 8QF.

Polygonum Mr J. R. L. Carter, Rowden Gardens, Brentnor, Near Tavistock, Devon PL19 ONG.

Polypodium The Northern Horticultural Society, Harlow Car Gardens, Harrogate, N. Yorkshire HG3 1QB.

Populus Lackham College of Agriculture, Lacock, Chippenham, Wiltshire SN15 2NY.

Potentilla fruticosa Barnsley Metropolitan Borough Council, Department of Amenities and Recreation, 12/18 Eldon Street, Barnsley, Yorkshire S70 2JB.

fruticosa Dr E. Hickey, Thomond College, Limerick, Ireland

fruticosa Mr W. R. E. Webb, Webb's Nurseries, Wychbold, Near Droitwich, Worcestershire WR9 0DG.

herbaceous Mr M. C. Swash, Long-

field Nursery, Oreton, Cleobury Mortimer, Shropshire DY14 0TJ.

Primula, allionii cvs. Mr J. Main, East Gate House, 7b Inverleith Row, Edinburgh EH3 5LP.

alpine auricula Leeds City Council, Department of Leisure Services, 19 Wellington Street, Leeds, W. Yorkshire LS1 4DG.

European spp. Mr & Mrs A. Quest-Ritson, Corsley Mill, Corsley, Warminster, Wiltshire BA12 7QA.

sect. Candelabra & Sikkimensis Newick Park Enterprises, Newick Park, W. Sussex BN8 4SB.

sect. Vernales cvs. Mr J. W. Martin, The Orchard, Longford, Market Drayton, Shropshire TF9 3PW.
Mrs D. L. Shaw, Tarn Cottage, West Lane, Cononly, Near Keighley, W. Yorkshire.

Auriculas (double) Mr D. W. Salt, Donington House, Main Road, Wrangle, Boston, Lincolnshire PE22 9AT.

sect. Vernales cvs. Mrs P. Gossage, Oakenlea, West Coker Hill, Yeovil, Somerset BA22 9DG.

marginata Mr M. D. Myers, Fairview, Smelthouses, Summerbridge, Near Harrogate, N. Yorkshire HG3 4DH.

Prunus, evergreen Wyevale Nurseries (Holdings) Ltd., King Acre, Hereford HR4 0SE.

Prunus serrulata Cunningham District Council, Moorpark House, School Road, Kilbirnie, Ayrshire KA25 7LD.

Prunus subhirtella and *speciosa* Mr E. Daniel, Handcross Park, Handcross, Haywards Heath, W. Sussex RH17 6HF.

Pseudopanax Ventnor Botanic Garden, The Winter Gardens, Ventnor, Isle of Wight PO38 1SZ.

Pulmonaria The Royal Horticultural Society, RHS Garden, Wisley, Woking, Surrey GU23 6QB.
Wigan College of Technology, Parsons Walk, Wigan, Greater Manchester WN1 1RR.

Pyracantha Writtle Agricultural College, Chelmsford, Essex CM1 3RR.

Pyrethrum Mr G.W. Goddard, 25 Mornington Road, Chingford, London E4 7DT.
Lamport Hall Trust, Lamport Hall, Northampton NN6 9IIB.

Pyrus, except *communis* cvs. Mr & Mrs C.A. Quest-Ritson, Corsley Mill, Corsley, Warminster, Wiltshire BA12 7QA.

Quercus The Hillier Arboretum, Jermyns Lane, Ampfield, Near Romsey, Hampshire.

Ranunculus ficaria Mr R.D. Nutt, Great Barfield, Bradenham, High Wycombe, Buckinghamshire HP14 4HD.

Rheum, spp. and cvs. The Northern Horticultural Society, Harlow Car Gardens, Harrogate, N. Yorkshire HG3 1QB.
Culinary cvs. The Royal Horticultural Society, RHS Garden, Wisley, Woking, Surrey GU23 6QB.

Rhododendron: forrestii agg. The National Trust, Bodnant Garden, Tal-y-Cafn, Colwyn Bay, Clwyd.
Ghent Azaleas The National Trust, Sheffield Park Garden, Uckfield, E. Sussex TN22 3QX.
Glenn Dale Azaleas Crown Estate Commissioners, The Great Park, Windsor, Berkshire SL4 2HT.

Knap Hill and Occidentale Azaleas Heaselands, Haywards Heath, W. Sussex RH16 4SA.
Azaleodendron hybrids Lord Porchester, Milford Lane House, Burghdene, Newbury, Berkshire RG15 9EL.
spp. (in part) Crown Estate Commissioners, The Great Park, Windsor, Berkshire SL4 2HT.
s. Maddenia The National Trust for Scotland, Brodick Castle, Isle of Arran KA27 8DE.
s. Falconera The National Trust for Scotland, Brodick Castle, Isle of Arran KA27 8DE.
s. Barbata The National Trust for Scotland, Inverewe Garden, Poolewe, Achnasheen, Ross-shire. IV22 2LQ.

Rhus Dr A. Plack, 'Rhus', Bridford, Exeter, Devon EX6 7LD.

Ribes, spp. and primary hybrids University Botanic Garden, Cambridge CB2 1JF
sanguineum cvs. Metropolitan Borough of Sandwell, Recreation and Amenities Department, Hales Lane, Smethwick, Warley, Sandwell, W. Midlands B67 6RS.

Ribes grossularia cvs. see Gooseberry.

Robinia Mr N.B. Junkers, Junker's Tree and Landscape Services, Stoke Cottage, Stoke St Mary, Taunton, Somerset.

Rodgersia Mr & Mrs Pope, Laundry Cottage, Hadspen House, Castle Cary, Somerset BA5 7NG.

Rohdea japonica Mr R. Grounds and Mrs D. Grenfell, Apple Court, Hordle Lane, Lymington, Hampshire SO41 0HU.

Rosa: pre-1900 shrub roses The

National Trust, Mottisfont Abbey, Near Romsey, Hampshire.

19th century shrub roses The National Trust for Scotland, Blue Cottage, Malleny House Garden, Balerno, Midlothian EH14 7AF.

Rambler Roses Mr & Mrs H. C. W. Robinson, Moorwood Farm, Cirencester, Gloucestershire GL7 7EB.

Roscoea Mr E. Needham, Derow, Keniwith, Feock, Truro, Cornwall TR3 6QZ.

Rosmarinus Messrs R. and M. Cheek, 35 Wembdon Rise, Bridgwater, Somerset

Rubus Clinterty Agriculture College, Kinellar, Aberdeen AB5 0TN.

Ruscus University Botanic Garden, Cambridge CB2 1JF.

Salix, lowland types The Forestry Commission Westonbirt Arboretum, Tetbury Gloucestershire GL8 8QS.

dwarf types Northumberland County Council College of Agriculture, Kirkley Hall, Ponteland, Newcastle upon Tyne, Tyne and Wear NE20 0AQ.

Mr C. N. Newsholme, Longwood, Cannsdown, Beaford, Winkleigh, Devon EX19 8AD.

Salvia Mr & Mrs P. Vlasto, Wyke End, 20 Belle Vue Road, Weymouth, Dorset DT9 8RY.

Sambucus The National Trust, Wallington Garden, Cambo, Morpeth, Northumberland NE61 4AW.

Mrs M. Barber, Cloverhill Farm, Old Toll, Ayr KA6 6LP.

Santolina Mrs L. Williams, Marle Place Plants, Marle Place, Brenchley, Tonbridge, Kent TN12 7HS.

Mrs C. Price, Stone Lea Nurseries, West Haddlesey, Near Selby, N. Yorkshire Y02 8QA.

Sarcococca Capel Manor Institute of Horticulture and Field Studies, Bullsmoor Lane, Waltham Cross, Hertfordshire EN7 5HR.

Sarracenia Messrs R. & M. Cheek, 35 Wembdon Rise, Bridgwater, Somerset.

Sasa Mr D. McClintock, Brackenhill, Platt, Sevenoaks, Kent TN15 8JH.

Mr D. A. Crampton, Drysdale Nurseries, 96 Drysdale Avenue, Chingford, London E4 7PE.

Saxifraga, European spp. University Botanic Garden, Cambridge CB2 1JF.

kabschia types Waterperry Horticultural Centre, Near Wheatley, Oxfordshire OX9 1JZ.

Scabiosa Mrs S. Parrett, Dinkling Green Farm, Whitewell, Clithero, Lancashire

caucasica The National Trust, Hardwick Hall, Doe Lea, Chesterfield, Derbyshire S44 5QJ.

Schizostylis Mr F. Shepherd, Bosbigal, Old Carnon Hill, Carnon Downs, Truro, Cornwall TR3 6LF.

Sedum Mrs S. Sage, Abbey Dore Court Gardens, Near Hereford HR 2 0AD.

Semiaquilegia/Paraquilegia Mr J. Drake, Hardwicke House, Fen Ditton, Cambridge CB5 8TF.

Senecio, woody spp. (New Zealand) The National Trust for Scotland, Inverewe Garden, Poolewe, Achnasheen, Ross-shire IV22 2LQ.

Shibataea Mr D. Crampton, Drysdale Nurseries, 96 Drysdale Avenue, Chingford, London E4 7PE.

Sidalcea Mrs M. Ramsdale, Walters Gift, Start Hill, Gt Hallingbury, Bishop's Stortford, Hertfordshire CM22 7TF.

Skimmia University of Leicester, Department of Botany, University Road, Leicester LE1 7RH.

Slieve Donard cvs. City of Belfast, Parks Department, Fernhill House, Glencairn Park, Glencairn Road, Belfast, Northern Ireland BT13 3PT.

Sorbaria The Paignton Zoological and Botanical Garden, West Lodge, 187 Totnes Road, Paignton, Devon TQ4 7EU.

Sorbus, spp. and cvs. University of Manchester, Department of Environmental Biology, Williamson Building, Oxford Road, Manchester M13 9PL.

sects. Aria and Micromeles The National Trust, Winkworth Arboretum, Near Hascombe, Godalming, Surrey.

Durham Agricultural College, Houghall, Durham DH1 3SG.

Spiraea Askham Bryan College of Agriculture and Horticulture, Askham Bryan, York YO2 3PR.

Stewartia Hon E. and Mrs Boscawen, The High Beeches, Handcross, Sussex RH17 6HQ.

Symphytum Mrs I. Strachan, Banner Lodge, 9 Newbattle Terrace, Edinburgh EH10 4RU.

Syringa Borough of Brighton, Parks and Recreation Department, Moulscoomb Place, Lewes Road, Brighton W. Sussex BN2 4GL.

Leeds City Council, Department of Leisure Services, 19 Wellington Street, Leeds, W. Yorkshire LS1 4DG.

Taxus University of Bath, Claverton Down, Bath, Avon BA2 7AY.

Thalictrum Mr & Mrs G. Buchanan-Dunlop, Broughton Place, Broughton, Biggar, Lanarkshire ML12 6JH.

Mr J. Ravenscroft, Bridgemere Garden World, Bridgemere Nurseries Ltd, Bridgemere, Near Nantwich, Cheshire.

Thymus Mr & Mrs F. Huntington, Quantock Herbs, Hethersett, Cothelstone, Taunton, Somerset TD4 3DP.

Tilia Viscount Devonport, Ray Demesne, Kirkwhelpington, Northumberland NE19 2RG.

Tillandsia Mr A.J. Jarlett, 103 Woodland Way, Marden Ash, Ongar, Essex CM5 9ET.

Tricyrtis Hardy Plant Society, The Old Sawmill, Castle Woods, Skipton, N. Yorkshire.

Trillium Mr A. Page, 38 Shaftesbury Avenue, Chandler's Ford, Eastleigh, Hampshire SO5 3BS.

Trollius Mrs A. Stevens, Ivy Cottage, Ansty, Dorchester, Dorset.

Tropaeolum Mr & Mrs G. Buchanan-Dunlop, Broughton Place, Broughton, Biggar, Lanarkshire ML12 6HJ.

Tulbaghia Mr S. Benham, Gardens Cottage, Knightshayes Court, Tiverton, Devon.

Tulipa, spp. and primary hybrids University Botanic Garden, Cambridge CB2 1JF.

florists' and old cvs. Mr D. Bromley, The Moortown, Near Wellington, Shropshire.

Veratrum NCCPG Surrey Group, 7 Lower Road, Fetcham, Leatherhead, Surrey KT22 9EL.

Verbena The National Trust for Scotland, Greenback, Clarkston, Glasgow.

Veronica, sect. spicata Mr & Mrs P. Foulsham, Kings Head House, Itchel Lane, Crondall, Farnham, Surrey GU10 5PR.

Viburnum Mr R. Robinson, Hyde Hall Garden Trust, Hyde Hall, Rettenden, Chelmsford, Essex CM3 5ET.

Derby City Council, Leisure Services, Roman House, Friar Gate, Derby DE1 1XD.

Vinca Mr J. Sharman, Church Lane Farm, Cottenham, Cambridge CB4 4SN.

Viola, bedding Violas and Violettas Leeds City Council, Department of Leisure Services, 19 Wellington St. Leeds, W. Yorkshire LS1 4DG.

odorata cvs. Mrs Y. S. Matthews, Cornwall. (address from Secretariat)

Viola and Violetta Mr R. G. M. Caw-

thorne, Lower Daltons Nursery, Swanley Village, Swanley, Kent BR8 7NU.

Watsonia Mr A. Goddard, Barton Manor, Whiffingham, East Cowes, Isle of Wight PO32 6LB.

Weigela City of Sheffield Botanic Gardens, Curators House, Clarkenhouse Road, Sheffield, S. Yorkshire S10 2LN.

Wisteria Somerset College of Agriculture and Horticulture, Cannington, Bridgwater, Somerset TA5 2LS.

Woodwardia Mr R. Grounds and Mrs D. Grenfell, Apple Court, Hordle Lane, Lymington, Hampshire SO41 0HU.

Yucca Somerset College of Agriculture and Horticulture, Cannington, Bridgwater, Somerset TA5 2LS.

Zelkova Mr R. and Mr W. L. Banks, Hergest Croft Gardens, Kington, Herefordshire HR5 3EG.

Index